His Brother's Keeper

Applied Psychoanalysis Monograph Series
of
The Chicago Institute for Psychoanalysis

edited by
George H. Pollock, M.D., Ph.D.

His Brother's Keeper:
A Psychobiography of
Samuel Taylor Coleridge

Stephen M. Weissman, M.D.

Copyright © 1989, Stephen M. Weissman

All rights reserved. No part of this book may be reproduced by any means, nor translated into a machine language, without the written permission of the publisher.

Library of Congress Cataloging-in-Publication Data

Weissman, Stephen M.
   His brother's keeper: a psychobiography of Samuel Taylor Coleridge / Stephen M. Weissman.
      p. cm.—(Applied psychoanalysis monograph series: monograph 1)
   Bibliography: p.
   Includes Index.
   ISBN: 1-4392-0392-X

   1. Coleridge, Samuel Taylor, 1772-1834—Biography—Psychology. 2. Poets, English—19th century—Biography. 3. Psychoanalysis and literature. I. Title. II. Series.
PR4483.W4 1989
821'.7—dc19
[B]   87-33293
                                                                      CIP

Manufactured in the United States of America

for Carole Horn

And the Lord set a mark upon Cain, that whosoever found him should not kill him.
—*Genesis* 4:15

Table of Contents

Foreword	ix
To the Reader	xi
Introduction	xiii
Prologue: Cain and Abel	xvii
1. The Rivals	1
2. School Days	15
3. My Brother's Keeper	33
4. Pantisocracy: A Tribe of Brothers	47
5. Honeymoon Radical Style	73
6. The Surveillance of Cain and Abel	91
7. Miracles of Rare Device	107
8. Fatal Interlude	131
9. Calm Before the Storm	153
10. The Eye of the Storm	163
11. Wedding Bells	183
12. Troubled Sleep	209
13. Bargaining with God	231
14. Exile's Return	255
15. An Archangel a Little Damaged	283
16. Coleridge the Psychologist	303
17. The Final Years	309
Epilogue: Posterity's Verdict: A Postmortem	323
Appendices	327
References	333
Author Index	337
Subject Index	339

Foreword

Although this book is a chronicle of events in the life of a gifted individual, it reads as though it were a novel; that is, it reads easily and the author carefully, though not completely, avoids technical terminology. As a psychoanalyst and psychiatrist, however, he tells his story from a particular point of view. Otherwise one might ask: why another biography of Coleridge? While the narrative is not technical, it is well documented, the evidence presented is pertinent to the author's thesis, and the references are authoritative. However, the data, independent of the author's hypothesis, allow the reader to consider alternative explanations of the threads and patterns in this life.

Although one can see the map of Coleridge's life laid out, a complete understanding of his genius and his personality evades us. The author presents his subject's life on a continuum and even with the selective inclusions one can see it progress in its tragic way. Along the road one gets the flavor of what in the world about Coleridge impacted on him, his family, his friends and colleagues, and on his work. That he was a master of many subjects and fields of thought is acknowledged. His speculations on memory and association anticipated some of Freud's discoveries. Yet he was addicted to opium, and his life was marked by the deaths of close family members, ill health, domestic unhappiness, arguments with close friends, flashes of insight that perished without being developed, procrastination, and an oscillation of mood and affect from exuberance and enthusiasm to despair and despondency—so much so that one might consider him a manic-depressive and his use of opium a self-therapy to keep his affects in some manageable equilibrium. It is indeed possible for one to suffer this disorder and still have quite separate though concomitant neuroses, character problems, and creative abilities. This combinatorial approach allows us greater depth and breadth of understanding and allows for multiple hypotheses as to what is going on in the individual.

We are still far from fully understanding creativity. Freud, in his Foreword to Marie Bonaparte's psychoanalytic interpretation of the life and works of Edgar Allan Poe, noted "how many of the characteristics of Poe's works were conditioned by his personality and [one] can see how that personality derived from intense emotional fixations and painful infantile experiences. Investigations such as this do not claim to explain creative genius, but they do reveal the factors which awaken it and the sort of subject matter it is destined to choose."

There are so many themes here of personal interest that restraint is difficult: Coleridge's childhood loss of his father, his brother's suicide, the deaths of his children, Wordsworth's abandonment of his illegitimate daughter, the use of opium to possibly curb manic-depressive behavior, the effect of opium on creative imagery in Coleridge and in De Quincey, mourning as Samuel Taylor Coleridge more or less tells us of it, symbiotic brother transferences, and many more.

To cite the excellence of this work is not to exempt it from discussion, criticism, and further elaboration. Although Stephen Weissman is bold in his correlations, he is careful in his conclusions. Some of these require no further proof; others call for further investigation. For example, Hartley Coleridge's behavior may be seen as identification with his illustrious father's behavior, as Weissman suggests, but it may also be viewed as a manifestation of manic-depressive behavior in the next generation. Readers will judge Weissman's interpretations using various frames of reference, but should recognize the risk of reducing the life of a creative genius to simple explanations. We can learn much by reflecting on Coleridge and on his many contributions to our insights about ourselves and those with whom we come into close contact. And we owe Stephen Weissman a debt of gratitude for bringing us closer to one of the most tormented yet creative lives our civilization has produced.

George H. Pollock, M.D., Ph.D.

Chicago

To the Reader

In the quotations from Coleridge and others, the spelling throughout this text has been modernized, except in the case of proper nouns and words which retain, in my opinion, the flavor of their original meaning without disrupting the reader's attention. Thus the word *burthen* remains the same, while the word *synonime* is changed to the modern spelling, *synonym*. The nineteenth-century tendency to capitalize many words has been replaced by a greater use of lower case letters, again in the interest of readability. Punctuation has largely been left intact except where numerous slash marks were originally used and where I think commas and periods best serve that purpose for the modern reader. I have tried not to alter the essential meaning of these passages but to improve their flow and readability.

Abbreviations have been used for citations to the four most frequently quoted sources: *CL* refers to the *Collected Letters of Samuel Taylor Coleridge*, *CNB* to the *Notebooks of Samuel Taylor Coleridge*, *PW* to *The Complete Poetical Works of Samuel Taylor Coleridge*, *JDW* to the *Journals of Dorothy Wordsworth*, and *LWDW* to the *Letters of William and Dorothy Wordsworth*. The numbers in references to the Notebooks refer to entries rather than pages.

Readers will find the entire source for the Prologue quoted in Chapter 7 and can decide for themselves what fanciful liberties, if any, have been taken in the rendering of this crucial event from Coleridge's boyhood.

Introduction

At the end of the eighteenth century, as the Industrial Revolution was altering the landscape of England and the French Revolution was democratizing its politics, another great revolution was taking place as well: the Romantic Revolution was giving birth to modern literature with its emphasis on subjective emotional experience. Together, Samuel Taylor Coleridge and William Wordsworth "fathered" modern poetry and that Romantic Revolution in literature.

No biography of Coleridge is complete without a study of his famous friendship with William Wordsworth. But previous works on the lives of both men have ignored the more controversial, unsavory aspects of their friendship. Taking what has become a standard "party line," their biographers have glossed over the less appealing aspects of their affection for one another.

By established tradition, William Wordsworth is remembered as Coleridge's closest and dearest friend, who loyally tried but failed in his heroic efforts to save Coleridge from his opium habit. But this study asserts an entirely different role for William, who, at a crucial turning point in the fall of 1800, actually helped push Coleridge into his addiction, thereby undermining him as both artist and man.

Central to this controversial interpretation is our ability to date precisely, for the first time, the onset of Coleridge's hard-core addiction: it occurred during that unhappy autumn of 1800. Thanks to the historical research of Dr. John Estes of the Pharmacology Department of Boston University Medical School (see Appendix C), it is now possible to calculate Coleridge's morphine dosages with a margin of error of only 20 percent. This allows us to trace the progressive increase in Coleridge's dosage requirements and to determine when he made the crucial shift from casual drug use to physical dependence.

Another shibboleth of standard Coleridge biography which modern psychopharmacology challenges is Coleridge's supposed "love" for Sara Hutchinson. By taking their cue from Coleridge himself, generations of sentimentally inclined biographers have waxed poetic over that tragic unconsummated love affair that purportedly led to Coleridge's addiction.

But no one has ever troubled to notice the sorry fact that Coleridge was suffering from a drug-induced psychosis at the time he first produced an explanation of his downfall and that he was therefore a less than reliable witness. In a series of maudlin diary entries penned three years after he met Sara—and written at a time when he was fully addicted and lost in the midst of opium-induced hallucinations—Coleridge hazily reconstructed how he had come to such a sorry state. It was a case of "love at first sight," Coleridge told himself, that had wrecked his marriage and driven him into drugs.

By taking Coleridge's retrospective rationalization at face value, previous biographers of Coleridge have chronicled his downfall as Coleridge wished to imagine it to have been. Both Coleridge and his biographers agree that his tragic undoing was his supposedly tumultuous love for Sara. But careful rereading of Coleridge's diaries and letters on a *day by day* basis reveals an entirely different story: Sara Hutchinson was merely the go-between, fantasy-vehicle for Coleridge's obsessive attachment to William Wordsworth—an unconsciously homosexual attachment which is also traceable in the poetry Coleridge was writing at that time (see the discussion of *Christabel* in Chapter 15.).

Understandably enough, Coleridge could not admit such feelings to himself. His denial took the form of pining for Sara, his link to William. By overidentifying with their subject and taking Coleridge's rationalizations as gospel, Coleridge's previous biographers have mistaken the smokescreen for the fire.

But the central view presented in this study is that the great and truly tragic love of Coleridge's life was his love for William Wordsworth. And if the depths of that love stemmed in part from neurosis and unconscious homosexual sources, it was also a powerful conscious quest for an idealistically creative, poetic brotherhood, and its story is the story of a failed dream.

This study's central premise is that every writer has a personal unconscious myth. Coleridge's was Abel and Cain. Just as his *Ancient Mariner* was a symbolically disguised retelling of that harrowing tale, so his tormented friendship with William Wordsworth was an equally well masked reliving of that myth. Thus while Coleridge's quest for brother-love was in part unconsciously homosexual in the broadest sense, it was not simply a sexual obsession in the narrower meaning of that term. The proposed thesis is not intended either as sensationalism or as a reductionistic psychological "cheap shot."

Also, there is an underlying set of theoretical assumptions about the psychology of the artist and the nature of the creative process in this study: what I elsewhere have called the "Loss-Restitution Hypothesis of Creativity" (Weissman, 1986, p. 192). Stated simply, the Loss-Restitution Hypothesis views the artist as a loss-sensitive, separation-prone individual both by inborn temperament and as the reaction to early developmental experiences of loss and separation. As a result of these twin factors, he learns as a child to rely upon his ability to create imagery (verbal, musical, visual, etc.) as a compensatory defense against losses and separations. Later, as an adult, the artist is a depression-prone, loss-sensitive individual who relies upon his capacity to create both as a coping mechanism and nondefensively, as a mode of identity formation.

Viewed from this perspective, art is a disguised form of nostalgically autobiographical remembering whose commemorative powers attempt to defy nature's inevitable forces of death, decay and loss by creating a work of permanence that can outlive its creator. In this way, creative activity defends against depression while the creative product itself (play, poem, painting, or what have you) is the symbolic denial of the loss.

But if creative activity allows the artist to temporarily fend off feelings of loss and empty depression, his original susceptibility can only be temporarily appeased but never remedied by the creative process, no matter how successful. Victorious artistic renderings are little better than failures. Just as Antony's Cleopatra awakens appetites where most she satisfies, the artist's muse holds him in equal paradoxical thralldom. His is a thirst for permanence that is only further incited by the memory of having been ecstatically quenched—to have known the exhilaration of creating a masterpiece and thereby achieving immortality ultimately begets a craving for more of the same. (See my discussion of *Kubla Khan* in Chapter 7.)

Another underlying assumption in this study is that had he lived today, Coleridge would probably have been clinically diagnosed as suffering from some form of underlying Mood Disorder. Moreover, it is well known that opiate abuse kindles latent Manic-Depressive tendencies in genetically susceptible individuals. In such people, opium can cause a full blown clinical depression to flare up and go out of control. Often they become caught in a vicious cycle: drug abuse intensifies a depression which then prompts the depressed individual to relieve his depression by taking more drugs.

In all likelihood, something like this happened to Coleridge. But for stylistic purposes of this narrative, I have intentionally avoided using such technical terms since they tend to transform people into medical categories and subtract from their individuality. As a literary strategy for the sake of the general reader, I have attempted to keep all technical psychiatric and psychoanalytic terms to a minimum. But I am sure that the clinician-reader can easily supply the appropriate technical terms that would enrich his understanding of Coleridge's case history.

The manuscript for this book was completed in 1987. While it was in the process of production, several important papers have appeared that I have not been able to address.

Finally, I would like to thank the many people who have helped with this book. First and foremost, I want to express my deep and tender gratitude to my wife Carole for her encouragement, ideas and editorial skills. Also to be warmly thanked are Charlie Fenyvesi, Michelline Frank, Ed Kessler, Nancy Mello, Jack Mendelson, Rachel Rosenblum, Danny Dayan and Neil Young for their suggestions and criticisms.

Prologue

Cain and Abel

> *Entinctured with a twine of leaves,*
> *That leafy twine his only dress!*
> *A lovely Boy was plucking fruits,*
> *By moonlight, in a wilderness.*
> *The moon was bright, the air was free,*
> *And fruits and flowers together grew*
> *On many a shrub and many a tree:*
> *And all put on a gentle hue,*
> *Hanging in the shadowy air*
> *Like a picture rich and rare.*
> *It was a climate where, they say,*
> *The night is more belov'd than day.*
> *But who that beauteous Boy beguil'd,*
> *That beauteous Boy to linger here?*
> *Alone, by night, a little child,*
> *In place so silent and so wild—*
> *Has he no friend, no loving mother near?*
> —*The Wanderings of Cain* [PW, p. 287]

In 1779, in the kitchen of a rural vicarage, a seven-year-old boy asks his mother to slice a piece of cheese so that he may toast it over the fire. He is capable of cutting it himself, but it is "no easy matter, it being a *crumbly* cheese" and his heart is set on a perfect slice (CL I, p. 352).

His mother indulgently slices the cheese and goes on with her housework. Delighted with his trophy, the youngster carefully sets it aside and saunters out into the garden for a few minutes. When he returns, he discovers his nine-year-old brother has deliberately crumbled the cheese. The smaller child lashes out at his taunting brother, striking the older boy on the side of the head. His big brother slumps to the floor and lies there motionless. Terrified, the small child hovers over the prostrate form, whimpering and moaning. His brother leaps to his feet, gleefully bellows out a horse laugh, and returns his brother's slap with a smack.

Blinded with rage, his face stinging and his pride wounded, the smaller child seizes a kitchen knife and lunges at his tormentor, the blade poised to strike. He will never be entirely certain if he intended to drive the weapon home to its mark or meant merely to strike terror in his bullying brother's heart—for suddenly his mother enters the room.

Aroused by the commotion, she has arrived just in time to catch her son's arm and pry the knife from his fist. Caught in the act, and aware that nothing he will say to his mother can justify the attack, he wrestles free from her grip and bolts from the Devonshire cottage into the autumn evening.

He darts down the lane which passes in front of the churchyard, heading instinctively for the river. He streaks along the bank for nearly a mile until he reaches a hillside which slopes to the river's edge. At the top of the hill he begins to catch his breath, but it takes much longer for his jumbled feelings to die down.

The sun sinks toward the horizon and storm clouds begin to gather. Downstream, calves in the fields beyond the river graze lazily, feeding before bedding down for the night. The boy stares around him. He sees no trace of pursuers. The river is no more than ten yards across at its widest point, but it looks more vast to him. Like that river, the enormity of his crime looms large in his young mind. Aware that he faces certain punishment when he returns, he cannot bring himself to go home and submit.

Rummaging through his breeches pockets, he comes across his shilling prayer book. He takes it out and starts to read by the fading light. He repeats his morning and evening prayers. But even while praying very devoutly, he gloats, with inward and gloomy satisfaction, over how miserable his mother must be.

When it grows too dim to read, he pushes the book back into his pocket and huddles in the darkness.

Her child has been gone for what feels like like an eternity to his mother, although in fact it is barely half an hour since he tore out of the house. Physical violence between her boys is nothing new to her, but at fifty-three she is beginning to be less unflappable and a bit less energetic. She has already raised six other sons, three to manhood, and tonight she is beginning to wish that her last two were full-grown as well.

She waits patiently for her youngster, until "the *sulks* had evaporated" (CL I, p. 353), a time-honored strategy, but she is troubled by the dreadful stormy night. It will be cold and wet, no night for a small child to be abroad. She cannot imagine this one running away from home. He is not the adventurous sort. But she underestimates the intensity of his ordeal with his brother.

Anxious to the point of distraction, she abandons her waiting game and dispatches several men and all the boys to search the village. They return empty-handed. Alarm sets in.

At ten o'clock at night the lost child is "cry'd by the crier," with a reward offered. Other men hurry to two nearby villages and raise the criers there to announce the search for the lost boy. The manhunt continues, with half the town up all night.

Outside the youngster sleeps fitfully. It is a dramatically stormy night—terrifying, but majestic—as if a sign of God's judgment. Well versed in the tales of the Bible, the boy already knows the story of Cain and Abel. Like Cain, he has struck out murderously against his brother; he is now an outlaw and a wanderer. For the rest of his life he will feel this mark of Cain.

About five in the morning he wakes, astounded to find himself entangled in the branches of a dry thorn bush. Groggily he recalls having suffered the penetrating cold in his fitful sleep and wrapping himself in what he thought was a blanket. Somehow he has rolled down the hill to within a few yards of the river. He is too wet and stiff and cold to move. His muscles ache and his joints are frozen. Nearby, the ponds and the river are being dragged for his body.

He sees a shepherd and some workmen and cries out for help, but so faintly that it is impossible to hear him even thirty yards away. He begins to whimper and sob to himself. It is these animal sounds which finally catch the attention of a determined member of one of the dawn search parties. Scooping the shivering child into his arms, he wraps him in his greatcoat and carries him nearly a quarter of a mile.

As they near the village, the man spies the boy's parents and shouts out the good news. Peeking over the edge of the greatcoat, the youngster spots his father among the people running toward him. While the child is grateful for his deliverance, thoughts of the flogging he expects have remained with him all night long. As they draw nearer, he can make out his father's features. The tears stealing down his face mark his relief and pleasure. And while his mother is somewhat more reserved, she is "outrageous with joy" to have him home safe.

Neither parent mentions the fight or the knife. But a woman from the village chimes in: " 'I hope, you'll whip him, Mrs. Coleridge!' " (CL I, p. 354). No one seems to take notice of her comment.

The child is carried home and put to bed. With careful nursing he recovers from the physical exposure and shock within a few days. But thoughts of his encounter with his brother and his ordeal on that stormy night remain buried inside him. And although he receives no further punishment for his deed, memories of his crime and deliverance will echo and reecho within him for the rest of his life.

It may have been in the same year—the exact date is uncertain—somewhere in the English borderlands, hundreds of miles up the Great North Road that snakes and stretches into Scotland, that another youngster, equally miserable, also grabs a blade in a fit of passion. Half furious, half disconsolate, he flees to his grandparents' attic, where he snatches a sharp dueling foil and seriously considers running himself through with that deadly weapon.

The first boy homicidal, the second suicidal, both are of equally stormy temperaments. Both have begun to learn what it means to feel like outsiders. As grown men their paths will cross; they are destined to share a great but tormenting friendship. This book is the story of the life of the first child, Samuel Taylor Coleridge, and tells of his remarkable intercourse with the second, William Wordsworth.

Chapter 1

The Rivals

*My namesake sprung from Jewish Breeder
Knew from the Hyssop to the Cedar—
But I, unlike the Jewish leader,
Scarce know the Hyssop from the Cedar—*

[CNB 1104]

On a wintry evening in 1780, an elderly gentleman and his small child paused to admire the night sky as they made their way home from a nearby farmhouse. Naming as many stars as time permitted, the man outlined the shapes of a few constellations and pointed out Jupiter's steady pinpoint gleam, which, he said, was the light from a far-off planet a thousand times larger than the earth on which they stood. He wanted the boy to realize that the universe was far more vast than his eyes could see.

Spellbound, the child would cherish memories of this conversation with the old man. As a budding author in his twenties, he credited it as one of the incidents that had kindled his creative imagination. Later in life he would take pains to share the legacy with his son. And by the time he grew to the old man's age, tears streamed down his face whenever he reminisced about that starry night.

It is impossible to know if the youngster was more enraptured by the majesty of the night sky or by the old man's eloquence. But certainly it was his father's words which made those remote lights come alive with meaning for the boy who "heard him with a profound delight and admiration" (CL I, p. 354). Father and son, the pair were uncommonly fond of one another. Sixty-one-year-old John Coleridge doted on eight-year-old Sam, fully as much as wide-eyed Sam was in awe of John's wisdom and erudition.

Teacher, minister, and community leader, the Reverend John Coleridge had made a lifelong career of uplifting and instructing others. To accomplish his lofty aims, he was not above using his knack for showmanship, his own homespun brand of ecclesiastic razzle-dazzle. A fluent Hebrew scholar steeped in the Old Testament, John leavened the sermons he preached to his rural flock with well-chosen snatches of Hebrew, peddled with a carnival man's flair as *"the immediate language of the Holy Ghost"* (De Quincey, 1970, p. 58). While Coleridge later recalled how his father delighted in astounding his congregation with his arcane knowledge, he was quick to add that John's charismatic charlatan streak was more than offset by his warmth and humanity. Coleridge went so far as to compare him with the lovable country parson of Fielding's *Joseph Andrews:* "in learning, good-heartedness, absentness of mind and excessive ignorance of the world, he was a perfect Parson Adams" (CL I, p. 310).

It was John's fondest hope that Sam would eventually follow in his footsteps and take Holy Orders. Intensely interested in his youngest son's education, he liked to teach the boy by taking him on his knee and holding long conversations with him. An apt pupil, Sam could read a chapter of the Bible before he was three.

But the evidence suggests that Sam was inspired to learn that biblical text more by love of his father than by love of God. Doggerel penned in later life (see this chapter's epigraph) reveals a clear-cut lack of identification with his biblical "namesake" Samuel, who like Coleridge had been destined for the priesthood by his parents' wishes.

While those lines may only reflect Coleridge's adult feelings about becoming a minister, he recalled how from his earliest years he had had "a feeling of dislike and disgust" connected with his Christian name: "S.M.U.L.—altogether it is perhaps the worst combination of which vowels and consonants are susceptible" (CL II, p. 1126). Although at first glance his objections to his name seem to be metrical, not spiritual, his spelling, *SMUL*, suggests that John taught the child the Hebrew derivation of his name, *Smu-El*, and its meaning: "a prayer heard by God"—the mark that destined Samuel for the priesthood. Given John's dreams for Sam and his storyteller's knack for overwhelming his listener's resistance with Old Testament texts, it seems clear that Samuel first learned of his biblical namesake's illustrious career in the priesthood from his ambitious father.

When John Coleridge told his son that tale, he found a receptive and wide-eyed listener. Already an avid reader by the age of five, Sam's vivid imagination was easily fired by such legends. Moreover, its central theme, the chosen child, matched Sam's view of his own special status as the gifted infant in this overcrowded family teeming with big brothers.

Sam's very definite impression was that he enjoyed the twin distinctions of being his "Mother's darling" (CL I, p. 347) and his father's favorite, "the child of his old age" (CL I, p. 354). But in order to maintain this cherished belief that he and he alone was the center of his parents' universe, young Sam was occasionally obliged to employ his own budding storyteller's imagination.

One of the tales he concocted concerning his family ran something like this: Once upon a time, there was a simple country parson who was blessed with many sons and daughters, twelve to be exact. Absentminded, impractical, and lovably bumbling, the good man was "an Israelite without guile; simple, generous, and . . . indifferent to the good and the evil of this world" (CL I, p. 355). A rustic scholar of sorts, the old man "had so little of parental ambition in him, that he had destined his children to be blacksmiths" (CL I, p. 354).

All of them, that is, but his youngest son. In the presence of that precocious child, the kindly old man was awestruck. Impressed by his little one's remarkable powers of speech, the humble preacher was jolted from his dreamy lethargy and vowed to teach his genius son what little he knew. Fate had shown the parson that his boy was destined for greatness.

In broad outline, this is the *tone* of the portrait Coleridge later painted of his father. As a grown man, Coleridge would delight in regaling his friends with anecdotes of John's forgetfulness: how once, in preparing for a trip her husband was about to take, Anne Coleridge packed a clean shirt for each day he'd be gone. On his return, she was alarmed to discover all his shirts missing. Flabbergasted, John could shed no light on the mystery until, undressing for bed that evening, he peeled off shirt after shirt, having absentmindedly followed his wife's instructions that he put on a fresh blouse each day.

On another occasion, when seated at a fashionable dinner party, someone discreetly whispered to John that his shirttails were out. Attempting to tuck them in while still absorbed in conversation, the good man proceeded to stuff half of his dinner partner's flowing white gown into his trousers before he was made aware of his *faux pas*.

Coleridge's stories were endless, and he spun a yarn so well that his biographers have accepted his characterization of his father and portrait of their relationship, even while taking the tall tales with a grain of salt. But there were glaring contradictions to this quaint paternal portrait.

Far from being unaspiring, simple, or unworldly, John Coleridge was in fact remarkably ambitious and encouraged and expected the same from each of his sons. And had Samuel actually been the only one of his "tribe of brothers" (L. Coleridge, 1905, p. 27) whom their father had destined for the ministry, it is likely he would have been more inclined to follow in his footsteps. But as Sam already knew by the age of eight, taking Holy Orders was no path to glory if his aim was to be one of a kind. His brother William (age twenty-two) had just been ordained, while his brothers Edward (age twenty) and George (age sixteen) were headed in that celestial direction with their proud father's blessings.

Faced with this contradiction of his childhood myth that he was the chosen son of the tribe, Sam resourcefully came up with an alternative hypothesis to account for his older brothers' successes: each had been driven along his career path by their mother's "pride and spirit of aggrandizing her family" (CL I, p. 354). According to Sam, their father barely seemed to notice his other boys. Dreamily absorbed in his homespun philosophical and spiritual cogitations, he left the education of the other children to his commonsensical wife. It was his mother, Sam insisted, who had already drafted John (age twenty-six) and James (age twenty-one) into the military and was now urging Luke (age fifteen) toward a career in medicine.

Since Anne Coleridge handled discipline and managed the family budget, it is easy to see how in his imagination Sam could invest her with additional powers. But it is the artificial neatness of Sam's division of his parents into the warm-hearted dreamer and the shrewdly calculating manager that raises the suspicion that the future mythmaker was engaging in caricature rather than portraiture.

So while young Sam disingenuously cast his father in the family drama as the moonstruck, lackadaisical scholar, muddling through life, lost in his reveries, John Coleridge appears in reality, to have had a good deal of personal drive and ambition. His own father, a failed entrepreneur "reduced to extreme poverty," gave sixteen-year-old John "the half of his last crown and blessing" before bidding his son farewell as he "walked off to seek his fortune" (CL I, pp. 303–304).

A gifted scholarship student at his local grammar school, adolescent John quickly obtained a post as schoolmaster in a nearby village. Saving his pennies and shillings, John "scraped up enough money" to attend Cambridge (CL I, p. 303), which he entered at the age of twenty-nine with a wife and two young children in tow.

Resettling in Devon after his ordination, John became a churchwarden and schoolmaster. Widowed at the age of thirty-two, he was left with the care of his three young daughters until his remarriage to Anne Bowden two years later. He proceeded to have ten children with Anne, including his "tribe" of nine boys, one of whom died in infancy.

John eventually became Master of the King's New Grammar School, Chaplain Priest of the Collegiate Church and Vicar of Ottery St. Mary, the second largest Devon parish and the town in which Sam was born on October 21, 1772. John's brood prospered and while Sam considered himself his father's magnum opus—the child of his old age—the other sons of this supposedly unambitious country parson would produce, marry, or beget power and wealth (including two bishops and a Lord Chief Justice) within two generations.

John's dynastic impulses and worldly successes do not belie the fact that there was also a dreamy, artistic side to his personality. The image Sam formed of his father was lopsided, but not inaccurate. Yet curiously, while Coleridge would always emphasize his father's visionary temperament, he downplayed John's literary interests as if they were little more than the amateurish strivings of a casual Sunday dabbler.

John's four major published works consisted of two school texts, a religious treatise, and a political sermon. He also wrote magazine articles with such whimsical titles as "On the Discovery of Elephant's Bones Near Dover," as well as composing verse. But the most striking example of this supposedly humble parson's literary ambitions are to be found in the draft of a letter he sent to David Garrick, the foremost actor of the day, accompanying a manuscript of a play he hoped to interest Garrick in producing at the Drury Lane.

Clearly an ambitious fellow with strong creative and procreative drives, John Coleridge was a man intent on leaving his mark on the world. And whether he intended it or not, he was inspiring his son to oblige him in that aim as he chatted with his small boy. Given Sam's need to win his father's love by uniquely living up to his aspirations and ideals, it is hardly surprising that he would eventually leave the arena of ecclesiastic glory to his brothers and opt for a literary career. Declining the honors of SMU-EL, Samuel would become a man of letters, even going so far as to rechristen himself STC by adopting his monogram as a nom de plume.

But if eight-year-old Sam was toying with ambition, there is room to suspect that he was also learning to curb and disguise his unbridled aggressive instincts, the raw energy so necessary for any poet or warrior intending to carve out his place, particularly if it is to be one of preeminence. And the peaceful calm of that starry night stood in sharp contrast to the stormy night on the hillside. It had been little more than one year since Sam had brandished the knife over a piece of cheese—or, to put it more precisely, for evidence of his mother's love unspoiled.

After that quixotic enterprise, he had begun to grow away from his mother and was starting to mold himself in his father's image, or in the image his father offered him. Sam later recalled how John made his way in the world:

> My father . . . walked off to seek his fortune. After he had proceeded a few miles, he sat him down on the side of the road, so overwhelmed with painful thoughts that he wept audibly. A gentleman passed by, who knew him: and enquiring into his

distresses took my father with him, and settled him into a neighbouring town as a schoolmaster. [CL I, p. 303]

Now, John Coleridge was by no means a man who relied exclusively on helplessness or on other men's charity. More likely, eight-year-old Sam was being taken in hand, and this episode from his father's boyhood was being used as a homily, a parable with which to instruct Sam by emphasizing the Christian virtues of meekness and modesty as the critical ingredients in John's success. For even before the stabbing incident, Sam's parents had been finding good reason to be concerned about teaching their high-strung prodigy to stop being such a show-off:

> I was fretful, and inordinately passionate, and as I could not play at anything, and was slothful, I was despised and hated by the boys; and because I could read and spell, and had, I may truly say, a memory and understanding forced into almost an unnatural ripeness, I was flattered and wondered at by all the old women—and so I became very vain, and despised most of the boys, that were at all near my own age—and before I was eight years old, I was a *character*—sensibility, imagination, vanity, sloth and feelings of deep and bitter contempt for almost all who traversed the orbit of my understanding were even then prominent and manifest. [CL I, p. 347]

Eventually Sam would go overboard in his attempts to control his arrogance and suppress his competitiveness. Not content to cultivate a surface image of humility to gloss over his precocity and ambitions, he would, at critical times, make it a point of honor to deny his own self-interest, even to the extent of refusing to stand up for himself and fight back when it was appropriate to do so. To compensate for this taboo against aggression, Sam would closely follow John's story of his boyhood by developing an uncanny knack for being discovered and taken care of: relying on the kindness of strangers would become his modus operandi.

Eventually Sam would master the fine art of the modest social entrance as part of life's stagecraft by demurely contriving to first be noticed by others and invited to speak before allowing his audience to discover his voluble brilliance. Yet even as a grown man, once given the floor Coleridge would never be able to resist the temptation to hog it with all the vestigial instincts of the childhood prodigy.

But on some of those later occasions Coleridge would appear to be driven by an urgent pressure of speech and a giddy flight of ideas whose remote sources he could neither fathom nor entirely control. In fact, there is room to suspect that some of Coleridge's personal inconsistencies and his tendency toward unstable mood shifts had a far more fundamental basis than can be accounted for by these comparatively late experiences in socialization. Desperately insecure but arrogantly confident, dreamily mild-mannered and stormily temperamental, young Sam was filled with glaring contradictions which suggest that he was either born with or soon developed quicksilver mood swings. (What is known in modern psychiatric parlance as Manic-Depressive or Cyclothymic mood disorders.)

It was not long before Sam found himself embroiled in the proverbial battles of childhood with his brother Frank. Two years Sam's elder, Frank Coleridge was a fitting temperamental match for Sam as co-star in the endless dramatic repertory of nursery theater, which ranged from tragedy to high comedy. Having previously enjoyed solo billing as star performer by dint of being the youngest, Frank naturally resented sharing the limelight with his brother.

Already cast as "the handsome Coleridge" by unanimous family acclaim (CL I, p. 311), Frank was as volatile and theatrical as Sam. By the time he was a thirteen-year-old serving in the military he was a swashbuckling "young dog . . . as fond of his sword as a girl of a new lover" (L. Coleridge, 1905, p. 30). And as a proud, high-strung, romantic fifteen-year-old, he would sign his letters to his sister Nancy with the flourish, "Your affectionate and Handsome Brother" (L. Coleridge, 1905, p. 30). Endowed with a more virile, animal intelligence than was Sam, Frank was, in his own way, equally dramatic.

Hamming and mugging in their lighter moments, this nimble pair of nursery players acted out such childhood classics as *the hero and the villain, partners in crime, comrades in arms,* and *the stooge and his master.* And of course there was that old perennial favorite, The Punch and Judy Show, or as Sam later put it,

Frank had a violent love of beating me—but whenever that was superseded by any humor or circumstance, he was always very fond of me—and used to regard me with a strange mixture of admiration and contempt—strange it was not—: for he hated books, and loved climbing, fighting, playing and robbing orchards, to distraction. [CL I, p. 348]

Sam's most poignant memory of Frank's tenderness was of an occasion when he was six, stricken with a contagious "putrid fever," and placed in quarantine: Frank loyally "stole up in spite of orders to the contrary, and sat by my bedside, and read Pope's Homer to me" (CL I, p. 348).

Such cozy companions that on good days they dined on a runcible spoon, on others they were capable of the most passionately violent arguments. The incident over the slice of cheese occurred the following year, when Sam was seven. Viewed from afar, that episode might appear to be a classic case of triangular rivalry—two small boys fighting over their mother's love. But Sam emphatically recalled that the geometry of his chronic conflict with Frank was actually four-sided, and involved a quartet rather than a trio:

> I was my mother's darling—in consequence, I was very miserable. For Molly, who had nursed my brother Francis, and was immoderately fond of him, hated me because my mother took more notice of me than of Frank—and Frank hated me, because my mother gave me now and then a bit of cake, when he had none—quite forgetting that for one bit of cake which I had and he had not, he had twenty sops in the pan and pieces of bread and butter with sugar on them from Molly, from whom I received only thumps and ill names.—So I became fretful, and timorous, and a tell-tale—and the schoolboys drove me from play, and were always tormenting me—and hence I took no pleasure in boyish sports—but read incessantly. [CL I, p. 347]

According to Sam's splayed sense of justice, it was equitable for Frank to have Molly, while he, Sam, possessed their mother exclusively, without brotherly acrimony. In theory, he saw no reason why Frank should object to this ingenious blueprint for domestic peace. But daily experience frustrated his dream of a harmonious quartet.

And so, Sam's "incessant" reading was aimed at finding a solution to his conflict with Frank. Back to the drawing board, researching the problem in his fairy tales, Sam located a case which explained precisely the weakness in his grand design for domestic bliss: he had miscalculated the nature of women.

The story he found fascinated him so much that he read it again and again. It became so important that he even developed a magical ceremonial ritual before pouring over it each day:

> I found the Arabian Nights' Entertainments—one tale of which (the tale of a man who was compelled to seek for a pure virgin) made so deep an impression on me (I had read it in the evening while my mother was mending my stockings) that I was haunted by spectres, whenever I was in the dark—and I distinctly remember the anxious and fearful eagerness, with which I used to watch the window, in which the books lay—and whenever the sun lay upon them, I would seize it, carry it by the wall, and bask, and read. [CL I, p. 347]

As young children often do, Sam chanced upon a story that reflected his own predicament. The similarities were close enough that repeated readings of the instructive fable offered consolation and hope. The tale (see Appendix A) was of two brothers, the Persian Kings Shahryar and Shahzeman. Banding together after they are betrayed by their wives, the disillusioned brothers travel, seeking one another's consolation.

Wandering along their way, they cross paths with an enormous, powerful genie whose cunning wife forces the brothers to cuckold the giant as he sleeps. Now, with final proof that all women are fickle and perfidious, and that even the most mature and powerful of men fall helpless victims to their wiles, the two brothers become confirmed misogynists.

The rest of the tale focuses on King Shahryar, who, after slaughtering his wife, remains bitter and depressed and opts for a life of pleasure and revenge. A compulsive seeker of virgins, Shahryar weds, beds, and beheads maidens on a nightly basis until he all but decimates the virgin population of his kingdom. At this point, Scheherazade steps in.

Determined to end the senseless bloodshed, she is intent on soothing the unhappy King and reawakening his trust. Unlike her luckless predecessors, who shared nuptial pleasures with the King immediately after the wedding ceremony, Scheherazade contrives to keep the King awake all night by telling him a bedtime story. Finally, after a thousand and one nights, she renews his faith in women and they live happily ever after.

Faced with the daily tribulations of his stormy domestic quartet with Frank, Mother, and Molly, Sam was mesmerized by this tale of two brothers who fell victim to the caprices of the women in their lives. By banding together, the two brothers liberated themselves from the tyranny of women and became fast friends. While Sam and Frank could not dispose of Mother and Molly by chopping them up, as Shahryar and Shahzeman had done with their wives, there certainly was a grain of truth in the idea that the rivalry between Sam and Frank centered on their relationship with women.

Nothing is known of the immediate aftermath of the battle over the cheese on that October night in 1779: how the two boys made up with one another or if they ever did. But it is known that they never had time to grow up together or to establish their brotherly relationship on an adult footing. For two years later, in the fall of 1781, Frank Coleridge left Ottery St. Mary and set out for sea as an apprentice midshipman in the Royal Navy. He was eleven years old—by no means an unusual age by the child-rearing standards of the day.

Handsome, fit, and bubbling with enthusiastic anticipation of his seafaring adventures, Frank had every ambition for a fair voyage in life. Judging from letters he sent home to his family with messages to Maria, his prospective fiancée, begging her to remain faithful and to wait for him, it seems that eleven-year-old Frank had informally proposed to the girl before leaving home. Little is known of Maria except that she set a high price on her hand, demanding Frank come up with a fortune of ten thousand pounds before she would consent to marry him.

While Maria's marriage bounty suggests a touch of vanity that was clearly the match of young Frank's warrior pride, the sum in question was not entirely beyond his grasp. And it is to the dashing young man's credit that he never stooped to quibble over her asking price but remained unflinchingly optimistic that he would be able to raise this princely sum and accomplish his matrimonial designs. Boys setting out to sea dreamed of the fame and riches to be won from captured naval prizes, and Frank Coleridge was no different.

And so when John Coleridge left for Plymouth to take Frank to his ship and see him off on that fall day in 1781, there was nothing in the nature of a punishment in an eleven-year-old boy's being sent to sea to make his fortune. But what was both cruel and unusual was the fact that in addition to bidding Frank good-bye, Sam would never again see his father. On the night of October 4—a date he would never forget—Sam awoke from his sleep in the middle of the night to the shriek of his mother's voice. He knew instantly that his father was dead.

John Coleridge was buried in a vault in front of the altar in the church where he had so long preached. He had died in bed on the night of his return from Plymouth, of undetermined causes, most likely of a heart attack. The vicarage was now emptier than it had ever been before. Sam's entire tribe of brothers were scattered to the four corners of the earth. Young John was in India, Frank was at sea, and George (age seventeen) and Luke (age sixteen) were away at school. His older brothers had long since departed. Only Mother, Molly, and his sister Nancy remained.

Soon a new parson and schoolmaster was found for Ottery St. Mary, and the family moved from the two-story vicarage into more modest quarters. Still attending John's school, Sam now returned home with daily tales of the new master's mistakes and criticisms of his teaching talents. Clearly no one could replace his father.

Meanwhile, plans were being made for the family's future. A place was found for Sam at the Christ's Hospital School in London, where he would prepare for the clergy in keeping with John's wishes. In April of 1782, six months after his father's death, Sam left for London.

Although Sam did not realize it at the time, he would rarely return home again—once at the age of thirteen and once again at nineteen—before beginning university. And for a family that saved and cherished their children's letters home, only one would survive from Sam to his mother. And that letter is striking in its coolness, its formality, and its emphasis upon duty rather than love.

Even though Anne Coleridge would live twenty-seven more years, dying at age eighty-two, Sam would visit her no more than two or three times once he became a grown man with a family of his own. A note that Sam later wrote to his own son Hartley, preparing him for a visit to his grandmother's that never materialized, suggests something of Sam's childhood view of his mother. Instructing Hartley how to behave at Ottery, he wrote:

> Specially, never pick at or snatch up anything, eatable or not. I know, it is only an idle foolish trick; but your Ottery relations would consider you as a little thief—and in the Church Catechism *picking* and *stealing* are both put together, as two sorts of the same vice—'and keep my hands from picking and *stealing.*' And besides, it is a dirty trick; and people of weak stomachs would turn sick at a dish, which a young FILTH-PAW had been fingering. [CL III, p. 10]

Even when Anne Coleridge lay on her deathbed in 1809, Sam would make no attempt to see her, although there was ample time for him to do so. After her death, Sam would remain curiously silent about his reaction to her passing. He would, however, unaccountably skip one edition of the one-man weekly newspaper he was publishing at the time. And during that two-week period there would be one cryptic entry in his diary that hinted of his feelings:

> In the comment of R[abbi] Akibah on Eccliastes, XII.i we have a story of a mother who having nothing else to blame her child for, or—it being some way deformed, and unwilling that it should be deemed to have been punished for some fault of hers, complained of her child, in earnest before the Judge, . . . that it kicked her unmercifully in the womb. [CNB 3614]

When and how Sam's feelings for his mother soured remains a mystery. Possibly he had already grown to distrust her by the time he read the Arabian Nights story. But, as that tale correctly suggests, most boys get over the inevitable disappointment of their romantic fantasy that they are their mother's darling.

It is likely, however, that Sam never forgave his mother for the much more real betrayal of sending him off to London so soon after his father's death. Unprepared to cope with yet another loss following so closely on the heels of Frank's departure, Sam was about to learn the meaning of the word homesick and might well have found reason to despise his mother for casting him out.

Six months was all too brief an interval for Sam to mourn his father, particularly if Anne Coleridge was dealing with her own feelings of loss with a stiff-upper-lip, business-as-usual approach. If Anne relied on grim optimism or tight-lipped stoicism to cope with her own grief, it is unlikely she could have permitted, much less helped, her son to express his.

But while grief can be postponed, it cannot be denied its eventual expression. Once settled at Christ's Hospital School, Sam would find time enough to discover how sorely he missed his father. And afterward, as a grown man, Sam would be puzzled by his peculiar tendency not to react to emotionally upsetting events except after long delays of time:

> If I were to judge of myself by what takes place in my consciousness after hearing or seeing any calamity or distressing occurrence, and by the freedom, I feel, to talk, chat, laugh, etc., I should think and often have thought myself utterly insensible/incapable of feeling deeply for myself or others. [CL II, p. 1046]

But try as he might to get to the bottom of it, Coleridge would never clearly connect his lifelong tendency toward delayed emotional reactions to the events leading to that coach trip to London in the spring of 1782. And as he looked back on those first few weeks in London years later, he would recall not his overwhelming loss, but the gaiety and excitement he first felt on encountering the throbbing vitality of that great city.

Chapter 2

School Days

> *At eve, sky-gazing in 'ecstatic fit'*
> *(Alas! for cloister'd in a city School*
> *The Sky was all, I knew, of Beautiful)*
> *At the barr'd window often did I sit,*
> *And oft upon the leaded School-roof lay.*
> —from an early version of *Dejection: An Ode*
> [quoted in Chambers, 1938, p. 8]

The Bull Inn at Aldgate in East London was a family enterprise run by Ann Nelson. Her son George drove the Exeter Defiance, the coach that ran from Ottery to London. The Bull was one of the finest coaching inns of the day—known for its great mahogany chairs and full-bodied port—both of which John Bowden no doubt enjoyed as he waited for his sister's boy to arrive from Devon.

Sam Coleridge received a cheerful welcome from Uncle John and was relieved to discover such a warm-hearted, friendly soul awaiting him at the end of the tiring journey from his sleepy market town of twenty-five hundred people to this metropolis of over a million. Equally pleased with his nine-year-old nephew's precocity, John declared Sam a prodigy and made up his mind to turn him into a man about town in the ten weeks they had to spend together before school started.

Never having had a son of his own, Sam later wrote, John "was very proud of me, and used to carry me from coffee-house to coffee-house, and tavern to tavern, where I drank, and talked and disputed, as if I had been a man" (CL I, p. 388). Sam—now fatherless—was thrilled to find a replacement for Papa even if Uncle John's conversation was inspired more by the liquor he drank than by the books he read: "my poor Uncle . . . was as generous as the air . . . but he was a sot" (CL I, p. 388).

But as Sam discovered in the taverns they frequented,

Uncle John was by no means the only one who drank too much. Half of London reeled and staggered on a Saturday night. While the shabby poor drowned their wretchedness in drams of Geneva in the seedy gin mills, working and middle class men snored on their sofas with their boots on, and even the mightiest in the land were seduced by the grape. Ambitious William Pitt, about to become his country's youngest prime minister, would die precociously (in his mid-forties) of alcoholism, while the heir apparent, the Prince of Wales, after coming of age in 1783, would alarm members of the royal household by drunkenly brandishing his sword in the air as he wobbled and staggered about his drawing rooms. Only his father, George III, known in some circles as "Farmer George" (Sherwin, 1960, p. 29), was known for his sobriety.

And though their fare was far less lethal than that of the taverns, the coffeehouses Uncle John frequented were just as intoxicating and lively for a nine-year-old boy just up from the country. The Virginia and Baltic on Threadneedle Street, only a stone's throw from John's tobacco shop, was undoubtedly one of John's regular haunts, as that was where the traders and sea captains offered samples of their freshly arrived shipments from the colonies. But more than marketplaces, the coffeehouses served as neighborhood centers where friends met in the smoky rooms to gossip, talk politics, and while away the hours. "Spoilt and pampered" (CL I, p. 388), Sam was delighted to be the center of so much attention and enjoyed himself thoroughly.

Given Uncle John's proclivities, he may have found scant time to show Sam the town, but London Bridge was a sight not to be missed. Like the streets of the city, the Thames was jammed with traffic—galleys, skiffs, barges, and other small craft filled and congested that river. Downstream, below the bridge and headed seaward, row after row of stately, tall-masted ships rode at anchor side by side, filed into blocks by nationality, creating a maze of boulevards and avenues out of the surrounding waters while gulls soared and floated through the mist, scavenging their Sunday dinners. It was a maritime age and it would not be long before Horatio Nelson forcibly demonstrated to the world that Britain commanded the seas.

Upstream, approaching the city and the bridge from

Greenwich, the first glimpse of London more often than not revealed a sprawling metropolis eerily shrouded in a dense mixture of thick smoke and heavy fog. On overcast days only the dome of St. Paul's towered above the smog, and through the hazy air its great bells tolled the hours. Since Elizabethan times, thousands of chimneys all across the city had belched out a fine gritty soot which settled on the buildings over the centuries, finishing them with a somber patina. And in the hospital dissection laboratories, kept well supplied with corpses through the nocturnal diligence of the grave-robbing "resurrection men," any observant medical student could tell you that the lungs of your city-bred cadaver were a "dingy thundercloud blue" (Quennell and Quennell, 1977, p. 176), in contrast to the robust pink of those of his country cousin.

The most startling sight on the bridge for a young boy fresh from the country were the rotting heads of traitors to the crown, suspended from the lofty parapets as a gruesome warning. Sam had never seen anything like it at Ottery; though his father had written a pamphlet on the American Revolution, this trip to London was his first exposure to a volatile center of social unrest, precariously balanced on the edge of mob violence. In fact, London was then still rebuilding from the effects of the Gordon Riots two years earlier. On a warm spring day an orderly group of sixty thousand demonstrators concluded their open-air rally in St. George's Fields by marching eight abreast across that same London Bridge in what had been planned to be a nonviolent protest at the Houses of Parliament. But drunks from the gin mills and disgruntled rabble from the slums began to smash and overturn carriages.

Afterward, for nearly a week, mobs roamed the city and arsonists' fires raged nightly across London, destroying ten times more property than would the storming of the Bastille. Watching the mayhem with his fellow law students, William Pitt had suffered the spectacle of his rooms at Lincoln's Inn "surrounded with flames on all sides" (Reilly, 1979, p. 64). He would never forget the violence of those crowds; when he assumed leadership of his country three years later, he personally began to shape a series of repressive policies toward radical reformers.

London was experiencing its latest crime wave, superimposed on its already high baseline rate following the troop demobilizations after the American War. Anne Coleridge had good reason to take comfort in the knowledge that her youngest child, as a student at the Christ's Hospital School, would soon be securely cloistered away from the dangers of street crime and political disturbances.

New boys found the shift from home to school abrupt and impersonal. To ease the transition, they were shipped to the Junior School at Hertford, twenty miles north of London, for a six-week orientation program before starting classes at the main campus. The fresh air, wholesome food, relaxed atmosphere, and brilliant summer green of the sun-dappled English countryside stood in stark contrast to the gray pavements of the city, and the life that awaited them.

Once back in London, young Coleridge—as he was now known to his schoolmasters and seven hundred classmates—was placed in the Lower Grammar School and assigned a bed. The boys were housed in twelve dormitories and took their meals together in the commons of the main building. School food was meager, unappetizing, and boring—sometimes repulsively inedible, barely a day short of rotten.

Boys fortunate enough to have friends or family in the city were free to supplement the drab institutional fare with tasty parcels and looked forward to hearty meals taken at a cheerful home table on their leave days. But while Uncle John may have pampered his nephew during their intoxicating ten-week adventure, it seems his affable generosity was fueled by the spirits he drank and evaporated just as quickly. Judging by the fact that Coleridge routinely spent his leave days alone traipsing around London, it appears that he did not often have the opportunity to visit Uncle John.

Instead, lost in the crowds, he stared vacantly into shop windows for hours on end, killing time as he waited for the hour when they were allowed to return. During his wanderings, Coleridge searched with longing for men in black—amiable clergymen willing to chat with him for a few minutes. Clearly, he missed his father.

Both clergyman and schoolmaster, the Reverend Matthew Field was the most logical substitute, as his role as Master of the Lower Grammar School put him in daily contact with the child. But Field was a self-absorbed fop whose general tendency to ignore his pupils led him to summarily dismiss Coleridge as a dull and unpromising boy. While Field's immediate impression may have been accurate, the mental sluggishness he observed was a sign of a clinical depression, not of inferior intelligence.

Coleridge's first two years at Christ's Hospital, from the ages of nine to eleven, were the most gruesome period of his childhood. He was suffering from profound melancholia after his father's death, and this was aggravated both by the stress of being sent away from home and by the grim authoritarian atmosphere of Christ's Hospital. Charles Lamb, entering the school at about the same time as Coleridge, later described his first day there:

> The sight of a boy in fetters, upon the day of my putting on the blue clothes, was not exactly fitted to assuage the natural terrors of this initiation.... I was told that he had *run away*. This was the punishment for the first offence. As a novice, I was taken soon after to see the dungeons. These were little square Bedlam cells where a boy could just lie at length upon straw and a blanket—a mattress, I think, was afterward substituted—with a peep of light let in askance from a prison orifice at top, barely enough to read by. Here the poor boy was locked in by himself all day, without sight of any but the porter who brought him his bread and water—who *might not speak to him*—or of the beadle, who came twice a week to call him out to receive his periodic chastisement, and here he was shut by himself *of nights*, out of reach of any sound. [Lamb, 1820–1825, p. 28]

Lamb went on to recall that there were cases of madness and even suicide in response to such harsh treatment.

But the enlightened educational psychology of the day taught that sparing the rod spoiled the child. Two of the school's major goals were to teach the boys respect for authority and to indoctrinate them into the system of rank and privilege so that they might become model citizens. The fact that a handful of graduates of this King's charity school went on to occupy some of the highest posts in the land—top-ranking military officers, judges, bishops, politicians—was considered proof positive of the virtues of this child-rearing philosophy.

Fagging and flogging were its mainstays; each new boy became fag to a senior who served as his mentor in return for such services as scraping and polishing his muddy shoes, or warming his icy bed sheets on a winter night. Designed to instill a keen sense of hierarchical social status, like the paternalistic system of rank and privilege that prevailed in English society at large, this schoolboy practice all too often deteriorated into a system of exploitation. The boys' cruelties toward one another were influenced by the example of their masters. Floggings were routinely used to test and reinforce rote memorization of Latin and Greek, to maintain order, and to teach respect for authority. Given the fact that the majority of these handpicked scholarship students came from impecunious backgrounds and thus were motivated to cooperate with the system in order to get ahead, the more drastic penal methods Lamb described were rarely necessary.

It was understood from the start that only a small percentage of the boys would enter university. And while overt displays of competitiveness were discouraged, it was also well known that each boy's future station in life began to be decided at an early age. Boys were first screened as potential university material at age eleven; at that age the promising students were drafted into the Upper Grammar School, while the less apt began to prepare for commercial life. By the age of sixteen an elite cadre of expert classics scholars, or Grecians as they were called, were chosen for the First Form. It was the Grecians who eventually won scholarships that allowed them to attend Oxford and Cambridge.

While most boys' academic destinies depended on their master's impression of their intelligence, Coleridge credited his good fortune in becoming a Grecian to Thomas Middleton, a generously inclined schoolmate two years ahead of him. Having escaped Reverend Field's notice in the classroom, Coleridge came to Middleton's attention in the cloisters. Impressed to discover an eleven-year-old reading Virgil for pleasure, Middleton reported the incident to the Master of the Upper Grammar School, James Bowyer.

Shortly afterward, Coleridge was admitted to the Upper School, where he rapidly became good friends with Middleton and devoted himself to the less easily gained goal of becoming "old Jemmy Bowyer's" protégé (Campbell, 1905, p. 2). A curmudgeonly man but a dedicated teacher who took an intense interest in his boys, the Reverend James Bowyer was a stern taskmaster who liberally wielded his flogging birch to reward shoddy scholarship. Finding Coleridge a promising pupil, Bowyer took a personal interest in his education. But unluckily for Coleridge, Bowyer gruffly demonstrated his affection by adding an extra stroke for good measure to Coleridge's periodic floggings, accompanied by an explanatory grunt: "for you are such an ugly fellow" (Gillman, 1838, p. 20). Nonetheless, Coleridge had finally found a clergyman-schoolmaster who cared about him.

Fortunately, Coleridge was soon able to rely on less ambivalently expressed affection. In 1784, when Coleridge became an Upper Boy, his brother Luke arrived in London to spend a year studying medicine and his spare time looking after Sam. Bound by a strong sense of loyalty, the Coleridge brothers took care of one another. Concurrent with Sam and Luke's reunion, Frank (age fourteen) and John (age twenty-nine) were renewing their acquaintance thousands of miles away. Frank had already spent three years at sea when his ship sailed south across the Equator, rounded the Cape, and made its way through the Indian Ocean. Landing at the port of Bombay, Frank had been discovered accidently by John, who immediately secured his discharge from the Royal Navy and obtained a commission for him in the Indian Army. Delighted, John wrote home to Ottery suggesting he do the same for Sam.

But John's offer was unnecessary, for just as Luke left London, George showed up to take his place. After graduating Oxford, George had become a clergyman-schoolmaster, and had taken a teaching post in a London suburb. Eight years Sam's senior, George quickly became a substitute parent for Sam—a role he would fill for the rest of Sam's schooldays.

With George's encouragement and Bowyer's tutelage, Coleridge's depression lifted and he began to blossom intellectually. Apart from his enormous appetite as a reader—enthusiastically devouring as many as two books a day—he was also beginning to develop his skills as a writer. Besides instructing Coleridge in formal metrics and the different poetic genres,

Bowyer was a tough critic who taught by saving up four or five of his cringing pupil's poems and reviewing the accumulated evidence of their shortcomings out loud, roaring and thundering in front of the entire class:

> In fancy I can almost hear him now exclaiming, 'Harp? Harp? Lyre? Pen and ink, boy, you mean! Muse, boy, Muse? Your Nurse's daughter, you mean! Pierian Spring? Oh, Aye! the cloister-pump I suppose.' [Coleridge, 1817a, p. 5]

Mortified but motivated, Coleridge struggled harder to win Bowyer's approval and was doubly delighted when finally allowed to copy a few of his best poems into his master's Golden Album—the ultimate sign of recognition.

These poems, Coleridge later estimated, were little more than the mechanical transcription of thought into verse. "Dura Navis," written when he was fifteen, addresses an adventurous youth at sea (possibly Frank), speculates on the dangers he faces, and wishes him godspeed and a safe return to dry land and domestic bliss. While its immature lines bear no resemblance to the graceful verse of the *Ancient Mariner*, it is nonetheless Coleridge's first poem about the hazards of nautical life and a sailor's hardships.

As Coleridge's academic confidence increased, he became less socially isolated. Besides Middleton, Coleridge's closest school friend was a handsome, good-natured boy named Robert Allen. Charles Lamb, somewhat younger, was just beginning to worship Coleridge for his brilliance, much as Coleridge idolized Middleton. Coleridge and Lamb were to be lifelong friends.

At the age of sixteen, Coleridge and Allen became Grecians. Soon afterward, their soaring spirits bolstered by their elite status, the pair went courting. Having met two attractive sisters—Mary and Anne Evans—they began to enjoy a weekly rendezvous with the girls:

> And oh! from sixteen to nineteen what hours of paradise had Allen and I in escorting the Miss Evanses home on a Saturday, who were then at a milliner's . . . and we used to carry thither, on a summer morning, the pillage of the flower gardens within six miles of the town with sonnet or love-rhyme wrapped round the nosegay. [Coburn, 1979b, p. 32]

Previously oblivious to matters sartorial, young Coleridge's letters to his brother George began to exude the confident tone of a man of the world as he importuned his guardian for extra pocket money with which to finance a new set of breeches he fancied.

But Coleridge's diaries also reveal that beneath this dashing facade and romantic bravado, he was plagued by sexual insecurities. Terrified of catching the "itch" in his blood from any sexual contact with Mary Evans (CNB 2398), his nominal sweetheart among the pair of sisters, Coleridge was unable to feel any physical attraction. Back at the Christ's Hospital dormitory after his Saturday outings with Allen, he lay awake at night "groaning and praying," afraid that he was a "eunuch" (CNB 2398n). Although his adolescent anxieties were perhaps irrational in their extent, the epidemic prevalence of gonorrhea and syphilis in the late eighteenth century was enough to warrant realistic concerns about catching the dreaded "pox."

While Coleridge's ardor for Mary was chilled by his sexual fears, he thoroughly enjoyed the camaraderie with Bob Allen that came with courting a pair of sisters. Hungry for domestic security, it was not long before Coleridge was addressing Mrs. Evans as "Mama" and "Right Reverend Mother," while her daughters soon became "my sisters" (CL I, p. 33). Encircled by this sense of family, Coleridge undoubtedly felt well cared for when in 1789 he was confined to an infirmary sickbed for a case of jaundice misdiagnosed as "rheumatic fever."

On a July day in 1789, all across the city, Londoners sat down to their morning coffee and opened the *Morning Post* to read the startling news that earlier that week a mob of Parisian men and women from the working class suburb of Saint-Antoine had risen up in fury and stormed the Bastille—a hated symbol of the tyranny they had so long suffered and one of the nobility's most effective weapons for safeguarding its prerogatives and privileges.

The news spread like wildfire throughout England, and the event became the most hotly debated political matter of the day. By the time of the London Revolutionary Society's annual November Fourth dinner at the London Tavern on Bishopgate Street—a meeting commemorating the anniversary of the Glorious Revolution of 1688—a spirit of fervent internationalism had so overcome the assembled members that they declared themselves "Citizens of the World" and "Friends of Liberty"; they enthusiastically pledged toast after toast to their French brothers' stunning victory over tyranny. On July 14 of the following year, the Society held a special dinner at the Crown and Anchor in the Strand to commemorate the fall of the Bastille. A stone from the hated prison was prominently displayed on the dais as Society members expressed their heartfelt sympathies by sporting the tricolor cockade.

Astutely capitalizing on this popular sentiment, Lebrun, foreign affairs minister at the French embassy, fueled the English radicals' enthusiasm with glowing bulletins describing the latest achievements of the heroic Revolution. So up to date were these bulletins that only a few short weeks after the *Marseillaise* was composed, groups of Englishmen were expressing their solidarity with their heroic French comrades by singing rousing stanzas of that stirring march from freshly printed copies, courtesy of Monsieur Lebrun. Too young (at least for one of his class and station) to participate directly in political demonstrations, yet nonetheless influenced by the democratic spirit just starting to sweep through English intellectual circles, seventeen-year-old Coleridge dashed off a poem fervently praising the Revolution: the "Destruction of the Bastille."

But in spite of his nascent leanings toward radical politics, Coleridge remained under his family's influence and acceded to their wishes by preparing for university with the goal of becoming an Anglican clergyman. As one of Christ's Hospital's leading scholars, he was accorded the honor of delivering the annual schoolboy Latin oration at the Lord Mayor's festivities on St. Matthew's Day, 1789. However, a privately circulated poem, "The Nose, an Odaic Rhapsody," in which he makes fun of the Lord Mayor's proboscis, suggests that Coleridge was already feeling irreverent, both toward signs of his own academic success and toward social rank and privilege generally. But at this point he was prepared to do no more than satirize convention. In his final year at Christ's Hospital (1790) he applied for and won a scholarship to Jesus College, Cambridge. The award was intended for young men with a high degree of motivation and showing promise for clerical careers.

School Days

Arriving at Cambridge early one morning in mid-October of 1791, having taken the night coach from London, Coleridge headed directly for Thomas Middleton's rooms at Pembroke College. After breakfast, Middleton got Coleridge settled into Jesus. It took no time at all for them to reestablish the big brother–little brother relationship of the old Christ's Hospital days.

A serious classics scholar destined to become a Bishop in the Church of England, Middleton hoped to win an academic fellowship that would allow him to remain on after completing his final undergraduate year. He had already begun to prepare for the exhausting competitive examinations scheduled for that December. Coleridge was delighted when Middleton suggested they keep each other company while they studied, but he was soon struck by the ferocity of his friend's self-discipline. One evening while the pair were working quietly—after Middleton had somehow managed to persuade his ever talkative companion to adhere strictly to a vow of total silence—Coleridge was startled by the sharp report of a pistol. Looking up, he was amazed to see Middleton in knee boots with a smoking gun at his side; he explained that he was shooting at the rats in order to drive them back into their holes so they would not eat the textbooks.

In addition to being rat-infested, the rooms at Cambridge were chilly and damp. In late November, Coleridge wrote his brother George:

> Cambridge is a damp place—the very palace of winds: so without very great care one is sure to have a violent cold. I am not however certain, that I do not owe my rheumatism to the dampness of my rooms. Opium never used to have any disagreeable effects on me—but it has upon many. [CL I, p. 18]

Dreary, damp, foggy, and marshy—the undrained lands of the Fen District on which Cambridge bordered was the part of England having the highest concentration of opium addicts throughout the eighteenth century and the first half of the nineteenth. Known in working class circles as "Mother's Blessing," opium was a popular home remedy, regularly used for a wide variety of ailments from cradle to grave (Mayhew,

1851–1864, V. 4, p. 245). Teething infants were given the drug to soothe them, young children received it for the rheumatic pains of ague, fretful women took it regularly for "female troubles," and manual laborers recreationally spiked their beer with opium to offset boredom and fatigue; the elderly Fen men—many of them lifetime addicts—used it for arthritis and other infirmities of old age. Home-grown opium was brewed in the form of poppy-head tea and "there was not a labourer's house . . . without its penny stick of opium," the commercial vending of which "was as common as the sale of butter and cheese" (Berridge, 1979, p. 298).

Coleridge encountered no difficulty in finding opium, as it was legally sold—as aspirin is today—by ordinary tradesmen as well as apothecaries, any of whom would no doubt have unhesitatingly suggested it to him as the treatment of choice for colds and arthritic pains. As Coleridge's letter to George suggests, he had tried opium even before coming to Cambridge. Most likely he had been given the drug for childhood agues and other minor illnesses; he perhaps received it for his bout of "rheumatic fever" at Christ's Hospital. Like the unsuspecting adults who originally administered it to him, Coleridge was unaware of opium's addictiveness and used it for his cold without mentioning any of its vivid mental effects.

Although George Coleridge was worried about his youngest brother, his concern was not about drugs. He wanted to know if Coleridge was associating with a certain William Frend, a Fellow at Jesus College. A Unitarian dissenter and disciple of Joseph Priestley, Frend was a godless man in George's eyes and a potentially dangerous influence on his Samuel's moral and spiritual welfare. Irritated by George's overprotectiveness, Coleridge waspishly replied that "Mr. Frend's company is by no means invidious" (CL I, p. 20) but also reassured George that he had not yet abandoned the Church of England.

George's anxieties were motivated by the widespread social upheaval taking place: everywhere people were challenging the established authority of England's religious and political institutions. Conservative monarchist and devout Anglican, George was concerned that Sam would join the avant-garde Cambridge radicals flocking to Unitarianism. Challenging the doctrine of the Trinity, Unitarians insisted that God was one and indivisible.

While this may seem a matter of theological hairsplitting today, the social implications of the controversy were profound.

Because it presented a profound paradox, the doctrine of the Trinity reinforced the need for a highly stratified clerical hierarchy that devoted itself to explaining God's mysterious ways to the uneducated common man, thereby preying upon his ignorance, it was argued by Unitarians, and undermining his confidence in his own ability to decide right from wrong. By contrast, Unitarianism demystified God into a simple, approachable force who could be petitioned directly, without what was condemned as the mumbo jumbo of the Latin liturgy and the hocus-pocus of the sacraments. Conscience was becoming more an individual concern than a policy matter dictated by a Church of England devoted to maintaining the status quo. This trend had no need of an elite schooled in Latin and Greek, a sign that men like George Coleridge might soon be out of a job—a concern that was beginning to worry His Majesty, George III, regarding his own line of work. Both Church and King were dispensable, as the French had just demonstrated by disestablishing the Catholic Church and capturing Louis XVI at the Varennes border and unceremoniously hauling him back to Paris under armed guard.

Faced with this anarchical prospect and its possible spread to England, the Establishment was fighting back by forming Church-and-King clubs to contain the godless democrats whose French-sympathizing societies were springing up with memberships running into the thousands, if not hundreds of thousands. By 1791, Coleridge's freshman year, English society had become polarized, and the country was on the verge of civil violence.

All across the country on July 14 the Friends of Liberty held dinner meetings. The most dramatic response occurred at Birmingham, where a huge mob of torchbearing Church-and-King demonstrators went on a three-day rampage, destroying three Unitarian churches and twenty-seven homes, including Joseph Priestley's. Radical-led mobs contributed their share to the mayhem, including a rampage at Sheffield that required two divisions of the King's Fifteenth Light Dragoons to be put down. As was the case in France, men were discovering that their humanitarian ideals involved more bloodshed than they had anticipated.

And so George Coleridge had good reason to worry that his misguided baby brother might fall under the influence of men like Frend. No doubt George was relieved to learn that Samuel had just been awarded a second fellowship reserved for future Anglican clergymen and that he was "reading Pindar, and composing Greek verse, like a mad dog" (CL I, p. 35).

Under Middleton's influence, Coleridge set his sights on competing for the Greek Prize Ode that spring and for a Craven Fellowship the next winter. Winning the Craven would insure staying on at Cambridge indefinitely, just as Middleton hoped to do.

By the time Christmas rolled around, Coleridge was ready for a break and spent a delightful fortnight in London with the Evans family, squiring the two sisters with Bob Allen, who was back from Oxford. Returning to Cambridge refreshed and in high spirits, Coleridge kept up a steady, bantering correspondence with all of the Evans women. Later that spring term even Middleton let up, once he learned he had failed to win the scholarship. Coleridge went out on his first wine-drinking party and was "baptized" in the River Cam when his sailboat capsized (CL I, p. 35).

In June Coleridge was awarded the gold medal in the Browne Greek Prize competition for his *Ode on the Slave Trade*. Afterward he left for the West Country and a long summer holiday. Pleased at having proven that he had not been merely a big fish in the small Christ's Hospital pond, twenty-year-old Coleridge was proud of his victory and bubbling with confidence over his successful first year as a Cantab. Next fall he would set his sights on the Craven.

After brief visits with his brothers Edward and James in Salisbury and Exeter, Coleridge arrived at his mother's home in Ottery. Anne Coleridge was now sixty-five and had been living alone in the village since her daughter Nancy's death the previous year. Proud of his recently acquired skill at making clever conversation while holding his liquor, the dashing Cantab was chagrined when his mother forbade him to drink a single drop of wine at her table. He was further dismayed with the conservative provincialism of Ottery.

His letters to George reflect an adolescently smug dismissal of the local gentry, whom he caricatured as country bumpkins. But intent on keeping in grammatical practice for the Craven, he wrote his gossipy satires entirely in Latin. A translated segment reads:

> I have written to our brother Francis—and entrusted the letter to Kesell. . . . Kesell is absolutely beside himself with the enjoyment of this little bit of glory. He has just come to meet me as I was walking down through the churchyard. 'Hallo! Mr. Samuel, how d'ye do! You know, I suppose, that Lord Shore, ahem! Lord Shore, you know, whom the King has just made Governor-General of all India, is the husband of my son-in-law's sister; ahem, I say my son-in-law's sister's husband! I should be glad, if you would write to Francis yourself (the post is always perfectly reliable); but I myself, ahem, will recommend him to the Governor-General very strongly, and I have no doubt but the Governor-General will deal with your brother's affairs in such a way that my recommendation, ahem, will be understood to be no ordinary one!'—Oh, how I missed the way we used to laugh! But I thought it better to suppress my amusement, and to feed and stimulate the man's folly by mildly agreeing with him, which I hope was not altogether blameworthy. What a puffed-up creature! What pomposity! Our mother positively drinks in his long-winded speeches and dreams of the most wonderful prospects. [CL I, p. 41]

While Coleridge was amused by his self-important Ottery neighbor's supercilious mannerisms, he was mildly irked by the tiresome way in which his mother clucked naively over the man's offer and dreamed rhapsodically of Frank's "wonderful prospects." Frank Coleridge had last written home in the fall of the previous year (1791), and it is likely that his letter was at Ottery at the time of Coleridge's visit. If so, Coleridge understood why his mother worried about Frank. Frank's letter had been penned at the edge of battle:

> September 20, 1791
> My ever honoured, ever beloved parent,
> Your letter has woke me amidst the din of arms to all the

softer feelings of nature. My mamma, think not because you have not heard of me that you have not been daily, nay hourly, in my mind. I call my Creator to witness I love you with such affection that does not despair of equality with my happier brothers, but I cannot like them tell you so every month, nor always every year. For these three years past I have been stationed nigh 1,400 miles from Calcutta . . . promoted and ordered to the European Battalion. . . . His Lordship in Council ordered me to succeed to the first vacancy in the Native Battalion up the country. He has since summoned me, with twelve other officers and 800 Sepoys, to attend the Grand Army previous to his laying siege at Seringapatam, the capital of the Mysore tyrant. Proud of such an honourable distinction, I join him with ardour, and if fortune crowns my wishes, will scatter the pearls of the Sultan at the feet of my Mamma. Mr. Tomkins lingers on board for any letter, for we are falling into the main ocean from the Ganges. I can detain him no longer, and must be concise. My health has never known disease, my character has never known a stain. My friends I have never lost. Enemies I have never made, and happy I have ever been, except when, Mamma, you call me across the ocean. God Bless you, best of parents; tell your children that their absent brother is what he ought to be, or if he has one fault it is that of being too partial to the banks of the Ganges. Molly, I kiss you! Would you know your favourite boy again? Live and you shall see him! . . . I am writing amongst hundreds of soldiers . . . Mamma, receive my dutiful, my eternal affection. On my knees I call for your blessing on your ever duteous child. Francis Coleridge [L. Coleridge, 1905, p. 48]

If Frank's letter or his mother's clucking over Frank's brilliant career prospects revived old rivalrous feelings in Coleridge, they do not show in his correspondence. His competitive feelings were exclusively focused on his fellow contestants for the Craven and the grueling examination that awaited them.

Returning to Jesus that September, Coleridge apparently devoted his last drop of energy to his studies. Now there were no bantering letters to the Evans sisters or poetry written for his own amusement. All of his letters were to George, mainly in Latin, to keep in practice for the Craven. As fall wore on, Coleridge grew weary of the grind. By November his face had broken out in acne from the strain.

There were seventeen contestants for the university-wide preliminary competition that December. After six days of constant examinations, the field was narrowed to four finalists, Coleridge among them. After a final round of tests, the four waited nervously for the results to be announced in early January of 1793.

Chapter 3

My Brother's Keeper

*A grief without a pang, void, dark, and drear
A stifled, drowsy, unimpassioned grief,
Which finds no natural outlet, no relief,
In word, or sigh, or tear. . . .*
—from *Dejection: An Ode* [PW, p. 364]

On 10 April 1794, twenty-one-year-old Trooper Silas Tomkyn Comberbache was released from company barracks and discharged, on grounds of insanity, from the King's Fifteenth Light Dragoons. While he was not actually insane, there was definitely something odd about Comberbache that people had noticed throughout his four-month cavalry stint. The recruiting sergeant had even attempted to talk him out of enlisting. Perhaps it was the young man's elegant speech or the fact that he walked into the recruiting office with several rare editions of books in Latin and Greek under his arm. Whatever the clues, the old trooper knew instinctively that Comberbache lacked the manner and bearing of a British dragoon, and other trained eyes soon sized him up the same way.

When the recruits arrived at company barracks and were mustered for inspection, the commander singled out Comberbache, ordered him to step forward, and asked skeptically if he thought he could run a bayonet through a Frenchman. Comberbache replied that he didn't know but allowed as how he would let a Frenchman run him through before running away. Satisfied, at least for the moment, the officer ordered Comberbache to return to ranks.

But training exercises soon confirmed the commandant's first impression: Comberbache was unable to handle his horse—the animal handled him, galloping out of control or throwing him from the saddle, time and again. Moreover, Comberbache's uniform was disheveled and his field gear a mess. When an inspecting officer picked up a carbine in obvious need of repair and inquired whose it was, Comberbache cheerfully replied that if it was rusty it must be his.

Yet there was nothing in the polite young man's manners to suggest a disobedient troublemaker. Good-natured and easygoing, Trooper Comberbache tried hard to please and got along well with his fellow enlisted men despite their obvious social differences. A great storyteller, he entertained his barracks mates with tales of Alexander the Great and the Peloponnesian Wars. Clearly an inventive fellow, Comberbache soon worked out an equitable exchange of services with his less literary comrades—writing gorgeous love letters to their sweethearts in payment for having his gear in order and his horse well groomed.

The officers were as puzzled by Comberbache as were the enlisted men. One evening, while standing guard duty at a regimental ball, Comberbache overheard two passing officers discussing the Greek drama. Begging their pardon for interrupting, Comberbache apologetically informed them that the *Oedipus* being quoted was by Sophocles not Euripides. These men did not know what to make of this new recruit any more than did the officer who found the words *"Eheu! quam infortunii miserrimum est fuisse felicem"* (Alas! how unfortunate it is to have been happy) scribbled on the stable door (Gillman, 1838, p. 61).

Comberbache was not entirely pleased with his image as the misfit. Anxious to win respect, he rose to the occasion when the opportunity presented itself. While his unit was out on maneuvers, one of the troopers came down with smallpox and fell into a delirious fever. When the regiment returned to barracks, Comberbache stayed behind in cramped quarantine quarters to nurse his stricken comrade. He described his vigil:

> The almost total want of sleep, the putrid smell and the fatiguing struggles with my poor comrade during his delirium are nearly too much for me in my present state—In return, I enjoy external peace, and kind and respectful behavior from the people. [CL I, p. 62]

By early February the mystery surrounding the trooper was dispelled. The company commander received a letter informing him that Silas Tomkyn Comberbache was actually a Cambridge student by the name of Samuel Taylor Coleridge who had vanished the previous fall. When confronted, Comberbache admitted he was the Coleridge in question.

Relieved at finally having located him, Coleridge's distraught family began to negotiate his discharge. Meanwhile, Coleridge continued to nurse the delirious trooper. The negotiations dragged on for several months until the company commander, realizing that the family could not afford to hire a substitute recruit, offered to discharge the young man on grounds of insanity, that he might return to Cambridge in time to avoid forfeiting his scholarships.

During the negotiations, Coleridge had ample time to reflect on his escapade. He spent February in the pesthouse with his stricken comrade. By mid-month, the trooper was no longer uncontrollably delirious and Coleridge could relax his vigil, leave the man unattended at times, and get some much needed sleep:

> Tonight I shall have a bed in a separate room from my comrade—and, I trust, shall have repaired my strength by sleep ere the morning—For eight days and nights I have not had my clothes off—My comrade is not dead—there is every hope of his escaping Death—Closely has he been pursued by the mighty Hunter! [CL I, p. 64]

Coleridge owed himself an accounting, and his family would expect one as well. He could explain why he had run away from Cambridge but had not given much thought to what was more puzzling: Why would an avowed pacifist change his name, join the cavalry, and then choose to spend more than a month nursing a delirious soldier? What was Comberbache's mission?

At the time of his discovery, Coleridge's contrite letters were filled with pleas for forgiveness and confessions of having fallen from grace. As a much older man, Coleridge would dismiss this incident by lightheartedly emphasizing its comic aspects. He never invited others to take it seriously and was at a loss himself to understand its deepest personal significance. As a result, Coleridge's biographers have graciously declined his youthful, tragic, self-pitying explanations; it has become a convention in Coleridge biography to treat the escapade as a comic adventure stemming from desperate finances and a broken heart.

The episode had actually begun with the announcement in early 1793 that Coleridge had lost the Craven, having tied with a man who was awarded the scholarship because he was younger. No longer the prodigy, Coleridge fashioned a new image for himself. He had really always been, he now claimed, the prodigal:

> To real happiness I bade adieu. . . . I became a proverb to the university for idleness—the time which I should have bestowed on academic studies, I employed in dreaming out wild schemes. . . . I fled to debauchery. . . . even for the university scholarship, for which I affected to have read so severely, I did not read three days uninterruptedly—for the whole six weeks, that preceded the examination, I was almost constantly intoxicated! My brother, you shudder as you read. . . . [CL I, p. 67]

While it is conceivable that he did not study as diligently as he appeared to, it is equally plausible that Coleridge was now covering up his mortification over defeat by concocting the alibi that he had not tried as hard as he might to win the Craven. A letter to Mrs. Evans, shortly after the Craven results were announced, reveals that Coleridge had indeed studied in earnest, had felt deeply wounded by his defeat, had tried to rationalize those feelings, and had, for a brief time, sought consolation in religion:

> The event of our examination was such, as surpassed my expectations, and perfectly accorded with my wishes. After a very severe trial . . . we . . . were declared equal . . . and the scholarship . . . awarded to the youngest. . . . I am just two months older than he is—and tho' I would doubtless have rather had it myself, I am not yet at all sorry at his success . . . he is sensible and unassuming. . . . So much for myself. . . . I have enclosed a little work of that great and good man, Archdeacon Paley. . . . the reasoning has been of some service to *me*. . . my hypochondriac gloomy spirit *amid blessings* too frequently warbles out the hoarse gruntings of discontent!—Nor have all the lectures, that the divines and philosophers have given us . . . on the vanity of riches, and the cares of greatness, etc.—prevented me from sincerely

regretting, that Nature had not put it into the head of some *rich* man to beget *me* for his *first born*—whereas now I am likely to get bread, just when I shall have no teeth to chew it—Cheer up, my little one! (thus I answers I) *better late than never*. . . . My dear Mrs. Evans! excuse the wanderings of my castle building imagination—I have not a thought, which I conceal from you—I *write* to others, but my pen talks to you. [CL I, p. 47]

Two days later, Coleridge wrote a long, chatty letter to Mary Evans filled with gossip and lighthearted witticisms. Far from being a sore loser, morbidly preoccupied with his misfortunes, he had hit upon the idea of soothing himself with music:

here comes my fiddling master—for—(but this is a secret—) I am learning to play on the violin.—Twit Twat—twat twit—pray, M. de la Peuche, do you think, I shall ever make anything of this violin?—'Un magnifique! Un superbe! Par honneur, Sir, you be ver great genius in de music—Good morning, Monsieur!'—This M. de la Peuche is a better judge, than I thought. . . . This new whim of mine is partly a scheme for self defence—three neighbours have run music-mad lately—two of them fiddle scrapers, the third a flute-tooter—and are perpetually annoying me with their vile performances, compared with which the grunting of a whole herd of sows would be seraphic melody. Now I hope by frequently playing myself—to render my ear callous—as a lady of quality, being reprimanded by her husband for having eaten onions, (or garlic) answered him—why don't you eat onions yourself, my dove, and then you would not smell them!—Besides—the evils of life are crowding upon me—and music is the sweetest assuager of cares. [CL I, p. 50]

But as Coleridge's cheerful letter also revealed, his rapid emotional recuperation was in fact due to another, more recently discovered sweet soother of cares, a walloping dose of that old Fen District cure-all, "Mother's Blessing." His letter ended on this ominous note:

Are you asleep, my dear Mary?—I have administered rather a strong dose of opium: however, if in the course of your nap you should chance to dream, that

> I am with the ardour of your fraternal friendship
> Your affectionate S. T. Coleridge you will never have dreamt a truer dream in all your born days. [CL I, p. 52]

Aware for a long time of opium's painkilling effect, Coleridge had recently discovered that the drug had the power to cheer him. (He had begun taking it for a dental extraction three days earlier.) He was, however, unaware that his irritable reaction to his neighbors' flute-tooting and fiddle-scraping was caused in part by the hypersensitivity to sound which opium produces. If he was starting to rely on opium for consolation, Coleridge's emotional hold must have been tenuous.

He was on shaky ground in any case. His dreams of an academic career as a Cambridge fellow were shattered; and while a career in the Church was still a possibility, his faith was slipping away. He was already ripe to leave school by the time the next piece of bad news arrived a few days later. This time it came from Ottery St. Mary.

Anne Coleridge had just received a packet from India containing a letter and a gold watch. The letter informed her that the watch belonged to her dead son, Francis. Given the distance and problems of shipping, it was the only part of Frank's remains that his cavalry regiment had been able to send. Even the news of his death had taken months to arrive.

The enclosed watch had been presented to Frank by Lord Cornwallis after the bloody siege of Seringapatam. Frank had ridden with the Fourteenth Battalion on a surprise nighttime raid in which many had died. Frank had fought bravely, but after the battle a delirious fever had set in. At some point in the midst of his delirium, he had been left unattended by his comrades and had shot himself.

Although Coleridge was unaware of how deeply affected he was by the news of Frank's suicide, Comberbache's mission had just been decided. Whether it was his habitual tendency to delay his emotional reactions, or the fact that he was still licking his wounds from his own disappointment, Coleridge seemed barely to register the news of his brother's suicide. The death seemed to him like a remote event that had happened to a stranger he had known in another life:

Poor Francis! I have shed the tear of natural affection over him.—He was the only one of my family, whom similarity of ages made more peculiarly my brother—he was the hero of all the little tales, that make the remembrance of my earliest days interesting!—Yet his death filled me rather with melancholy than anguish.—I quitted Ottery, when I was so young, that most of those endearing circumstances, that are wont to render the scenes and companions of our childhood delightful in recollection, I have associated with the place of my education. [CL I, p. 53]

Coleridge made no other detailed mention of his immediate reactions to Frank's suicide. We do not know if he continued using opium frequently or regularly. But we do know that Coleridge began to socialize rather hectically (if not hypomanically).

Talking nonstop, "he was ready at any time to unbend his mind in conversation. . . . his room was a constant rendezvous of conversation-loving friends" (Gillman, 1838, p. 53). Charismatic and voluble, Coleridge took refuge from his recent personal losses by immersing himself in nightly debates on the burning social issues that were emerging as a result of the fast-moving chain of events sweeping through England and the Continent.

The week of the Craven announcement was the same one in which Louis XVI was beheaded. News of Frank's death arrived just as France declared war on England. Cambridge was alive with heated discussions and it was easy for Coleridge to turn away from his personal losses. An omnivorous reader, he plunged into the running duel in print taking place between Thomas Paine and Edmund Burke. Soon his thoughts were far from Frank and far from the Craven.

The raging debate was whether ends justify means. Paine argued that violence and revolution are necessary to secure the natural rights of all men over the property rights of the overprivileged. Prosecuted for treason by Pitt's government, Paine had fled to France a declared outlaw, a fact which enhanced his romantic appeal to Coleridge and other student radicals.

Accusing Paine and his Jacobin supporters of a conspiracy to overthrow Church and State, Burke's credibility rested on his clairvoyance. From the very beginning, in 1789, he had condemned the French Revolution as atheistic and prophesied that it would result in anarchy and bloodshed—a forecast that now was proving tragically correct.

While Coleridge had been studying for the Craven in the fall of 1792, Citizen Jean Paul Marat had been belched up from the sewers of Paris, dressed in rags, caked with grease, an oily bandana around his forehead. A disgruntled, paranoid former physician with a twitching face and wild eyes, Marat declared himself "the rage of the people" (Loomis, 1968, p. 94). Bitter, among other things, that his treatise on Newton's *Optics* had never been recognized by the Royal Academy, Marat unleashed his megalomaniacal fury by orchestrating the September Massacres.

While idealistic English radicals chanted the heroic marching song of the men of Marseilles, a hand-picked group of hardened criminals, among them the scum of the prisons of that city, were busy in Paris butchering fifteen hundred men, women, and children. For seven nights the gutters of the Rue de Seine ran crimson with the blood of the Revolution's "enemies" before Marat's lust for revenge was spent.

The French Revolution had been comparatively orderly, bloodless, and civilized until Marat's grisly *Septembriseurs*. But as Burke had predicted all along, the new republic was now becoming an anarchy. Its emerging leaders—Marat, Danton, and Robespierre—were skillfully pandering to the prejudices of working class mobs, drawing their power from the roaming wolfpacks.

Across the Channel, liberals were divided: some turned away from the movement, others discounted the reports as exaggerated. The more militant radicals hailed the bloodshed as a necessary dialectical step in this shift away from a middle class revolution and began to display their allegiances by abandoning wigs and wearing full-length trousers like the sansculottes, their working class French brothers. Still wearing his own hair unpowdered several years later, Coleridge would nostalgically describe himself as "a genuine *sans culotte*, my veins uncontaminated with one drop of gentility" (CL I, p. 303).

Coleridge's dreamy elitist yearning to be the firstborn son of a rich man—hatched on the eve of the Craven and confided to Mrs. Evans—was rapidly replaced by an identification with the working class underdog sansculottes. Coleridge was by no means the only one to be swept up in this whirl of controversy—all of English society was becoming polarized. The formerly sedate London Corresponding Society (LCS) had just begun to recruit working class members into its swelling ranks and was sending donations of money and supplies to the brave "Soldiers of Liberty" at Calais, who replied in turn with offers of "fraternity and assistance to all who wish to recover their liberty" (Goodwin, 1979, p. 19). Fearing the worst, Pitt fortified The Tower, stepped up recruitments and ordered regiments like the King's Fifteenth Light Dragoons to stand by to repel foreign invaders and suppress domestic rebellions.

Back at Cambridge, the mood of crisis reached a feverish pitch. While Church-and-King conservatives burned effigies of Thomas Paine in torchlight rallies, the radical students rose up in irate support of their hero, William Frend. In search of a cause and well primed to react to an injustice, Coleridge dove headlong into the controversy with manic energy.

Anticipating the truth of Talleyrand's remark that treason is a matter of dates, William Frend had become a cause célèbre—dismissed from the faculty for his ill-timed pamphlet supporting English nonintervention in France, which rolled off the press just as war was declared. Removed from his residence at Jesus, Frend was placed on academic trial for subversion.

The university exploded. Angry demonstrators, Coleridge in the forefront, chalked slogans of "Frend for Ever!" (Chambers, 1938, p. 20) across school walls, while bonfire rallies were held with the ominous words *Liberté* and *Egalité* etched in flaming gunpowder on the college lawns. Frend's trial was held in spite of mass protests denouncing it as an academic witch hunt. Coleridge himself disrupted the sedate trial proceedings with loud applause for Frend, and rapidly became identified as an unruly troublemaker and ringleader by the university authorities.

Coleridge somehow managed to escape academic expulsion and by the end of the spring semester of 1793 was a confirmed antiwar pacifist with strong Unitarian leanings. He was also in financial straits, having lived beyond his means. Whether he was abusing opium at this time was unclear, but it was inexpensive at the dose range he would have required and could not have been the source of his debts. (It is known that three years later Coleridge required only a grain of opium—thirty grains being considered a "pennyworth" back then.)

Leaving Cambridge for the summer, Coleridge nonetheless headed for Ottery in high spirits, flirting with several women on his coach trip and writing poetry for them. Once back home he took another party of young ladies on a tour of a local cave known as the "Pixies' Parlour," and commemorated that visit with a poem gallantly dedicated to the fair maidens who accompanied him on that gay outing. Filled with stock pastoral images, there is nothing in Coleridge's "Song of the Pixies" that sheds a clue on the curious fact that in little more than a month he would become acutely suicidal and plunge into a deep depression.

But perhaps his visit to that cave reawakened memories of the dead. A fine secret meeting spot for boys, the Pixies' Parlour had served as the Coleridge brothers' playground—in fact Coleridge was delighted to discover the precise spot where they had carved their initials on the wall. The monograms were still visible and he delighted in showing them to his entourage, perhaps with lighthearted vignettes of Frank, "the handsome Coleridge." No doubt his Ottery vacation provoked other childhood memories of their times together as well.

Given the events of the past year, Coleridge was a prime candidate for the depression that was about to descend upon him. He had lost Frank through suicide and had suffered blows to his pride and career plans and identification with the gentry by losing the Craven. He had responded to these losses by throwing himself into a hypomanic frenzy of radical demonstrations, identifying with the lower class sansculottes, and into stormy political debates. He also had his first experiences at sexual carousing with the local Cambridge prostitutes, largely at the instigation of his friends. Swept up in a desperately gay carnival of despair, Coleridge had never given himself time to grieve over Frank or to put his disappointment over the Craven into perspective by formulating new life plans for himself.

Still denying the emotional significance of the two events, Coleridge became morbidly preoccupied with his financial status as summer wore on. Heavily in debt to his college tutors, Coleridge cringed at the prospect of facing George and confessing his "follies" (CL I, p. 59). Finally mustering the courage, he approached his older brothers, who agreed to bail him out. But fearing their ire, he did not disclose the full amount (one hundred forty-eight pounds), intending instead to break the bad news by slow degrees.

By now he was a man on a tightrope. After receiving the money, he headed for college but detoured to London for a few days before returning to school. Remaining at Cambridge less than a week, he caught a night coach back to London, where he stayed for three nights before returning to Cambridge once more. Acutely suicidal, he moved from place to place with frenzied desperation, as if he could escape his destructive feelings by changing his locale. After one more week at Cambridge, he again fled to London. Out of control, he spent the money his brothers had given him with a reckless abandon the sources of which he could not fathom.

Down to his last few shillings, he bought a ticket for the Irish sweepstakes, hoping to reverse his fortunes. While awaiting the results of the lottery drawing with a magical sense that his life hung in the balance, he grew more depressed.

When he learned that his ticket had not been chosen in the drawing on November 26, he interpreted the lottery-oracle as a message from fate that his destiny was death. For the next few days and nights, he struggled to find the courage to act.

In later recalling what this period had been like for him, Coleridge would describe himself as *delirious* and *suicidal:* tortured by "enfever[ed] . . . dreams" (CL I, p. 63), his "agitations were a delirium" (CL I, p. 68)—a delirium prompting him to kill himself. Fighting off his suicidal impulses, he staggered the streets of London long into each night, resting on the stoops of houses in a daze, giving his few remaining pennies to the beggars that approached him.

At dawn on the morning of December 1, Coleridge managed to fight off the latest wave of suicidal feelings long enough to stumble into a Chancery Lane recruiting office, where he attempted to enlist in the cavalry. In spite of his pitiful condition, one glance was enough to tell the recruiting sergeant that he was dealing with an educated gentleman, desperate and down on his luck.

The kindly trooper tried to talk Coleridge out of enlisting, gave him some money and told him to get some rest and think things over. A few hours later Coleridge returned, intent on joining the Fifteenth Regiment of Light Dragoons. Trooper Comberbache enlisted on December 2 and marched forty-eight miles to join his unit at Reading, where he was officially inducted on December 4, 1793.

Remaining incommunicado from his family for more than two months, Coleridge then tried in his way to become a soldier. But it was only after Comberbache's heroic mission of nursing a delirious comrade that Coleridge felt up to leaking the news of his whereabouts to friends he knew would inform his family.

Holed up in the Henley pesthouse while his comrade recuperated and his family negotiated his release, Coleridge attempted to make sense out of the events of the past few months. "My mind is illegible to myself" (CL I, p. 63), he wrote George, adding that he was mystified by the "gloomy *huddle* of eccentric actions, and dim-discovered motives" (CL I, p. 67) that had impelled him. Apparently, Coleridge never stopped to wonder how on the anniversary of his having first learned the news of Frank's delirium and suicide—and two months after feeling delirious and suicidal himself—he found himself nursing another delirious soldier back to health.

There had been other clues along the way. Once again he was running away from his family, just as he had done as a child of seven after trying to stab Frank. On both occasions, his conflicted feelings toward his mother were prominent. This time, he wrote a friend,

> there is a pleasure doubtless an exquisite pleasure mingled up in the most painful of our virtuous emotions—Alas! my poor Mother! What an intolerable weight of guilt is suspended over my head by a hair of one hand.... [CL I, p. 63]

He had known that same "pleasure" as a seven-year-old when, sitting on the hillside on that stormy night in Devon, he had taken out his shilling book with its morning and evening prayers and "devoutly repeated them—thinking *at the same time* with inward and gloomy satisfaction, how miserable my Mother must be!" (CL I, p. 353).

Back then he had tried to kill Frank and felt both justified and appalled by his behavior. But now Frank was really dead and—as if in dire penance—Coleridge's only option was self-murder. And so S. T. Coleridge disappeared and Trooper Comberbache emerged as an alternative to suicide. While Trooper Comberbache proved a sorry substitute for the soldierly Frank Coleridge, Comberbache could at least prevent another delirious warrior from suffering Frank's fate.

No evidence exists to suggest that Coleridge consciously connected his crisis with Frank, or even thought of him. Frank was dead and gone—a stranger from another life. Coleridge had forgotten how much he had loved his brother, how passionately he had hated him, and how deeply involved with one another they had been. He had been unable to grieve for his dead brother. And yet he had felt an odd compulsion to assume a fictitious identity and nurse a delirious stranger—symbolically making up for the lack of nursing that had led to Frank's untimely death.*

Coleridge behaved as if his own past destructive feelings could be magically undone by a symbolic act, and in a sense it worked. Comberbache's conscientious nursing of his stricken comrade gave Coleridge peace of mind. Now that Trooper Comberbache's mission was accomplished, Coleridge was ready to leave the army (April 1794).

But on that stormy October night back in Devon, Cain's mark had been seared into young Sam Coleridge's consciousness, and the pain of it would continue to haunt and torment him for the rest of his life.

---

*Translating into the primary process language of the unconscious, for Silas Tomkyn Comberbache read: *Sigh, alas! To my kin, come back!*

Chapter 4

Pantisocracy: A Tribe of Brothers

Innocent foal! Thou poor, despis'd forlorn!
I hail thee Brother, spite of the fool's scorn!
And fain I'd take thee with me in the Dell
Of High-souled Pantisocracy to dwell;
Where Toil shall call the charmer Health his bride,
And Laughter tickle Plenty's ribless side!
—from *Address to a Young Jack-Ass and It's Thether'd Mother*
[CL I, p. 143]

In the burning summer of 1794 a heat wave scorched England's wheat fields, rocketing the price of bread above the record high of the previous year, when heavy harvest rains had rotted the grain in the fields, drowning hopes for enough to feed a hungry populace. That hot summer eighty thousand people fled England for America. And many more Englishmen—faced with unemployment, inflation, food and draft riots, bankruptcies, drastic curtailment of civil liberties, and an unpopular war with France that was provoking mounting hysteria over an imminent French invasion—were tempted to leave that troubled island. Among those considering Philadelphia as a destination was a twenty-year-old radical from Oxford, Robert Southey, who wrote a friend announcing a plan to found a utopian commune by the banks of the Susquehanna River: "When Coleridge and I are sawing down a tree we shall discuss metaphysics; criticize poetry when hunting a buffalo, and write sonnets whilst following the plough" (Coleridge, 1795, p. xxiii). Coleridge and Southey's choice of locale was influenced by the fact that Joseph Priestley, their political hero, had just escaped persecution in England and settled in nearby Northumberland, Pennsylvania.

Having decided to cast their lot together as brothers, though they had known each other barely two months, Southey and Coleridge were prepared to brave all manner of hardship and danger in the name of their glorious cause, which—Southey informed his correspondent—Coleridge had christened *Pantisocracy*, a Greek coinage meaning "rule equally by all." Southey's announcement came as no surprise to his friends.

While Trooper Comberbache—his regulation military wig at full tilt—had been engaging in regimental training maneuvers, Southey had been dreamily weaving transatlantic scenarios for his own comedy of despair. But unlike that dashing cavalry recruit, the cautious Robert Southey had kept his wanderlust in check by reminding himself of the dangers of being "cooked for a Cherokee, or oysterized by a tiger" (Haller, 1966, p. 125) should he embark on his reckless plan alone, with no sidekick or boon companion.

Of a more orderly temperament than Coleridge, Southey had even observed the nicety of obtaining an official leave of absence from Oxford before taking the fall semester off to search his soul and contemplate his future. Southey's family, like Coleridge's, expected their charge to forgo his interest in radical politics and literature and take Holy Orders in the Church of England. Recoiling from the hypocrisy and conservatism of the Established Church, Southey had appeased his family by halfheartedly committing himself to a medical career he was forcing himself to pursue, when Samuel Taylor Coleridge breezed into his rooms at Baillol College, and into his life, on a balmy June day in 1794.

When the two compared notes on the social irrelevance of their respective curriculums, Coleridge discovered that Southey shared his fascination with the political thinkers of the day—Paine, Priestley, Rousseau, and Burke. And while Southey had dedicated his spring term to Aesculapius, Coleridge had spent his with Demetrius Phalareus, the author of a dusty tome in ancient Greek which he had been assigned to translate in full as penance for his unauthorized leave. Now that the term was ending, both men looked forward to emancipation from such drudgery.

Having decided to set out on a walking tour of Wales for his summer holiday, Coleridge was stopping over at Oxford for a few days' visit with Bob Allen. After catching up on old times at Christ's Hospital and the Evans sisters, Allen had told Coleridge there was a Baillol man—a fellow poet and political radical from the West Country—whom he thought Coleridge might enjoy meeting.

Allen's hunch proved correct. As soon as they began to read each other's works in progress, a magical rapport began to develop between the two poets. Southey had recently completed the first draft of his epic *Joan of Arc*, which was dedicated to "Liberty" and packed with stanzas honoring the heroic French Revolution. Coleridge's praise for the poem won Southey, who in turn, declared Coleridge's work to be "of the strongest genius, the clearest judgement, the best heart" (Haller, 1966, p. 127).

Most exciting was the discovery that they were kindred spirits politically. Rebellious by nature and romantic by temperament, Robert Southey was a staunch idealist who had been expelled from his boarding school for his provocative scatological essay, "On Flogging," which he had published in *The Flagellant*, a magazine he had founded. But the sources of Southey's antiestablishment sentiments ran deeper than mere schoolboy rebellion. He had seen his father die, broken in spirit, after a brief stint in a debtors' prison. Thoroughly radicalized and already believing "that society requires desperate remedies" (Haller, 1966, p. 119), young Robert Southey had been quick to pin his hopes for a better world on the experiment in France that began with the fall of the Bastille.

Yet as Coleridge and Southey reviewed the five years since that great event, both confessed to the same ideological dilemma that was plaguing so many English radicals in the spring of 1794. While each was deeply committed to the principles of the French Revolution, both were in a quandary over the bloody turn of events that began with the Reign of Terror. Willing to dabble in treason only so long as there were clear-cut differences between the governments of William Pitt and Maximilien Robespierre, both Coleridge and Southey were starting to wonder if the justice being dispensed at the *Conciergerie* was any better than that at the Tower of London.

In July of 1793 had come Charlotte Corday's attempt to liberate her country of tyranny, sensationally depicted in the lithographs of the day which showed her stabbing Marat to death as he lay soaking in his copper-lined hip bath, shaped like a high-button shoe. Taking over the leadership of the all-powerful Committee of Public Safety, Robespierre had cleverly used that incident as evidence of a widespread conspiracy. By September his Law of Suspects, which provided for neighborhood vigilance committees of informers, had allowed his terror tactics to silence completely the voice of any rational opposition.

In October, Marie Antoinette's head had rolled, followed in November by the heads of twenty-one members of the moderate Girondist party, who went to their deaths singing the *Marseillaise* in an ever diminishing chorus as, one by one, their voices were stilled by the executioner's blade. Samson—the public executioner—was the busiest man in France. His hair tied neatly behind his head so that his skillful hands could work unencumbered, Samson performed his efficient *toilette* on forty or fifty prisoners a day before loading his tumbrels and setting off for the Place de la Revolution, where huge crowds waited, joking in a holiday mood about how they had come to see the famous barber "shave" the citizens of France with the national razor.

Under Robespierre's guidance, the process of justice had already been speeded up so that most cases were concluded in less than twenty-four hours: a morning "trial," followed by a midday *toilette* and a trip to the guillotine by late afternoon. As a result of this heavy traffic, the stones of the square had become permanently coated with blood and as a concession to the irate property owners whose neighborhood homes had begun to depreciate in value, Robespierre had recently allowed the guillotine to be moved to a less densely populated square. He did not realize that by midsummer the infernal machine would be returned to the Place de la Revolution in his own honor.

But to Coleridge and Southey, English justice did not look very much better that spring. In May, William Pitt had suspended habeas corpus, thereby gaining the power to incarcerate arbitrarily his political enemies. Pitt had lost no time in imprisoning without hearings twelve of the leaders of the London Corresponding Society (LCS) and the Society for Constitutional Information (SCI) on charges of high treason. Incarcerated in the Tower of London, they came to be known as the Twelve

Pantisocracy: A Tribe of Brothers

Apostles (Goodwin, 1979, p. 369), and their martyrdom would become a rallying point for English radicals.

As if not to be outdone in his contest with Pitt as to who could more drastically curtail his nation's civil liberties, Robespierre had on June 10 passed a law which abolished all defense and made accusation sufficient to obtain a conviction. Repulsed equally by Pitt and by Robespierre, Coleridge and Southey agreed that choosing between France and England was like choosing between Lucifer and the deep blue sea.

Sharing his long-cherished dream of emigrating to America, Southey proposed the deep blue sea. More philosophically inclined, Coleridge invented a form of government and a set of principles for the venture. They would found a commune whose system of operation—Pantisocracy—included equal rule by all. Any acquired property, Coleridge added, would be held in common by the members of this new republic, under a principle he christened *aspheterism*. Selfishness could be abolished by eliminating its cause—private ownership.

By now the mood was electric in Southey's rooms at Baillol. Other young men, including two of Southey's friends, George Burnett and Robert Lovell, were rapidly drawn into the scheme. The plan would be to recruit a tribe of brothers—"twelve gentlemen of good education and liberal principles" (Lefebure, 1975, p. 133)—who would set sail for the colony with twelve young ladies in tow and one hundred twenty-five pounds apiece for land and equipment. The men would till the soil, the women would rear the children, and everyone would cultivate his mind and "enjoy his own religion and political opinions" (Lefebure, 1975, p. 134). If the French experiment had conclusively shown that political freedom was not for the common man, then Pantisocracy's programs were designed for and by university-educated gentlemen—a form of democracy for the intellectual elite.

By the time he left Oxford three weeks later, Coleridge felt better than he had in months. Having discovered a soulmate in Southey, he was exhilarated at the prospect of moving to America with a group of friends his own age. By sharing a sense of camaraderie and brotherhood, they could attain the democratic ideal he believed in so deeply, while at the same time gratifying a desperate emotional need that had already driven him blindly into the Reading barracks and the Henley pesthouse. With the help of this new family of brothers, he could break his ties with Ottery and become his own man.

Robert Southey and George Burnett accompanied Coleridge through the Cotswolds toward Gloucester and Wales before turning off for their own homes in Bristol and Somerset. Coleridge agreed to rendezvous with Southey in Bristol later that summer, at which point they would iron out the few remaining wrinkles in their plan. Coleridge's spirits were soaring.

Throughout his life, Coleridge's euphoric moods were infectious—he could captivate and spellbind whole drawing rooms and rivet lecture halls full of people with his startling conversation and flight of ideas. In Abergeley, a Welsh seaside resort, he delighted an entire village with his antics: having parted company with his walking stick, he turned the town upside down by having the crier announce:

> Missing from the Bee Inn, Abergeley—a curious walking stick. On one side it displays the head of an eagle, the eyes of which represent rising suns, and the ears Turkish crescents. On the other side is the portrait of the owner in wood-work. Beneath the head of the eagle is a Welsh wig—and around the neck of the stick is a Queen Elizabeth's ruff in tin. All adown it waves the line of beauty in very ugly carving. If any gentleman (or lady) has fallen in love with the above-described stick and secretly carried off the same, he (or she) is hereby admonished to conquer a passion, the continuance of which must prove fatal to his (or her) honesty; and if the said stick has slipped into such gentleman's (or lady's) hand thro' inadvertance, he (or she) is required to rectify the mistake with all convenient speed.—God save the King. [CL I, p. 93]

Curiosity seekers flocked to the crier like the Pied Piper as the procession wended its way through the village lanes, spilled across the town beach, and wound back to the Bee, where an apologetic, absentminded old man returned the stick. A beautiful young lady leaned from her carriage window and begged for a copy of the crier's announcement, which Coleridge presented with a gallant flourish "that lighted up a blush on her cheek, and a smile on her lip" (CL I, p. 94).

Uninhibited when it came to flirting with strangers, Coleridge could be worse than shy with women he cared about. Encountering Mary Evans's sister Eliza at a crowded church in Wrexham, Coleridge pretended not to recognize her and beat a hasty retreat to his inn. Later, Mary and her sister passed by the window of his room and, catching a glimpse of him, walked back and forth on the street below, obviously trying to decide if it had been Coleridge after all. Feeling sick almost to the point of fainting, Coleridge hid. Shaken by his narrow escape, he wrote Southey: "My fortitude would not have supported me, had I recognized her—I mean, *appeared* to do it!—I neither ate or slept yesterday—but love is a local anguish—I am 16 miles distant, and am not half so miserable" (CL I, p. 88). Coleridge had not communicated with his former Christ's Hospital sweetheart for a year and a half, not since he had mysteriously broken off all contact with her immediately after writing his euphoric "opium letter" after the announcement of the Craven. By now a changed man—thoroughly radicalized and no longer the brilliant young man on his way up the career ladder of conventional success—Coleridge fled Mary in order to avoid explaining his actions and the transformation he had undergone.

But Coleridge possessed more courage in his intellectual disagreements with men. Getting into a heated political debate with some local villagers at a rural inn at Bala, he almost provoked a fistfight by toasting Joseph Priestley and General Washington. Coleridge portrayed himself in his bulletins to Southey that July as leaving a dizzying after-impression in his wake as he evangelically preached Pantisocracy on his rambles through the Welsh countryside. His tour ended by midsummer, and he arrived in Bristol on the fifth of August.

A thriving commercial city near the head of the channel dividing the West Country from Wales, Bristol's busy port rivaled that of London and Liverpool. Its wharves were lined with African slavers, American tobacco ships, and West Indiamen, imparting an international flavor to the city. Its politically sophisticated inhabitants would be receptive to hearing what Coleridge and Southey had to say about the recent events in London and Paris and their new Pantisocracy movement.

Having grown up in Bristol and in nearby Bath, Southey

had many ties in both communities, including a most ardent one to a Miss Edith Fricker, whose family he had known since childhood. Southey had spent July writing poetry, resuming his courtship of Edith and preaching Pantisocracy to all who would listen. A daily visitor at the Frickers', Southey found that family a captive audience as he sang his praise of both Coleridge and Pantisocracy, laying the groundwork for his new friend's welcome.

Southey's fiancée, twenty-one-year-old Edith, lived at home and had gone to work to contribute to household finances now that the family had fallen on hard times. Having grown up better off, Edith and her sisters had attended a genteel young ladies' boarding school before their father's financial decline and eventual death. Inept or unlucky in matters of money, Stephen Fricker had lost his wife's dowry of ten thousand pounds in a variety of business schemes and had died bankrupt, leaving his wife and six children to fend for themselves.

Coming from a prosperous and cultivated family, Mrs. Fricker had taken great pains to insure that her vivacious daughters attained a higher level of education than most young women in their sagging circumstances managed to achieve. Mary Fricker read Latin and Greek, Sarah knew Italian and French, and Southey's Edith worked as a teacher. Mrs. Fricker had perhaps been a lively and charming woman in earlier times, but by now financial anxieties and the care of her two youngest, George and Eliza, had worn her out. There was something grim, stoical, and slightly martyred in Mrs. Fricker's manner in spite of the fact that all the older girls had cheerfully pitched in to keep the family afloat. Sarah (age twenty-four) and Martha (age seventeen) worked as milliners, while Mary (age twenty-two) had earned her living as an actress until her recent marriage to Robert Lovell, Southey's friend and a local poet.

Lovell had been visiting at Oxford that June and had been present at that glorious historical moment when the Pantisocracy movement was first conceived in the boiling brain and sprung just as rapidly from the eloquent lips of its charismatic founder, Samuel Taylor Coleridge. Swept up in the excitement, Lovell had volunteered himself and his new bride as the first married pair of Pantisocrats. Returning to Bristol, he informed his wife of the good news; she in turn told her sisters. And so, by the time of Coleridge's much heralded arrival in that city, the entire Fricker family's curiosity had been whetted. The stage had been set for his entrance.

From the start, he injected an air of mirth and hilarity into the Fricker home. His utopian scheme was exciting and he presented it eloquently and exuberantly. Sarah Fricker proved one of the most attentive members of his audience, and Coleridge had long since developed a weakness for sympathetic listeners, especially if they were female.

Petite, dainty, dark-haired Sarah was the prettiest of the sisters. She was also known within the family circle to be the most high-strung. Growing up, the other girls had lived in dread of their eldest sister's terrible temper, often looking forward to the end of holidays and peace and quiet when Sarah returned to boarding school. But all of the Fricker sisters were on their best behavior with the two gallants present, and it did not take long for an attraction to develop between Coleridge and Sarah, who happened to be the most available for matters matrimonial.

Although by no means an intellectual, Sarah was an appreciative woman and thoughtfully nodded her approval as Coleridge declaimed the lofty philosophical principles of Pantisocracy in the Fricker parlor, located, as chance would have it, at the top of Redcliffe Hill, which commanded a panoramic view of Bristol Harbor. Given Coleridge's powers of monologue and the physical setting, it seemed the easiest thing in the world to step onto a boat and set sail for America.

Or, that is, almost the easiest thing in the world. There still remained the ticklish issue of money—enough to pay everyone's passage to Philadelphia and cover the cost of land and equipment. But resourcefully determined not to be denied his cherished dream, Robert Southey came up with the idea of raising some quick cash by writing a play.

L'incorruptible, Maximilien Robespierre, had just been executed, and the newspapers were filled with graphic accounts of the event: the tumbrel processional along the *via dolorosa* of Paris's streets, Robespierre dressed in his coat of robin's egg blue and jonquil breeches as he rode to his own beheading in the midst of the worst heat wave in recent memory. Tossing their hats in the air with glee, the onlookers had jested or screamed curses while groups of women festively danced the *carmagnole* in circles around the slowly moving death cart. Over a thousand Frenchmen had perished under Robespierre in the past month, and eight thousand more were in prison awaiting that fate on the day of his execution.

After some discussion, Coleridge, Southey, and Lovell agreed that Robespierre's end would make a fit subject for a play. Coleridge took the first act, Southey the second, and Lovell the third. Staying up all night and working furiously, they knocked out *The Fall of Robespierre* in twenty-four hours, with Southey picking up the slack when Lovell proved unable to hold up his share of the bargain.

Little more than a versified rendition of newspaper accounts, their play was finished in record time. All that remained was to publish it, collect the money, and catch the next boat for Philadelphia. They contacted a young Bristol bookseller by the name of Joseph Cottle who, while taken with Coleridge and Southey and sympathetic to their Pantisocratic cause, was unwilling to take a chance on their play.

Faced with this unanticipated obstacle, it began to dawn on the young men that it might take more time and planning to raise the necessary capital. Pantisocracy could be realized in weeks and months, but not in hours and days. Perhaps Coleridge could peddle the Robespierre manuscript in London or Cambridge when he returned to university that fall.

Exhausted after their literary marathon, the two poets decided to unwind by touring Somerset. Stopping over at Bath to call on Southey's mother, Coleridge found the visit so congenial that he was addressing her elatedly as "our mother" by the time they left (CL I, p. 99). Sightseeing and preaching Pantisocracy as they went, both men enjoyed the heady glow of brotherhood until a sleepless night at a Cheddar inn, where Southey declared Coleridge a "vile bedfellow" (Haller, 1966, p. 130), as it began to dawn on him that it might be better if being brothers did not mean being one in all things.

Proceeding on their way, they dropped in on George Burnett at Huntspill and were delighted to learn that he was still committed to Pantisocracy. From there they walked to Nether a well-known Somerset liberal whose prize possessions were his extensive library and what was said to be a lock of George Washington's hair.

A self-educated man with leadership ability, twenty-nine-year-old Poole commanded the respect of his conservative community to the extent that he was even able to dissuade the local townspeople from engaging in the increasingly popular national pastime of burning Tom Paine in effigy. Although his suspicious neighbors were alarmed by news of the arrival of two Jacobin poets, Poole managed to calm things down in spite of Southey's rash praise of Robespierre as "a ministering angel of mercy, sent to slay thousands that he might save millions" (Haller, 1966, p. 154). Poole was more favorably impressed with Coleridge and, after listening thoughtfully to his Pantisocracy scheme, heartily approved of its principles. While unprepared to join them, he indicated a willingness to support their cause. Later, Poole would prove an invaluable resource for Coleridge.

From Stowey, the brothers returned to Bristol and the Frickers. Only three days remained before Coleridge was slated to leave for Cambridge. He had not yet informed his family of his new plans to immigrate to America, though he vowed to Southey that they would set sail by the following March.

As if to cement that promise, Coleridge surprised everybody, perhaps himself most of all, by proposing to Sarah Fricker, who promptly accepted. Was his proposal a passionate declaration of love, or was it a more obliquely framed request that Sarah be his partner when the time came to pair up and go to America? How much did he desire Sarah and how ardent was his wish to be bonded to Southey? Married to Edith and Sarah, the two friends could be linked for life, in a quartet.

Regardless of whether it was intended as a commitment to Sarah, a statement to Southey, or a pledge to Pantisocracy, Coleridge's proposal was taken to mean an actual commitment. If Coleridge—always the poet—thought he was speaking in metaphor to convey his feelings of the moment, he would soon discover that he had been taken quite literally by everyone at the Fricker home.

He had arrived in Bristol on August 5 and departed for London on the twenty-first. During those frenzied sixteen days, he wrote a play with Southey, refined their immigration scheme, made a whirlwind tour of Somerset, and proposed to Sarah Fricker. Exhausted and emotionally drained by the time he reached London, he instinctively headed for his old Christ's Hospital haunts, taking a room at the nearby Angel Inn off Newgate Street. Evenings were spent recuperating in the back room of the Salutation and Cat alehouse, a favorite neighborhood rendezvous of older Grecians and recent graduates.

Ricocheting from the utopian excitement of the future to the comfortable security of the past, he attempted to get his bearings and steer a steady course between giddy elation and a gnawing uncertainty about the future. Despite his "melancholy mood" (CL I, p. 97), he wrote Southey, he was keeping the faith: peddling Robespierre by day and preaching Pantisocracy by night. Spending his evenings holed up in the smoky back room of the Salutation and Cat with some of the older Grecians, as well as with Charles Lamb, Coleridge dissolved his cares in the grape and waxed eloquent on his new utopia —inspiring some of the boys to beg to join the scheme once they finished university.

The many bumpers of punch and porter by the hearthside in that alehouse back room, he rationalized to Southey, were part of an extensive research and development program he was conducting for their Susquehanna enterprise. Beyond recruiting future generations of Pantisocrats, he was gathering invaluable information on bisons, mosquitoes, and hostile Indians from a drinking companion who worked as the London agent for an American real estate company. Reassuring Southey that he had it on the best authority that "literary characters make *money* there," he ended: "remember me to your mother—to our mother—am I not affiliated?" (CL I, p. 99).

Ten days later, Coleridge wrote: "Tell Mrs. Southey, I had the nightmare last night—I dreamt (vision of terrors!) that she refused to go to America! God bless her!" (CL I, p. 101). Although Robert Southey's mother was nominally involved in the actual immigration plans, the fact that Mrs. Southey figured prominently in Coleridge's nightmare suggests she played a more important symbolic role in Coleridge's unconscious. While at a conscious level Coleridge was working on a political utopia, at an unconscious level he was attempting to create an ideal family. The feasibility of the latter would prove as questionable as that of the former.

Back in Cambridge by mid-September, Coleridge ably defended the impeccable logic of Pantisocracy in nightly sessions with his fellow Cantabs. While by no means actually committed to embark, he was absolutely dedicated to the idea of the plan and the ideals for which it stood. His ardor for Miss Fricker proved capricious by comparison.

Yet Coleridge was shocked to receive a self-righteously angry letter from Southey questioning his commitment to Pantisocracy and sternly reprimanding him for not having written Miss Fricker since leaving Bristol. In case he had forgotten —Southey reminded him—he had in fact proposed to Sarah. Deeply wounded, Coleridge indignantly protested that he still loved Miss F., defensively adding that he had already written Sarah before Southey's letter arrived.

But Coleridge soon gave Southey even more reason to doubt his sincerity by describing his latest dalliance with a certain Miss Brunton—a beautiful actress who was in Cambridge that fall on tour with a provincial theater company. Curiously, Coleridge naively offered this news by way of trying to reassure Southey of his loyalty: he was *forcing* himself to see Miss Brunton for Miss Fricker's sake.

According to Coleridge, he was falling in love with one woman in order to get over another, so that he might better love a third. He reasoned as follows: In early October he had received a touching letter from Mary Evans, writing, as a friend who had once loved him, because she was alarmed to learn of his rash plan to immigrate to America. Mary added that she was also concerned because she had heard—from a source who would remain unnamed—that Coleridge had become an atheist and a political extremist.

Mary's letter had rekindled old feelings of love, Coleridge confessed to Southey, and in order to cure himself of this passion, he was spending all of his time with Miss B. In her daily company, he hoped to forget Mary—an eminently sensible plan, he maintained, as Miss B. would soon be leaving Cambridge, thus freeing him of his feelings for her as well as for Mary Evans, allowing him to return his affections to their rightful owner, Miss Sarah Fricker:

> I was constantly at the theatre here till they left us—I endeavoured to be perpetually with Miss Brunton—I even hoped, that her exquisite beauty and uncommon accomplishments might have cured one passion by another. The latter I could easily have dissipated in her absence—and so have restored my affections to her, whom I do not love—but whom by every tie of reason and honor I ought to love. I am resolved—but wretched! [CL I, p. 110]

And so his plan backfired, and he found himself out of love with Miss Fricker.

Although he mooned over Mary Evans constantly, he did not reply to her letter for more than a month. He was in love with her still, or so he told himself. But just as it was the idea of Pantisocracy to which he had pledged himself faithfully, so it was the memory of Mary that he loved. He had fled her in Wales, and now he made no effort to see her, although she had put him on notice in her letter that she was on the verge of giving her heart to another. While mourning her loss (with gusto), Coleridge made no bid to regain her affection.

Given the social delicacy of a young woman taking the initiative and contacting a former sweetheart whom she had not seen in three years, Mary's letter may have been so discreetly worded that Coleridge may have been genuinely confused as to what extent she was inviting him to renew their courtship and to what extent she was simply writing at the request of her unnamed informant.

Baffled and alarmed by his baby brother's latest transformation, George Coleridge was Mary Evans's "unnamed informant." He had begged her to write in the hope that she could talk some sense into Sam. In George's eyes, Sam was drifting away from God, the Church, serious scholarship, sensible politics, and England itself. While Coleridge saw himself as casting off ties with his Church-and-King family, they thought him in danger of losing his moorings or, as George put it, becoming "deranged" (CL I, p. 118).

Meanwhile, Southey was faring little better with his conservative relations, who had thrown him out of their house on a rainy night after learning of his rash plan. Faced with such turbulent trials with their families, Coleridge and Southey supported one another in a constant flow of letters. Southey faced disinheritance and banishment, while Coleridge was threatened with "being confined" (CL I, p. 118) in a lunatic asylum.

Like two ships in a storm, Coleridge and Southey exchanged distress signals while trying to keep up each other's flagging spirits by reassuring one another that Pantisocracy was alive and well. However, in spite of their fraternal utterances, crippling doubts had begun to creep in on both sides. Southey was dismayed by Coleridge's fickle behavior with Sarah Fricker. And Coleridge was equally appalled when Southey blithely mentioned in passing that, naturally, they would be taking personal servants with them to their Susquehanna colony.

But by far the most constraining consideration was the fact that they were still short of cash. Although *The Fall of Robespierre* had been published in Cambridge, it had not yielded the fabulous profits they had dreamed of. And on the international scene, it looked as if England and America might declare war any day, turning the North Atlantic into an impassable combat zone.

Yet in spite of these uncertainties, Coleridge realized that the time had come for him to make his own way in the world. By early November he was determined to confront George in person, resolve his tie to Mary Evans, and permanently sever his connection with Cambridge. He headed for London and his old Newgate Street digs, the Angel Inn and the Salutation and Cat.

Coleridge arrived to find all of London, and Newgate Street in particular, abuzz with the latest sensational event in radical politics. The first victim of William Pitt's witch hunts—one of the Twelve Apostles—had just been acquitted of a charge of high treason by an Old Bailey jury, thereby saving his head from public display on Temple Bar or London Bridge. Exhausted after the ordeal of the trial, Thomas Erskine, defense attorney for the accused, had attempted to slip out of the courtroom quietly and return home for a much needed rest. But outside the Old Bailey on Newgate Street, thirty thousand radical sympathizers had been assembled all day, waiting for the test case verdict. Exploding with joy, the mob unharnessed the horses of the carriages of both Erskine and his client, Thomas Hardy, and triumphantly pulled each man's vehicle home while the Light Horse Volunteers and an Artillery Company nervously stood guard in a drizzling rain, in case violence and rioting broke out. As chance would have it, it also happened to be Guy Fawkes Day. But by ten-thirty that night the streets were quiet and the soldiers went home.

Swept up by the thrill of this stunning victory for English civil rights, Coleridge dashed off a sonnet in praise of Erskine which he sent to the editors of the *Morning Chronicle*, who promptly published it. Having stationed himself in the center of the action, which was only just beginning to unfold at Newgate Prison and the Old Bailey next door, Coleridge settled down to his nightly routine of declaiming upon the events of the day with his friend Charles Lamb at the Salutation and Cat. The trials of the remaining eleven Apostles were about to start, and Coleridge would keep apace of the events in verse, writing a series of topical sonnets addressed to Pitt, Burke, Priestley, Lafayette, and others, all published in the *Chronicle*. The trials were the climax of a six-month period which was the English equivalent of Robespierre's Reign of Terror.

The previous May, Pitt's agents had descended on the homes of the London radical leaders in a lightning series of well-coordinated, middle-of-the-night raids in which they broke down doors, smashed personal belongings, seized the twelve men, and snatched their private papers as well as the membership records of the LCS and SCI. Since then the twelve had been held and interrogated for months without hearings or trials in the heavily fortified Tower, under a tight security guard of soldiers with fixed bayonets. Pitt was taking no chance of another Bastille.

Thomas Hardy, the first radical tried, was a Scottish shoemaker who had founded the working class LCS, so sympathetic to the sansculottes. Unable to prevent the jury from making the crucial distinction between high treason and the intention to reform Parliament by constitutional means, Pitt had nonetheless used Hardy's trial as a propaganda device to rehearse every shred of evidence against *all* radical societies in order to foster national hysteria over the dangers of a widespread violent conspiracy. But Pitt's credibility was about to take a nosedive.

Next up on the docket was the Reverend Horne Tooke, an eccentric, one-eyed radical parson and leader of the SCI, who had militantly vowed to "dye his black coat red" (Goodwin, 1979, p. 47). During his trial, the defense attorney succeeded in putting Pitt in the witness box and sent the courtroom into an uproar by cleverly catching Pitt in a lie. Tooke was acquitted and Coleridge's sensational sonnet in the *Chronicle* drew an acid comparison between the "Iscariot" Pitt (PW, p. 83) and his illustrious father, who had himself been Prime Minister.

By mid-December, after the unsuccessful prosecution of John Thelwall—a skillful orator known for his inflammatory rhetoric—Pitt dropped the charges and freed the remaining prisoners. Attending the victory dinner thrown by the proprietors of the *Chronicle* for the twelve radicals, Coleridge could see that each man had paid an enormous personal price for the political triumph. Hardy's shop had been looted and his wife had suffered a miscarriage. Horne Tooke's health had been destroyed, and Thelwall's family had been harassed by Pitt's agents—consequences which Coleridge filed away in his memory as precautions for his own future radical activities. And in spite of widespread popular support for the restoration of habeas corpus, Parliament would vote to continue Pitt's powers of arbitrary imprisonment in the interest of national security.

Coleridge had become so caught up in political events that he had lost sight of his original reason for coming to town—to reassure brother George that he was no flaming Jacobin. He had hoped that a face-to-face chat would allow him to clarify George's misconceptions concerning the crucial semantic distinction between a bloodthirsty democrat and a peace-loving Pantisocrat. But whatever light he had initially been able to shed on his brother's confusion was dimmed as George read Sam's inflammatory poems in the *Chronicle*.

The second goal of Coleridge's trip to London—as ill-fated as the first for much the same reason—had been to seek a "reconciliation" with Mary Evans. But as with George, Coleridge's approach to Mary was filled with patent self-contradictions. While professing his ardent wish to be reunited with her, Coleridge did everything in his power to lose her. His first move had been to delay responding to her letter for more than a month. But finally breaking nearly two years of total silence,

Coleridge summoned the courage to explain himself in a letter to Mary.

To his credit, he owned up that he had vanished abruptly without explanation after losing the Craven because he found the circumstances too painful to discuss at the time. With his career prospects shattered, he lacked the resources to marry and thought, therefore, that the gentlemanly thing to do was to withdraw.

Of course he glossed over the fact that he never consulted her on this delicate matter. And then, in what amounted to an orgy of self-pity which made him appear extremely unappealing, Coleridge informed Mary that he would understand perfectly if she had already given, or was in the process of giving, her affections to another. He added, with great nobility of spirit, that he would even learn to unselfishly "love" her new husband if that was her choice.

Having set the stage for a final rejection by writing his maudlin letter rather than attempting to woo her in person, Coleridge holed up in the alehouse back room with Charles Lamb, acting the part of the anxious suitor, dangling in suspense awaiting his lover's reply. Mary's answer, a negative one, arrived just before Christmas. Two down and one to go before he could count himself a free man again, Coleridge turned his full attentions to Robert Southey.

Anxious to be let off the matrimonial hook, Coleridge described the crushing blow Mary Evans had dealt him:

> To lose her!—I can rise above that selfish pang. But to marry another—O Southey! bear with my weakness. Love makes all things pure and heavenly like itself:—but to marry a woman I do *not* love—to degrade her, whom I call my wife, by making her the instrument of low desire—and on the removal of a desultory appetite, to be perhaps not displeased with her absence!— Enough! . . .
>
> Mark you, Southey!— I *will do my Duty.* [CL I, p. 145]

But wriggle and squirm as he did in the many letters he wrote to Southey that December—protesting that he did not love Sarah Fricker—Coleridge pleaded to deaf ears. Southey self-righteously expected Coleridge to do his duty.

Unable to obtain a reprieve, Coleridge resorted to stalling tactics. While promising daily that he was on his way back to Bristol, he settled into the alehouse with Charles Lamb. Smoking pipe after pipe of Oronoco tobacco, drinking egg-hots and eating Welsh rabbits, the pair nostalgically reminisced on the old days at Christ's Hospital and endlessly discussed politics and poetry. It was an experience Lamb never forgot: "I think I hear you again. I imagine to myself the little smoky room at the Salutation and Cat, where we sat together through the winter nights, beguiling the cares of life with poesy" (Lamb, 1848, p. 25). As winter wore on, Bristol seemed more distant, the back room more snug, and the prospect of Miss Fricker more chilling.

Meanwhile, back in Bristol, Southey grew more impatient and irritated with Coleridge by the minute. Finally, in mid-January, unwilling to brook any further delay, he came to London to fetch Coleridge, whose response was: "I am glad you are come . . . and yet I am not glad" (CL I, p. 149).

Coleridge returned to Bristol out of a sense of duty and obligation to Robert Southey—not to Sarah Fricker or Pantisocracy. Having spent less than two weeks with Sarah, he barely knew her. And while neither Southey nor Coleridge openly admitted it, they both knew that their idealistic plan to move to America was on the rocks, due to their shared ambivalence as well as to real financial obstacles.

While he owed Sarah Fricker and the American plan nothing, he owed Southey a great deal. They had become brothers and Coleridge felt compelled to honor that bond. His urgent quest for a brother had been set in motion after Frank's suicide, and Southey had generously stepped in to fill the place of Coleridge's lost childhood companion. They had struck an emotional bargain, and Southey was insistent that Coleridge live up to his half of the arrangement.

Apart from Charles Lamb, who had grown deeply attached to Coleridge, the landlord at the Salutation and Cat was the sorriest to see him leave. Personally fond of Coleridge and aware that his nightly conversation had attracted many customers to the pub's back room, the proprietor tearfully offered him free lodging if he stayed on indefinitely. Of a less sentimental turn of mind, the innkeeper at the Angel demanded

Coleridge leave a bundle of clothes as security for his unpaid bill.

It was with the utmost delicacy that Sarah Fricker informed Coleridge of the two suitors who had appeared in his absence—particularly the one of comfortable means whom her uncle was urging her to marry. Presented with this loophole and the fact that Sarah was insisting demurely only that he make up his mind one way or the other, Coleridge was free to withdraw from his obligation to Miss F., albeit by jilting her. But it was Southey, not Sarah, whom he could not leave in the lurch.

At first, relations between the two friends were idyllic. Along with George Burnett, they rented a room in a College Street boarding house which served as Pantisocracy headquarters by day and doubled as lodgings by night. Still faced with the lack of money to finance their commune, Coleridge and Southey decided to give a paid subscription series of lectures to raise capital. In spite of their cramped living quarters, Southey was thrilled: "Coleridge is writing at the same table; our names are written in the book of destiny, on the same page" (quoted in Chambers, 1938, p. 39).

Joseph Cottle, the bookseller, agreed to print and sell the tickets for the series. Southey decided to give all his lectures on history, while Coleridge planned to diversify his and give three on politics, six on religion, and one each on the slave trade and Pitt's Hairpowder Tax. Although by no means a regular church-goer, Coleridge had remained religious and was relishing the opportunity to give his views on how society could be reformed only within a religious framework, essentially Unitarian in nature.

In Coleridge's eyes, the godless French democrats had perverted the Revolution from brotherhood to fratricide through a lack of guiding religious principles, while on the home front, the Church of England had become the equally corrupt hand-maiden of aristocrats: "the religion of mitres and mysteries, the religion of pluralities and persecution, the eighteen-thousand-pound-a-year religion of Episcopacy" (Coleridge, 1795, p. 66). He looked forward to pulpitizing to the world how revolution and Christianity fit together by demonstrating how the teachings of each supported the other.

Throughout that winter and the early spring of 1795, Coleridge and Southey spent their days at the boarding house researching and writing their lectures together. Evenings, they visited with Sarah and Edith, an inseparable foursome, and, much to his surprise, Coleridge found himself again falling in love with Sarah. Clearly the odd man out except for running errands and being useful in a good-natured way, George Burnett was unable to persuade Martha Fricker to marry and was not called upon to lecture by Coleridge and Southey.

In preparing for his lectures, Coleridge had learned an important lesson from the Twelve Apostles: the necessity of taking precautions. As the Old Bailey proceedings had demonstrated, Pitt's spies and paid informers were everywhere and were even willing to perjure themselves if need be. Careful to create a written record to serve as evidence in any future treason proceedings, Coleridge published his talks. The printed versions were greatly watered down compared to the fiery rhetoric of his in-person delivery, which provoked "mobs and mayors, blockheads and brickbats, placards and press gangs... [and]... two or three uncouth and unbrained automata [who] have threatened my life" (CL I, p. 152).

Reviewing both the violence of the French Revolution and the recent wave of political repression in England, Coleridge passionately advocated yet one more revolution—a bloodless one based firmly on religious principles and conducted by an educated elite who were fit to govern until the masses were better prepared through universal education. While Coleridge's carefully edited, printed texts cannot recapture the spirited flavor of his evangelical harangues, a later reminiscence does:

> Speaking in public at Bristol... after a turbid stream of wild eloquence I said—"This is a true Lord's Supper in the communion of darkness! This is a eucharist of hell! A sacrament of misery!—over each morsel and each drop of which the spirit of some murdered innocent cries aloud to God, This is *my* body! and this my blood!" [CL II, p. 100]

Dipping down deep into family tradition, the twenty-two-year-old Samuel had obviously drawn on the Reverend John Coleridge's gift for sermonical oratory, although he was clearly putting them to a different use than his father would have imagined. Or, that is, in some ways a different use. As his lectures moved from politics to revealed religion, it became clear that Coleridge had not departed from an essentially religious framework, despite his revolutionary vision. Advocating what in essence amounted to a Christian form of socialism, based on the Bible, which he quoted both chapter and verse, Coleridge outlined a system with Jesus as the salvation for the world's woes. But while John Coleridge's Jesus had been a godhead of mystery, Samuel's was an ordinary man of Unitarian invention, as outlined by Joseph Priestley and others.

Or as Coleridge summed up, "I have asserted that Jesus Christ forbids to his disciples all property—and teaches us that accumulation was incompatible with their salvation!" (Coleridge, 1795, p. 226). Documenting this assertion with quotes from Matthew and St. Paul, Coleridge drove home the point to his flock. But while his image of Christ clearly owed a great deal to Priestley, his views on private property must have been inspired by some other source, since at that very moment Priestley was busily enegaged in real estate speculation in the Susquehanna Valley.

Bristol's Church-and-King reactionaries were less than thrilled by Coleridge's attempt to overthrow the status quo with Jesus and love. They were even less pleased with his scathing indictment of that important local industry, the slave trade. Coleridge did, however, receive a warm welcome from the Bristol intelligentsia, who admired the "happy union of wit, humor and argument" and applauded his "arch manner of recitation" (Coleridge, 1795, p. xxx). While commenting favorably on his talks, the local newspapers took pains to point out that they might be better received if he would improve his sloppy, unkempt bohemian-radical appearance by wearing clean stockings and combing his hair.

Yet Coleridge's personal magnetism suffered little as the result of his appearance: Sarah Fricker held her head high on her evening promenades through Bristol, arm in arm with her celebrated Samuel. But while their lecture series may have made Coleridge and Southey celebrities, they were failing to accomplish their aim of raising capital. Pantisocracy remained stalled in spite of the fact that by now the glorious American adventure had been scaled down to a modest trial run in Wales. Unable to make ends meet, the two men were living off Joseph Cottle's generosity. As their dream began to flounder, ominous signs of friction began to develop.

The first evidence of open discord appeared in early June when the quartet, accompanied by Cottle, went on a two-day outing to Tintern Abbey to celebrate the end of the grueling lecture series. While dining at the Beaufort Arms in Chepstow, Coleridge and Southey got into an argument over the fact that Coleridge had failed to deliver one of Southey's lectures after specifically asking to give the talk. Tempers flared and each accused the other of a waning commitment to Pantisocracy.

Sarah sided with her Samuel and Edith took Southey's side in the argument. After a discussion agitated to the point of tears, they patched up their differences and continued on their torchlight tour of Tintern Abbey. But mistrust and resentment were building on both sides.

Southey was bitter, he claimed, because he had been contributing the lion's share to their joint financial support. Industrious by nature, Southey resented that while he was composing furiously at the writing table, Coleridge dreamily wandered about the room, frequently interrupting Southey's concentration by meditatively chewing over his ideas out loud for hours on end. And by now, Coleridge's brilliant conversation seemed less spellbinding to Southey. Living with Coleridge on a daily basis, he had heard the same extraordinary flashes of insight tiresomely repeated almost verbatim to different people, night after night. In Southey's moral—if not moralistic—eyes, Coleridge suffered from laziness and a tendency to sponge off others.

And to Coleridge's idealistic thinking, Robert Southey had begun to reveal that most un-Pantisocratic sin of all sins, selfishness—an unwillingness to *aspheterize* for the common good. In early spring, Southey had heard from an old friend who hinted that when he came into his inheritance he would consider setting up an annuity for Southey of a hundred and sixty pounds a year. Although the gift was a long way off and would never actually materialize, Southey had revealed his true colors by making it abundantly clear that, should his ship come in, he would be unwilling to *aspheterize* its cargo.

By August, the rift between Coleridge and Southey was already deepening when a wealthy uncle of Southey's invited him to spend six months in Portugal, all expenses paid, and offered to finance his nephew's legal training upon his return. Southey accepted. Coleridge was wounded by Southey's decision to leave. Pantisocracy was dead, and they were definitely at odds with one another. Their lovely fraternal dream died an undignified death as, filled with icy rage, Southey and Coleridge politely nodded whenever they crossed paths. "Unsaluted and unsaluting," Coleridge "passed by the man to whom for almost a year I had told my last thoughts when I closed my eyes, and the first when I awoke!" (CL I, p. 168).

But Coleridge was by now very much in love with his loyal Sarah, who had stood by him, and he made up his mind to marry her as soon as possible. And although he had decided to go to Portugal with his uncle, Southey planned to marry Edith secretly before leaving England.

Sarah Fricker and Coleridge were married on October 4, 1795 at St. Mary Redcliffe Church in Bristol. Mrs. Fricker and Josiah Wade, a wealthy Bristol tradesman and close friend of Coleridge's, were witnesses at the ceremony. No longer on speaking terms with Coleridge, Southey did not attend. And if Coleridge missed his brother, he did not let it show, since by all accounts he appeared to be very happy on his wedding day.

Six weeks later Robert Southey married Edith Fricker in that same church and set sail for Portugal alone immediately after the ceremony. Coleridge did not attend the wedding or see Southey off at the ship. But on the eve of Southey's marriage, Coleridge wrote an impassioned letter summarizing the history of their friendship. At the end of his letter, Coleridge conveyed his deep sense of loss:

> You have left a void in my heart—I know no man big enough to fill it. Others I may love equally and esteem equally: and some perhaps I may admire as much. But never do I expect to meet another man, who will make me unite attachment for his person with reverence for his heart and admiration of his genius! I did

not only venerate you for your own virtues, I prized you as the sheet anchor of mine! [CL I, p. 173]

Perhaps it was no coincidence that Coleridge chose the fourth of October as the date of his own wedding. It was a date already associated in his mind with two losses: his father had died that day, just after Frank had gone off to sea. We can only speculate whether Coleridge chose that anniversary date because he now associated his marriage with the loss of Robert Southey as well. In Southey he had found a replacement for Frank, albeit a temporary one, just as earlier he had providentially found a substitute for his father in his brother George.

Coleridge's ties with both men were now painfully ruptured, and if a future need for symbolic replacements arose, he would have to look elsewhere. But confident in his love for Sarah, Coleridge felt for the moment secure. In marrying her, he was declaring his independence from childhood and family ties and making the statement that he would be his own man.

Chapter 5

Honeymoon Radical Style

> *Ah! quiet Dell! dear Cot, and Mount sublime!*
> *I was constrain'd to quit you. Was it right,*
> *While my unnumber'd brethren toil'd and bled,*
> *That I should dream away the entrusted hours*
> *On rose-leaf beds, pampering the coward heart*
> *With feelings all too delicate for use?*
> ....
> *I therefore go, and join head, heart, and hand,*
> *Active and firm, to fight the bloodless fight*
> *Of Science, Freedom, and the Truth in Christ.*
> —from *Reflections on Having Left*
> *a Place of Retirement* [PW, pp. 107–108]

Excited by his honeymoon adventure, Coleridge dashed off a wedding announcement describing "the solemn joy I felt—united to the woman I love best of all beings. We are settled—nay—quite domesticated at Clevedon" (CL I, p. 160). Their honeymoon cottage was nestled near the rolling coombes of the West Country in a sleepy fishing village on the Bristol Channel. Bathing in the sea by day, they lay awake at night listening to the murmur of the waves. The topmost buds of a rose "peep'd at the chamber-window" (PW, p. 106), while aromatic myrtle and jasmine blossoms wreathed the front door, mingling their odors with fragrances from the nearby bean fields, wafted in on the fresh sea breezes.

Declaring the view "more *various* than any in the kingdom" (CL I, p. 160), Coleridge was as intoxicated by the sights as he was by the scents and sounds. "Mine eye gluttonizes" (CL I, p. 160), he said as he surveyed the sloping forests and lush fields surrounding their village. From a hillside perch he could see the Bristol Channel filled with white sails and speckled with islands, with the Welsh coast off in the distance and the remote spires of Bristol barely visible over the horizon.

But most inebriating of all to the young groom was the realization that he was actually married: "Mrs. Coleridge—MRS. COLERIDGE!!—I like to *write* the name. Well—as I was saying—Mrs. Coleridge desires her affectionate regards to you ..." (Cl I, p. 160). "I love and am beloved and I am happy," he told a friend (CL I, p. 164). Instinctively turning to poetry to express such strong feelings, Coleridge dedicated nine poems to Sarah during their courtship and honeymoon.

The Aeolian Harp is by far the best—a close-up portrait—with an interior view of the cottage, their relationship, and Coleridge's moods. His verse captures the moment: he and Sarah are sitting peacefully together at twilight, listening to the music of a wind harp in their casement window. Her cheek is softly resting against his arm as they drink in the distant sound of the sea, the smell of the bean fields, the glow of the evening sky at sunset, and the touch of each other's bodies. They bathe in this mélange of sensations until Coleridge breaks the spell by allowing his mind to wander off into flights of speculative fancy. No longer involved in the pleasure of the moment, he ruminates on the nature of God and the universe. Gently chiding her husband for distancing himself from her, Sarah reminds him that a simple, unquestioning belief in God could ease his need to ponder such unanswerable philosophical questions.

But of a restless temperament, Coleridge at times hungered after ultimate truths. At one moment a consummate idealist, the penniless poet took pride in the fact that his marriage to his dowryless bride was not calculated on material considerations. Other truths, however, were less welcome to him: shortly after their wedding, Coleridge introduced a slip of the pen into his letters and diaries that would persist indefinitely—a glaring miscalculation making himself older than he was by a year and a day. Perhaps he sensed that the disparity in his and Sarah's ages might make for an unequal relationship.

If this liaison between a protractedly adolescent twenty-two-year-old who had never supported himself, much less another, and a near-spinster of twenty-four, well accustomed to assuming financial responsibility in her family, was intended by Coleridge to curb the heady excessses of his radical idealism,

Honeymoon Radical Style

it would take some doing. Perhaps, however, Sarah intended to be the one to adjust, to accommodate patiently to her husband's restless energies. As she already knew, his whims might demand uprooting and impermanence.

By mid-fall, after a six-week honeymoon, Coleridge was back in Bristol leading an antiwar counterdemonstration at Guildhall. News of his reemergence on the political scene made the London dailies:

> After a considerable time spent in fruitlessly calling 'Mr. Mayor! Mr. Mayor!' in a tone... which would have fascinated the attention even of a Robespierre; Mr. Coleridge began the most elegant, the most pathetic and the most sublime address that was ever heard, perhaps, within the walls of that building. [Coleridge, 1796, p. xxvii]

The Tory mayor had convened the townspeople to demonstrate Bristol's loyal support of George III and to gather signatures for a petition endorsing two pending acts of Parliament designed to silence any dissent against the King or his government.

Cut short by the Mayor and not permitted to address the crowd further, Coleridge and his comrades hired a hall at the Pelican for their own protest meeting and began soliciting signatures on a counterpetition. The fight was on. The two acts, if passed, effectively spelled the death knell for radical dissent. Coleridge explained to Sarah that his services were needed, and by December they were back in Bristol, temporarily living at his mother-in-law's as Coleridge prepared to combat William Pitt's latest treachery.

Since the successful defense of the Twelve Apostles, the ranks of the LCS had swelled despite Pitt's holding the trump card of suspended habeas corpus. By Spring 1795 there were forty divisions in the London branch alone, and on June 29 they assembled, one hundred thousand strong, at St. George's Fields to demand universal male suffrage, an annual Parliament, and an end to the war with France.

By October the London branch had doubled to eighty divisions and another mass demonstration attracted a crowd so huge that they were addressed from three rostrums simultaneously by a group of speakers that included John Thelwall and William Frend. Again it was an orderly assembly, but three days later the window of George III's carriage was shattered by a stone or a marble shot from an air gun as he rode through St. James Park on his way to Parliament. Interpreting this chain of events as proof that political demonstrations incited the mob to regicide, Pitt introduced two "Gagging Acts" designed to restrict freedom of speech and the right of public assembly.

The first measure redefined the scope of treason to include any attempt, whether in print or in speech, to exert pressure on the King or to "intimidate" Parliament. Only two witnesses were required for conviction. The second measure gave local magistrates discretionary power over all meetings of more than fifty people. Refusal to disband was punishable by death, with magistrates indemnified in advance for any injuries or loss of life resulting from their attempts to break up such meetings.

The month remaining before Parliament voted was the last opportunity for radicals to prevent enactment of these harsh measures. Throughout England the opposition massed to collect signatures and to demonstrate in hopes of influencing the vote. Mass rallies in London held by the LCS in mid-November and early December attracted four hundred thousand people each. And while Coleridge did not officially belong to the LCS—his platform of Christian reform did not permit such an affiliation—he organized and addressed local meetings of Bristol radicals and collected signatures at the Pelican.

But the petitions fell on deaf ears. On December 18, the "Gagging Acts" became the law of the land and Pitt was equipped with the legislative machinery he needed to break the back of the radical movement. Only time would tell how far Pitt would go, a limit Coleridge seemed eager to test.

In late December Coleridge met with Josiah Wade and a group of prosperous Bristol tradesmen of liberal persuasion to present his plan for a one-man magazine to advance their political views and serve as a showcase for his poetry. In a "flaming prospectus" he outlined his two main objectives: repeal of the "Gagging Acts" and universal male suffrage (Coleridge, 1796, p. xxxii). Designed to "preserve freedom and her friends from the attacks of robbers and assassins" (Coleridge, 1796, p. xxxii), his magazine was christened *The Watchman*.

Having obtained local backers, Coleridge barnstormed the nearby Midlands in search of subscribers. Exploiting the one loophole in the "Gagging Acts"—that they placed no restriction on religious services, no matter how large—Coleridge mounted the pulpits of Unitarian churches. "My sermons spread a sort of sanctity over my sedition," he declared (CL I, p. 179). Dressed informally in street clothes rather than clerical robes, Coleridge gave talks "preciously peppered with politics" (CL I, p. 176) and delivered with a crusader's fervor. Jesus was on his side:

> Mr. Fellowes gave one of my prospectuses to an aristocrat. He glanced on the motto: 'That All may know the Truth, and that the Truth may make us free.'
> 'A *seditious* beginning!' quoth he.
> 'Sir!' said Mr. Fellowes— 'the motto is quoted from another author.'
> 'Poo!' quoth the aristocrat. 'What odds is it whether he wrote it himself or quoted it from any *other seditious dog?*'
> 'Please (replied Mr. F.) to look in the 32nd Chapter of John and you will find, Sir! that that *seditious* dog was Jesus Christ!'
> .... This is one proof among thousands that aristocrats do not read their bible. [CL I, p. 179]

Coleridge's tour included Birmingham, Sheffield, Manchester, Derby, and Worcester. Along the way he saw firsthand evidence of Pitt's intentions. The editor of the Sheffield *Iris* was in prison, while the previous editor had been forced to flee England. The London publisher he sought for his magazine was indisposed owing to a previous engagement—he was doing time at Newgate for publishing Paine's *Rights of Man*.

Coleridge was just starting to consider the precautions he would take with *The Watchman* when he learned he would have to be even more careful—he was about to become a father. "Distressed and sorely agitated" on learning that his bride of five months was mysteriously ill (CL I, p. 180), he returned to Bristol in time to learn that Sarah's "illness" was the first trimester malaise of an unplanned pregnancy. The timing could not have been worse.

Insecure over the prospect of becoming a father while penniless and walking the political tightrope of his publishing enterprise, Coleridge grew panicky, by no means an uncommon reaction among prospective young fathers. More serious, however, was the fact that he soothed the cares of impending fatherhood with "Mother's Blessing." For two weeks in late February he took opium almost nightly to steady his nerves as he struggled to meet the printer's deadline for the first issue of *The Watchman* and tried to comfort Sarah, who was contending with her pain and the threat of a miscarriage. But by mid-March Coleridge, with a sigh of relief, informed a friend that prospects for both the new baby and the new magazine were looking up.

By the end of March the Coleridges were settled in new lodgings, which doubled as offices for *The Watchman*. Slaving away on this one-man weekly, Coleridge found it impossible to fill its thirty-two advertisement-free pages entirely with original material. Excerpting national news from the London dailies and relying on occasional contributions from William Frend and Thomas Poole, Coleridge also devoted large sections to verbatim transcripts of relevant Parliamentary debates; these he punctuated ironically with italics, exclamation points, and capitals.

About a third of the magazine was original material: Coleridge attacked the Church of England, ridiculed the miracles of the New Testament, preached his Christian socialism, advocated revolution, and attacked Pitt, sometimes directly, sometimes in fictitious letters to the editor signed with pseudonyms. The poems in *The Watchman* were his lesser efforts; his best were already in press with Joseph Cottle, who was bringing out his collected poems.

Early issues of the magazine were pro-French. Coleridge's loyalties, like those of many other English intellectuals, transcended patriotic nationalism and embraced the ideal of international brotherhood. But as spring wore on, public opinion rapidly began to turn as it became patently clear—even to Coleridge—that the recently formed five-man Directory that had replaced Robespierre intended to pursue a policy that went beyond mere national defense.

On the day Coleridge recited his wedding vows at St. Mary Redcliffe, an unknown artillery captain had spent his afternoon stationed in front of the Church of St. Roche near the Tuileries, where he handily dispatched a Royalist mob with what he modestly described as a "whiff of grapeshot" (Loomis, 1968, p. 233).

His reward for subduing that uprising had been promotion to the rank of Brigadier. And by April, as *The Watchman* went into its second month, that recently promoted General —Bonaparte—was successfully leading a full-scale invasion of Italy. While Pitt had begun to show a willingness to listen to popular opinion and put an end to the bloodshed by negotiating with the French, the Directory had turned a deaf ear to Pitt's overtures and was stalling for time as their invading armies chewed up more and more European real estate.

The romantic war of ideology was fast becoming one of empire. Before 1796, many English radicals had even welcomed the prospect of a French invasion as a liberation from the combined tyranny of George III and William Pitt. But now, filled with patriotism and aware of the need for self-defense, many of the same people who had objected most violently to Pitt's "Gagging Acts" were beginning to accept them as necessary wartime security measures.

In the course of six months, from December 1795, when *The Watchman* was first conceived, to May 1796, when it folded abruptly for lack of subscribers, a drastic change had taken place in England's political climate. As Coleridge was forced regretfully to conclude in his tenth and final issue: "O Watchman! thou hast watched in vain!" (Coleridge, 1796, p. xxvii). Or, as he would later put it, "I have now seen my error. I have accordingly snapped my squeaking baby-trumpet of sedition, and have hung up its fragments in the chamber of penitences" (CL I, p. 240). By mid-spring Coleridge's twin honeymoons—with Sarah and with radical politics—were at an end.

Sarah was now in her fifth month, providing Coleridge a daily visible reminder of his need to find a reliable means of supporting his family. His *Poems on Various Subjects* had just come out, but he had long since spent Cottle's advance of thirty pounds and still faced debts for expenses incurred by *The Watchman*. Coleridge was just starting to feel the financial pinch when he received a heartwarming surprise from Thomas Poole, the liberal tanner he had met during his walking tour of Somerset two years earlier.

Poole had settled an annuity of forty pounds on Coleridge (approximately $1400 a year by 1980 standards; see Appendix

B) so that he might continue his literary efforts. Besides Poole, the list of patrons included Josiah Wade and J. J. Morgan, a Bristol lawyer. A week later, Coleridge received a ten-pound award from the Literary Fund of London in recognition of his *Poems on Various Subjects*, which had just begun to receive favorable reviews. And finally, Josiah Wade stepped in and agreed to absorb the debts *The Watchman* had incurred.

Although these windfalls were not enough to comfortably support a family of three, they provided breathing room for Coleridge to contemplate his next career move less desperately. Should he seek extraliterary sources of income, or attempt to balance the family budget with his pen? Publishing his own magazine had proven risky, and although the volume of poems was well received, it was failing to produce the much needed family nest egg. And there were no immediate prospects for his idealistic dream of *aspheterizing* both his fortunes and his anxieties with a brother poet.

Although Southey had just returned from Portugal, their literary partnership was at an end. After taking lodgings across the street from the Coleridges, Southey broke the ice by sending a one-line note quoting Schiller: "Fiesco! Fiesco! thou leavest a void in my bosom, which the human race, thrice told, will never fill up" (CL I, p. 294). But if Southey had remembered their parting more realistically, he would have better begun his note, "Fiasco! Fiasco!" Although the two men resumed speaking terms, it was clear to Coleridge that the old feelings could not be recaptured.

Using the summer of 1796 to get his bearings, Coleridge investigated job opportunities and sought counsel from others. He visited his family in Ottery, where, as he described it, he was "received by my mother with transport, and by my brother George with joy and tenderness and by my other brothers with affectionate civility" (CL I, p. 232). But by now, both during the visits he made to Stowey and in the steady correspondence developing between them, Coleridge found himself turning to Thomas Poole for advice and support in preference to his brother George.

Mature, realistic men, both George Coleridge and Thomas Poole held many of the same attractions for Coleridge —thoughtfulness, stability, benevolence, and integrity. But ever since his arrival in the West Country two years earlier, Coleridge had been relying increasingly on Poole and had formed a close friendship in spite of the fifty miles that separated Stowey from Bristol. During his visits to Poole, Coleridge had come to admire the man's rustic simplicity and the uncomplicated country life he led.

In warm weather the pair sat in Poole's orchard, drinking the local cider and talking politics long into the night. Unlike brother George's Church-and-King conservatism, Poole's level-headed liberalism appealed to Coleridge and provided a steadying balance to his own tendency to react in extremes.

As Coleridge informed Poole, he was leaving no stone unturned in his search for security. For a while he considered an offer of a job as reporter for the *Morning Chronicle* in London but was filled with reservations about relocating Sarah and their new baby to "the felon-crowded dungeon of a great city" (CL I, p. 155). The more he and Poole talked about life, the more Poole became the source of inspiration for Coleridge's latest ideal: the self-sufficient rural man. And Poole's tiny hamlet of Nether Stowey rapidly became Coleridge's utopia.

But if Coleridge intended to drop out of radical politics and avoid corrupt city life in favor of rural simplicity, he still needed a realistic way to support his family. Searching for prospects, he retoured the Midlands, where he considered opening a small private school or serving as tutor for a wealthy family. On his way back to Bristol that August, he stopped in Birmingham and renewed acquaintances with twenty-one-year-old Charles Lloyd, an amateur poet and the son of a wealthy Quaker banker. A fervent admirer of Coleridge's poetry, Lloyd proposed that Coleridge become his paid private tutor and that he move in as a boarder with Coleridge and Sarah.

Having demonstrated neither aptitude nor inclination for commerce, Charles Lloyd had long been a source of worry to his father, both as a result of his literary interests and the strange fits of psychomotor epilepsy to which he was prone. The senior Lloyd was favorably inclined to pay both for Coleridge's tutorial services and for his informal custodianship of his erratic son, if only he could be assured that Coleridge was no longer a flaming Jacobin who might lead the young man astray. For their part, the Coleridges would have to decide if there would be room in their household, particularly with a new baby on the way, for a pupil prone to uncontrollable fits of delirium which required the same type of nursing and physical restraint that Coleridge had performed at the Henley pesthouse. More susceptible than the average person to the allure of caring for a delirium-prone brother poet, Coleridge was strongly tempted by the Lloyds' offer of eighty pounds a year.

On September 20, while negotiating with the Lloyds, Coleridge received news of the birth of his son and dashed back to Bristol with his new pupil in tow. Naming his son David Hartley Coleridge in honor of the philosopher, Coleridge adamantly refused to have the child baptized.

While his first reaction was "I have seen handsomer babies in my life" (CL I, p. 236), it took only a few short weeks before Papa Coleridge was dashing off poetry to Hartley and proudly declaring him "the very miniature" of himself (CL I, p. 243). By mid-October the budding patriarch declared his intention to relocate to the country, where "my children should be bred up from earliest infancy in the simplicity of peasants, their food dress and habits completely rustic" (CL I, p. 240).

With beseeching sweetness, Coleridge wrote Poole that he yearned to be "near ... to see you daily, to tell you all my thoughts in their first birth, and to hear yours, to be mingling identities with you" (CL I, p. 249). He implored Poole to do all in his power to help him make the move to Stowey:

> My heart has been full, yea crammed with anxieties about my residence near you. I so ardently desire it, that any disappointment would chill all my faculties, like the fingers of death. And entertaining a wish so irrationally strong, I neccessarily have *daymair* dreams that something will prevent it—so that since I quitted you, I have been gloomy as the month which even now has begun to lower and rave on us. [CL I, p. 242]

Aware that his moody young friend was prone to momentary bursts of enthusiasm, Poole cautioned Coleridge that Stowey was only a three-street market town in the middle of nowhere. Poole advised Coleridge to first experiment with rural living by moving to the outskirts of Bristol, before hastily uprooting his family. Deeply wounded by Poole's suggestion, which he misinterpreted as personal rejection, Coleridge lamented that in the suburbs of Bristol he would "be perpetually haunted . . . [by] the hideous ghost of departed hope.—O Poole! how could *you* make such a proposal to me?" (CL I, p. 272).

The "hideous ghost" Coleridge feared most at this turning point in his life would seem to be the nagging spectre of his missing father. Fatherlesss since the age of nine, he felt panicky and ill-equipped to cope with the demands of being a father himself: "O Thomas Poole! Thomas Poole! if you did but know what a father and a husband must feel, who toils with his brain for uncertain bread! I dare not think of it—the evil face of frenzy looks at me!" (CL I, p. 275). Feeling a desperate need for paternal guidance, Coleridge hungered for Poole's "instruction, daily advice, society—everything neccessary to my feelings and the realization of my innocent independence" (CL I, p. 274).

Satisfied that he had at least gotten Coleridge to consider seriously the potential drawbacks of relocating so far from Bristol, Poole became more sympathetic and agreed to help him resettle. But local housing was scarce, and it took time for Poole to locate an adequate rental within the Coleridges' budget. Faced with delay, Coleridge developed a pain in his face. "My medical attendant decides it to be altogether nervous. . . . My beloved Poole! in excessive anxiety, I believe, it might originate! I have a blister under my right ear, and I take twenty-five drops of laudanum* every five hours. . . . I am anxious beyond measure to be in the country as soon as possible" (CL I, p. 250).

Coleridge's attack lasted less than a week, after which Charles Lloyd developed a series of somnambulistic "delirious vision[s]" (CL I, p. 257) requiring around-the-clock nursing and, eventually, removal to his family's home for recuperation. By late December of 1796, Poole located a cottage with an acre

---

*Twenty-five drops of laudanum was approximately the equivalent of 6.5 mg. of oral morphine every five hours. See Appendix C for method of calculation. Goodman and Gillman (1970) describe 6 to 15 mg. of oral morphine as an average adult therapeutic dose. Coleridge's dose was at the lower end of the spectrum, suggesting that at this point he was by no means addicted; one would expect an addict to require much higher levels for the relief of pain. He was, however, developing a stress-related pattern of episodic opium use.

and a half of cultivable ground at a rent of eight guineas per year.

Arriving in the dead of winter with their four-month-old son, his nanny, and a wagonload of furniture, the Coleridges were delighted with their small thatched-roof cottage. Although the living quarters were cramped, the property abutted on Poole's backyard. Delighted to be living so near his mentor, Coleridge reassured Poole of his intention:

> to work *very hard*—as cook, butler, scullion, shoe-cleaner, occasional nurse, gardener, hind, pig-protector, chaplain, secretary, poet, reviewer, and omnium-botherum shilling-scavenger—in other words, I shall keep no servant, and will cultivate my land-acre and my wise-acres, as well as I can. [CL I, p. 266]

Learning of his friend's latest adventure, Lamb quizzed, "Is it a farm you have got? And what does your worship know about farming?" (Lamb, 1980, p. 60). Undaunted, Coleridge purchased some geese and ducks and a couple of pigs. Poole talked him out of buying a cow, offering a steady supply of milk from his own animal. Relying on Poole for agricultural advice, Coleridge started a garden and began raising his own potatoes and vegetables. Finally he was leading the orderly, self-disciplined life of which he had always dreamed:

> I never go to Bristol—from seven to half past eight I work in my garden; from breakfast till 12 I read and compose; then work again—feed the pigs, poultry etc, till two o'clock—after dinner work again till tea—from tea till supper *review*. So jogs the day and I am happy. I have society—my friend, T. Poole and as many acquaintances as I can dispense with. [CL I, p. 308]

And on Sundays, Coleridge even found time to preach at Unitarian meeting houses in nearby Taunton and Bridgwater.

Socializing with his neighbors in the evenings, Coleridge amused them with his witty puns and riddles and was particularly pleased over the fact that he was learning to dance. Sarah began making friends with the women of the village, many of whom had children Hartley's age. All in all, moving to Stowey seemed to have been a good decision:

We are *very* happy—and my little David Hartley grows a sweet boy—and has high health—he laughs at us till he makes us weep for very fondness.—You would smile to see my eye rolling up to the ceiling in a lyric fury, and on my knee a *diaper* pinned, to warm. [CL I, p. 308]

While Coleridge's panic at Hartley's birth over being ill prepared for fatherhood may have lent a desperate urgency to his wish to relocate near Poole, there had been nothing rash or impulsive in his choice of men. In selecting Poole as teacher, guide, mentor, and father-figure, Coleridge could not have made a more sensible choice.

A thoughtful, unassuming man who had prepared to take over his family's prosperous tanning business by forgoing a university education in order to learn the ropes by working as a common laborer in a tannery, Poole was progressive in his attitudes and cared deeply about his employees' welfare. He had already formed a working men's benevolent society and would later found one for women, build a school, and serve as trusted friend and counselor to many of the poorer families in the neighborhood. Remaining a bachelor all his life, Poole would focus his strong need to nurture on community welfare projects rather than on a family of his own.

Drawn by Poole's sense of fatherly responsibility and managerial competence, Coleridge hoped those traits might rub off so that he might put his life on a steadier keel. And for his part, Poole keenly regretted his lack of formal schooling and had painstakingly taught himself makeshift Latin and Greek, which daily contact with Coleridge could easily improve. In fact, Poole was as much in awe of Coleridge's literary abilities and academic erudition as Coleridge was impressed by Poole's common sense and managerial skills.

As part of his impulse to self-improvement, Poole had accumulated an immense library, stocked with the classics and the modern political philosophers. Sitting in Poole's "great windy parlour" (CL I, p. 643) long into the cold winter nights, Coleridge rummaged through Poole's collection, browsing and borrowing volumes that interested him, and commenting on the texts to Poole's edification.

Coleridge was also writing at a steady pace, with Poole's

encouragement. While Poole had little to offer on the technical side in terms of line by line literary criticism, he was nonetheless teaching his younger friend a great deal about regular, industrious habits. Coleridge was hard at work revising his verse for the second edition of his collected poems. Influenced in part by the rustic life he was leading, and perhaps by Poole's straightforward speech as well, Coleridge was pruning out the flowery excesses in some poems and discarding others altogether. Refining his craft by simplifying his diction, Coleridge promised Cottle nothing but his "choicest fish, pick'd, cleaned and gutted" (CL I, p. 312).

Coleridge's confidence as an author was steadily growing and in early February, after receiving a request to write a tragedy from the manager of the Drury Lane in London, he decided to make his first solo effort at writing a play. The London offer arrived just as Charles Lloyd turned up, recovered from his epileptic delirium and looking forward to resuming his literary apprenticeship. No longer available to spend time tutoring Lloyd, Coleridge terminated their financial arrangement but eventually yielded to his former pupil's entreaties by generously inviting him to remain on as a boarder and agreeing to include some of his poems in the forthcoming second edition of the collected poems.

Lloyd gratefully accepted. Coleridge began writing his tragedy, *Osorio*, while Lloyd set to work on his poems. Domestic life in the crowded cottage settled down to a steady routine until early March, when Coleridge was forced to turn from his play and attend again to the drama of real life, as night after night Lloyd fell into fits of *"agoniz'd delirium"* (CL I, p. 315). Exhausted and bleary-eyed after more than a week of nursing the stricken man, Coleridge finally accepted the fact that Lloyd needed more expert medical attention than he could provide.

Shortly after Lloyd's departure for a sanatorium in Lichfield, Coleridge plunged into a deep "depression too dreadful to be described.... even now I am not the man I have been —and I think never shall. A sort of calm hopelessness diffuses itself over my heart" (CL I, p. 319). Mystified by his melancholia, Coleridge did not consciously fathom the source of his depression: his failure to nurse Lloyd back to health. The hectic delirium of psychomotor epilepsy had raged far beyond the self-limited course of smallpox's delirious fever, and Coleridge had blamed himself. At Henley he had triumphantly announced that he had defeated "the mighty hunter" and had felt elation, but this time he was unable to rescue a stricken comrade and was plunged into depression.

Coleridge's despair gradually subsided, and by the time spring arrived he was once again in robust good spirits. His collected poems had just been released with Lloyd's verse tacked on, and by early May he had finished the first four acts of *Osorio*.

It was no coincidence that at the same time Coleridge began writing *Osorio*, which dealt with the theme of a reunion with a lost brother, Coleridge had invited Lloyd—like a brother—to become a member of his household. Both fraternal expressions were, it turned out, fraught with problems.

In *Osorio* an older brother, Albert, is in love with a young woman. Forced to depart on a long sea voyage, Albert gets Maria to promise she will faithfully await his return. But filled with jealousy, Albert's younger brother, Osorio, secretly arranges for Albert to be murdered at sea. After Albert's departure, Osorio pursues Maria, who rebuffs him, remaining loyal to Albert.

Meanwhile, Albert discovered the plot and escapes unharmed but undergoes many hardships and delays before he is able to return home to claim his bride and confront his brother. Shocked at the sight of Albert, Osorio thinks he is a ghost returned from among the dead, until Albert explains his escape. Mortified, Osorio attempts suicide. Filled with forgiveness, Albert stops Osorio and absolves him of his crime.

Coleridge's play concludes with the understanding that Osorio will either become a self-exiled, guilt-haunted wanderer, or will be executed for another crime. While the finale is ambiguous, the grisly verdict is clear: no matter what, fratricide must not go unpunished, and the wish is as bad as the deed.

Like Osorio, seven-year-old Sam Coleridge had also come to grief with his older brother over a woman's love, and in a fit of passion had wished, even attempted, to do away with his rival. And two years later, midshipman Frank Coleridge had set out to sea, secure in the promise of his sweetheart Maria that she would faithfully await his return.

Coleridge's play was sketchily autobiographical, its conclusion provoked unconsciously by his failure to save Lloyd from his delirium. And just as Comberbache had atoned earlier for Coleridge's "crime" against his brother, restoring the young man's mental balance, now his character Osorio bore the guilt but was forgiven by his brother, thereby rescuing Coleridge from another depression.

It is striking that while Coleridge was imaginatively transforming his life story into art during that first winter at Stowey, he had also begun to remember consciously and to record carefully Frank's fate and his reaction to it. One month into *Osorio*, Coleridge wrote Poole:

> The 9th child was called Francis: he went out as a midshipman . . . his ship lay on the Bengal Coast—and he accidentally met his brother John—who took him to land and procured a commission in the army.—He shot himself (having been left carelessly by his attendant) in a delirious fever brought on by his excessive exertion at the siege of Seringapatam: at which his conduct had been so gallant, that Lord Cornwallis payed him a high compliment in the presence of the army and presented him with a valuable gold watch, which my mother now has.—All my brothers were as inferior to Francis as I am to them. He went by the name of 'the handsome Coleridge.' [CL I, p. 311]

Coleridge's emerging memories of Francis during the writing of *Osorio* were no coincidence. At Poole's suggestion, Coleridge was engaged in a new project, systematically writing an autobiography in the form of a series of letters which he addressed and sent to the older man.

Before moving to Stowey, Coleridge had begged Poole to teach him how to become self-sufficient, and the letter-writing device was a powerful tool toward that end. And if psychotherapy can be viewed a self-healing process involving orally re-creating one's life story with the unobtrusive help of a guide and auditor, the task Poole assigned Coleridge served much the same end. Writing down his story was providing Coleridge a sense of continuity with his past, some appreciation of its influences, and a more coherent personal identity.

But an even more remarkable by-product of Poole's assignment was the way in which incompletely remembered childhood experiences—mobilized but not recaptured by Coleridge's conscious efforts at recall—were instead being elaborated in Coleridge's art by means of his poetic imagination. What Coleridge could not directly recollect as fact he was "remembering" indirectly in the disguised form of creative imaginings which could then be used in poems and plays to "solve" the conflicts he could not face directly.

But if narrating his life story to Poole was providing Coleridge the key to rich material that which could be used in his art, the results were by no means impressive. Coleridge's skill was not yet equal to his fantasies. As the manager of the Drury Lane would soon confirm, much to Coleridge's dismay, *Osorio* was no masterpiece.

Although Coleridge was getting closer to writing a major work now that he had begun to tap powerful themes of deeply personal significance, he still lacked a mature poetic voice with which to express himself. And the fatherly Poole was no better able to help Coleridge acquire that voice than he could fill that painful fraternal void that had originated with Frank's death. If Coleridge still craved the creative sweetness of poetic brotherhood that he had tasted briefly in his collaboration with Southey and searched for vainly with Lloyd, he would have to look elsewhere.

Chapter 6

The Surveillance of Cain and Abel

On Mr. Ross, usually cognominated Nosy.
*I fancy whenever I spy nosy
   Ross
More great than a Lion is Rhynose-
   ros.*

[CNB 432]

By 1797, as England and France entered the fourth year of their bloody war, it had become apparent both at 10 Downing Street and in the small house on the Rue de la Victoire where Bonaparte lived that the two nations were in the grip of a struggle for survival, not just an economic contest for foreign markets. While England, bereft of allies, was suing for peace, the French were contemplating a full-scale invasion of Great Britain.

By February, France had already tried a test landing of a small raiding party on the west coast at Ilfracombe. But after that effort failed, the Directory turned to France's brilliant twenty-seven-year-old military hero for leadership. By October, with great public ceremony and fanfare, "Citizen General" Bonaparte would be appointed head of the Army of England and would personally tour his Channel ports, dispatch privateers to reconnoiter the English coast, and place large orders for cannon of a British type that could be loaded with captured ammunition once his army was ashore. Preparing his people, Pitt told them to "expect the French any dark night" (Lawrence, 1970, p. 102).

Eventually, the coast defense maps in the Home Secretary's office would resemble chessboards dotted with castles, as the entire British seaboard became ringed with strategically placed

Martello towers. Built with five-foot-thick brick walls, the squat towers perched defiantly, like a series of sentry bulldogs, at potential enemy landing sites. From these platforms the English hoped to pour down a hail of deadly grapeshot to repel the invading French hordes.

But in August of 1797, Britain's defenses were far from fully mobilized and an air of panic and xenophobia pervaded that land, particularly in the vicinity of Ilfracombe, as well as in nearby Bath, Bristol, and Somerset. Back in London, at the Home Secretary's office, all rumors and reports of saboteurs were being taken seriously, and secret service agents were being dispatched to investigate any suspicious occurrences.

And so it was only natural that the Duke of Portland acted with speed in sending out one of his men after receiving a letter from a physician in Bath describing "a very suspicious emigrant family who have contrived to get possession of a mansion house at Alfoxton" (Blunden and Grigg, 1970, p. 80). Arriving at the tiny hamlet of Stowey, which lay three miles from the Alfoxton mansion, the secret agent began making inquiries about the new foreign couple and discovered that they were English, not French, but spoke in a dialect unlike West Country speech. He learned also that the odd couple spent most of their time with another man who had recently moved into the area. Placing the trio under twenty-four-hour surveillance, he confirmed reports that they clandestinely wandered the countryside by day and by night in both fair and foul weather.

The female suspect was a short, animated, high-strung woman in her mid-twenties with brilliant, wild gray eyes and deeply tanned skin, as dark as a gypsy's. The man claiming to be her "brother" was tall and wiry, with thick red-brown hair, a gaunt face, thin lips and a protuberant nose which made his intense eyes appear more deeply set than they actually were. Taciturn if not sinister looking, the male suspect appeared when alone to be by turns stern, morose, and menacing. At such moments of solitude, he could be seen muttering to himself in a manner that might suggest to a biased observer that he was hatching a diabolical plot.

However, the gaunt-faced suspect appeared less severe and forbidding in the company of his two cronies. No longer brooding, he could be seen convulsively laughing at the playful antics

The Surveillance of Cain and Abel 93

of the other man, who was shorter in stature, less menacing in appearance, and more talkative, if not voluble. Slightly round-faced, with thick full lips, gray eyes, and wavy dark hair worn long and unkempt, the second man's softer features might have tempted the agent to describe his face as flabby and unintelligent looking, except for the fact that it was constantly animated with thought and conversation.

Although both male suspects were in their mid-twenties, the wiry, angular one looked much older, and this fact, coupled with the impression he gave of a shrewd, methodically calculating intelligence that was always at work, made him seem the ringleader of the group. The gypsy woman and the pudgy-faced man both deferred to him.

All three suspects wore old clothes, and rumor had it that the pair that called themselves brother and sister godlessly did their laundry on the Sabbath. But even more alarming than their habits and appearance was the fact that the tall gaunt man regularly carried a spy glass on their outings, while his chubby-faced friend scribbled copious observations in the notebook he constantly carried. Suspecting that they were surveying the Somerset coast in preparation for an enemy landing, the secret agent cautiously managed to eavesdrop from behind a sand dune and his ears perked up when he heard one of them mention Spy Nosy. Having mistaken the philosopher's name for that of another agent—possibly the mastermind behind the operation—the Home Office man remained hot on the trail of this dangerous trio for three weeks.

While he may have mistaken the little band's purpose as dangerous, the secret agent was correct in sensing something conspiratorial about the trio as they roamed the Somerset countryside, investigating every nook and cranny from the hillside glens and forests to the sloping brook that wandered into Bristol Channel. Spinoza was not the only subject of their intense conversations, as they animatedly discussed politics, philosophy, and poetry for hours on end. But the eavesdropping agent ultimately concluded that the plot they were hatching was literary and not political.

Reporting to Whitehall, the agent informed his superiors that the suspicious trio was a group of harmless poets who did not bear further watching. The conspiracy they were plotting was the radical overthrow of the traditions of English literature; in little more than a year they would publish their revolutionary manifesto, *Lyrical Ballads*. And later, in the years to come, it would remain a standing private joke among Coleridge and his two old friends, William and Dorothy Wordsworth, that they had been considered enemies of the state because of their interest in the philosopher Spy Nosy.

However, far from being old friends or literary partners at the time of their surveillance that August, Coleridge and the Wordsworths were just getting to know one another. Becoming acquainted, Coleridge-style, meant a nonstop marathon of daily and nightly outings designed to speed up that exhilarating process. As Coleridge put it, they were becoming "three persons with one soul" (Ellis, 1967, p. 124).

From her first glimpse of him loping along the dusty Dorset highway, Dorothy Wordsworth was struck by Coleridge's energetic exuberance. Arriving from his forty-mile, two-day hike in high spirits—so high in fact that he "leaped over a gate and bounded down a pathless field" (Lefebure, 1975, p. 212) —Coleridge impressed Dorothy as a carefree, warmhearted spirit who dispensed with such first-time formalities as a proper entrance via the front door. Only casually acquainted with Wordsworth, Coleridge was returning a visit that William had made two months earlier.

Like their boyish guest, twenty-seven-year-old William and twenty-five-year-old Dorothy were also walking enthusiasts who enjoyed solitary nature hikes. But recently the local farmers had become suspicious of William and were half convinced he spooked their cattle when, tramping the countryside spy glass in hand, he recited his own verses out loud. Yet, as Coleridge knew, it was essential that poets read their verse aloud, that they might hear how the words sound.

Anxious now to renew the acquaintance, the two men wasted no time in reading their recent compositions to each other and to Dorothy, who had a fine ear and was an astute critic. Like Coleridge, William was writing his first play, *The Borderers*. Interestingly, Wordsworth's drama, like that of his new friend, dealt with a vicious rivalry between two brotherlike figures. But unlike Coleridge's Osorio, who ineffectually plots his rival's defeat only to turn his destructive guilt upon himself, William's protagonist was more diabolical; through sinister scheming, he dupes his brother into destroying himself.

As awkwardly written as *Osorio*, Wordsworth's play would receive from the London theatrical community no warmer a reception than did Coleridge's. But either blinded in his judgment, or hoping to start off his first visit on a friendly note, Coleridge compared William's play favorably with those of Shakespeare and offered to use his connection with the Drury Lane to get William a reading. And as if to demonstrate his goodwill even further, Coleridge dashed off an enthusiastic note to Joseph Cottle praising *The Borderers* to the skies.

Coleridge was in turn pleased to discover that William was favorably impressed with *Osorio*. But dour and reserved by nature, the lean and angular Wordsworth did not lavish praise so excessively as did his sanguine, pudgy-faced guest. He did, however, offer terse encouragement. Coleridge wrote:

> Wordsworth admires my tragedy—which gives me great hopes. Wordsworth has written a tragedy himself. I speak with heartfelt sincerity and (I think) unblinded judgement, when I tell you, that I feel myself a *little man by his* side; and yet do not think myself the less man, than I formerly thought myself.—His drama is absolutely wonderful. [CL I, p. 325]

Aware that Wordsworth was a "strict and almost severe critic" (CL I, p. 326), Coleridge found William's skimpily worded praise all the more delicious and set about finishing his drama with renewed vigor.

In fact, stretching his brief visit into a stay of three and a half weeks, Coleridge began blocking out new scenes. William too resumed his writing, and whatever free time remained was spent walking and talking together. The two men soon discovered that they shared more in common than an interest in literature and similar life styles.

Although both of these subsistence "farmers" had attended Cambridge, their time there barely overlapped, as there was a two-year difference in their ages. William's younger brother Christopher had been in the same literary club as Coleridge, but far more important than common social connections was a shared political outlook—each had traced out a literary career by resisting pressure exerted by a provincial and conservative middle class family to enter the Anglican clergy.

Like Coleridge, William had briefly considered establishing a political magazine dedicated to the struggle against Pitt's government. Inspired by the idealism of the radical French experiment, William had gone one step further than Coleridge by making a romantic pilgrimage to witness the Revolution in person. But securely tucked away in the provincial towns of Blois and Orleans, where he studied French, Wordsworth had had almost no involvement with the fast-paced political events unfolding in Paris. He had in fact complained to his older brother Richard, then living in London, that the latter was in a better position than he to follow the Revolution's daily progress, through the up-to-date English newspapers. Eventually, however, he had managed to spend some time in Paris, around the time the Terror was ushered in by Marat's massacres. Shortly afterward, William wisely beat a hasty retreat to the relative safety of England.

While Wordsworth's involvement in the Revolution had been marginal at best, in Coleridge's eyes William's continental adventures were quite romantic. For Coleridge, William had the rugged masculine appeal of someone who had stood at the barricades. And that Wordsworth remained tight-lipped about his experiences in France served only to heighten his romantic appeal for Coleridge, who saw him as a strong and silent hero.

But William's silence did not stem from modesty. Though Coleridge could intuit the tense, brooding unhappiness in Wordsworth's lachrymose pauses whenever he spoke of France, he could not have fathomed the source of his new friend's reserve. William had undergone a personal disappointment in France which he found too painful to discuss with anybody except his sister Dorothy, who knew the whole story.

During his stay in Orleans, William had begun an affair with a young Frenchwoman by the name of Annette Vallon. She had become pregnant, and their daughter Caroline had been born on the very eve of the Terror. Fearing for his personal safety, William had fled France without ever seeing his child. Although William and Annette had apparently vowed to marry, opposition from both families, William's lack of financial security, social turmoil, and their own ambivalence had conspired to prevent the match.

Unclear whether he had left his lover and child by circumstance or by choice, Wordsworth had become depressed. Even now, five years later, he brooded guiltily over those events. Much of the poetry he was writing dealt with the theme of abandoned women left to fend for themselves, and for their children, by husbands and lovers whom William portrayed as ostensibly blameless victims of the social system.

Keenly aware of William's unhappiness and deeply solicitous of his welfare, Dorothy Wordsworth was delighted with Coleridge's admiration of her brother, which she saw as a much needed boost to his morale. And Coleridge's respect for William's talents as a writer, his eagerness to promote his literary career, his astute technical criticism of his friend's manuscripts, and his spontaneous warmth all left Dorothy with the impression of "a wonderful man . . . so benevolent, so good tempered and cheerful" (LWDW I, p. 188). Personally charmed by Coleridge and grateful for his ability to draw her moody brother out of his self-preoccupation, Dorothy exuded a warmth which more than compensated for William's stiffness.

Returning to Stowey, Coleridge described Dorothy in equally positive terms. But glowing as his first impressions of her were, Coleridge had already formed his primary attachment to the strong and silent William: "a very great man—the only man, to whom *at all times* and in *all modes of excellence* I feel myself inferior" (CL I, p. 334). Triumphantly describing his latest conquest to his brother-in-law, Coleridge enthusiastically wrote Southey: I had been on a visit to Wordsworth's . . . and I brought him and his sister back with me and here I have *settled them*" (CL I, p. 334).

But if Coleridge's rhapsodic note made it sound as if he had swept William off to Stowey with the hypnotic charms of the Pied Piper, more mundane considerations had in fact inspired the Wordsworths' hasty decision to relocate. Their tenancy of the Dorset farmhouse was due to expire, and they needed a place to stay. It was true, however, that they chose Somerset in order to be near Coleridge and to pursue the literary exchange and budding friendship on a daily basis.

And while William had blossomed in response to Coleridge's warmth, it was also the case that Coleridge had needed a new hero. He first began to focus those intense idealizing energies on William largely as a matter of chance, when Wordsworth had happened to drop by the previous April. Having crossed paths in Bristol for a few hours at a time during William's rare stopovers there, the two men had been little more than casual acquaintances at the time of Wordsworth's visit.

But the timing of William's social call had been propitious, coinciding uncannily with the ten-day period during which Coleridge had plunged into a "depression too dreadful to be described" (CL I, p. 319). Arriving just as Coleridge had begun to feel the void left by Lloyd's illness and departure, William had been unable to rouse Coleridge from his despondency. But deeply appreciative of Wordsworth's company, Coleridge had gratefully promised to return William's social call with an extended visit to Dorset in June. And so when Coleridge leapt over the fence two months later, he was ripe for confrontation with Wordsworth as part of his undiminished hunger for a spiritual brother.

Coleridge departed from the Dorset farmhouse on June 28 and returned four days later with a one-horse chaise to transport the Wordsworths and their belongings to Stowey. Dorothy rode with him while William set out on foot for lack of room. As Coleridge and Dorothy—the two voluble members of the trio—drove along those rutted roads on their forty-mile trip, Coleridge learned more about William and Dorothy's background.

Growing up in the northernmost reaches of England, close to the Scottish border, William and Dorothy had been born twenty-one months apart, the second and third in a series of five children. Their father had worked as an agent for Sir James Lowther, one of the richest, most powerful, and politically corrupt men in England. Apart from his own seat in the House of Lords, Lowther controlled nine in the House of Commons, his MP's being known as "Sir James' ninepins" (Purkis, 1970, p. 24). Among others, William Pitt had been launched in his parliamentary career by representing one of Sir James's pocket boroughs.

An attorney by training, William and Dorothy's father

managed Sir James's properties and worked as a behind-the-scenes political henchman, bribing local officials and fixing elections for his Tory boss. He was able to provide handsomely for his family, who lived in a red brick manorial home with spacious rooms, marble fireplaces, and a comfortable number of servants.

Their terraced grounds overlooked the scenic river Derwent, whose "ceaseless music" (Moorman, 1957, p. 1) remained the earliest, most cherished memory of William's childhood. Next in emotional importance was his nostalgic recollection of the carefree way in which he and Dorothy roamed the forests and gardens as young children, growing up in a permissive atmosphere lovingly created by their mother, Anne Cookson.

Despite the difference in their ages, Anne baptized Dorothy and William together, as if she knew intuitively that they were destined to become inseparable childhood playmates and lifelong companions. And almost from the time of William's birth, his twenty-three-year-old mother noticed something about the boy that set him apart from her other children. "He will be remarkable," she said, "either for good or for evil" (Ellis, 1967, p. 5).

Not long after Anne's sudden death from pneumonia when William was eight, his maternal grandparents delivered their unsympathetic verdict: bad seed. Bereft and miserable over the loss of his mother, William became a surly, unpleasant child. Looking after their dead daughter's five children with none of her permissive gentleness, the elderly Cooksons rapidly singled William out as the defiant troublemaker in the lot.

The Cooksons made no particular effort to identify the all-too-apparent reasons for their grandson's misery, and the list of William's domestic crimes multiplied rapidly. On one occasion, after unsuccessfully daring his brother into doing it for him, William angrily tore a whip through the canvas of an ancestor's portrait that hung in his grandparents' home. Severely punished for such infractions, William was a proud child who licked his wounds in private. Once, fleeing to his grandparents' attic, he seriously contemplated suicide by running himself through with a sharp dueling foil.

Apparently William's father neither effectively consoled the boy nor prevented the Cooksons from scapegoating him.

Depressed and demoralized after his wife's death, John Wordsworth never recovered from that loss and did not remarry. In keeping with Anne's dying wish, he sent six-year-old Dorothy off to be raised by a maternal cousin many miles away. Then, one by one, John sent each of his four boys to the Hawkshead Grammar School in the nearby Lake District, where, fortunately, they lived together as boarders in the home of a local woman who looked after them with maternal tenderness.

As Dorothy put it, the children had been "squandered abroad" (LWDW I, p. 16). And as Coleridge may have realized sympathetically as their carriage bumped along, both he and William had been nine-year-olds when sent off to boarding school shortly after losing a parent. While William had been as unhappy as young Sam Coleridge, he did not turn inward to the same degree, however, and did not seek consolation in the solitary world of books.

Unlike the citybound Sam, William turned to the out-of-doors. Roaming the countryside and roughhousing with his classmates, William snared birds, scaled cliffs, skated, boated, and rode ponies in the countryside. Clearly in love with nature, at this point in his life Wordsworth celebrated its joys in boys' play rather than with the more reflective appreciation of its consoling powers that he later developed.

When William was thirteen and Dorothy eleven, their father died suddenly. Leaving no will, he created a complex legal tangle which was compounded by Sir James Lowther's refusal to pay his outstanding debts to John's heirs. As those debts were the bulk of their father's estate, the Wordsworth children were left in financial jeopardy and at the mercy of their Cookson grandparents. Not until 1802, five years after William and Dorothy had taken up with Coleridge, would the debt be collected, but then the Wordsworths would recover more than eighty-five hundred pounds.

The most important legacy John left William was his love of poetry. Having learned from his father long passages by Milton, Shakespeare, and Spenser, William began writing poetry shortly after his father's death. Less boisterous now, he sought the reflective solitude of time spent alone in nature and began to develop a spiritual empathy for the solitary peddlers, vagrants, and wanderers he met on his Lake District walks. His perceptions of these people resonated with the lonely sense of self-sufficiency he was struggling to develop now that he was an orphan, disliked by his Cookson guardians.

Four years later, as a seventeen-year-old about to begin Cambridge, William was reunited with Dorothy after nearly ten years' separation. "Endeared to each other by early misfortune," as Dorothy put it (Davies, 1980, p. 67), the pair of former playmates recaptured their intimacy. Unlike the Cooksons, Dorothy intuitively appreciated the pain and loneliness behind William's unpleasantly stiff exterior.

Reabsorbed in their childhood bond as soulmates and constant companions, they roamed the countryside together and dreamed of the time when they would be old enough and in a financial position to live together in a small cottage of their own. Over the next three years, William spent as much time as he could with Dorothy and even wrote a long poem in her honor.

When the time came for William to leave Cambridge, he was still too poor and Dorothy too young to pursue their dream of a rustic cottage. Resisting family pressure to take Holy Orders, William stalled for time and went to France, where he began his affair with Annette, with its disastrous consequences.

When he returned home, his self-esteem and love of mankind both badly shattered, William wandered Wales and England, staying with friends and writing poetry, some of which was published—though with less acclaim than Coleridge received for his early works, and to no greater financial benefit. But upon receiving a generous nine-hundred-pound legacy from a dying man he had befriended and nursed in the last stages of his illness, he finally found himself in a financial position to live with his sister. By investing the money and living frugally, William and Dorothy were realizing their old dream. The inexpensive housing that Coleridge described would be an important consideration to Dorothy, who was anxious to ensure their security.

By the time the Wordsworths' carriage rattled into town and pulled up on Lime Street, Coleridge was enthusiastically looking forward to introducing Dorothy to his home, to Sarah, and to nine-month-old Hartley, his "minute philosopher" (Ellis,

1967, p. 104). While Sarah and Dorothy were cordial, it was clear from the start that they were not destined to become close friends. Intelligent but not intellectual like Dorothy, Sarah was devoted to child care and keeping a comfortable home. Her busy domestic schedule left little time for reading and literary matters. For her part, Dorothy much preferred intense intellectual discussions with men to household talk with women.

Anxious to be a gracious hostess to her husband's new friends, Sarah warmly welcomed the Wordsworths and extended her hospitality. A few days later, when Charles Lamb and his sister Mary arrived for a one-week visit, Sarah's cottage was crammed so full of guests that there was scarcely space to catch her breath, much less talk with Dorothy. In the hubbub, Sarah accidentally spilled a skillet of hot milk on Coleridge's foot. Unable to go off on walks with the Lambs and the Wordsworths, Coleridge stationed himself in the garden where, seated beneath a lime tree, he wrote a poem about his enforced confinement which he dedicated to Lamb—*This Lime-Tree Bower My Prison*. Lamb was pleased with the verse and Sarah was relieved to see her husband good-naturedly transform his misery into art.

Stepping in to relieve the Coleridges' overcrowding, Poole located a spacious house for the Wordsworths to rent in Holford, three miles from Stowey. The townspeople were suspicious of the odd foreign couple from the start; as the Duke of Portland's secret agent may have noted, their lease had been signed on Bastille Day. But far more ominous than that chance coincidence of dates was the fact that within weeks of the Wordsworths' arrival in Somerset, one of the Twelve Apostles showed up.

Short, stout, and jovial, there was nothing in John Thelwell's physical appearance to justify the terror he struck in the hearts of the townspeople. But having done time in the Tower and in Newgate, there was also nothing in Thelwall's gentle manner that could offset his frightening reputation as a political agitator and dangerous revolutionary. Hounded wherever he went throughout England, he had turned up in Stowey at Coleridge's suggestion, to look the town over as a place to retire.

Delighted with the presence of such a political celebrity, Coleridge and the Wordsworths took long country strolls with

Thelwall. In their animated political discussions, they took to addressing each other in the French manner as Citizen John or Citizen Samuel. It was shortly after Thelwall's departure that the secret agent turned up and began his surveillance of the trio.

All in all, it was a busy, happy summer. The Coleridge cottage hummed with activity and was packed to the rafters with houseguests. Hartley thrived, Sarah bustled and fussed, and Coleridge got lost in a hectic schedule of back-and-forth socializing with William and Dorothy.

Pregnant once again, Sarah miscarried in late July. Taking it in stride, she appeared minimally affected by the experience. An August visitor found her,

> as I have continued to find her, sensible, affable and goodnatured, thrifty and industrious, and always neat and prettily dressed. I here see domestic life in all its beauty and simplicity, affection founded on a stronger basis than wealth—on esteem. Love seems more pure than it in general is to be found, because of the preference that has been given in the choice of a lifefriend, to mental and moral rather than personal and material charms, not that you are to infer that Coleridge and his wife have no *personal* recommendation. Mrs. Coleridge is indeed a pretty woman. [Cornwell, 1973, p. 168]

And within a few short weeks of his pretty wife's miscarriage, Coleridge managed to find time in his busy schedule to get her pregnant yet again.

Coleridge's agricultural husbandry did not keep pace with his domestic husbandry. His farming enterprise fell by the wayside as the result of his daily outings with William and Dorothy. Although he was also neglecting his writing, the three friends constantly discussed literature. As a result of these conversations, Coleridge began to reappraise his earlier poems, which now seemed embarrassingly juvenile to him, replete as they were with flowery excesses of emotion. Wordsworth's understated personal manner and his technique of portraying those simple feelings in plain English had begun to influence Coleridge to the point that he compared his own verse to a dose of ipecac.

In a satirical attempt to mock his former style, he dashed off three poems pseudononymously intended as a good-natured burlesque of himself, as well as of Lamb and Lloyd, who had both contributed verse to the second edition of his collected poems. Deeply hurt and offended, the two men withdrew their works from the forthcoming third edition and Lloyd began to mount his own special revenge in the form of a novel about Coleridge, *Edmund Oliver*. Having mistaken the third poem in the series as aimed at him, Robert Southey also took umbrage and encouraged Lloyd by spitefully furnishing him with biographical details of Coleridge's life. (Clearly violating Coleridge's privacy, the novel described the Comberbache escapade. In passing, it portrayed Edmund Oliver as an extremely casual, part-time user of opium—indirectly confirming the impression that at this stage in his life Coleridge was by no means habituated or addicted to the drug.)

Coleridge was bewildered by his friends' anger, since he knew his comic verse mocked himself as well as them. But what he did not realize was that Lamb, Lloyd, and Southey were becoming increasingly jealous of his infatuation with Wordsworth. By now, Coleridge was completely taken with William as a friend and a poet. He admired his virile simplicity and stark, understated writing. "Of all the men I ever knew," he later said, "Wordsworth has the least femininity in his mind. He is all man! He is one man of whom it might have been said, 'It is good for him to be alone' " (Ellis, 1967, p. 83).

Coleridge was amazed to discover that writing poetry—with Wordsworth—had the thrill of a strenuous male exercise. He could use his mind as an active, virile organ—not as a traditionally passive receptacle for flowery, exaggerated sentiments. Later commenting to William on the masculine ease with which ballads could be written, Coleridge rambunctiously bragged that all a poet had to do was "jog on . . . between a sleeping cantor and a marketwoman's trot. . . . [He] must be troubled with a mental strangury, if he could not lift up his leg six times at different corners, and each time piss a canto" (CL III, p. 292).

Coleridge's bravado about ballad writing and his deep admiration of William as "all man" reflected a lifelong insecurity about his own masculinity which helps explain the magnetic power of Wordsworth's attraction for Coleridge. To Coleridge, William embodied the qualities he personally lacked as a writer and as a person. He interpreted William's dour terseness and emotional self-containment as signs of personal strength. Those traits were particularly appealing to Coleridge, the self-styled chatterbox whose compulsive eloquence stemmed in part from loneliness and insecurity.

Accurately or not, he saw Wordsworth, as he had seen his brother Frank, as manly and independent to an extreme degree. He was unaware that his tough hero had recently fled the responsibilities of fatherhood and marriage in France, life commitments which Coleridge had chosen to face, with however much anxiety. And while he romanticized Wordsworth as one who was strong enough to go it alone, he overlooked the glaring fact of William's retreat to a cloistered life with his doting sister and childhood companion, Dorothy. Twenty-eight-year-old William could also be viewed as highly reliant and shying away from his own independence, at least for the moment.

But objective realities were not the issue: Coleridge needed to find a lost brother in William, and Wordsworth needed to be seen and admired as more masculine and independent than Coleridge. In six short months, Coleridge had become totally enamored with William Wordsworth, as a result of what he later ruefully described as his "idle trick of letting ... [my] wishes make romances out of other mens' characters" (CL II, p. 751).

It was not the first time he had romanticized another man in his quest for a brother. Willing to drop everything and migrate to the ends of the earth after barely becoming acquainted with his fellow Pantisocrat, he had been similarly passionate about Southey. And he had embraced Charles Lloyd, nursed him tenderly, and offered him literary fraternity through co-publication.

Now his intense hero worship was riveted on Wordsworth. Barely half an inch shorter than William in height and already enjoying a somewhat greater literary reputation than Wordsworth, Coleridge self-effacingly demoted himself to the status of a "little man" (CL I, p. 325), extravagantly comparing his friend's third-rate play, *The Borderers*, with the dramatic works of Shakespeare. While William Wordsworth would in fact become a masterly poet over the next decade, it is crucial to remember that in 1797 he was an unknown who had neither published nor written anything that merited Coleridge's accolades.

Emotionally sustained by Coleridge's admiration and intellectually catalyzed by his aesthetic appreciation of his experiments at simplifying poetic diction, Wordsworth would persist tenaciously in challenging prevailing literary conventions by writing about ordinary people, using everyday language. Like any innovator he would be heckled by his critics, and he would turn to Coleridge for encouragement, time and again.

Profoundly influenced by the French Revolution's emphasis on common human values rather than aristocratic elitism, Coleridge could keenly appreciate Wordsworth's stylistic innovations as the natural extension of democratic ideals into literature. Pruning ornate imagery from poetry was like stripping titles and gaudy displays of wealth from royalty—or like viewing Christ as mortal rather than divine, as the Unitarians did. Uncertain as to the value of his literary innovations, Wordsworth was grateful to Coleridge for formulating their aesthetic rationale.

But if Coleridge's self-effacing veneration of his friend appears on the surface to have been one-sided, his idealization of William was about to lead to a creative explosion for Coleridge as well. Stimulated in part by the glorifying "romance" he was making of Wordsworth's character, Coleridge was about to tap some core memories concerning his brother Frank. He was to use them in a far more profound way and with much greater skill than he had in *Osorio*.

Resuming his autobiography while basking in the glow of this new friendship—half reliving and half remembering his childhood—Coleridge was about to write two masterpieces that symbolically recapture and commemorate his relationship with Frank. *Kubla Khan* and the *Ancient Mariner* would prove as innovative as Wordsworth's verse—breaking fresh literary ground with startling, fantasy-laden, visionary writing. Inspired rather than squelched by his idolatry of Wordsworth, at least for the moment, Coleridge was about to catapult to new artistic heights.

Chapter 7

Miracles of Rare Device

> *The shadow of the dome of pleasure*
> *Floated midway on the waves;*
> *Where was heard the mingled measure*
> *From the fountain and the caves.*
> *It was a miracle of rare device,*
> *A sunny pleasure-dome with caves of ice!*
> —from *Kubla Khan* [PW, p. 298]

Shillingless and hard pressed with a second baby on the way, Coleridge wrote a friend in mid-October of 1797 that he was considering becoming a Unitarian minister "as a lesser evil to starvation—for I get nothing by literature" (CL I, p. 349). Their quarterly rent was coming due, he owed the nanny back wages and was in debt to the village shoemaker and the local chandler to the tune of almost half of next year's income. Winter loomed and he faced a substantial bill for last year's coal supply as well as skyrocketing fuel costs due to wartime inflation and French naval raids on the Newcastle colliers.

Unable to make ends meet, he was weary of trying to provide for his family with his pen and the garden spade. Although he had just finished *Osorio* and sent it off to the Drury Lane for a reading, he held hollow hopes for that play. By now he was filled with "indescribable disgust, a sickness of the very heart, at the mention of the tragedy" (CL I, p. 356).

While his conscious feelings of dissatisfaction were focused on the obvious flaws in this clumsily written play, Coleridge's heartsickness and disgust stemmed from another source. Finishing his fratricidal drama was unearthing shards and relics long since buried in the graveyard of forgotten childhood experience. Just as the original impulse to write *Osorio* had been an outgrowth of his second autobiographical letter to Poole, completing the play was in turn releasing fresh childhood memories. The repulsion Coleridge felt toward his completed manuscript was in part a reaction to the reemergence of the painful memories it had begun to stir.

Within days of putting the finishing touches on *Osorio*, Coleridge jotted down those recollections in his third autobiographical letter to Poole:

October 9, 1797

My dearest Poole,

From March to October—a long silence! but as I may have been preparing materials for future letters, the time cannot be considered as altogether subtracted from you.

From October 1775 to October 1778

These three years I continued at the reading-school—because I was too little to be trusted among my father's schoolboys. After breakfast I had a halfpenny given me, with which I bought three cakes at the bakers close by the school of my old mistress—and these were my dinner on every day except Saturday and Sunday—when I used to dine at home, and wallowed in beef and pudding dinner.—I am remarkably fond of beans and bacon—and this fondness I attribute to my father's having given me a penny for having eaten a large quantity of beans, on Saturday—for the other boys did not like them, and as it was an economic food, my father thought, that my attachment and penchant for it aught to be encouraged.—My father was very fond of me, and I was my mother's darling—in consequence, I was very miserable. For Molly, who had nursed my brother Francis, and was immoderately fond of him, hated me because my mother took more notice of me than of Frank—and Frank hated me, because my mother gave me now and then a bit of cake, when he had none—quite forgetting that for one bit of cake which I had and he had not, he had twenty sops in the pan and pieces of bread and butter with sugar on them from Molly, from whom I received only thumps and ill names.—So I became fretful, and timorous, and a tell-tale—and the schoolboys drove me from play, and were always tormenting me—and hence I took no pleasure in boyish sports—but read incessantly.... I read thro' all the gilt-cover little books that could be had at that time, and likewise all the uncovered tales of Tom Hickathrift, Jack the Giant-killer, etc etc... and I used to lie by the wall, and *mope*—and my spirits used to come upon me suddenly, and in a flood—and then I was accustomed to run up and down the churchyard, and act over all I had been reading.... At six years old I remember to have read Belisarius, Robinson Crusoe and Phillip Quarll—and I found the Arabian Nights' Entertainments—one tale of which (the tale of a man who was compelled to seek for a pure virgin) made so deep an impression on me (I had read it in the evening while my mother was mending stockings) that I was haunted by spectres, whenever I was in the dark—and I distinctly remember the anxious and fearful eagerness, with which I used to watch the window, in which the books lay—and whenever the sun lay upon them, I would seize it, carry it by the wall, and bask, and read. My father found out the effect, which these books had produced—and burnt them.—So I became a *dreamer*—and acquired an indisposition to all bodily activity—and I was fretful, and inordinately passionate, and as I could not play at anything, and was slothful, I was despised and hated by the boys; and because I could read and spell, and had I may truly say, a memory and understanding forced into almost unnatural ripeness, I was flattered and wondered at by all the old women—and so I became very vain, and despised most of the boys, that were at all near my own age—and before I was eight years old, I was a *character*—sensibility, imagination, vanity, sloth and feelings of deep and bitter contempt for almost all who traversed the orbit of my understanding, were even then prominent and manifest.

From October 1778 to 1779

That which I began to be from 3 to 6, I continued from 6 to 9.—In this year I was admitted into the grammar school, and soon outstripped all of my age.—I had a putrid fever this year—my brother George lay ill of the same fever in the next room.—My poor brother Francis, I remember, stole up in spite of orders to the contrary, and sat by my bedside, and read Pope's Homer to me—Frank had a violent love of beating me—but whenever that was superseded by any humor or circumstances, he was always very fond of me—and used to regard me with a strange mixture of admiration and contempt—strange it was not—: for he hated books, and loved climbing, fighting, playing and robbing orchards, to distraction.

My mother relates a story of me, which I repeat here—because it must be regarded as my first piece of wit.—During my fever I asked why . . . our neighbor did not come and see me.—My mother said, she was afraid of catching the fever—I was piqued and answered—Ah—mama! the four angels round my bed aint afraid of catching it.—I supposed, you know the old prayer—

Matthew! Mark! Luke! and John!
God bless the bed which I lie on

> Four angels round me spread
> Two at my feet and two at my head—
>
> This prayer I said nightly—and most firmly believed the truth of it.—Frequently have I, half-awake and half-asleep, my body diseased and fevered by my imagination, seen armies of ugly things bursting in upon me, and these four angels keeping them off.—In my next I shall carry on my life to my father's death.—
> God bless you, my dear Poole! and your affectionate
>
> S. T. Coleridge
> [CL I, pp. 346–350]

Unlike his previous autobiographical letter, which is largely a family history based on other people's anecdotes, this letter breathes vivid personal images. Here Coleridge had tapped a more dynamic mode of recollection, one that would furnish richer raw material for the forthcoming *Kubla Khan* than had been available to him while working on *Osorio*. His childhood came alive—materializing before his eyes like some genie from the Arabian Nights.

Papa's pupils towered above him. Scapegoated by Molly and Frank, he had felt miserable. "Fretful" and "timorous," he became a tattletale, which only made him "despised and hated by the boys," who teased him for being unathletic and scorned him as the village sissy; "flattered and wondered at by all the old women" of Ottery, he was shunned and scapegoated by the boys for his vanity and effeminacy.

And so he sought consolation in reading and daydreaming—hypnotizing himself with the Arabian Nights tale of Shahryar and Scheherezade. Entering that world of make-believe, he sought refuge from his own, in which he felt so vulnerable and powerless. Dreamily basking in the sunlight pouring through the vicarage window, he licked his wounds in the privacy of his imagination. Curling up with that tale, sometimes he was entranced by sadistic Shahryar, other times by seductive Scheherezade—the powerful Tartar emperor who ruled by decree, and the beautiful, bewitching woman who could turn the King into jelly when it suited her whim.

But like the poet's view of forbidden Xanadu, it had been an all too fleeting glimpse of paradise for six-year-old Sam. Discovering his son's obsessive preoccupation with this erotic tale and its hypnotic power over him, John Coleridge burned the book in hopes of bringing his boy back to earth.

Five days after writing that memory-evoking letter, Coleridge retired to a remote farm that lay on the Somerset seacoast. The farmhouse straddled a green hillside that gracefully sloped down to the sea. Although Coleridge never explained what prompted him to go there, it seems he felt a strong urge to be alone. Among the few things he took with him were some opium and a copy of Samuel Purchas's seventeenth-century travelogue, *Purchas' Pilgrimage*, which told the story of another great Tartar emperor, Kubla Khan.

Later, Coleridge would claim, somewhat defensively, that he brought opium along for "dysentery" (CL I, p. 349). His explanation is perfectly plausible, but it is equally imaginable that he was using the drug for pleasure since he was well aware of its ability to produce euphoric reveries and completely in the dark as to its dangerous addictive effects. The dysentery rationale was given at a much later period of his life, when he was ashamed of having become addicted to opium. By then Coleridge wanted his readers to think of him as an unwitting victim who had taken opium only out of necessity and never purposely for pleasure or for "inspiration."

But regardless of his intentions, he brought opium and the book about the Tartar emperor along with him that day. And while the composition of *Kubla Khan* may have been as accidental as Coleridge later claimed it was, his "creative accident" was of the same order of coincidence as the well-known dream of the coiled snake that led to the discovery of the benzene ring. While the apparently "effortless" discovery of benzene's chemical structure first appeared to its inventor in a miraculously inspired dream—just as Coleridge claimed that his poem was delivered to him fully formed in an opium dream—the scientist had been mulling over the problem for quite a while before the solution was revealed to him in his sleep.

Coleridge's preoccupation with his creative problem, too, went back a long time. Since early boyhood he had been struggling to reconcile his masculine and his feminine traits, to create a harmony between his *animus* and the *anima* which seemed to set him apart from Frank and the other boys of the village. As a six-year-old he had been obsessed and fascinated by the enchantress Scheherezade and the powerful Tartar emperor.

Coleridge's memories of those childhood fantasies had just surfaced and, with them, the realization that he had changed relatively little since then. He still delighted in daydreaming and reading—he liked nothing better than curling up with a good book and losing himself in it.

And if the make-believe world of daydreams was not as readily accessible as when he was a boy, with the help of opium he could still drift off lazily and recapture the thought processes of a child's imagination. But his Tartar hero now had a different identity. The Persian King Shahryar had been replaced by the Mongol emperor, Kubla Khan.

Several entries in Coleridge's literary notebooks reveal his preoccupation with Khan at this time. But more striking is a diary note describing an exotic oriental scene fit for a king:

> In a cave in the mountains of Cashmere an image of ice, which makes its appearance thus—["]two days before the new *moon* there appears a bubble of ice which increases in size every day till the 15th day, at which it is an ell or more in height: then as the moon decreases, the image["] does also till it vanishes. [CNB 240]

Coleridge was fascinated by the passage he quoted (from Thomas Maurice's *History of Hindostan*), which demonstrates how a physical landscape can be transformed through suggestive sexual imagery to depict masculinity and femininity in nature. The image of an ovumlike ice bubble—cyclically resonating in size to the phases of the moon as it lies hidden from the night sky in a womblike cave—evokes the rhythmical flux of the menstrual cycle. Struck by Maurice's literary invention, Coleridge was about to use it to create a rare device of his own in *Kubla Khan*.

But if Maurice's passage lent stylistic inspiration to *Kubla Khan*, the germ of the poem emerged from the memories just mobilized by Coleridge's autobiographical letter. He had recalled how, ostracized by a jeering circle of boys for his "sissy" traits, he had made a daily ritual of poring over the tale of the powerful Tartar ruler of a magnificent empire. Repeating in action what he had just recalled in his letter, Coleridge retreated to that lonely farmhouse to curl up and read once more.

What happened next is well known. Coleridge became intoxicated on opium while reading Purchas and drifted into a trancelike reverie lasting several hours. He never got past the first few lines of the book:

> In Xanadu did Cublai Can build a stately Palace, encompassing sixteene miles of plaine ground with a wall, wherein are fertile Meddowes, pleasant Springs, delightful Streames and all sorts of beasts of chase and game, and in the middest thereof a sumptuous house of pleasure, which may be removed from place to place. [quoted in Lefebure, 1975, p. 253]

Like Proust's madeleine, those first few lines triggered a gorgeous stream of associations evoking his old dream of the powerful oriental emperor and the bewitching woman who controlled him. All this he recorded in his poem *Kubla Khan*. He entered the wondrous world of ambiguous sexual mysteries seen through a child's imagination—an exotic paradise of womblike caves issuing forth life itself and hillside breasts flowing with milk while the panting earth orgastically spews and spurts its masculine force, which mazily meanders into nature's feminine chambers. It was a world where one could be both Shahryar and Scheherezade and experience the dreamlike thrill of merging masculine power (Kubla Khan) with feminine lyricism (the Abyssinian Maid)—a safe dream so long as there were no dangerous enemies lurking about and no reprisals for tasting such forbidden pleasures.

But while sensuously surveying his exotic kingdom, Khan hears the strain of "ancestral voices prophesying war." The spectacular harmony of *animus* and *anima* is shattered, and in the second part of the poem the poet is allowed a final glimpse of his rapidly receding vision now vanishing over the waters. In the end he can only recall with pangs of deep regret nature's fabulous bisexual splendor. Only if he dares once more to encompass in himself the Abyssinian Maid serenading Khan with her siren song, reflecting the glory of the imaginary empire they have created together (just as Scheherezade had mesmerized Shahryar with her tales), then, and only then, can the poet transport himself back to Xanadu:

> Could I revive *within me*
> Her symphony and song,
>   To such a deep delight 'twould win me,
> That with music loud and long,
> I would build that dome in air,
> That sunny dome! those caves of ice!
> And all who heard should see them there,
> And all should cry, Beware! Beware!
> His flashing eyes, his floating hair!
> Weave a circle round him thrice,
> And close your eyes with holy dread,
> For he on honey-dew hath fed,
> And drunk the milk of Paradise.   [PW, p. 298; italics mine]

Modern critics have often noted the bisexual images in *Kubla Khan*. More important, Coleridge himself was among the earliest theorists to hint speculatively at the crucial role that bisexuality plays in creativity. Many years after composing *Kubla Khan*, when he had become a critic whose special area of interest was the psychology of the creative imagination, he remarked that "a great mind must be androgynous" (Coburn, 1979b, p. 44). Did lingering memories of his experience composing *Kubla Khan* lie behind that intuitive comment?

Coleridge may well have sensed that at some unconscious level he had drawn the images of *Kubla Khan* from his own androgyny. Perhaps that was why he later labeled the poem a "psychological curiosity" (Campbell, 1905, p. 592). But other readers have taken this remark to suggest that he considered his poem nonsense verse with no underlying meaning.

At the strictly psychological level of interpretation, other levels of meaning (such as the philosophical or allegorical) aside, there is at least one underlying statement coherently presented in the poem: Read as a psychological commentary on the creative mind, *Kubla Khan* is a poem whose subject is poetry. It constructs a poetic image of paradise, comments on the psychological struggle involved in creating that image, and measures the price the poet pays for daring to inseminate himself and give birth to his poem.

With sensory immediacy, it presents the reader with a poetic vision, poignantly depicts its rapid fading, and speaks finally of the poet's requirement for an androgynous harmony if he is to create new—or recapture old—visions of Paradise. Only when blissfully in tune with his own *animus* and *anima* can he create—or re-create—such visions. The splendors, both of mythical Xanadu and of the poetic vehicle that transports us there—the text of *Kubla Khan*—are the result of an expert blending of these twin life forces. But instead of didactically spelling out this message, the poem indirectly educates the reader through the enjoyable experience of its orgastically explosive imagery. Just as it requires a blend of *animus* and *anima* to compose such a poem, so it requires a happy harmony of these same forces in the reader to respond intuitively to the beauty of the work at this level. Readers who insist that *Kubla Khan* is nothing more than nonsense verse are uneasy permitting themselves that experience, insisting instead that it is not there.

Coleridge himself alludes to the emotional vulnerability involved in bisexual reveries. Even for the most powerful of emperors, Kubla Khan, it is not safe to indulge his *anima* in the presence of enemies—his enjoyment of the androgynous beauty of his fantasy empire is abruptly shattered by "ancestral voices prophesying war."

And the psychological reasons behind the poet's interruption of his character's bemused delight stemmed from complex sources, as Coleridge was about to remember: it is one thing for a small boy to feel delightfully feminine in the privacy of his imagination, but it is an entirely different matter to be branded a sissy and a Mama's boy in a derogatory manner, as part of a power struggle with a stronger rival.

Two days after the reverie in which he composed *Kubla Khan*, Coleridge vividly recalled those "ancestral voices prophesying war" in his next autobiographical letter to Poole:

October 16, 1797
Dear Poole:
From October 1779 to October 1781
I had asked my mother one evening to cut my cheese *entire*, so that I might toast it; this was no easy matter, it being a *crumbly* cheese—My mother however did it—I went into the garden for some thing or other, and in the mean time my brother Frank *minced* my cheese, 'to disappoint the favorite.' I returned, saw the

exploit, and in an agony of passion flew at Frank—he pretended to have been seriously hurt by my blow, flung himself on the ground, and there lay with outstretched limbs—I hung over him moaning and in a great fright—he leaped up, and with a horse-laugh gave me a severe blow in the face—I seized a knife, and was running at him, when my mother came in and took me by the arm—I expected a flogging—and struggling from her I ran away, to a hill at the bottom of which the Otter flows—about one mile from Ottery.—There I stayed; my rage died away; but my obstinacy vanquished my fears—and taking out a little shilling book which had, at the end, morning and evening prayers, I very devoutly repeated them—thinking *at the same time* with inward and gloomy satisfaction, how miserable my Mother must be!—I distinctly remember my feelings when I saw a Mr. Vaughan pass over the bridge, at about a furlong's distance—and how I watched the calves in the fields beyond the river. It grew dark—and I fell asleep—it was towards the latter end of October—and it proved a dreadful stormy night—I felt the cold in my sleep, and actually pulled over me a dry thorn bush, which lay on the hill—in my sleep I had rolled from the top of the hill to within three yards of the river, which flowed by the unfenced edge of the bottom.—I awoke several times, and finding myself wet and stiff, and cold, closed my eyes again that I might forget it.—In the mean time my mother waited about half an hour, expecting my return, when the *sulks* had evaporated—I not returning, she sent into the churchyard, and round the town—not found!—Several men and all the boys were sent to ramble about and seek me—in vain! My mother was almost distracted—and at ten o'clock at night I was *cry'd* by the crier in Ottery, and in two villages near it—with a reward offered for me.—No one went to bed—indeed, I believe, half the town were up all one night! To return to myself—About five in the morning or a little after, I was broad awake; and attempted to get up and walk—but I could not move—I saw the shepherd and workmen at a distance—and cryed but so faintly, that it was impossible to hear me 30 yards off—and there I might have lain and died—for I was now almost given over, the ponds and even the river near which I was lying, having been dragged.—But by good luck Sir Stafford Northcote, who had been out all night, resolved to make one other trial, and came so near that he heard my crying—He carried me in his arms, for near a quarter of a mile; when we met my father and Sir Stafford's servants.—I remember, and never shall forget, my father's face as he looked upon me while I lay in the servant's arms—so calm, and the tears stealing down his face: for I was the child of his old age.—My mother, as you may suppose, was outrageous with joy—in rushed *a young lady* crying out—'I hope, you'll whip him, Mrs. Coleridge!'—This woman still lives at Ottery—and neither philosophy or religion have been able to conquer the antipathy which I *feel* towards her, whenever I see her.—I was put to bed—and recovered in a day or so—but I was certainly injured—For I was weakly, and subject to the ague for many years after.

My father (who had so little of parental ambition in him, that he destined his children to be blacksmiths, etc and had accomplished his intention but for my mother's pride and spirit of aggrandizing her family) my father had however resolved, that I should be a parson. I read every book that came in my way without distinction—and my father was fond of me, and used to take me on his knee, and hold long conversations with me. I remember, that at eight years old I walked with him one winter evening from a farmer's house, a mile from Ottery—and he told me the names of the stars—and how Jupiter was a thousand times larger than our world—and that the other twinkling stars were suns that had worlds rolling round them—and when I came home, he showed me how they rolled around. I heard him with a profound delight and admiration; but without the least mixture of wonder or incredulity. . . .

Towards the latter end of September 1781 my father went to Plymouth with my brother Francis, who was to go as midshipman under Admiral Graves; the Admiral was a friend of my father's.—My father settled my brother; and returned Oct. 4th, 1781—. He arrived at Exeter about six o'clock—and was pressed to take a bed there by the Harts—but he refused—and to avoid their entreaties he told them—that he had never been superstitious—but the night before he had had a dream which had made a deep impression. He dreamt that Death had appeared to him, as he is commonly painted and touched him with his dart. Well he returned home—and all his family, I excepted, were up. He told my mother his dream—; but he was in high health and good spirits—and there was a bowl of punch made—and my father gave a long and particular account of his travel, and that he had placed Frank under a religious captain, etc—At length, he went to bed, very well, and in high spirits. —A short time after he had lain down he complained of a pain in his bowels, which he was subject to, from the wind—my mother got him some peppermint water—and after a pause, he said—'I am much better now, my dear!'—and lay down again. In a minute my mother heard a noise in his throat—and spoke to him—but he did not answer—and she spoke repeatedly in vain. Her *shriek* awaked me—and I said, 'Papa is dead.'—How I came to think of his death, I cannot tell; but so it was.—Dead he was—some said it was the gout in the heart—probably, it was a fit of apoplexy—He was an Israelite without guile; simple, generous, and, taking some scripture texts in their literal sense, he was conscientiously indifferent to the good and the evil of this world.

God love you and S. T. Coleridge [CL I, pp. 352–356]

He had not thought of that fight with Frank in years: how, pushed past his limit, he finally fought back without running back to his mother, proving he was no sissy or tattletale. He had almost murdered Frank in the process. He never intended to kill him, at least he didn't think so. Or had he? The knife *was* in his hands. It had happened too fast and was over too soon for him ever to be sure what might have happened had his mother not shown up.

That night on the hill, lost in the storm, was long and lonely. His mind had been in a turmoil: Was God angry? Would he be struck by lightning? As night wore on, he desperately wanted to go home. Did he dare? What would his father do?

But Papa was wonderful. He was forgiving. And afterward, his father spent more time with him than ever—taking him on long walks, showing him the mysteries of the heavens, spellbinding him with his talk. And then that night of horror when his father had died. Roused by his mother's shriek, he awoke to a living nightmare: death had visited Papa twice—first in a dream, and then in reality.

After that, he was alone, both brotherless and fatherless. Later he learned that Frank's ship had sailed for India. And still later he heard that Frank had killed himself. He barely cried. What did that dead man in India have to do with the brother he remembered? That man had been a delirious stranger.

During the next few weeks Coleridge visited frequently with Wordsworth, taking long walks with him. The more he got to know William, the closer he felt to him. William was Frank's age, or the age Frank would have been had he lived.

There was something about Wordsworth that Coleridge couldn't put his finger on, though he described it to Cottle: from the start, he felt *small* in comparison to William. Somehow, Wordsworth seemed much bigger. And yet he did not belittle Coleridge or tower above him physically. Wordsworth just seemed older, more gifted. He was confident, manly, and, in Coleridge's eyes, the better poet. He wanted to learn from Wordsworth, to work with him. Perhaps they could write a poem together.

Both men were short of cash, so late one November afternoon, while they were out on a walk together, Coleridge suggested they write a five-pound ballad for a magazine. He would write the first canto, Wordsworth the second, and so on, until the ballad was done. Why not retell the tale of Cain and Abel?

Coleridge had been reading Gessner's *Death of Abel* and was fascinated by his imaginative dramatization of the old Bible story. The author depicted the long-standing rivalry between the two brothers as suddenly culminating in an unpremeditated, impulsive murder. In a split second, Cain awoke from a dream and clubbed Abel to death before he knew what he was doing. It happened as quickly as young Sam Coleridge had lunged at his brother with a kitchen knife. Afterward, Cain had been seared by the wrath of God, a guilt-haunted wanderer.

Good-naturedly, Wordsworth agreed to try reworking Gessner's tale. They would call their poem *The Wanderings of Cain*. Coleridge made a promising start with his canto (see the epigraph to this book's Prologue), but Wordsworth found himself blocked. The theme did not appeal to William; the poem clearly belonged to Coleridge. Encouraging his friend to continue, Wordsworth offered to serve as sounding board and advisor. As they discussed *Cain*, Coleridge's plan shifted: he would recast the tale in a supernatural setting and create a character of his own to tell Cain's story, using a symbolic crime as a substitute for the original fratricide.

Coleridge hit on the idea of replacing Cain with a mariner. The sailor would still be a guilt-haunted wanderer, but the circumstances would be entirely different: he was someone returned from a long sea voyage during which an impulsive crime had been committed, perhaps a crime against nature. Coleridge was stymied over how to symbolize the deed until Wordsworth suggested that the mariner had slaughtered an innocent sea bird, the sort said to bring good luck on voyages. Coleridge liked the idea and decided to use it.

But if his theme was to be a symbolic crime—impulsive murder—followed by perpetual guilt and eternal atonement, Coleridge still needed a stylistic approach. Years later he told De Quincey that "before meeting a fable in which to embody his ideas, he had meditated a poem on delirium, confounding its own dream-scenery with external things and connected with the imagery of high latitudes" (De Quincey, 1970, p. 39). And so Coleridge decided to depict the sea voyage through the eyes of a delirious man, and to tell the tale of that feverish soul's adventures at sea.

The vivid seascapes are transmogrified by the mariner's delirium. But if one strips away the fantastic explanations and images of *The Rime of the Ancient Mariner*, one is left with a straightforward account of a sea voyage from England to India. The mariner's fabulous visions are the very sights one would see today if one were to retrace the mariner's route.

The mariner's ship sails the Atlantic, crosses the Equator, rounds Cape Horn or slips through the Straits of Magellan, and finds its way into the Pacific and then the Indian Ocean. Sailing that same route today, one encounters the stormy gales off the North Atlantic and the steady blow of the Equatorial Trades. The area around Cape Horn and the Straits is fantastic to the eye due to the extraordinary mists and cloud forms created by the icy wind and water of the Antarctic mingling with the oven-hot South American currents and breezes. Optical illusions and phantasmagorical shapes have been reported for centuries and it has always been superstitious mariners' lore to tell of ghost ships and apparitions looming in those mirages. Albatrosses are known to wing their way over these waters.

Entering the Pacific is equally dramatic, though different. There are dead spots along the coast of South America—cesspools of currentless water where slimy giant jellyfish and monster-sized squid collect and float like an oily surface slick glistening in the noonday sun. And there are the Doldrums, windless patches of sea where vessels lie listlessly becalmed for days on end, waiting for a stirring breeze.

Since Sinbad's time, the Indian Ocean has been considered

a magical sea because of the extraordinary phosphorescence of its microscopic marine life. At times that ocean takes on a milky gleam, boiling over with light. On such nights, ships appear as black shadows sailing on a sea of liquid fire, and even small fish leave long serpentine trails of light in their wake. The night sky is pitch black and mariners on night watch report an eerie glow on each other's faces when they lean overboard.

All of these nautical phenomena remain well known in the present century, and Coleridge read about them in travel accounts published in his own day. But a far more intriguing question is whether he first learned of them by reading Frank Coleridge's account of his boyhood voyage to India. Only five of Francis's letters written during the nine years he was away from Ottery survive, and none of them contains descriptions of that edge-of-the-world voyage seen through the eyes of a sixteen-year-old.*

But in any case, *The Rime of the Ancient Mariner* is intimately connected with Frank's death. Coleridge's unconscious feelings of grief and responsibility are woven into the narrative plot and emotional tenor of his poem. The chain of events leading to its composition affords a fragmentary glimpse of how the creative process may have worked.

A few weeks after remembering the childhood stabbing incident, Coleridge came up with the idea of writing a ballad about Cain's fratricide. The delayed timing suggests that he probably did not consciously connect his childhood memory with the idea for the poem. His recollection faded from awareness for a few weeks. After enough time had passed for him to forget those unhappy details, Coleridge's conflicted memory resurfaced in the form of a creative impulse. During that dormant period, Coleridge had unconsciously hatched a plot. By the time his memory reemerged for creative consideration, it had been reorganized into an idea for a poem on fratricide, a universal, less personal theme.

---

*Both Frank and the mariner sail a route from England to India. Frank undoubtedly went via the Cape of Good Hope, the mariner by way of Cape Horn. They are not identical voyages except in the unconscious mind. Literally, Frank sailed to Bombay while the mariner's ship only goes into the Indian Ocean, metaphorically retracing Frank's route.

But that theme was still too personal for Coleridge to write about without conflict. The "crime" was still too close to home, even though he could overtly disavow it as biblical, or as Gessner's. More likely than not, had Coleridge actually attempted to finish *The Wanderings of Cain*, he could not have let his imagination run free, and it would have deteriorated into a clumsy imitation of Gessner's work.

In order to ventilate his old memories and the feelings they evoked less self-consciously, Coleridge needed the privacy of a disguise. His artistic decision to symbolize the crime and camouflage the theme of fratricide was crucial to his poem's development. Once the explicit crime was hidden in symbolism, more personal elements could slip in. By backing away unconsciously from autobiographical material, Coleridge was able to put more of his conflicted feelings into the poem. The mariner's delirium is Frank's, the mariner's guilt is Coleridge's, and the mariner's ship retraces Francis Coleridge's passage to India and the calamity that befell him. Coleridge's wedding had occurred on the anniversary of Frank's departure and his father's death—and it is a wedding celebration the mariner interrupts with his gripping tale.

In one sense, Coleridge's poem was an unconscious attempt at repairing his haunting loss by bringing Frank back from the dead once more—the latest in a series of symbolic attempts to do so. Having succeeded at the Henley pesthouse, Coleridge found peace. After failing with Lloyd, he became depressed. Comforting both men, much as Frank had comforted him when he was a feverish six-year-old with a "putrid fever," Coleridge gave them the critical nursing care his brother had never received in his fatal delirium. He paid them the debt he had never been able to repay Frank.

But this time Coleridge was repairing his loss with words, not deeds—using his creative imagination to "rescue" his brother. His mariner sets sail with every promise of a fair voyage, just as Frank had departed with high hopes about his future. Coleridge directs his ship's wondrous but harrowing passage to India, filled with painful hardships and extraordinary spectacles.

Then his mariner sinks into a dangerous delirium, drifting in and out of consciousness, alone and on the brink of death.

Just at the worst moment, Coleridge invokes a poetic miracle, rescues the mariner, and returns him home safely—a frightening spectacle to the wedding guest, who sees him as a ghost returned from among the dead, a ghost who keeps him from the good fellowship of the celebration within.

The mariner is Frank, of course, but he is also Coleridge. All things are possible in the unconscious: a sailor can be both murderer and victim as easily as a poet can be both an emperor and his siren. Coleridge had already successfully fantasized himself as both Shahryar and Scheherezade, Kubla Khan and the Abyssinian Maid. In his mariner he evokes a single character who is both himself and Frank, Cain and Abel.

For just as Coleridge's poem was intended symbolically to repair a loss, it was also meant to appease his irrational sense of responsibility for that loss. Many critics have complained that the poem's one flaw lies in its psychologically unrealistic depiction of the mariner's guilt, claiming that the punishment does not fit the crime. They are correct, if we think of the mariner as tormenting himself solely for the killing of a bird.

But the mariner's haunting guilt and perpetual atonement make a great deal more psychological sense when we think of him as savagely punishing himself for surviving a disaster in which everyone else perished. Unable to make peace with himself and forget, he compulsively relives the events, both in his mind and in conversations with strangers. His excessive self-blame may make him seem like a gray-bearded loon, but his lunacy represents, in reality, a syndrome not well described until after World War II.

Experiences with catastrophes have taught us a great deal about such reactions. Some people who survive catastrophic experiences cannot emotionally accept their good fortune. Instead of successfully integrating such experiences, they relive their harrowing ordeals over and over again in their dreams and waking thoughts, conscientiously blaming themselves for what befell those who perished. Concentration camp survivors were among the first in whom the syndrome was described, but those who are part of natural disasters in which others perish may be equally susceptible.

Like the mariner, a survivor of such a disaster does not fit in. He is unable to adjust to the business-as-usual mood of the world at large, because he has much more serious business of his own: to reconcile himself to what has happened to him, and to its far-reaching consequences, by compulsively reliving and replaying the events in his mind.

Beyond his need to assimilate the experience is the need to make sense of it by answering the question *Why me?* Implicitly, at least, the question has two facets: *Why did this happen to me?* and *Why am I the only one to survive?* Of course there are no satisfactory answers to such questions, and behind them lies a terrible doubt: *Do I deserve to live and to enjoy life?*

For if the survivor's flashbacks are intended at one level to gain control over psychic pain through familiarization, at another they inflict more suffering as a form of punishment. Like some infernal machine that has been overloaded and runs amok so that it no longer efficiently files memories away, putting them in proper perspective, the survivor's mind diabolically plays and replays the painful events without ever gaining mastery. This attempted desensitization gone haywire leads instead to a self-reinforcing hypersensitivity—like tonguing a sick tooth in anticipation of pain and thereby causing it.

Endlessly reliving such harrowing memories is a brutal way to atone for survival. Mentally replaying such ugly memories is a cruel way to spoil the joy of a wedding, and in a sense this is what the mariner does. And if we ask why some survivors continue to detach themselves from life's festivities long after their tragedies have faded, we can only infer that they believe they do not deserve life's pleasures.

These unhappy outsiders are unable to answer *Why me?* with acceptance: *That's life.* Instead, immediately after a disaster, conscious fault-finding focuses on replaying the events of the actual tragedy. The survivor recriminates himself for failing to take more practical or more heroic measures to help those who have died. (In *The Ancient Mariner* the mariner blames himself for killing the bird that protected the lives of sailors, that brought good luck.) But unconsciously the survivor's feelings of guilt begin to resonate with earlier experiences—with guilt left over from past childhood "crimes" or with vividly recollected instances of terrifying childhood helplessness. Among survivors, old childhood nightmares are reexperienced with striking frequency.

The majority of survivors gradually recover from the traumatic impact of a catastrophe. As they "heal," their childhood nightmares subside, perhaps to resurface with later stresses. But for the unhappy few—like the mariner—the recurring nightmares become part of a lifelong nocturnal process of suffering. And the themes of childhood dreams are interwoven with the larger catastrophe until they are consolidated into terrifying recurrent nightmares blending the old with the new. Interpreting the present in the light of the past, the unconscious mind has come up with its own explanation: *You are suffering now for what you once did. You are getting what you have always deserved.*

Coleridge's poem may be used to illustrate this mechanism. For the moment, assume that it represents a nightmare he suffered in the aftermath of Frank's (and his father's) death. The fact that it came five years later need not be a problem; survivor nightmares may persist a lifetime. The first task is to identify the day residue of the nightmare, the elements in daily waking life that have revived the old feelings and conflicts which the nightmare presents in symbolic form.

The search for the day residue is usually confined to the waking events preceding the night of the dream. Assume, then, that this poem, which was in fact written over several months, occurred as a dream in a single night. Extending the analogy, allow the weeks preceding the start of work on the poem to serve as the period in which to look for the day residue.

In compressed form, the events of the "day" preceding Coleridge's "nightmare" were as follows: He wrote a long letter to Tom Poole—a fatherly man—describing his vivid memories of how as a young boy he had tried to stab his brother Frank during a fight over who was their mother's favorite. Finishing the letter, Coleridge thought in passing of Frank's death and how little he had felt when informed of that event in far-off India. But in a rush, as he so often was, he had no time to dwell on these thoughts. He had big plans to spend the day with his new friend, William Wordsworth. William, as old as Frank would have been had he lived, in various ways reminded Coleridge of his dead brother. Masculine and stoical, William too had been an active, athletic, mildly rebellious boy, though he robbed birds' nests rather than farmers' orchards. It had been an enjoyable outing with William, one of those glorious autumn days with the fall wind blowing through the Quantock Hills, rustling the leaves. They had talked about many things, including a poem on Cain and Abel—it had occurred to Coleridge that it might be fun for the two or write it together. William encouraged him to write it alone, however, and suggested that a symbolic crime be substituted for the fratricide. William remembered how as a boy he had once killed a bird for the cruel sport of it, and how afterward he had felt guilty and terrified, like a criminal. William never really knew why he had done it, but it had happened during an unhappy period in his life, shortly after his mother's death. Wasn't that the kind of feeling Coleridge was trying to capture in his poem?

Their conversation proceeded to more agreeable subjects, but Coleridge began to have a gnawing feeling of uneasiness —mildly disagreeable and apparently unconnected with what was going on between William and himself. By now Coleridge was only half listening. His disquiet lingered and threatened to spoil the day. Nothing ever materialized, though there were moments when Coleridge thought he might be falling ill—his muscles ached and his joints felt stiff, as if he had caught a chill and an arthritic ague was coming on. His malaise was short-lived, however, and by the time Coleridge went to bed that evening he was feeling a warm glow of satisfaction over the day he had spent. About to fall asleep, he thought of how good life had been to him: happily married, he had a lovely son in fine health, a good friend in Tom Poole, and a deepening bond with William Wordsworth. His thoughts drifted as he luxuriated in his sense of well-being. From time to time, though, his body ached and he felt the slightest twinge of anxiety. Could it all be too good to be true? Superstitiously, he dwelt on that thought for a moment but then let it pass. Eventually he fell asleep.

Around four in the morning, perhaps, he hears the deep resonance of a bassoon like the one in the church at Stowey. A wedding is taking place. A stranger appears and a ship looms up from nowhere. Terrifying things begin to happen, and by four-fifteen Coleridge is wide awake, sitting bolt upright in bed, sweating profusely, his skin cold and clammy. Sarah asks groggily if he is all right; he tells her to go back to sleep.

Interpreted as a survivor's nightmare, *The Rime of the An-*

cient Mariner casts light on Coleridge's inability to enjoy life in the present after suffering an early tragedy. He sleeps uneasily and is bothered by disquieting premonitions during his waking hours. What are the sources of these queasy feelings?

Recall the conversation between the two men in the dream—the sailor and the wedding guest. If it is assumed that these figures represent two sides of the dreamer, then a *crude* translation of their symbolic dialogue might run something like this:

> Oh! So you're off to a wedding, are you? Well, I've got news for you. You're not going to enjoy any weddings—yours or anyone else's! And I'll tell you why: you don't deserve to. You're selfish and competitive, not entitled to share others' joys. Remember Southey's wedding? The reason you missed it was simple: you were too destructive to share your friend's happiness. You're incapable of being a good brother.
>
> You won't enjoy your own wedding either. You're not entitled to a happy marriage or to a woman of your own. And let me remind you why, just in case it slipped your mind: Do you remember your 'tribe of brothers' and your beloved Papa? You were all one happy crew till you spoiled it. How? By trying to kill Frank. You tried to stab him, don't you remember? You tried to murder him. Don't tell me it was a child's act, like killing a bird; we both know better than that.
>
> That was when the trouble started. Before that it had been smooth sailing. But you got selfish and wanted Mama all to yourself—you wanted them all out of the way, the whole crew. Well you got your wish. Papa's dead and so is Frank. You tried to pretend that it was just luck, a roll of the dice, that left you alive with Mama, instead of dead with the others. But it was what you wanted all along.
>
> And let me remind you of how unhappy she was to lose them all. She was half dead with grief, a living nightmare. She missed them even if you didn't. Oh, you did miss them? You wish you had died too? It wasn't your fault? Then how do you explain that stabbing?
>
> It was after that that everything began to go wrong—first Papa, then John, then Luke, and finally Frank. Well how do you explain that? Bad luck! Well you're free to believe that if you can. But even if it was bad luck, face it, you're jinxed. You're

going to suffer as much as Frank did. Why should you be happy and him dead?

What's that? You have already suffered? You atoned at the Henley pesthouse? And again with Lloyd? Then you'll suffer more. You're not fit to be friends with other men, no matter how you try. What's that? Oh! Your new friend William, that hermit. It'll be different with him, you'll make up for what happened with Frank? His love will shrive you? We'll see about that! Oh, you've changed? Don't make me laugh, your kind never change. You're doomed to wander alone and unhappy. . . .

But poems, like dreams, are condensed and have many levels of meaning. It is equally plausible to think of shooting the bird as the dreamer's symbolic destruction of his own sexuality—his male ability to soar—or to picture the dreamer's crime as the murder of his own creativity—his imaginative ability to soar. There are no contradictions in the unconscious between these creative and procreative interpretations of the bird symbol. It is even plausible to think of the bird's flight as opium-induced intoxication (getting high), with the metaphorical fatality representing the fall into addiction, becoming one of the living dead. From that perspective, the mariner's physical ordeals might be seen as alternating states of drug reverie and drug withdrawal—the windless breeze represents the drug rush; the delirium, the painful effects of withdrawal.

The possibilities are rife and the temptation to pursue them compelling, but too many liberties have perhaps already been taken. Although Coleridge's ballad was in fact based on a fragment of an actual dream of a phantom ship, it was a friend's dream, not his own. And though this structural modeling after a dream lends some credence to the interpretation attempted here, it remains a gross oversimplification to view the poem exclusively as if it were a clinical specimen.

A dream is a dream and a poem is a poem. The analogy simply allows an assessment of how closely the poem's surface plot—the mariner's tale—depicts the behavior and feelings of someone suffering from survivor guilt. Although the machinery of the poem is supernatural, there is nothing psychologically improbable in the story. While the mariner's punishment may not "fit" the crime, Coleridge intuitively knew a great deal about survivor guilt and depicted it with great accuracy and great artistry.

And if he was portraying something that seems highly probable in human experience, he was not conjuring it from thin air. He wrote about survivor guilt because he was suffering from it, and though he did not fully fathom its sources, he knew what he was talking about. In writing the *Mariner* Coleridge was achieving a certain degree of mastery over the powerful feelings that haunted him periodically. But as the mariner warned, relief was only temporary. He had done penance but would do still more.

Chapter 8

Fatal Interlude

> *O let a* titled *Patron be my Fate.*
> *That fierce Compendium of Ægyptian Pests—!*
> *Right Reverend Dean, Right Honourable Squire,*
> *Lord, Marquis, Earl, Duke, Prince, or if aught higher,*
> *However proudly nicknam'd, he shall be*
> *Anathema Maranatha to me.*
>
> [CNB 293]

Even before his *Osorio* manuscript wended its way home, albatross-fashion with a note from the Drury Lane's manager, Coleridge had been toying with the idea of supporting his growing family by becoming a Unitarian minister. But the news that he had failed to erase their rising debts by writing a successful play for the London stage hardened his resolve. Aware that his five-pound magazine ballad would barely cover the rent, Coleridge set the *Ancient Mariner* aside. By year's end he located a vacant curacy in Shrewsbury and began preaching to the congregation on a three-week trial basis.

While he had fared no better with the Drury Lane's management than his father had before him, the preacher's boy had at least been well steeped in the stagecraft of sermonical oratory. A member of the congregation recalled his sonorous, silvery delivery:

> It was in January, 1798, that I rose one morning before daylight, to walk ten miles in the mud, and went to hear this celebrated person preach. Never, the longest day I have to live, shall I have such another walk as this cold, raw, comfortless one, in the winter of the year 1798. . . . When I got there, the organ was playing the 100th psalm, and, when it was done, Mr. Coleridge rose and gave out his text, 'And he went up into the mountain to pray, HIMSELF, ALONE.' As he gave out this text, his voice 'rose like a

steam of rich distilled perfumes,' and when he came to the last two words, which he pronounced loud, deep, and distinct, it seemed to me . . . as if the sounds had echoed from the bottom of the human heart, and as if that prayer might have floated in solemn silence through the universe. The idea of St. John came into mind, 'of one crying in the wilderness, who had his loins girt about, and whose food was locusts and wild honey.' The preacher then launched into his subject, like an eagle dallying with the wind. . . . I could not have been more delighted if I had heard the music of the spheres. Poetry and Philosophy had met together. Truth and Genius had embraced, under the eye and with the sanction of Religion. This was even beyond my hopes. I returned home well satisfied. [Armour and Howes, 1940, pp. 243–244]

Coleridge's startling performance satisfied everyone's requirements—his musical eloquence was clearly the match of that remarkable poetic voice with which he had begun to write. Requiring no further proof, the church elders wasted no time in beginning negotiations for Coleridge to tend their flock permanently. But they were not the only ones who had fallen under the hypnotic spell of his language.

Two days later, Coleridge received a letter from Thomas and Josiah Wedgwood, wealthy sons of the founder of the pottery empire. Intent on persuading him not to abandon literature for the ministry, they were offering a guaranteed lifetime annuity of a hundred and fifty pounds a year, no strings attached. The purpose? To give him the artistic freedom to write, free from financial anxieties. For once in his life, Coleridge was speechless. Barely acquainted with twenty-seven-year-old Tom Wedgwood, and on even less familiar terms with his older brother, Josiah Jr., Coleridge was stunned. Two comparative strangers had volunteered seventy-five pounds apiece per year—the purchasing power of approximately $5280 a year by 1980 standards—for his *lifetime* support!

The annuity had been Tom's brainchild, and it was by no means the first time he had astonished someone with his generosity. Two years earlier, he had bestowed a similar gift on an impecunious scientist-mathematician who had served as his paid traveling companion during a four-month walking tour of Germany. Having attempted that trip to recuperate from a severe depression, Wedgwood had been deeply grateful for the constant company of a friend during one of those black periods when he so dreaded being alone.

Impulsively generous but headache-prone and already subject to the severe mood swings that would dog him the rest of his life, Tom had experienced his first nervous breakdown when he was twenty-one. Laid low by that depression, he had abandoned his "silver pictures" (Wedgwood and Wedgwood, 1980, p. 123), a promising series of scientific experiments using nitrate of silver to study light—a technique that anticipated the development of modern photography. Having already delivered two papers on light to the Royal Society before he was twenty-one, Wedgwood immodestly advertised himself as the family genius on the basis of his unfulfilled youthful promise (laurels which his nephew, Charles Darwin, would later win from his uncle).

Committed to the betterment of mankind, Tom Wedgwood fancied himself a philanthropic talent scout and was prepared to foot the bill for men of proven or promising genius. He had been taken with Coleridge's voluble brilliance and emotional spontaneity when they first met during a brief Somerset visit a few months earlier. By contrast, Wordsworth's dour reserve and stiff manner ill served him in the competition for the largesse of this patron saint of impoverished intellectuals.

Wedgwood's attraction to Coleridge is perhaps explained by their temperamental similarities. Like Coleridge, Wedgwood was restless and hungered for new experience. Propelled by his depressions and by his scientific curiosity, he had recently begun to dabble in mood-altering drugs—a list which would eventually include opium, hashish, and laughing gas. And there was also the bond created by a shared political outlook.

In spite of enormous family wealth, the Wedgwood boys had been raised in an intellectual atmosphere that emphasized nonconformity and humanitarian values. Their father, Josiah Sr., had idealistically supported a wide variety of liberal-Unitarian causes, including the abolitionist movement and the French Revolution. Anxious to see his youngest and most gifted son's melancholia cured by that time-honored English remedy for depression—a trip abroad for one's health—Josiah Sr. deliberately selected Paris as the twenty-one-year-old Tom's destination. Arriving just in time to celebrate the third anniversary of the Bastille's fall, young Tom had renewed his sagging spirits by dedicating himself to the democratic idealism that was sweeping through France.

Startling, then, as the offer of a lifetime subsidy from a casual social acquaintance may have seemed, there had been a strong affinity between Coleridge and Tom Wedgwood from the very start.

Finishing up his three-week preaching stint before going on to the Wedgwood's home to accept the annuity in person, Coleridge dashed off letters describing his good news to his two closest friends. Poole replied:

> your last letter made me so happy that I went to a party here in town, and was never so cheerful; never *sung* so well, never so witty, never so agreeable—so I was told ten times over! They little knew the cause which made joy beam from every feature and action. [Hanson 1962, p. 242]

And Wordsworth commented to a friend, "No doubt you have heard of the munificence of the Wedgwoods towards Coleridge. I hope the fruit will be good as the seed is noble" (CL I, p. 377). After visiting with the Wedgwoods for a few days, Coleridge made what he called his "strange and abrupt departure" (CL I, p. 385) from their Bristol mansion:

> If you have never been a slave to the superstition of impulses, you will marvel to hear that I . . . awoke at 5 in the morning, and was *haunted* by a strange notion that there was something of great importance that demanded my immediate presence at Stowey. I dressed myself, and walked out to dissipate the folly—but the Bridgwater coach rattling by, and the coachman asking me if I would get in—I took it for an omen—the superstitious feeling recurred—and in I went—came home and found—my wife and child in good health! [CL I, p. 385]

But unlike his father before him, who fled Exeter after an encounter with Death only to meet with him later that night in Ottery, Coleridge found no disaster awaiting him when he arrived home in Stowey. His pregnant wife and young son were both well; and the tiny village lay peacefully lost in a quiet winter's sleep. He could find nothing to explain his forebodings.

Over the next month, Coleridge explored the childhood roots of these uneasy feelings in a final autobiographical letter to Poole and in a poem, *Frost at Midnight*. The letter supplied the facts, while his poem captured the feelings.

The Wedgwood annuity was by no means the first time that his fortunes had changed overnight. In his letter he recalled the equally sudden reversal in his fortunes that had taken place after Frank's departure and his father's death. Recalling the domestic upheaval and financial insecurities that descended upon him, he traced his move from Ottery to Christ's Hospital and painted a vivid portrait of what school life had been like in those days. But he did not mention his homesickness, loneliness, and depression. His poem picks up where his letter left off.

The poem opens in the still calm of a frosty February night. Coleridge is alone in his parlor except for his infant son, sleeping in his cradle. From time to time the silent, windless night is pierced by the cry of an owl. Otherwise, there is nothing to explain his mounting uneasiness. The village slumbers. The surrounding sea, hills, and woods are also still. Unable to understand his uncanny feeling that something is about to happen, he spies a thin film of ashes on the fireplace grate. Now it all makes sense—old wives' tales teach that a film on a firegrate means a visitor will arrive.

But the midnight calm persists. No one arrives. His queasy feelings linger as he stares into the fire. Present time and place dissolve—he becomes a Christ's Hospital schoolboy staring at the fire, hoping someone from home will visit. And now—having once more become that small homesick child mesmerized by the flames—he can hear the churchbells of Ottery peeling their announcement of a gay summer fair day, bittersweet sounds of the home he has just left behind.

The telescoping of memory is dramatic: he remembers and then remembers himself remembering in a vivid pictorial fashion—a flashback and then a flashback with a flashback. Sensory and immediate, his memories are sights and sounds.

Time and place dissolve again. He startles. Once more he is the grown man in the Stowey parlor and realizes that his ominous dread stemmed from the threat of those painful childhood feelings spoiling his present sense of peace. The flashbacks prevent him from fully losing himself in the tranquil beauty of the present. Turning toward his sleeping son, he half vows, half prays, to protect his boy from ever suffering similar insecurities. The poem ends with the hope that Hartley, unlike himself, will fully enjoy frosty midnights like this one, unblighted by painful memories.

Frost at Midnight marks a milestone in Coleridge's maturity both as artist and parent. One year had passed since his panicky move from Bristol to Stowey. Sympathetic to his desperation, Poole had fathered him well, and by now Coleridge was enjoying that sense of steady competence he had sought to acquire from his mentor. The autobiography project had helped Coleridge to internalize Poole, "whom I feel so consolidated with myself that I seem to have no occasion to speak of outside myself" (CL I, p. 391). But beyond stimulating Coleridge's personal growth, those letters had also proven a fertile source of creative ideas.

Coleridge had blossomed as a poet and was writing with a lucid fluency of images and rich musicality of cadence and intonation. But if Poole had served as his fatherly anchor, he also owed much to his brother-poet, William Wordsworth, for the apparent ease of execution with which he was now composing. Their artistic debt was mutual, and neither was keeping a strict tally of his obligations to the other. Meeting daily, virtually living in each other's homes, they read and criticized each other's poems—offering plot suggestions as well as images, sometimes even supplying whole lines for works in progress.

Coleridge returned William's help with the *Mariner* by giving him a hand with the plot of *Peter Bell*, supplying lines for *We Are Seven*, and probably suggesting the idea for *Goody Blake*. And if Coleridge's conversational simplicity of diction and language in *Frost at Midnight* bore the stamp of William's influence, the loan was amply repaid when Wordsworth later borrowed Coleridge's device of the psychological flashback sequences for his own *Tintern Abbey*.

If there were underlying feelings of rivalry—if either man was struggling to outdo the other—it was done in such a good-natured manner as to stimulate and incite his friend toward further achievement. Like a pair of evenly matched athletes training together, each helped the other to improve. The fact that both men either completed or began much of their greatest poetry during the first two years of their friendship attests to the altruism operating between them.

William's sister Dorothy helped set the tone for this remarkable atmosphere of creative generosity by working with both men on their poetry and encouraging them to do the same for each other. A fine writer and astute observer of nature, she unstintingly shared her ideas and never objected when both men—after reading her notebooks—borrowed phrases verbatim and inserted them in their poems.

Relaxed in expressing her feelings, Dorothy's easygoing demonstrativeness helped make it possible for the two friends to share unselfconsciously their affection for one another. It is hard to tell exactly how fond Dorothy was of Coleridge—her diaries hint at an unreciprocated "crush" with great delicacy. But what is clear from her letters and journals is that she was keenly aware of the extraordinary creative stimulation and intellectual cross-fertilization taking place between her brother and Coleridge. Which explains why Dorothy became so forlorn on learning that their lease would not be renewed, that their days at Alfoxden were numbered.

Feeling the pressure to decide their next move, William and Dorothy invited the Coleridges for a ten-day visit that March in what amounted to an informal planning session. They wanted to clarify to what extent, if any, they would be linking their plans. As they discussed alternatives, they came up with the idea of moving to Germany—an old dream of Coleridge's. He had always wanted to learn the language, so that he might read the modern poets and philosophers in the original.

William was completely taken with the "delightful scheme" (LWDW I, p. 213)—except for the delicate matter of finances. In spite of the nine hundred pounds he already possessed, Wordsworth's finances were limited. (Wordsworth's nine hundred pounds had an approximate purchasing power of $31,500 by 1980 standards. He had lent three hundred pounds to a friend at 10 percent interest, and the remaining six hundred was conservatively invested at 9 percent. Although the loan to his friend was eventually repaid in full, with interest, at this point the payments were in arrears.) The logical solution for William was to raise cash by publishing his poems, but he confided to a friend that the prospect filled him with fear and loathing:

> There is little need to advise me against publishing; it is a thing which I dread as much as death itself. This may serve as an example of the figure of speech by rhetoricians called hyperbole, but privacy and quiet are my delight. [LWDW I, p. 211]

Hypersensitive to criticism, William dreaded the reviewers' ridiculing reactions to his unconventional literary experiments (for the defensive tone of Wordsworth's concerns, read both the original introduction to *Lyrical Ballads* and the Preface to the second edition). Gloomy over the prospect of exposing himself to the corrosive wit of the critics, but resigned to the economic facts of life, Wordsworth cheered up when Coleridge offered to spare him the aggravation of negotiating with a publisher by doing it for him. By now a seasoned veteran when it came to dealing with the anxieties of publication and taking the critics in stride, Coleridge was already preparing a third edition of his poems for Cottle. He planned to include the *Ancient Mariner* if he could finish it on time.

In addition to dickering over his own forthcoming volume, Coleridge served at William's agent by negotiating a contract with his publisher for Wordsworth's poems as well. Cottle came up with a generous offer of thirty pounds apiece for each man's collected poems. The volumes would be published independently, under each author's name. Cottle's proposal was completely in keeping with Coleridge's original plans for himself and also met Wordsworth's financial requirements.

But now Coleridge abruptly changed his tune: he and Wordsworth would only be willing, Coleridge replied, to publish their poems *jointly* in one volume, with the strict stipulation that the authorship remain *anonymous*. Quite sensibly, Cottle objected that anonymous publication would injure the book's sales. Unaware of Wordsworth's hypersensitivity regarding the critics, Cottle did not further suspect that the two friends might be opposed to separately authored volumes in order to avoid any comparisons of their books' sales and reviews.

Nonetheless, Cottle managed to read between the lines of

Coleridge's letter enough to sense that he was concerned about Wordsworth's feelings. But misinterpreting the complex nature of that concern, Cottle sought to rectify matters by offering to publish *two* volumes of William's poems, while still publishing Coleridge's in one. Coleridge set Cottle straight:

> Wordsworth and I have *maturely weigh'd* your proposal and this is our answer . . . to the publishing of *his poems* in two volumes he is decisively repugnant and oppugnant. He deems that they would want variety etc etc. If this apply in his case, it applies with tenfold force to mine. We deem that the volumes offered you are to a certain degree *one work* . . . and that our different poems are as stanzas, good relatively than absolute. [CL I, p. 411]

Clearly Coleridge and Wordsworth were determined to be unified with one another. But the aesthetic rationale that they considered their poems "one work" was farfetched from a stylistic point of view. Stretching the imagination, a case could be made that their verse nominally followed a ballad format—hence the title, *Lyrical Ballads*. But the difference between Coleridge's fantastic supernaturalism and Wordsworth's homespun realism was like night and day.

Their vehement insistence on anonymous authorship for *Lyrical Ballads* was intended to emphasize their literary brotherhood and to minimize competition. Coleridge truculently informed Cottle that neither he nor Wordsworth cared a straw for his petty commercial arguments concerning sales and reputation: "As to anonymous publications, depend on it, you are deceived, Wordsworth's name is nothing—to a large number of persons mine stinks" (CL I, p. 412). His pugnacious rebuttal was exaggerated. By now, Coleridge had a moderately popular reputation which would have helped sales. But he also had the financial cushion of the Wedgwood annuity and could afford to ignore monetary considerations, at least for the moment.

In fact, when Cottle eventually paid the thirty pounds for *Lyrical Ballads* the proceeds apparently were given entirely to Wordsworth. Coleridge's main motive in the negotiations had been to help William raise the cash for their trip and to express his friendship through copublication. Summarizing his feelings for Wordsworth, he wrote:

> I have known him a year and some months, and my admiration, I might say, my awe of his intellectual powers has increased even to this hour—and (what is of more importance) he is a tried good man.... His genius is most *apparent* in poetry—and rarely, except to me in tete a tete breaks forth in conversational eloquence. [CL I, p. 410]

While Coleridge looked up to William, his hero worship was not squelching his own output. In fact he was keenly appreciative of the fact that his friendship with Wordsworth had stimulated his creative momentum. Finishing the *Mariner* in late March, Coleridge began *Christabel* that April, completing the first book before leaving for Germany.

Unable to talk sense into his two stubborn authors, Cottle capitulated. Of the twenty-three poems in *Lyrical Ballads*, four were Coleridge's and nineteen Wordsworth's. Although William contributed the larger number, the *Ancient Mariner* occupied one third of the book and was given pride of place as lead poem in the volume. Cottle ran off a few copies that summer but by then was already in the process of retiring from publishing.

Lyrical Ballads was transferred to J. & A. Arch, who published the book on October 4—an anniversary date already charged with deeply personal meanings for Coleridge. It was the day Frank had departed and his father had died, as well as the day of his wedding to Sarah. Now it stood for the joyous occasion of his giving birth to a slim volume of poems with his dear friend William.

Coleridge and the Wordsworths had already landed in Hamburg by the time *Lyrical Ballads* was published. Sarah remained behind in Stowey, having recently given birth to their second son, Berkeley, named after his proud papa's current favorite philosopher. Both Coleridge and Sarah felt that traveling with the infant was too risky, and Coleridge had been tempted to cancel the trip until Poole persuaded him to go with repeated reassurances that he would look after the family. Poole was the only man whose presence could allay Coleridge's superstitious dread that harm might befall his wife and children in his absence. Hoping to keep in close touch with his family through the post, Coleridge sent a total of twenty-one extremely long letters home during his ten-month absence, fourteen to Sarah and seven to Poole.

Sarah was relieved to learn that her husband's ship had successfully evaded the French warships and privateers that constantly marauded Channel shipping. His first letter ended:

> Kiss my Hartley and Bercoo Baby Brodder. Kiss them for their dear father, whose heart will never absent from them many hours together!—My dear Sara—I think of you with affection and a desire to be home; and in the full and holiest sense of the word ... will be, I trust, your Husband faithful unto death. [CL I, p. 148]

By way of a postscript he added, "The sky and colours are quite English just as if I were coming out of T. Poole's homeward with you in my arm" (CL I, p. 418).

Coleridge and William proved an avid pair of tourists as they roamed the streets and lanes of Hamburg, from the central marketplace and cathedral to the outermost suburbs, including a brief tour of its red light district, famous even then. And they managed to meet with Friedrich Klopstock, one of Germany's best known poets.

Having penned his laudatory *Ode to France* in 1789, Klopstock had traced out the same ideological pilgrimage as his two youthful visitors, first embracing and then recoiling from the Revolution. By now a rheumy septuagenarian with dropsically bulging limbs, Klopstock spoke no English, forcing Coleridge to take a back seat while William conversed in French, translating as he went. Appreciative of Klopstock's poetry but flabbergasted by his views on English literature (he ranked the now forgotten Richard Glover above Milton), Wordsworth and Coleridge remained respectfully deferential as the aging bard pontificated to them. But in their private conversations, Coleridge convulsed William by nicknaming their host "Klubstick" (De Quincey, 1970, p. 63).

They would have rolled along merrily had they remained together, but both men detested what Coleridge described as the "huddle and ugliness, stench and stagnation" (Hanson, 1962, p. 314) of Hamburg. Coleridge wanted to move to the quaint lakeside town of Ratzeburg, where he hoped to become fluent in spoken and written German by living among the natives. But faced with a more restricted budget, the Wordsworths chose rural Goslar, at the foot of the Hartz mountains, where they heard living was cheap. Many miles would separate them and, as winter wore on and the icy roads grew impassable, the post would become increasingly irregular.

Arriving in Ratzeburg in early October, Coleridge encountered no difficulty meeting Germans interested in extending their hospitality to a young *Englander*. "To be an Englishman is in Germany to be an angel—they almost worship you" he announced to Sarah (CL I, p. 435), and he went on to describe how the band greeted him with *Rule, Britannia!* as he entered a concert hall.

Having arrived by chance at the same moment as the news of Nelson's brilliant victory on the Nile, Coleridge found Ratzeburg's citizens "frantic with joy" (CL I, p. 420) that the balance of power had finally tipped in England's favor. After Bonaparte's recent campaigns in Italy and Switzerland, which had terrified the Rhinelanders that all of Europe might soon be living under French rule, Napoleon had given every indication that his next objective was England itself. But while cleverly keeping the British in check for months by focusing attention on the well-publicized activities of his "Army of England," Bonaparte had all the while been planning a massive Mediterranean expedition.

In May of 1798, with a force of forty thousand men and an armada of three hundred vessels, including thirteen ships of the line, Napoleon had quietly slipped out of France, conquered Malta in a matter of days, deftly skirted Nelson's patrols, and landed his men on the outskirts of Alexandria. In spite of the fierce resistance they encountered from the defending Mameluke hordes, renowned as savage warriors, Bonaparte's men had dispatched them as handily as they had the most modern armies of Europe. It was beginning to look as if France could conquer the world if she so chose. But on the first of August, ten English men-of-war sailed into Aboukir Bay and engaged the thirteen French ships of the line in a blistering

Fatal Interlude

battle in which the French lost eleven ships and fifty-two hundred men without sinking a single enemy vessel—the greatest naval victory in English history.

The people of Ratzeburg were relieved by the proof that Napoleon was not invincible, taking great comfort in the fact that England controlled the seas. As much the result of his nation's prestige as his own native wit and personal charm, Coleridge found himself wined, dined, and lionized by the Germans. With good-natured amusement, he described to Sarah how patent medicines, clothing, playing cards, even sticking plasters, were advertised as English or made in the English manner. Just as the nobility and bourgeoisie of King George's Hanover loved nothing better than an outing in an English style *Kaffeehaus*, so the young intellectuals were becoming passionately interested in English literature, particularly Shakespeare.

While Coleridge's antic moods were stimulated by the Anglomania he encountered, he enjoyed his popularity only as long as he knew things at home were secure. In late November his peace of mind was shattered by the month-old news from Sarah that both children had fallen seriously ill after receiving smallpox innoculations. Although she went on to say that they had recovered and were recuperating, Coleridge was deeply shaken to learn of their close brush with death. He wrote Sarah, describing how her letter had plunged him into "fits of weeping" (CL I, p. 449).

Vexed that Coleridge's preoccupation with his children might interfere with his progress in learning German by driving him into one of his bouts of depression, Poole wrote:

> let me entreat you not to over-interest yourself about your family and your friends here; not to incapacitate yourself by idle apprehensions and tender reveries of imagination concerning us. Those things are wrong. They can do no good . . . if you indulge in them. Mrs. Coleridge has sent me from Bristol the letter you wrote her. Was it well to indulge in, much less to express, such feeling concerning *any* circumstance which could relate to two infants? I do not mean to check tenderness, for in the *folly* of tenderness I can sympathise—but be *rational*, I implore you—in your present situation, your happiness depends on it. [Hanson, 1962, p. 325]

Firmly convinced that Coleridge's mission in Germany was crucial to his intellectual development, and fretful on learning that his high-strung protégé had "cried [himself] blind about Berkeley" (CL I, p. 453), Poole made up his mind to see to it that in future Coleridge would not be unnecessarily upset by unpleasant domestic news.

Although Coleridge was as depressed and homesick as Poole guessed, the two did not agree as to how his domestic affairs should be handled. Coleridge wrote Sarah and explicitly instructed her *never* to keep him in the dark in matters pertaining to herself and the children. As he put it:

> In a sense of *reality* there is always comfort—the workings of one's imagination ever go beyond the worst that nature afflicts us with—they have the terror of a superstitious circumstance.... Enough, that you write me always the truth. Direct your next letter thus—An den Herrn Coleridge, a la Post Restante, Gottingen, Germany. [CL I, p. 459]

Having mastered German, Coleridge had left Ratzenburg for Gottingen to enroll in its university, renowned throughout Europe for its brilliant community of scholars anad impressive library. He attended lectures in physiology, anthropology, and natural history, studied biblical criticism and several linguistic variants of Medieval German, and read extensively in German history, literature, and philosophy. He also began taking notes on the life and works of Lessing, a major literary figure about whom he hoped to eventually write a biography.

The European winter of 1798–99 proved one of the coldest of the century. There were painfully long stretches when the frozen rivers and icy roads halted all mail from England for weeks at a time. Although he met some fellow countrymen who were also studying at the university, their company did little to relieve his homesickness and the dull ache that he felt.

As spring rolled around, the days grew longer, the roads thawed to mud, and the rivers once more became navigable. Coleridge became more hopeful that a letter from home might make it through. On the sixth of April, he finally heard from Poole. After some preliminary remarks vaguely hinting that all was not well at home, Poole wrote,

> Perhaps even by reading so far, you *feel the reason* for my wishing to write you before Mrs Coleridge. I suspect you feel it by the anticipations in your last letter. You say there that you have serious misgivings concerning Berkeley—well—you now, my dear Col., know the worst. I thus give you to understand the catastrophe of the drama, without heightening it by first narrating the circumstances. . . . [Hanson, 1962, p. 334]

As Coleridge noted, Berkeley had died of consumption on the tenth of February; Poole's letter was dated March 15, 1799. Poole owed him an explanation as to why he had waited five weeks:

> I have thus, my dear Col., informed you of the whole truth. It was long contrary to my opinion to let you know of the child's death before your arrival in England. And I thought, and still think myself justified in that notion, by the OVER-ANXIETY you expressed in your former letters. . . . [Hanson, 1962, p. 334]

Attempting to console his friend by minimizing the emotional significance of a parent's attachment to a baby that age—perhaps not entirely inappropriate to an era known for its astronomically high infant mortality rate—Poole expounded his philosophical views on parent-infant relationships. Hoping to soften Coleridge's loss, Poole argued that because infants lacked reason, their attachment to parents was mere animal instinct.

Although Poole was well intentioned in his attempt to orchestrate the Coleridges' lives, he had inserted himself between husband and wife and made it more difficult for them to share their tragedy directly and to console one another. By delaying five weeks, he effectively denied Coleridge the chance to decide whether to cut short his trip in order to be with Sarah in her grief. Furthermore, according to Poole, the crisis had passed. Sarah was over her miseries and for Coleridge to either return home *or* share his own feeling by mail would be to reopen old wounds unnecessarily. Poole advised:

> Only let your *mind* act, and not your *feelings*. Don't conjure up any scenes of distress which never happened. Mrs Coleridge felt as a mother . . . and, in an exemplary manner, did all a mother

could do. *But she never forgot herself.* She is now perfectly well, and does not make herself miserable by recalling the engaging, though, remember, mere instinctive attractions of an infant a few months old. [Hanson 1962, p. 335]

Taking his cue from his mentor, Coleridge turned to philosophy and the question of whether unintelligent creatures—like infants—had souls and were immortal. Such was his frame of mind as he began his consolation letter to Sarah later that day:

> It is one of the discomforts of my absence, my dearest Love! that we feel the same calamities at different times—I would fain write words of consolation to you; yet I know that I shall only fan into new activity the pang which was growing dead and dull in your heart. [CL I, p. 481]

Puzzling over God's unfathomable ways, he informed Sarah of his gnawing doubts regarding Priestley's doctrines and Unitarianism because they both doubted or denied "the future existence of infants" (CL I, p. 482). Ending his letter on a slightly less philosophically impersonal note, he wrote:

> I trust my dear Sara! that this event which has forced us to think of the death of what is most dear to us, as at all times probable, will in many and various ways be good for us—To have shared—nay, I should say—to have divided with any human being any one deep sensation of joy or sorrow, sinks deep the foundations of a lasting love. [CL I, p. 483]

It took three more weeks before he finally heard from Sarah herself:

> My dearest Love,
> I hope you will not attribute my long silence to want of affection. If you have received Mr Poole's letter you will know the reason and acquit me. My darling infant left his wretched mother on the 10th of February, and though the leisure that followed was intolerable to me, yet I could not employ myself in reading or writing, or in any way that prevented my thoughts from resting on him. This parting was the severest trial that I have ever yet undergone, and I pray to God that I may never live to behold the death of another child. For, O my dear Samuel, it is a suffering beyond your conception! You will feel and lament

the death of your child, but you will only recollect him a baby of fourteen weeks, but I am his mother and have carried him in my arms and have fed him at my bosom, and have watched over him by day and by night for nine months. I have seen him twice at the brink of the grave, but he has returned and recovered and smiled upon me like an angel,—and now I am lamenting that he is gone! [Hanson, 1962, pp. 339–340]

Sarah's letter indicated that she had very much grieved and was, in fact, still mourning. And though she had ignored her husband's plea that she share the news of trouble *while it was happening*, it is also clear that Poole had urged her to remain silent.

On the day after Berkeley's death, Sarah had written Poole:

O! My dear Poole! I have lost my dear dear child. At one o'clock on Sunday Morning a violent convulsive fit put an end to his painful existence, myself and two of his aunts were watching by his cradle. I wish I had not seen it, for I am sure it will never leave my memory; sweet babe! . . . I am perfectly aware of everything you have said on the subject in your letter; I shall not yet write Coleridge, and when I do—I will pass over all disagreeable subjects with the greatest care, for I well know their violent effect on him—but I account myself most unfortunate in being at a distance from him at this time, wanting his consolation as I do, and feeling my griefs almost too much to support with fortitude. . . . Southey has undertaken the business of my babe's interment and in a few days we shall remove to his house at Westbury which I shall be rejoiced to do for this house at present is quite hateful to me.

I thank you for the kind letters you sent me and depend on your writing again—I suppose you will have received from Coleridge the promised letter for me. I long for it—for I am very miserable! [Ellis, 1967, p. 142]

Time would prove Sarah correct in her prophecy. Scenes of her harrowing ordeal with Berkeley's death could never be erased entirely from her memory. Letters written years later confirm that fact.

When Coleridge finally learned what Poole knew all along—that Sarah was sorely grieving—he faced a choice. As he had pointedly remarked to Sarah, thus far they had *divided*, not *shared*, their tragedy. Should he cut short his trip, or remain in Germany and finish his work?

Sarah had given mixed messages: while revealing more of her sufferings than she originally intended, she also went out of her way to reassure Coleridge that Southey was taking good care of her. But the fact that in that same letter she gratuitously informed Coleridge that nobody thought much of *Lyrical Ballads* hints that she may have been feeling resentful and was expressing it indirectly.

Faced with conflicting signals from Sarah, whose psychological blind spot had proven to be a knack for self-appointed martyrdom that was clearly the match of her sainted mother's, and urged to stay on in Germany by his mentor, whose bungling myopia when it came to understanding feminine psychology would eventually doom him to an unwanted perpetual bachelorhood, Coleridge added his own neurotic tendencies to the decision-making process. Given both his habits of procrastination and his predisposition toward delayed emotional reactions, his choice of a June departure date was no surprise.

But if Sarah had volunteered to shoulder the burden of grief for both of them, only to discover too late that it was heavier than she had anticipated, she had unwittingly left her superstition-prone husband with the burden of irrational guilt. In his earlier letter, begging her to inform him of all family emergencies, Coleridge explained that "in a sense of *reality* there is always comfort—the workings of one's imagination ever go beyond the worst that nature afflicts us with—they have the terror of a superstitious circumstance" (CL I, p. 459). By early May he had begun to discover the truth of this remark. "There are moments," he wrote Poole, "in which I have such a power of life within me, such a conceit of it, I mean—that I lay the blame of my child's death to my absence—*not intellectually;* but I have a strong sort of sensation, as if while I was present, none could die whom I intensely loved . . ." (CL I, p. 490). "What a gloomy spring," he added, and morbidly went on to describe at length the gruesome details of a particularly tragic suicide that had recently taken place in Germany. His melancholy noted ended: "O Poole! I am homesick . . . my poor Muse is quite gone—perhaps she may return and meet me at Stowey. . . . My dear Poole! don't let little Hartley die before I come home.—That's silly—true—and I burst into tears as I wrote" (CL I, p. 493).

Aware that the rustic charm of their cozy cottage would forever be marred by painful reminders of Berkeley, Coleridge asked Poole to locate a new home for himself and Sarah. No matter what, he emphatically reassured him, they would remain in Stowey:

> Wordsworth and his sister passed thro' here, as I have informed you—I walked on with them 5 English miles, and spent a day with them. They were melancholy and hypp'd—W. was affected to tears at the thought of not being near me, wished me, of course, to live in the North of England near the Sir Frederic Vane's great library. I told him, that independent of the expence of removing, and the impropriety of taking Mrs Coleridge to a place where she would have no acquaintance, two insurmountable objections, the library was no inducement.... Finally, I told him, that *you* had been the man in whom *first* and in whom alone, I had felt an *anchor!* With all my other connections I felt a dim sense of insecurity and uncertainty, terribly uncomfortable.—W. was affected to tears, very much affected; but he deemed the vicinity of a library absolutely *neccessary* to his health, nay to his existence. It is painful to me too to think of not living near him; for he is a *good* and *kind* man, and the only one whom in all things I feel my superior.... But my resolve is fixed, *not to leave you till you leave me!* I still think that Wordsworth will be disappointed in his expectations ... and I think it highly probable, that where I live, there he will live.... [CL I, p. 490]

Astonished and moved by Wordsworth's tears—coming as they did from a man who rarely showed his emotions—Coleridge overlooked the obvious explanation that William's tears expressed sympathy for his recent bereavement. Instead, Coleridge wishfully misinterpreted his friend's display of emotion as proof positive that William was prepared to follow him anywhere. But Wordsworth had been plain in outlining his plans.

While he regretted living so far from Coleridge, he and Dorothy would temporarily stay with friends in the North until they located an inexpensive cottage in Yorkshire or the Lake District. The news was no surprise: the Wordsworths had already told Coleridge of their search for a permanent home in their letters from Goslar that winter. As Dorothy put it, they intended to "decoy" Coleridge north on a long visit once he got back to England, in hopes of inducing him to settle there permanently (LWDW I, p. 238).

William and Dorothy wasted no time launching their campaign to persuade Coleridge to move north. During a stopover in Gottingen that spring, William, aware of his learned friend's fondness for well-stocked libraries, had tried his best to lure Coleridge to the Lakes with his tempting descriptions. For in spite of their adamant determination to move north, both William and Dorothy were aware of the great void in their lives that Coleridge's absence occasioned.

Having not seen him since their Hamburg days with "Klubstick," the Wordsworths had missed his daily society, living as they did in total seclusion, barely mixing with the Germans. Drinking daily from "Kubla" (Moorman, 1957, p. 412)—their affectionate nickname for their water can—the Wordsworths reminisced nostalgically about the missing member of their trio. And during those long months apart, William had begun to write his autobiography in blank verse—addressed and dedicated to Coleridge.

But if writing his life story for his friend was cementing Wordsworth's attachment to Coleridge, his search to recapture his childhood memories was impelling William to return to his native North Country. Intensely involved in recollecting his boyhood, Wordsworth was just starting to hit his full stride as a poet: his autobiographical project had already begun to yield the same sort of artistic results (the Lucy poems and the start of *The Prelude*) as Coleridge's had.

For Wordsworth, all roads led north. But overly confident of the crucial role he had recently played as William's literary partner in *Lyrical Ballads*, as well as his present one as auditor-catalyst-advisor for Wordsworth's autobiography, Coleridge half believed that William and Dorothy would be waiting to greet him upon his return to Stowey. Accompanying his friends along the Gottingen highway for the first few miles of their homeward journey, Coleridge bid them farewell.

During the next nine weeks, with the exception of one off for sightseeing, Coleridge worked eight to ten hours a day. Numbing his sorrow by poring over medieval German texts and tediously transcribing notes, he tried to finish his projects quickly. To shorten transcription time, he purchased two trunks full of modern books to bring back with him and then proceeded to fret, nervously unsure if he could make his extravagant thirty-pound purchase pay with the books he hoped to write (by 1980 standards, he had spent approximately $1050 on the books). On June 24, one day past the date on which he had promised Sarah he would be home, Coleridge departed Gottingen.

Chapter 9

Calm Before the Storm

> Well! If the Bard was weather-wise, who made
> The grand old ballad of Sir Patrick Spence,
> This night, so tranquil now, will not go hence
> Unroused by winds, that ply a busier trade....
> —from *Dejection: An Ode* [PW, pp. 362–363]

Coleridge's muse was not waiting to greet him when he arrived home that July. Death had desecrated their cottage. Its snug, welcoming rooms had been transformed into gloomy cells whose emptiness shrieked at the returning wayfarer, urging him to turn in his tracks and resume a nomad's life until he might find an unspoiled haven. The spark was gone from his marriage; Coleridge was developing a dread of his own home. Perhaps a mere change of houses would solve matters. If not, a change of locale might be necessary.

Of course that meant losing Poole. Although Coleridge was overjoyed to see him, a shift had occurred in their relationship. Far worse than having been unable to stave off disaster from the Coleridge household, Poole's bungling efforts to help once misfortune struck had only compounded the alienation between husband and wife. Sarah's love had been blighted by her solitary ordeal with grief, while Coleridge's had been disfigured by irrational guilt.

Both were disappointed in their expectations of his homecoming; in a letter Coleridge spoke of "domestic affliction ... hard upon" him (CL I, p. 523). The tender reunion each had yearned for during the long months apart was not to be. Now they needed to put the past behind them and make a fresh start, but first Coleridge would have to regain his wife's faith. Overdrawn on the Wedgwood annuity as the result of his stay in Germany, they were once again in debt. Skeptical of her husband's abilities as a provider, Sarah was unimpressed by *Lyrical Ballads*, with its slow sales and poor reviews.

Given Sarah's hot temper and Coleridge's instinctive dread of arguments, particularly with women, it is hardly surprising that he avoided confronting his wife and dodged her recriminations. Instead he chose a less direct method of restoring harmony to his marriage. He turned to Southey. Swallowing his pride, he wrote his estranged friend a grateful letter, graciously thanking him for taking care of Sarah in her moment of need. In his note, Coleridge attempted to convince his brother-in-law that the time had come to bury the hatchet.

Southey, still holding a grudge, had gleefully relished the opportunity to ridicule *Lyrical Ballads* in a magazine review written while Coleridge was in Germany. But far more painful to Coleridge than his injured literary vanity was the fact that Southey had skillfully managed to discredit him in Sarah's eyes by convincing her that his book was devoid of all merit. Aware of the longstanding rift between the two men, Sarah might under ordinary circumstances have taken Southey's views with a grain of salt. But feeling very much alone after Berkeley's death, and deeply grateful for Southey's comfort, Sarah Coleridge had by now elevated her brother-in-law to the status of an authority in most matters.

And so, determined to win back his wife's goodwill by regaining Southey's affection, Coleridge redoubled his conciliatory efforts when this initial overture was rejected. He not only wrote a second letter to his scornful brother-in-law but talked Poole into writing one as well, testifying that he had never heard Coleridge utter a single word of disrespect regarding Southey. And if Poole's testimony was not enough, Coleridge offered to furnish Southey additional proof from the Wordsworths. Finally, his pride satisfied, Southey relented.

By August the Coleridges and the Southeys were as inseparable as in the old days. Bantering stanzas while shaving or sitting at the breakfast table, the two former Pantisocrats began writing light verse together. Their major opus—a short piece of comic doggerel—was published in the *Morning Post*. Touring Devon together, the foursome visited Ottery, where Southey finally got to meet Coleridge's seventy-two-year old mother:

We were all a good deal amused by the old lady. She could not hear what was going on, but seeing Samuel arguing [politics] with his brothers, took it for granted that he must have been wrong, and cried out, 'Ah, if your poor father had been alive, he'd soon have convinced you.' [Hanson, 1962, p. 356]

Although there clearly was a gulf between Coleridge's liberal outlook and his family's Church-and-King politics, the Ottery visit went well. Having mended his ties with Southey and his Ottery kin, Coleridge was in good spirits by the time he and Sarah returned to Stowey in late September. There they were able to settle into a more contented domestic routine.

A few weeks later, Coleridge left for Bristol to visit Cottle and hunt for his two trunks of books, which had not yet arrived from Germany. In search of medical advice after a two-week bout of "rheumatic fever,"* Coleridge dropped in at the Pneumatic Institute, a Wedgwood-sponsored foundation for medical research, where he met a young researcher named Humphry Davy. Apart from admiring Davy's flair for amateur verse, Coleridge was impressed by the scientific idealism that prompted the twenty-one-year-old to experiment on himself with potentially lethal drugs in order to understand their pharmacology. He was currently working with nitrous oxide and, having recently discovered its intoxicating properties, obliged Coleridge by letting him inhale some, just as he had done for the ever curious Tom Wedgwood.

In the midst of his Bristol visit, Coleridge received a letter filled with "alarming accounts of Wordsworth's health" (CL I, p. 545). Dropping everything, he struck out for the North to visit William. Arriving in Sockburn, a small Yorkshire farming village, on the twenty-sixth of October, he found William in fine condition, the report having proven a false alarm. If Dorothy was the culprit who had sounded the false alarm, as part

---

*Coleridge's symptoms consisted of stabbing pains from the small of his back to both calves, "rheumatic" pains in his head and shoulders, and periodic twitching of the muscles in his arms and thighs. Although he called this attack "rheumatic fever," he mentioned no swelling, redness, or tenderness in his joints and, apparently, no fever—symptoms one might expect in a full-blown attack of that disease. Also of interest is the fact that Coleridge made no mention of requiring opium to control his pain.

of a previously declared plan to "decoy" Coleridge north, she was not there to face charges, having left on an extended visit with friends.

Delighted to see William after six long months, Coleridge was in hilarious good spirits and treated his hosts, the Hutchinsons, to one of his more dazzling displays of wit and charm. Having heard the Wordsworths reminisce fondly about their old friends the Hutchinsons, Coleridge made himself one of the family, disarming their North Country reserve with his humor.

Like the Wordsworths, the Hutchinsons were a close-knit family of brothers and sisters whose being orphaned at an early age had tightly woven the bonds among them. Growing up together in nearby Penrith, the children of both families attended the same schools. As teenagers, Mary Hutchinson and Dorothy Wordsworth had formed an inseparable trio with William during his summer visits as a Cambridge student.

Tall, fair, and slender, Mary Hutchinson at twenty-nine created, through her graceful feminine movements, gentle manners, and radiant smile, a pleasing impression of beauty which a more critical, feature-by-feature analysis of her plain face would not have borne out. From the fact that she alone of the Hutchinson women was mentioned by Coleridge in his diary, it is clear that he was initially drawn to her in preference to the twenty-four-year-old Sara, who was plain, short, dark, and pudgy, though considerably more verbal and intellectually agile than her older sister. Lavishly punning and flirting in a good-natured way, Coleridge left a favorable impression with all the Hutchinsons by the time he and Wordsworth departed a day later.

Hiking vigorously, they toured the Lakes for three weeks, as William nostalgically shared the breathtaking majesty of the land of his boyhood. Both Coleridge and Wordsworth were particularly struck by the beauty of Grasmere and a quaint old house, formerly an inn, known as Dove Cottage. William wrote Dorothy a note describing the village and the charming house he had seen.

Near the end of their journey, Coleridge received a letter from Daniel Stuart, editor of the *Morning Post*. Anxious to hire Coleridge, Stuart offered to pay his travel and living expenses, guaranteed his mornings free, and agreed to pay him the salary of a featured correspondent. Short on cash and always open to new experiences, Coleridge accepted. Stopping at the Sockburn farmhouse on his way to London, Coleridge rested for several days, possibly amusing himself by flirting with the Hutchinson sisters, although his diary entries for those days make no mention of it.

Arriving in London in late November, Coleridge began writing for the *Post* on a four-month trial basis. Locating lodgings, he sent for Sarah and Hartley, who arrived in early December. Having heard nothing from her husband since his departure for Bristol five weeks earlier, Sarah was undoubtedly miffed. It is unclear if the report of William's ill health had held much water with Sarah. Nor is it known what role Coleridge may have played in "decoying" himself to the Lakes in order to scout the area out with a mind toward settling there—a move he knew Sarah would oppose, as it would whisk her away from friends and family. But it would seem that relations between the Coleridges were fairly cordial nonetheless, as within a month of their London reunion Sarah was pregnant again.

Like most marriages, the Coleridges' always went more smoothly when there was money to pay the bills. By accepting the lucrative newspaper job, Coleridge tabled the touchy question of where they would settle next and enjoyed for a time a life of domestic peace. Hartley, now three, was delighted over the prospect of a new sibling but was still puzzled as to the fate of his old one; he prattled and quizzed—much to his papa's droll amusement—about his missing brother Berkeley, who had gone up to the sky to live with the stars in the heavens.

Although they were not living exactly in fortune's lap, the Coleridges' spacious quarters made for a pleasant home life. The handsome salary that Stuart provided was enough to allow Sarah to meet the greengrocer without wincing. She was Mrs. Coleridge, wife of the *Post* reporter. Their credit was impeccable—an exhilarating experience given their recent ups and downs and her earlier experiences with a feckless father.

But Coleridge's boss, Daniel Stuart, was not renowned for his philanthropy. As Coleridge put it, "Dan's a Scotchman who is content to get rid of the itch when he can afford clean linen"

(Coleridge, 1968, p. lxvii). Stuart expected—and got—a profitable return on his investment. In addition to averaging six columns a week, Coleridge wrote editorial pieces and occasionally contributed poetry. Given this rather hectic schedule, it was fortunate for the Coleridges' domestic life that it was only a short walk from their lodgings to the gilded globe that hung over the *Post*'s front door—a glittering reminder of its worldwide news coverage and Coleridge's assignment as political commentator on the war.

Having electrified the world by escaping Nelson's clutches and slipping back to France after his Egyptian defeat, Napoleon had just appointed himself First Consul and was raising French morale by framing a new constitution. Meanwhile, Pitt and his allies were overemphasizing the strategic importance of Nelson's victory and ignoring their own recent setbacks in the Netherlands and Switzerland. Confident of their ability to pursue a rapid military conclusion to the war, they had cast a greedy eye over their maps and declared Europe "ripe or rather rotten, for destruction" (Reilly, 1979, p. 366). That conviction would help prolong the war another fifteen years.

Pro-peace in outlook, Coleridge was appalled by the senseless carnage and dismayed by Pitt's leadership, though he no longer compared him to Judas or wished he would be struck by lightning, as he had in the *Watchman* days. And while the plucky Corsican's charisma appealed to his romantic imagination, he was equally repulsed by Bonaparte's thirst for power. Writing long into the night, Coleridge often did not make it home until dawn, just as the hawkers hit the pavements with the day's edition. But hard as the work was, he enjoyed his challenging assignments and found political journalism as exhilarating as it was exhausting.

There were also lulls during which he found time to attend fashionable dinner parties with writers, painters, politicians, and professional men. To relax and unwind, he loved to talk shop and debate politics. Most everyone he met was favorably impressed with his startling command of language, as both writer and speaker. Publishers repeatedly approached him with book offers and, half tempted by their contracts, he wrote Southey describing the gold mine he had discovered. If only he would come to London, there would be guineas enough for both of them and a spacious flat to share on Buckingham Street.

Having seen the miracles that the Southeys' daily company worked on his marriage, and craving the brotherhood of a fellow poet, Coleridge began to feel Southey out regarding the prospect of their setting up a joint household after his stint with the *Post* was over. Southey, however, was suffering from "nervous exhaustion" due to overwork (Haller, 1966, p. 302), and was planning a trip abroad.

Meanwhile, the Wordsworths continued their wooing of Coleridge. Anxious to regain their friend's daily companionship, William kept up his campaign to lure Coleridge to the Lakes. His charming descriptions of how he and Dorothy roamed the wild Cumberland countryside wistfully conveyed that Coleridge was always on their minds as they wandered, almost as if he were with them. Wordsworth's glowing letter ended with a generous postscript: "Take no pains to contradict the story that the L.B. [*Lyrical Ballads*] are entirely yours. Such a rumour is the best thing that can befall them" (LWDW I, p. 281).

Tempted by the overtures from Dove Cottage, Coleridge broached the subject of a move to the Lakes, but Sarah vetoed the suggestion. Halfheartedly inclined to give in, Coleridge asked Poole to find a new house for them. But even as he described what they were looking for, his thoughts kept drifting north:

> I would to God, I could get Wordsworth to retake Alfoxden—the society of so great a being is of priceless value—but he will never quit the North of England—his habits are more assimilated with the inhabitants there—there he and his sister are exceedingly beloved, enthusiastically. Such difference do small sympathies make—such as voice, pronunciation, etc—for what other cause can I account for it—. Certainly, no one, neither you, or the Wedgewoods, altho' you far more than anyone else, ever entered into the feeling due to a man like Wordsworth—of whom I do not hesitate in saying, that since Milton no man has *manifested* himself equal to him. [CL I, p. 582]

Poole's response was prompt, critical, and jarring. Coleridge replied:

You charge me with prostration in regard to Wordsworth. Have I affirmed anything miraculous of W? Is it impossible that a greater poet than any since Milton may appear in our days? Have there any *great* poets appeared since him? . . . Future greatness! What if you had known Milton at the age of thirty, and believed all you now know of him? [CL I, p. 584]

Zoning in on Coleridge's blind spot, Poole had focused not on the merits of Wordsworth's poems but on Coleridge's hero worship of William. Sensitive to the point of defensiveness, Coleridge was arguing at cross purposes in order to deny Poole's charge of idolatry and all that it implied. But while he could not tolerate his mentor's trenchant observations concerning his overattachment to William, he agreed completely with another of Poole's criticisms: that journalism was ephemeral and that Coleridge should be writing for posterity.

Determined to regain his literary momentum but still obliged to pay his debts, Coleridge accepted an offer from Thomas Longman, a London publisher, to translate Schiller's *Wallenstein* in his spare time. Aware that his popular correspondent had been feeling like a "caged lark" (Coleridge 1968, p. lxxxvii), Stuart offered to lighten his load and keep him on at full pay. More than satisfied with Coleridge's performance and his popularity with the *Post*'s readers, Stuart hoped to hire Coleridge on a permanent basis. No longer assigned to all night debates in Parliament, Coleridge faced the meticulous work of translation refreshed after a full night's sleep.

Spread thin by his commitments to Longman and Stuart, Coleridge had little time left over for his family, and so in early March Sarah and Hartley returned to the West Country to await his return. The plan was to meet in Bristol in April and proceed to Stowey, where they would search for a new house.

As the prospect of rattling around the now empty London flat did not appeal to Coleridge, he was grateful when Charles and Mary Lamb invited him to move into their place. Having long since reconciled their differences, Lamb and Coleridge were once again the best of friends.

The daily company of the Agnus Dei and the Virgin Mary—Coleridge's favorite nicknames for Charles and Mary—made his life infinitely more bearable, while Lamb jubilantly reveled in the "continuous feast" of Coleridge's conversation (Lamb, 1980, p. 68). No doubt the former Grecians' continuous feasting included liberal amounts of punch and Oronoco tobacco, transforming the Lambs' parlor into a reasonable facsimile of the smoky back room of the Salutation and Cat.

In mid-March Stuart and Coleridge met to discuss the latter's continued employment. Offering to hire Coleridge on a permanent basis, Stuart informed him that the deal might eventually include stock in both his newspapers if the arrangement continued as smoothly as it had until now. Tallying his tantalizing offer into pounds and shillings, Stuart reckoned that in a short time Coleridge might be worth as much as two thousand pounds a year (approximately seventy thousand 1980 dollars). Having delivered this bombshell, Stuart sat back in his chair, confidently awaiting Coleridge's reply.

He could do nothing but stare in amazement when Coleridge blithely informed him that he considered money "a real evil," needed nothing more than two hundred fifty pounds a year to get by, and much preferred "the lazy reading of old folios" while snugly tucked away in some remote corner of the English countryside to a journalist's life and the glitter of London (CL I, p. 582). Indicating his willingness to contribute freelance articles to the *Post*, Coleridge kept the meeting free of acrimony. Nonetheless, Stuart walked away shaking his head in disbelief. He had offered Coleridge the opportunity of a lifetime.

But Coleridge had been taking stock of his life and had reached the conclusion that he was at a turning point in his career. Over the past few years he had time and again allowed himself to be sidetracked by temptations and distractions. He had gone from poet to German scholar to political journalist to professional translator, as well as to would-be biographer of Lessing. Going back further in time, he could add political lecturer, publisher of his own periodical, playwright, and Unitarian minister to his list of occupations. He seemed to have an insatiable hunger for the challenge of new experiences, and others had always been quick to admire his versatile talents.

Everyone seemed to respond to the incendiary glow of his intellect and his burning enthusiasms. Recognition had come early and from many quarters. They wanted him in Shrewsbury, the Wedgwoods staked him to an annuity, German society lionized him, London publishers waved book contracts before his eyes, and now Stuart was pursuing him as well, promising him the moon. Most everyone seemed spellbound by his conversational brilliance and, as he had discovered during this London interlude, he was in the process of becoming a celebrity whose charismatic talents could magically open the drawing room doors of the wealthy, the fashionable, and the powerful.

However, if he was a brilliant young man on the move, he also had those private moments of self-doubt in which he felt like a desperate young man on the run. Hounded by his own expectations, and those of others, of what he might achieve if only he set his mind to it, he had not stayed put long enough in any one place to risk the challenge of facing up to his promise. But he was now twenty-seven, his wife was in the midst of her third full-term pregnancy, and they had no permanent home. And, most important, his life and career lacked any definite sense of direction.

He had cautioned Humphry Davy not to sell out by confusing the glamorous appeal of popular recognition for the more hard-won satisfaction of enduring achievement. Could he follow his own advice? On returning from Germany he told Southey: "I am resolved to write nothing with my name till my Great Work" (CL I, p. 535). But that had been six months ago. And two full years had passed since he had attempted a major poem. He had made a promising start with the first book of *Christabel*, and now the time had come to finish that poem, regain his creative momentum, and move on to other works.

Once he had made his decision, he found it difficult to brook any further delay. As March dragged on he champed at the bit, barely able to wait to be free from his scribbler's life as a "galley slave" (CL I, p. 569). Finally, spring arrived. Bidding Charles and Mary a warm good-bye, Coleridge took his leave. But after wending its way through the crowded London streets that April day in 1800, Coleridge's coach headed for the Great North Road. Describing his house guest's last-minute change of plan, Lamb wrote a friend: "Coleridge has left us, . . . on a visit to his god Wordsworth" (Hanson, 1962, p. 409).

Chapter 10

The Eye of the Storm

> *He that hateth his Brother, is a Murderer. This includes the emotions/passions of that part of the soul with which we feel anger.*
> [CNB 3293.6]

In March of 1801—one year after his departure from London—Coleridge triumphantly announced to Poole that he had just settled the philosophical problem of time and space and predicted that he was about "to solve the process of Life and Consciousness" (CL II, p. 706). Aware of the importance of his mission, Coleridge was prepared to pay the price—working night and day at a hectic pace. Nothing short of such an all-out effort would do if he were to achieve the definitive synthesis of all the major currents in Western thought. Reading in Greek, Latin, French, German, and English, Coleridge had been studying Plato, Aristotle, Pythagoras, Descartes, Voltaire, Leibniz, Kant, Bacon, Hobbes, Hume, Berkeley, Locke, and Newton, in addition to a host of lesser known figures.

Exhausting but exhilarating, his was a labor of love. Or almost a labor of love. In point of fact, Coleridge had a philosophical bone to pick. Adamantly opposed to the arid eighteenth-century materialist philosophers whose cause and effect reasoning dominated the times in which he lived, Coleridge was girding himself for battle. Locke and Newton were to be his principal adversaries. While they may have ushered in the scientific era, Coleridge considered it a scientific error for them to have assumed that the logic of their method should be applied to philosophical enquiry into the mysterious nature of the universe. As Coleridge saw it, the insertion of scientific metaphors into the language of philosophical discourse amounted to little more than a semantic sleight of hand: Locke claimed the universe ran *like* an orderly clock. *Ergo:* the Diety—if indeed there was one—was an expert clocksmith. While there was still room for mystery, the new enigma was, When and how had God become a master horologist?

Just as today computer terminology influences everyday language, subtly shaping daily thinking, so the technological breakthroughs of Coleridge's day influenced him. The machine had become the metaphor: the world operated like clockwork. Every educated man knew that. But Coleridge deplored this trend as little more than the disguised worship of scientific progress.

The scientific method was paying off: Newton had discovered the laws of optics and gravity, and others were appplying these laws to create the emerging technology. The Industrial Revolution had begun. New machines were being invented, and factories and mills were springing up all over England. Who could argue with such tangible proofs?

But Coleridge had no qualms about taking on the giants, and set about reexamining the original evidence from which progress had sprung. Planning to systematically repeat Newton's experiments, he asked Poole to ship him optical prisms as he transformed his bedroom-study into an experimental laboratory. He began keeping notes:

> Wednesday—Afternoon. Abed—nervous—had noticed the prismatic colours transmitted from the tumbler—Wordsworth came—I talked with him—he left me alone—I shut my eyes—beauteous spectra of two colors, orange and violet—then of green. . . . [CNB 925]

After seeing Coleridge at work, William became alarmed:

> At Wordsworth's advice or rather fervent intreaty I have intermitted the pursuit—the intensity of thought, and the multitude of minute experiments with light and figure, have made me so nervous and feverish, that I cannot sleep . . . [yet] it seemed to me a suicide of my very soul to divert my attention from truths so important, which came to me almost as revelation. [CL II, p. 707]

There was something quixotic about Coleridge's attempt to replicate Newton's research. Lacking laboratory training, he was not equipped to repeat the experiments. And there was something grandiose about Coleridge's sense of revelation and his flip assertion that "the souls of 500 Sir Isaac Newtons would go to the making up of a Shakespeare or Milton" (CL II, p. 709).

Coleridge would make that judgment himself. Two and a half years later, he begged Poole to destroy

> that letter which in the ebulliency of indistinct conceptions I wrote to you respecting Sir Isaac Newton's Optics . . . to my horror and shame . . . a letter which if I were to die and it should see the *light* would damn me forever, as a man mad with presumption! [CL II, p. 1014]

Four months later, he again implored:

> Poole! if you have not already (as I so earnestly requested) destroyed that letter and all copy of that letter in which I wrote you with dream-like imagination respecting Sir Isaac Newton, and my hope of optico-metaphysical discovery, I pray you do it now and tell me, that it is done. I never was anxious about any letter, saving that. [CL II, p. 1046]

If Coleridge's original objections to Newtonian materialist philosophy had merit, why did he become so ashamed of his own scientific enterprise? Switching political hobbyhorses or changing philosophical opinions had never before prompted him to destroy his letters in order to cover his tracks. Nor was he secretive about the fact that his life's path was strewn with half-completed projects like these optical and ocular experiments. His unusual hypersensitivity in this instance came from quite another source.

Looking back ruefully, Coleridge realized that those feverish experiments marked the start of his addiction to opium. At the time of his foray into Newton's *Optics*, he had begun to use the drug regularly and unwittingly was becoming addicted. During those self-deluding experiments filled with cosmic revelation, he had been unaware of what was happening.

The optical exercises consisted of becoming intoxicated and studying the properties of light with a drugged fascination. By day the rainbow refractions of the sun were the objects of his reveries. Nights he gazed into candles until dawn. By meticulously recording his observations in his diary, he could convince himself that his project was strictly scientific:

> Mem. In spectra, the luminous fringes inclosing a space some imperfectly circular some parallelograms—Item/motion communicated to the object by any motion in any part of the body. ex.gr. of the hand moving to and fro the flesh of the leg.—This important. [CNB 1039]

By the time he could secretly admit to himself in coded Greek cipher that laudanum was the basis of his beautiful visions, it was too late. Fully addicted, he could only stare in dumbfounded bewilderment as a pheasant's glorious plumage decayed into excrement before his eyes:

> one o'clock or near it—after much excitement, very very far short of intoxication, indeed not approaching to it to the consciousness of the understanding, tho' I had taken a considerable quantity of λαυδανυμ [laudanum] I for the first time in my life felt my eyes near-sighted. . . . I then put out the candles, and closed my eyes—and instantly there appeared a spectrum, of a pheasant's tail, that altered thro' various degradations into round wrinkly shapes, as of horse excrement. . . . I started out of my bed, lit my candles, and noted it down . . . something like horse dung. . . . O that I could explain these concentric wrinkles in my spectra! [CNB 1681]

Eventually he even played with his own excrement in intoxicated fascination. By then his handwriting was large and loopy, and often, absentmindedly, he would write words and phrases twice over: "What a beautiful thing urine is, in a pot, brown yellow, transpicuous, the image, diamond shaped of the of the candle in it . . ." (CNB 1766).

But if opium triggered Coleridge's regression, it was to his own past that he returned. Not all addicts nod at candles or gaze dreamily at the sun's rays: sunlight and firelight had always mesmerized him. As a six-year-old he had been entranced by the sunlight streaming through the vicarage window as he waited for the rays to fall on the copy of the *Arabian Nights* before picking up that book. Then, basking in the exact spot where the sun warmed the floor, he had transported himself to the hot desert sands of Shahryar's kingdom. Later he stared in dismay as his book went up in flames, confiscated and destroyed by his father. As if to turn his son's attentions in a more ethereal direction, John Coleridge had taken the boy stargazing and hypnotized him with tales of the heavenly fires that made the planets glow. Still later, as a homesick youngster at Christ's Hospital, Coleridge gazed into the fire, searching for the good luck sign of ash films on the grate. And even as a grown man, Coleridge loved nothing better than staring at the flames licking the logs of a roaring fire whenever he felt lonely or homesick.

In fact, Coleridge's earliest memory was his fascination with fire at the age of two: "I was carelessly left by my nurse—ran to the fire, and pulled out a live coal—burnt myself dreadfully.... [Was it] at all ominous?" (CL I, p. 312). We can only conjecture the wide range of meanings that fire images later assumed for Coleridge, but in two instances he made explicit reference to flames—in connection with love and with poetic imagination. One of the earliest entries in his journal reads: "The flames of two candles joined give a much stronger light than both of them separate—evid. by a person holding the two candles near his face, first separate, and then joined in one" (CNB 13). Immediately after this note, Coleridge wrote himself a memo to use the image of two candles for a poem on marriage that he never wrote.

On another occasion, a burning candle stood for his creative imagination. In March of 1801—the time of his experiments—he described how his poetic candle had just been snuffed out:

> You would not know me—!... The poet is dead in me—my imagination (or rather the somewhat that had been imaginative) lies, like a cold snuff on the circular rim of a brass candlestick, without even a stink of tallow to remind you that it was once clothed and mitred with flame. [CL II, p. 714]

Convinced he could never again write poetry, he went on:

> If I die, and the booksellers will give you anything for my life, be sure to say—Wordsworth descended on him, like the Γνωθι δεαυτον [Know thyself] from Heaven; by showing to him what true poetry was, he made him know, that he was no poet. [CL II, p. 714]

A dramatic change had taken place. When Coleridge left London in April of 1800, he had decided to devote himself to poetry. Scarcely a year later he was announcing that the poet in him was dead. But even more striking, Coleridge directly attributed the death of his poetic imagination to Wordsworth—previously his most vital source of nurturance as a poet. A malignant transformation had occurred.

Back in Somerset, he and William had kindled one another's imaginations—their poetic candles burned brightest together. *Lyrical Ballads* attested to that. Now Coleridge declared that his poetic imagination was lifeless. But his dead candle image was ambiguous. Did he believe his flame had *burned out* or had *been snuffed out*? While there is ample evidence to support the notion that Coleridge's creative loss was a drug-induced burnout phenomenon, there is also convincing evidence to support the notion that Wordsworth helped snuff out that flame. The alternatives—literary homicide and literary suicide—are by no means mutually exclusive.

The difficult decision as to where to settle permanently was experienced by Coleridge as momentous but not ominous. While Poole, Wedgwood, and Lamb all warned of his overattachment to William, Coleridge turned a deaf ear to their concerns. On literary grounds, he could so so with impunity. Although Wordsworth was not yet popularly recognized as a major literary figure, he would in fact be recognized by posterity as the only major poet of Coleridge's generation—that is, except for Coleridge himself.

Coleridge adamantly refused to consider that his friends' concern over his Wordsworth-worship were psychological comments about himself, not literary judgments of William. And so, determined to resume writing poetry, Coleridge had felt magnetically drawn to the Lake District by the time he left Lamb's home that spring. He visited with William and Dorothy for six weeks. When he departed Grasmere, two major decisions had been reached: a second edition of *Lyrical Ballads* would be forthcoming and he would move to the Lakes. He had located a suitable house for his family at Keswick, thirteen miles from Dove Cottage.

Coleridge informed Sarah that his plan to move north was final. She would have to understand that it was crucial for him to live near a brother poet if he were to resume writing poetry. As evidence of his willingness to compromise, he could point to his earlier efforts to set up a joint household with the Southeys. But that overture had failed; now his writing came first.

While in Bristol, Coleridge dropped off some poems with Humphry Davy, who generously agreed to correct proofs and supervise the local printing of the second edition of *Lyrical Ballads*. On hearing Coleridge's relocation plans, Davy reacted: "He has done wrong, I think, in removing so far from his other friends, and giving himself wholly to Wordsworth; it is wrong on his own account, and more so on his wife's, who is now at an unreachable distance from all her sisters" (Cornwell, 1973, p. 283). And not Davy alone, but most everyone, sensed something bizarre about Coleridge's attraction to Wordsworth.

By July the Coleridges were installed in Greta Hall, their new home in Keswick. Delighted with the panoramic view from his study, Coleridge could already feel his poetic juices stirring. "Looking slant," he wrote in a letter,

> direct over the feather of this infamous pen, I see the setting sun—my God! what a scene—! Right before me is a great *camp* of single mountains—each in shape resembles a giant's tent—and to the left . . . is the lake of Keswick, with its islands and white sails and glossy lights of evening—*crowned* with green meadows, but the three remaining sides are encircled by the most fantastic mountains, that ever earthquakes made in sport; as fantastic, as if nature had *laughed* herself into the convulsion, in which they were made.—Close behind me at the foot of Skiddaw flows the Greta, I hear its murmuring distinctly—then it curves round almost in a semicircle, and is now catching the purple lights of the scattered clouds above it. . . . [CL I, p. 614]

The letter ended: "My wife will not let me stay on. . . . I must go, and unpack a trunk for her—she cannot *stoop* to it—thanks to my late essay on population!" (CL I, p. 616). After helping Sarah, eight months pregnant, to unpack, Coleridge left the rest of settling-in to her, in order to dedicate his energies to the painstaking mechanical work of readying *Lyrical Ballads* for the press.

In view of the fact that it offered no chance for him to improve his shaky finances, Coleridge's devotion to the tedious and time-consuming publication process amazed his friends and distressed Sarah. If the entire proceeds of the first edition had gone to William, the same applied to the second. And in spite of the Wedgwood annuity and the lucrative stint with the *Post*, the Coleridges were again in debt as a result of their heavy moving expenses.

Nor would the second edition advance Coleridge's literary reputation. *Lyrical Ballads* would no longer be anonymous. William Wordsworth would be listed as sole author and in his introduction would graciously thank his anonymous friend for contributing the small handful of poems that were not his.

Quick to defend this one-sided arrangement, Coleridge could argue that he did not deserve to share the limelight. The vast majority of new poems were William's—he had been composing steadily and had maintained a creative rhythm. It had been two years since Coleridge had written a major poem, and he was rusty. But if he could regain his creative momentum by reconnecting with William, Coleridge reasoned, that would be payment enough for undertaking the scut work of publication.

Apart from *Kubla Khan*, which was being withheld, Coleridge had but one major poem to contribute, and that poem, *Christabel*, was far from finished. Only the first book was written, and to publish it as it stood would be to present his readers a cliff-hanger, a mere fragment of the tale. But now that he and William were back in harness, he felt it would be no time at all before he would regain his momentum, polish off that ballad, and move on to bigger fish.

And so Coleridge was willing to undertake the massive amount of work required in preparing the two volumes for press: each poem had to be transcribed by hand in legible fair copy and sent by mail coach to the Bristol printer, hundreds of miles away. Any later revision of a word or line required a detailed explanation to insure that the printer understood the corrections. Afterward, the printer's proofs had to be checked and the galleys returned with fresh corrections.

The bulk of the tedious work of transcription fell to Coleridge and Dorothy. Most of the poems were William's, and he was busy revising and adding finishing touches. At Wordsworth's suggestion, Coleridge made major revisions in the *Mariner*, modernizing the diction. By mid-July he sent a revised table of contents for the first volume to the printer. The new format revealed that the *Mariner* was no longer the lead poem. If Coleridge felt hurt about giving up his place of honor, he did not let it show. His collaboration with William proceeded smoothly all through the summer.

Although they lived thirteen miles apart, they were usually together, staying in each other's homes for days at a time to facilitate their work. During their free moments, they discussed poetry. They incorporated one another's ideas into their revisions and gradually hit upon a plan to write a long preface for *Lyrical Ballads*, stating their views on poetry. While that forty-page introduction was eventually written by Wordsworth alone, it included Coleridge's views. In fact Wordsworth wrote that "our opinions on the subject of poetry almost entirely coincide" (Roper, 1940, p. 18), and Coleridge agreed that the preface was "half a child of my own brain" (CL II, p. 830).

But if the ideas came from both men, the writing bore the stamp of Wordsworth's personality. Although his preface made many positive assertions about the widening scope of poetic language and subject matter, there also was a defensive tone that reflected William's dread of criticism. Sometimes he pedantically talked down to the reader, informing him exactly how the poems ought to be read. While some of the generally critical response to the long preface was of course aimed at the unconventional views on poetry it presented, part of the negative reception was surely engendered by Wordsworth's occasional tone of self-protective arrogance.

And while Coleridge claimed the preface contained their joint opinions, there were parts he apparently never read until the book was published. Most notable was a long passage on the *Mariner*. Wordsworth wrote:

> I cannot refuse myself the gratification of informing such readers as may have been pleased with this poem, or with any part of it, that they owe their pleasure in some sort to me; as the author was himself very desirous that it should be suppressed. This wish had arisen from a consciousness of the defects of the poem, and from a knowledge that many persons had been much displeased

with it. The poem of my friend has indeed great defects; first, that the principal person has no distinct character, either in his profession of mariner, or as a human being who having been long under the control of supernatural impressions might be supposed himself to partake of something supernatural: secondly, that he does not act, but is continually acted upon: thirdly, that the events having no necessary connection do not produce each other; and lastly, that the imagery is somewhat too laboriously accumulated. Yet the poem contains many delicate touches of passion, and indeed the passion is everywhere true to nature; a great number of the stanzas present beautiful images and are expressed with unusual felicity of language; and the versification, though the metre is itself unfit for long poems, is harmonious and artfully varied, exhibiting the utmost powers of that metre, and every variety of which it is capable. It therefore appeared to me that these several merits (the first of which, namely that of passion, is of the highest kind,) gave to the poem a value which is not often possessed by better poems. On this account I requested of my friend to permit me to republish it. [CL I, p. 602]

Coleridge's reaction to Wordsworth's discussion is unknown; but Lamb's response was as follows: "I am hurt and vexed that you should think it necessary with a prose apology to open the eyes of dead men that cannot see" (Roper, 1940, p. 337). Touchy to the point of defensiveness, Wordsworth would quibble with Lamb's objections, but would in later editions remove much of his insulting apology for Coleridge's poem.

Coleridge was not at Wordsworth's house when William sent the *Mariner* passage off to the printer that fall. He remained at Keswick because his infant son was seriously ill. On the fourteenth of September Sarah gave birth to a boy they named Derwent, after the river that flowed into the Greta, which in turn flowed by their house. The choice of this name was highly sentimental, as the Derwent was the river of William's childhood. Wordsworth wrote of its gurgling sounds as his earliest memory from infancy, and Coleridge's naming of his son was his way of honoring William. Moreover, Coleridge's idealization of William was so intense during this period that, shortly before Derwent's birth, Coleridge wrote a friend, inviting him to visit the Lakes: "But here you will meet too with Wordsworth 'the latch of whose shoe I am unworthy to unloose" (CL I, p. 620).

But if he was metaphorically groveling at William's iambic feet, Coleridge was nonetheless trying to get back on his own feet as a poet. As repayment for Coleridge's help with the second edition of *Lyrical Ballads*, Wordsworth had agreed to end the second volume with *Christabel*. Coleridge was struggling to finish that poem in order to meet the printer's deadline. William had already written a generous introduction:

> For the sake of variety and from consciousness of my own weakness I have again requested the assistance of a friend who contributed largely to the first volume, and who has now furnished me with the long and beautiful Poem of Christabel, without which I should not yet have ventured to present a second volume to the public. [CL I, p. 631]

The first book of *Christabel* had already gone off to the printer, and William was waiting to hear the second part as soon as it was finished.

Always a sentimental symbolizer—in life as well as art—Coleridge arranged to read his final version to William on the fourth of October: *Lyrical Ballads'* original publication date as well as the marker of Coleridge's wedding anniversary, his brother Frank's departure, and his father's death. Coleridge's diaries and letters present no record of his activities on the day before his visit to Wordsworth. Presumably he was hard at work finishing *Christabel*. However, through Dorothy's diary we have an unusually vivid glimpse of William's activities and thoughts on that day and, given the events that followed, the details are worth reviewing.

The third was a Friday. It was raining when William arose, just as it had the day before. After lunch, by which time the rain had stopped, William walked to Ambleside, a small village three miles from Grasmere. Dorothy accompanied him part of the way, and they talked about his preface for *Lyrical Ballads*. She then made her way back to Dove Cottage on her own.

While William was gone she read in the newspaper that Joseph Cottle's brother Amos had just died. She thought of going out to meet William and tell him the news but decided to wait until he got home. It had begun to drizzle and her teeth ached.

It was late when William returned, although it was still light out. No doubt upset by their discussion of Cottle's brother's death, William and Dorothy decided to go for another walk. At some point along their way, they were struck by the strange sight of an old man, bent over double and walking with the aid of a stick. He had a nightcap on his head, a coat draped over his shoulders, and an apron over his clothes. His face struck Dorothy as interesting. Although his dark eyes and long nose made him look Jewish, he told Dorothy that he was of Scottish parents but born abroad, where his father had served as a soldier.

William found something moving about the bizarre-looking old man. Although his physical deformities gave the impression of one who had been crushed by life, he retained his dignity and neither pitied himself nor appeared defeated. He matter-of-factly told William that he had been married but his wife was now dead. Their ten children had also preceded him, save one, a sailor with whom he had long since lost touch.

Continuing his narrative with equanimity, the old man explained his crippled posture by describing for William how he had been run over by a cart. His leg had been broken and his skull fractured. Though badly mangled, he had been knocked unconscious at the moment of impact and thereby spared the pain and terror of witnessing his mutilation.

He earned his livelihood by collecting leeches, which he sold for medicinal purposes. However, he stoically added, the leech population in the Lakes had been decreasing for quite some time, and it was becoming harder and harder to make ends meet. Sometimes he was forced to support himself by begging or by selling odds and ends.

What impressed William most about the leech gatherer was the self-respect with which he told his story. Although William might have wished to hear more of the old man's tale, night was falling fast. Bidding the stranger good-bye, William and Dorothy made their way home in the dark.

Memories and after-impressions of that incident lingered with William long after the old man had disappeared into the Cumberland night. Here was a man who had nothing, yet could be at peace with himself. Mulling over their chance encounter, William wondered if it had been an uncanny omen. Like Coleridge, William firmly believed in the mysterious and placed great faith in omens and signs. Had this one been intended for him?

William had been brooding about *Lyrical Ballads* that day. One concern that was becoming increasingly irksome to William was his fear of publishing alone. He had written about it in his new preface for all the world to see. William had said that he would not have ventured to publish a second volume without that poem from his anonymous friend, and he meant just that.

Given what the anxiety of poetic composition was like for Wordsworth, his aversion to solo publication was not surprising:

> I have now been more than a fortnight at home, but the uneasiness in my chest has made me beat off the time when the pen was to be taken up. I do not know from what cause it is, but during the last three years I have never had a pen in my hand for five minutes, before my whole frame becomes one bundle of uneasiness, a perspiration starts out all over me, and my chest is oppressed in a manner which I cannot describe. This is a sad weakness, for I am sure, though, it is chiefly owing to the state of my body, that by exertion of mind I might in part control it. ... the extent to which it exists nobody can well conceive. ...
> [LWDW I, p. 407]

Like a man with a phobia asking a friend to accompany him along a dreaded byway, William had been deeply grateful for Coleridge's collaboration on the original publication of *Lyrical Ballads*. But if the prospect of publishing alone made William uneasy, he also had little patience for such weaknesses in himself.

From earliest childhood William had prided himself on his own independence, and much of his poetry reflects that preoccupation. Just as Coleridge cultivated a supremely casual air of genius to deny his insecurities over his intellectual limitations, so Wordsworth made it a point of honor to assume a posture of fierce self-sufficiency. Having experienced severe dislocations early in life, William devoted his energies to reassuring himself that he needed no one. He would rely, William believed, on Nature. (Presumably, Dorothy's doting presence was dismissed as her reliance upon him.)

But his dependence on Coleridge was a different matter, and not so easily rationalized. Coleridge's poems had been like talismans for Wordsworth. He had needed the *Mariner* in order to muster the courage to publish what he now privately believed to be *his own* first volume of poems; moreover, he was beset by that need all over again. And William, it seemed, did not like his irrational feelings of childishly superstitious dependency.

Stewing and mulling over *Lyrical Ballads*, then learning about Cottle's brother, and finally witnessing the eerie spectacle of the solitary leech gatherer emerging from the twilight and then fading into the night was an uncanny concatenation of events, by William's way of thinking. Taking the chance meeting with the old man as a mystical sign, William described what that encounter signified to him in his poem *Resolution and Independence*. His title tells the story in a nutshell—he had made up his mind that the time had come to go it alone. Such a move necessitated shedding his emotional dependence on Coleridge, a step William felt ready to take now that he had been given guidance in the form of an omen:

And the whole body of the Man did seem
Like one whom I had met with in a dream;
Or like a man from some far region sent,
To give me human strength, by apt admonishment.
                              [Moorman, 1957, p. 451]

His courage braced, Wordsworth was all business when he met with Coleridge on the next day, the fourth of October, to discuss *Lyrical Ballads*. Coleridge arrived at Dove Cottage with his completed draft of *Christabel*, and William was tactful enough to have Coleridge read it twice before informing him that although he liked it, he had decided not to include it in *Lyrical Ballads*. The next day, William wrote to inform the Bristol printer of his decision. Instructing the printer to kill whatever portions of the poem were already set, he announced his willingness to personally absorb the expense.

That same day Coleridge wrote a friend:

> If I know my own heart, or rather if I be not profoundly ignorant of it, I have not a spark of ambition; and tho' my vanity is flattered, more than it ought to be, by what Dr. Johnson calls 'colloquial prowess,' yet it leaves me in my study. This is no virtue in me, but depends on the accidental constitution of my intellect—in which my taste in judging is far, far more perfect than my power to execute. And I do nothing, but almost instantly its defects and sillinesses come upon my mind, and haunt me, till I am completely disgusted with my performance, and wish myself a tanner, or a printer, or anything but an author. [CL I, p. 628]

Two days later, Coleridge wrote to Davy explaining the decision to kill *Christabel:*

> The Christabel was running up to 1300 lines—and was so much admired by Wordsworth, that he thought it indelicate to print two volumes with *his name* in which so much of another man's was included—and which was of more consequence—the poem was in direct opposition to the very purpose for which Lyrical Ballads were published—viz—an experiment to see how far those passions, which alone give any value to extraordinary incidents, were capable of interesting, in and for themselves, in the incidents of common life. [CL I, p. 631]

Although Coleridge tried to sound as if he were taking the decision in stride, his pride had been deeply wounded. *Christabel* was in fact only 677 lines long. By exaggerating its length, Coleridge was trying to save face by making Wordsworth's decision sound objectively merited. Moreover, his own view of the artistic merits of his poem had been badly shaken. His note continued:

> I assure you, I think very differently of CHRISTABEL—I would rather have written Ruth or Nature's Lady [poems by Wordsworth] than a million such poems but why do I calumniate my own spirit by saying, *I* would rather—God knows—it is as delightful to me that they are written. I *know* that at present (and I *hope*, that it *will* be so,) my mind has disciplined itself into a willing exertion of its powers, without any reference to its *comparative* value. [CL I, p. 632]

He *had* accomplished his original purpose. By completing the second book of *Christabel*, he regained his creative momentum and proved he had both the imagination and the self-discipline to write poetry. But a fatal note of self-pity had begun to creep in. Like Christ and Abel—whose names lay buried in his poem's title—Coleridge was beginning to feel more and more the sacrificial victim. His letter to Davy ended with a description of the river Greta, whose murmur had previously soothed him so:

> By the by, Greta, or rather Grieta, is exactly the cocytus of the Greeks—the word literally rendered in modern English is 'The loud lamenter'—to griet in the Cumbrian dialect signifying to roar aloud for grief or pain—: and it does *roar* with a vengeance! [CL I, p. 632]

But far more distressing than Coleridge's imagery of grief, pain, and lamentation—all suggesting his wounded feelings—was the sorrier fact that the Greta's soft sounds now roared in his ears. Coleridge's perceptual distortion suggests that, having reached for the laudanum bottle to ease his pain, he was now experiencing the hypersensitivity to sound that opium in heavy doses produces.

Two days later, Coleridge wrote Poole. Attempting to get a grip on his feelings and too chagrined to admit the folly of his move to the Lakes to the friend who had counseled against it most vehemently, Coleridge kept up his pretense that *Christabel* had been rejected for its length. To paint an even more convincing case, he tacked another one hundred imaginary lines to his poem. Now it was a leviathan of some fourteen hundred lines. And to minimize Poole's impression of his emotional dependence on William, Coleridge casually mentioned that he saw Wordsworth no more than once a month, maybe every three weeks at most.

Too mortified to admit as much to Poole, Coleridge had begun to regret his move. He wrote Josiah Wedgwood:

> My situation here is indeed a delightful situation; but I feel what I have lost—feel it deeply—it recurs more often and more painfully, than I anticipated—indeed, so much so that I scarcely ever feel myself impelled, that is to say, *pleasurably* impelled to write to Poole. I used to feel myself more at home in his great windy

parlour, than in my own cottage. We were well suited for each other. . . . indeed, my dear Sir, with tears in my eyes, and with all my heart and soul I wish it were as easy for us all to meet. . . . Yet when I revise the step, I have taken, I know not how I could have acted otherwise than I did act. [CL I, p. 643]

By the time Coleridge could openly "grief" and roar aloud to Poole, three more months had passed. And by then he was so heavily addicted to narcotics that the few hundred miles that separated him from Poole seemed an eternity's voyage rather than a short coach ride away, as he blinked and peered through the hazy fog that opium created in his mind. Bewildered and helpless, he wrote Poole:

O my dear Friend! that you were with me by the fireside of my study here, that I might talk it over with you to the tune of this night wind that pipes its thin doleful climbing sinking notes like a child that has lost its way and is crying aloud, half in grief and half in hope to be heard by its mother. [CL II, p. 669]

In the course of four months—from October 1800 to February 1801—Coleridge had gone from casual opium use to the downward spiral of addiction. His cry for help was too late.

He had been unable to share his misery with Poole and seek his advice earlier because he had been unable to admit his dilemma to himself. He had rationalized his emotions to the point of denying any feelings of resentment or betrayal toward Wordsworth over his unilateral decision to cancel *Christabel*. In a letter to Longman, the publisher of *Lyrical Ballads*, Coleridge wrote as follows: "I am especially pleased that I have contributed nothing to the second volume, as I can now exert myself loudly and everywhere in their favor without suspicion of self-interest or vanity" (CL I, p. 654). Not allowing himself to suspect any selfish motive on William's part, Coleridge accepted his friend's decision as an impartial artistic judgment and a marketing strategy. But at the same time, he fatally misinterpreted William's rejection as an accurate reflection of their comparative talents. As Coleridge put it, "he is a great, a true poet—I am only a kind of metaphysician" (CL I, p. 658).

By the end of October Coleridge had developed a full-blown case of writer's block. A journal entry read: "He knew not what to do—something, he felt, must be done—he rose, drew his writing-desk suddenly before him—sat down, took the pen—and found that he knew not what to do" (CNB 834). Coleridge was bewildered by his artistic block—everything had suddenly gone haywire in a mysterious fashion he was at a loss to explain.

Unless, that is, he was afflicted by some undiagnosed malady:

> My sickness has left me in a state of mind, which it is scarcely possible for me to explain to you—one feature of it is an extreme disgust which I feel at every perusal of my own productions, and which makes it exceedingly painful to me not only to revise them, but I may truly add, even to look on the paper, on which they were written. [CL II, p. 715]

Given the fact that his writer's block consisted of physical sensations—waves of nausea when looking at the pages of his manuscripts—it is easy to see how he believed his problem to be organic. He spoke of the "crazy machine" of his body and mind (CL I, p. 650).

But Coleridge's hypothesis failed to explain the strange fact that while his own pages swam before his eyes, provoking violent waves of disgust, the printer's proofs of Wordsworth's poems did not have the same effect. Or, if they did, he was nonetheless able to carry on fitfully and proofread the galleys. For in spite of his disabling symptom, Coleridge continued to work on getting William's two volumes into final shape.

Nothing if not a gentleman, Coleridge was determined to rise above any petty feelings of hurt. Nursing his grievances with a laudanum bottle, Coleridge did not let such minor resentments interfere with the task at hand. Goggling over those final printer's proofs to the point of strain, Coleridge's eyes became inflamed and bloodshot. He described his condition: "If you are writing any poems and want a lively idea of murder personified, it is a pity you cannot see *me*—: for I have two blood red eyes that would do credit to massacre itself" (CL I, p. 656). Describing the extent to which his creative talents had been massacred—either by his own or by another's hand—he wrote: "As to poetry, I have altogether abandoned it, being convinced that I never had the essentials of poetic genius and that I mistook a strong desire for original power" (CL I, p. 656).

But while Coleridge could hint indirectly at his feelings of having been massacred as an explanation of his abandoning poetry, he could not make the connection straightforwardly. Psychologically, he was shutting his eyes to the situation. And in doing so, he was inflicting the age-old punishment that Oedipus exacted upon himself. He was blinding himself —metaphorically and psychosomatically.

With his eyes painful and bloodshot, unable to write poetry, Coleridge retreated to his bedroom-study with his opium, candles, and books of philosophy. Instead of facing his conflict, he chased beautiful spectra in the deluded belief that he had found the ultimate answer to the mysteries of life. By the time he could open his eyes to the reality of what he had done, it was too late. By the time his beautiful visions had degenerated into horse manure he was already fully addicted.

The first nightmare came swiftly. It happened while he was staying at Dove Cottage, working on the printer's proofs. Ironically, it was Wordsworth who awoke to Coleridge's shrieks of terror. The other people in the house that night were Dorothy Wordsworth and Sara Hutchinson, who had arrived two weeks earlier. Coleridge had not seen her in a year. His journal read:

> Friday night, Nov. 28, 1800, or rather Saturday morning—a most frightful dream of a woman whose features were blended with darkness catching hold of my right eye and attempting to pull it out—I caught hold of her arm fast—a horrid feel—Wordsworth cried out aloud to me hearing my scream—heard his cry and thought it cruel he did not come, but did not wake till his cry was repeated a third time—the woman's name Ebon Ebon Thalud—When I awoke my right eyelid swelled. . . . [CNB 848]

The woman's name was the name of an apothecary in the *Arabian Nights*. And apart from the classic interpretation of the universal symbolism of this dream, as denoting castration, the dream language expressed two other ominous thoughts. Coleridge's dream seemed to be warning him that he was now in the grip of drugs and that a strange woman had caught his eye.

Chapter 11

Wedding Bells

> *Sly Beelzebub took all occasions*
> *To try Job's constancy & patience.*
> *He took his Honor, took his Health,*
> *He took his Children, took his Wealth,*
> *His Servants, Horses, Oxen, Cows—*
> *And the sly Devil did not take his spouse.*
>
> *But Heaven, that brings out good from evil*
> *And loves to disappoint the Devil,*
> *Had predetermin'd to restore*
> *Twofold all he had before,*
> *His servants, Horses, Oxen, Cows—*
> *Short-sighted Devil! not to take his Spouse.*
>
> —STC in the *Morning Post*, September 26, 1801
> [CNB 625]

Two years later, on October 4, 1802, William Wordsworth and Mary Hutchinson were wed in a small Yorkshire church. William's marriage was a fresh start for the thirty-two-year-old poet. It had taken him seven years to get over his affair with Annette Vallon. In fact, just before his wedding, Wordsworth went to France to see his former mistress and their daughter, both to clear his conscience and to assure himself that they held no claims upon him that could spoil his wedding plans.

There were other considerations that kept William from marrying until now. Scrimping and sacrificing, he had devoted himself to his poetry with single-minded tenacity. It had taken him five years to write the current edition of *Lyrical Ballads*, which, though by no means a bestseller, had finally begun to provide a modest cash flow which William intended to supplement with the income from his forty-three hundred pounds capital.*

---

*The approximate purchasing power of $150,000 in 1980, which, if invested conservatively at 9 percent, would have yielded approximately 400 pounds

William's lack of confidence as a poet had been as important as his tenuous financial situation in preventing him from marrying till now. Publishing *Lyrical Ballads* under his own name had been an important step toward establishing himself as a writer and providing him the sense of professional security he needed in order to support a family.

As cautious in matters emotional as in arrangements financial, Wordsworth was being anything but impulsive in his choice of a wife. He was marrying a woman he had known almost his entire life. Deep roots and a shared heritage made this a match well-designed for raising a family.

Like Dorothy, who was too choked with emotion to attend the ceremony, Coleridge did not make it to William's wedding. Instead, he was home at Keswick on Wordsworth's wedding day. Although it was also the Coleridges' seventh wedding anniversary, they were not celebrating this year. Nor had they the year before, when Coleridge first began to realize that he no longer loved Sarah.

In fact, there were times when Coleridge now wondered if he had ever loved her. At this point in his life he believed himself in love with another woman. And that woman, Sara Hutchinson, was in Yorkshire celebrating her sister's wedding.

From Coleridge's point of view, his was a hopeless love. He considered his marriage vow a holy bond which left divorce out of the question, and extramarital affairs ran counter to his moral principles. Depressed and at a dead end, he saw himself doomed to a lifetime of unhappiness.

To commemorate his good friend William's marriage, Coleridge had made special arrangements to publish a poem in the *Post* on Wordsworth's wedding day. His poem, *Dejection: An Ode*, was in this early version addressed to Wordsworth and expressed the significance of the occasion for each of them. Using the backdrop of a March landscape, the poem contrasts their responses to that scene in order to depict very different states of mind.

a year, the 1980 equivalent of $13,500. According to Davies (1980), by July 1802 William and Dorothy learned the Lowther debt was finally settled and their share would be 3000 pounds. Also according to Davies, Mary Hutchinson came with a dowry of 400 pounds.

Coleridge, the ostensible speaker in the poem, is unable to respond emotionally to the physical changes of spring about to erupt. Looking at the lifeless land, he senses the silent forces of revitalization already at work. But he finds no joy in that knowledge. Deaf to the faint murmurs of seasonal rebirth, all he hears is the howl of the March wind piping its doleful tune across the wasteland.

Out of harmony with the processes of renewal taking place—both the rebirth of the landscape in the poem and the real-life wedding ceremony the poem commemorates—Coleridge describes the depression that is blocking his emotional responsiveness:

> A grief without a pang, void, dark, and drear,
> A stifled, drowsy, unimpassion'd grief,
> Which finds no natural outlet, no relief,
> In word, or sigh, or tear. . . . [PW, p. 1077]

The poem goes on to contrast Coleridge's morbidity with Wordsworth's "gay, fancy, cheerful eyes" and "lofty song" of joy. And with remarkable generosity of spirit for a depressed man who claimed to have just lost his own creative abilities, Coleridge ends the *Morning Post* version of his poem:

> O lofty Poet, full of life and love,
> Brother and Friend of my devoutest choice,
> Thus may'st thou ever, evermore rejoice! [PW, p. 1081]

The poem had been started six months earlier, on the occasion of William's consolidation of his plans and the setting of a date for his wedding. As Wordsworth well knew, he was choosing a date filled with meaning for Coleridge. That day marked the occasion of his having merged his love with Sarah's and his talents with William's. It marked also the loss of Coleridge's father and brother, and was a painful reminder of that more recent occasion when William had informed him that *Christabel* would not appear in the new edition of *Lyrical Ballads*.

By the time of Wordsworth's wedding, it seemed as if all of Coleridge's dreams had turned sour. While William was flourishing—marrying, starting a family, and writing great poetry—Coleridge was addicted to opium, unhappily married, unable to write, and in love with a woman he could never allow himself to have.

Or so it appeared to Coleridge. But he was in the middle of a depression, and melancholia is notorious for playing tricks with the mind. It twists events and mangles memories till they bear but the remotest of resemblance to objective fact. Psychic pain does not remain localized; the part infects the whole.

While there is no doubt Coleridge was morbidly dejected, there is a question about how literally his account of his misfortunes should be taken. Some claims were patent exaggerations. How, for instance, could he believe his poetic abilities had deserted him entirely when the very instrument for stating that belief was one of the finest poems Coleridge had ever written?

As often happens in cases of melancholia, self-pity had eroded his thought processes. Not only was he exaggerating his loss of creative power, he was also distorting his memory of the chain of events that led to his depression. With a flair for tragic self-dramatization and a knack for oversimplifying, Coleridge had come to the conclusion that he was depressed because he was unhappily married. Overlooking any role that his recent disappointments with Wordsworth might have played, he blamed his wife entirely and bent over backward to deny his feelings of hurt and betrayal where Wordsworth was concerned.

Through the process of retrospective falsification he was rearranging his sense of the past. Never had he loved Sarah Fricker. Forced to marry her by Southey, he had acted against his will and better judgment. As Coleridge now saw things, it had been love at first sight with Sara Hutchinson, the one and only true love of his life. Thus the explanation of his misery was simple: he was depressed because he could not have Sara.*

In fact, Coleridge eventually rewrote the chain of events leading up to the onset of his depression and the start of his addiction to suit his rationalization. In a maudlin diary entry written in 1803—four years after he first met Sara—Coleridge recorded one of their earliest encounters:

---

*Although Coleridge spelled his wife's first name both with and without an *h*, for purposes of this narrative Sarah will always refer to Sarah Coleridge and Sara to Sara Hutchinson.

November 24th—the Sunday—conundrums and puns and stories and laughter—with Jack Hutchinson. Stood up round the fire, and pressed Sara's hand a long time behind her back and then, for the first time, love pricked me with its light arrow, poisoned alas! and hopeless. . . . [CNB 1575]

In another entry written during that period of historical revision four years later, Coleridge took pains to reassure himself that he was unaware of Wordsworth's attachment to Mary.

But Coleridge's 1799 diary tells a different tale. Slim, fair, graceful Mary Hutchinson is the only woman he comments on. No notice is taken of short, plump, plain Sara Hutchinson in either the October or the November entries during his Sockburn visits.

If he was smitten, his journals reflect not even a superficial laceration from cupid's arrow—much less a serious wound. In the hilarity of his enthusiasm over being reunited with William, Coleridge may well have flirted with both sisters in an unnoteworthy fashion. But his playacting at romantic conquest was designed to cement his bond with William by making him partner to the innocent fun.

By half-comically focusing his coy attentions on the sisters of the moment, Coleridge had reestablished his tie with his closest male friend of the moment. He had done the same with Southey much earlier in Bristol. In fact, even as far back as his Christ's Hospital days with Bob Allen and the Evans sisters, he had been partial to this quadrangular pattern of brotherly conquests.

But as Coleridge once put it, "love is a local anguish" (CL I, p. 285). A year passed after his Sockburn departure before he encountered Sara again. During that period he neither wrote to her nor mooned over her, as a love-struck man might be expected to do.

They next crossed paths in the winter of 1800–1801, when Sara was a houseguest at Dove Cottage for four months. Almost all of Coleridge's encounters with Sara took place in his wife's presence, sometimes in fact in the Coleridges' home. Known for her hot temper, Sarah Coleridge would not have permitted, much less welcomed, Sara Hutchinson into Greta Hall if she sensed any philandering or even a hint that her domestic security was being threatened.

But as Sarah Coleridge already knew, much to her regret, and as Sara Hutchinson was about to discover, much to her dismay, Coleridge was a changed man by then. He was preoccupied that he was about to be struck by death's dart, not by love's arrow.

The change in his appearance and demeanor since their Sockburn meeting was dramatic. While there were still a few glittering moments of gaiety and charm, the old Coleridge panache was a thing of the past. Terrified that his mind and body had become a "crazy machine" (CL I, p. 650), Coleridge was depressed; he suffered writer's block and was well on his way to opium addiction.

And while an oppressive mood of apprehension hung over the Coleridge household, husband and wife had not yet declared war on each other in November 1800. Anxious over her husband's health—which had taken a mystifying turn for the worse since the fourth of October—Sarah Coleridge was nursing him as best she could while also tending to her infant son.

Disabled by periodic bouts of arthritis, Coleridge had taken to his bed for long stretches of time. Kept awake nightly by pain and by the gnawing fear that he would die in his sleep like his father before him, he read philosophy long into the night. But while Sarah worried, she was also relieved that sometimes he was restored to health, as if by a miracle. During these dramatic recoveries, he felt well enough to trek the thirteen miles to Dove Cottage, where he devoted his energies to readying *Lyrical Ballads* for the printer.

Seeking an explanation for his cyclic illness, neither Coleridge nor Sarah considered the possibility that his trips to Grasmere lay at the root, that each fresh encounter with William triggered the next wave of misery, arthritis, and self-doubt. Nevertheless, Coleridge had just begun to make what would become his often repeated comparison between his blood-red eyes and the thought of murder, claiming that he "might as well write blindfold" (CL I, p. 647).

The baffling periodicity of his illness made Coleridge wonder if he was suffering from gout—the disease which, he believed, killed his father. Or maybe it was the damp Lake District climate. But at the time of Sara Hutchinson's arrival, he had not yet produced his fatal hypothesis that his mental and physical anguish were largely the result of his unhappy marriage.

And it was Psyche, not Cupid, who first hinted that Sara Hutchinson posed the threat of romantic entanglement. That enigmatically coded warning—unheeded because undeciphered—materialized in Coleridge's sleep on the night of November 28 when, having felt well enough to walk to Dove Cottage to help Dorothy transcribe William's poems for the printer, Coleridge was forced by bad weather to spend the night. It was on that occasion that he awoke the entire household with shrieks of terror as Ebon Ebon Thalud—the exotic female apothecary—snatched at his right eyeball as he lay sleeping.

But if Sara was the strange woman who caught his eye, Coleridge struggled desperately in his dream to resist her grip, suggesting the danger he sensed in such an involvement. Hardly reflecting a case of love at first or even second sight, the nightmare suggests at most that he may have begun to notice Sara. The fact that a nightmare resulted indicates that his alarm system had gone off, alerting him to the twin dangers of opium and exotic women.

Moreover, Coleridge's letters and diaries at the time do not reflect that he was in love with Sara during that winter, or that he was plunging headlong in that direction. The only three diary entries in which she is even mentioned reveal a joke Coleridge told her, an occasion on which he read aloud, and his dictation of a long alphabetical list of five hundred English plants to her from a botanical encyclopedia—all probably taking place in his wife's presence during the extended back-and-forth visits between the two families around the Christmas holidays.

What Coleridge's letters and diaries *do* reflect is that his major preoccupation that winter was "health, hope and a steady mind ... the 3 clauses of my hourly prayer" (CL II, p. 709). But unfortunately, none of his prayers were answered that Christmas.

The holidays found the entire Coleridge family at Dove Cottage. Sarah and the children arrived a few days early while Coleridge remained at home catching up on some last-minute correspondence. Having just seen *Lyrical Ballads* through the press, he described his "delight" in having contributed nothing to the second volume so that his praise and promotion could not be misconstrued as self-interest—an ugly word in his vocabulary. Then he dashed off Christmas greetings to two other friends, describing his massacred eyes and his decision to abandon poetry.

He was feeling none too well by the time he arrived at Dove Cottage. Seized by a painful attack of arthritis on the walk over, he immediately took to a sickbed, where he remained flat on his back for the entire visit. After the New Year, he had to be carried home in a chaise.

If any of his symptoms were in part psychosomatically induced by his conflicted feelings toward Wordsworth, Coleridge kept it well hidden from himself and from William. January of 1801 brought the publication of *Lyrical Ballads*, a worsening of his depression, and a deeper retreat into opium and philosophy. While filled with physical nausea when he attempted his own writing, he was nonetheless able to compose a series of promotional letters for *Lyrical Ballads*, designed to boost the book's sales.

Meanwhile, Sarah Coleridge responded with less and less sympathy to her bedridden husband's growing list of infirmities. She was confronted daily with the dire consequences of Coleridge's illness. Behind on the rent and overdrawn on the Wedgwood annuity, they were in debt to Poole, Lamb, Stuart, Wordsworth, and the Keswick merchants.

Furthermore, they were confronted daily with signs that they were living in financially troubled times. Vagabonds begged at their door with increasing insistence, while the newspapers described the economic unrest pervading the country. The war was dragging on with no end in sight, as the new century was being ushered in by that familiar guerdon of economic progress known in modern industrial society as combined inflation and recession.

Led by a Prime Minister whose hands had begun to tremble with the palsy of chronic alcoholism, and who was being lampooned in the broadsides of the day as seeing double on his way to the House of Commons, England was becoming the greatest imperial power since Rome. Soon, nearly one million of her men would be at war. While Coleridge continued to gulp down his laudanum, Pitt slugged huge quantities of port to steady his nerves. But fortunately for England, Pitt held his port better than Coleridge his opium. Nonetheless, out of nine and a half million people in that country, a full million and a half were paupers. And Coleridge was beginning to worry that he was on his way to being one of them. "But my country is my country; and I will never leave it, till I am starved out of it" (CL II, p. 711), he wrote Poole.

The final straw was a dunning letter from a London attorney threatening a lawsuit if Coleridge did not immediately return a publisher's advance for a book he had failed to write. A diary note written shortly afterward suggests the impact of that notice on the Coleridge household: "arguing in a circle ... we whirl round and round in perpetual and vertiginous agitation—agitation and vertigo" (CNB, p. 909). But, as Coleridge confided to Poole, he was literally unable to write, in spite of "the gloom and distresses of those around me for whom I aught to be labouring and cannot" (CL II, p. 722).

Blocked as a poet, Coleridge had already declared that he was leaving that field to Wordsworth. Besides, he was now interested in physical science. Asking Davy to ship him equipment for a chemistry laboratory, he had Poole send him optical prisms, while Wordsworth obliged by purchasing a set of botanical microscopes.

Unable to write poetry and deeply ashamed of his shortcomings as husband and provider, Coleridge hoped to conquer those feelings by unlocking the mysteries of the universe. His laboratory investigations would yield ultimate philosophical truths as well as remedies to England's economic problems. At one point he believed he had hit on a foolproof solution to the current food shortages by rotating acorn crops with corn crops.

And when he came down to the breakfast table, bleary-eyed after his nightlong optical experiments, he did little more than engage six-year-old Hartley in deep philosophical discussions. Helpless in the face of his addiction, there was nothing he could say to console Sarah or to defuse her angry frustration—except that he did not expect to live much longer.

By now Sarah's anxieties and criticisms were driving him deeper and deeper into self-pitying hypochondriasis. Convinced that the Lake District climate was fatal to his health, he toyed with the notion of taking a job as slave driver on the West Indian sugar plantation of some wealthy Bristol friends.

Toward the end of February 1801, Sara Hutchinson spent two weeks visiting the Coleridge family at Greta Hall. While the strained silences punctuated by occasional flare-ups between husband and wife were undoubtedly unpleasant, she was not the cause of their friction. She was welcomed by Sarah Coleridge and, judging from Coleridge's correspondence, his mind was on other matters.

Intent on remaining in Josiah Wedgwood's good graces, Coleridge was trying to impress upon his patron the seriousness and importance of his current philosophical investigations. Toward this end, he devoted his scant remaining energies during Sara's stay to the time-consuming task of composing four rambling philosophical letters which stretched on for pages and pages. His letters displayed an erudition sufficient to baffle or intimidate all but the most highly trained philosophical minds. Although Wedgwood found the letters unreadable, the annuity continued. But there is no way of knowing whether it was ever in serious jeopardy or if Sarah Coleridge had simply goaded her husband into writing because of her mounting sense of economic insecurity.

A few weeks after Sara Hutchinson's uneventful departure, William Wordsworth came over to Keswick to see Coleridge. Troubled by reports of his bedridden brother's sagging spirits and desperate finances, William wanted to reassure Coleridge of his willingness to help. Coleridge was on the verge of overthrowing Newton's *Optics* by the time Wordsworth arrived. Worried if not alarmed by what he saw, William returned with Dorothy in April to spend a full week with their friend.

Wordsworth had several long bedside chats with Coleridge. After his first visit, to ease Coleridge's troubled mind, he wrote to the London publisher saying he would assume responsibility for the thirty-pound advance. But apart from the help Wordsworth had come to offer, he was also seeking advice from his friend about a momentous decision he was then contemplating. Judging from a later diary note, Coleridge considered their bedside talk a turning point in his own life as well as Wordsworth's: "O God! if it had been foretold me, when in my bed I—then ill—continued talking with Wordsworth the whole night till the dawn of the day, urging him to conclude on marrying Mary Hutchinson" (CNB 3304).

Since Coleridge recorded his memory of this conversation seven years later, it is not surprising that his biographers are unsure of when the momentous talk took place. Some agree that it occurred during Wordsworth's March or April visit. But others place it later and argue that Wordsworth could not have talked about his marriage plans before because he was not yet in love.

Moorman, Wordsworth's biographer, provides a clue into the curious nature and timing of William and Mary's courtship:

> Throughout the autumn of 1800 and the early spring of 1801 he wrote to her frequently, and with warm affection, often addressing her as 'thou' and calling her 'my dearest Mary.' One might take them for love letters, save that the main subject is William's second edition of *Lyrical Ballads*. [Moorman, 1957, p. 472]

Puzzled by the paradox that William's love letters could have been unromantically filled with his professional preoccupations and literary vanity, Moorman summarizes her careful study of Wordsworth's prenuptial correspondence by concluding that "there can seldom have been a more unobtrusive wooing" (Moorman, 1957, p. 549).

Extremely private if not secretive, Wordsworth was habitually shy and cautious when it came to expressing his feelings or revealing his plans. And while at first glance it appears an odd way for a man to behave with the sweetheart he was thinking of marrying, Mary had known William a long time and could be expected to read between the lines of his notes.

As the publication date approached, Wordsworth thought of little else but his book. And since he saw himself as virtually penniless, Mary understood why their marriage hinged on the success of *Lyrical Ballads*. Sending her news of the book was the same as making wedding plans. Half in prudence, half in superstition, Wordsworth had linked the destiny of his courtship to the fate of his book.

If this interpretation of Wordsworth's courtship seems astonishing, Coleridge's "O God!" note reflects how much he had been taken by surprise on that fateful night when William first told him he was thinking of marrying Mary. But why was Coleridge shocked by the news? His emotional radar was finely tuned to his closest friend's romantic attachments: he had intuitively sensed that tie from the moment he walked in the door at Sockburn, just as he had with Southey on first entering the Fricker home.

But Wordsworth was less candid than Southey, and Coleridge had failed to estimate correctly the depth and seriousness of his attachment to Mary. William had kept his matrimonial designs a well-guarded secret and the news that he had long been thinking of marrying Mary now took Coleridge by complete surprise. But far more important than having received a confidence, Coleridge was suddenly finding that something else was finally beginning to make sense.

As their all-night conversation drew to a close, the sun came up over the Cumbrian mountains. Through his bedroom window he could see the peaks far off in the distance, silhouetted by the day's first rays. On his arrival in the Lakes those peaks had reminded Coleridge of tents sportively pitched by giants. But now that his poetic imagination had fled, he could find only abstract geometrical forms in that view, as the pieces of a baffling puzzle finally came together. At last the basis of his fatal misunderstanding with Wordsworth began to dawn on him.

Originally published on his wedding anniversary, *Lyrical Ballads* had symbolized marriage in Coleridge's mind. Setting aside reputation and pecuniary considerations, he had publicly wedded his talent and imagination with William's back in 1798. But now that *his* book was published, Wordsworth was telling Coleridge that he wished to marry Mary. For the first time he saw how much William had all along been pinning his wedding plans on the second edition of *Lyrical Ballads*.

Now Coleridge sensed their colossal misunderstanding: while he had slaved selflessly over *their* book to maintain his creative marriage with William, Wordsworth had toiled with single-minded energy over *his* book in order to marry Mary. Finally, William's proprietary behavior over *Lyrical Ballads* made sense.

There had been more at stake for Wordsworth than just

a book and a professional friendship. Moreover, until Coleridge's recent setbacks in health and finances, it had been easy for William to justify his point of view. Why not keep the book's original title and reputation and claim the privilege of sole authorship on the title page? After all, he had written most of the poems—killing *Christabel* had been a way of justifying his claims by further emphasizing the imbalance of their contributions.

In William's eyes, Coleridge could easily absorb the minor loss of prestige involved in the unequal liquidation of their professional partnership. Coleridge already had a wife and family, as well as the Wedgwood annuity to support them. Taking the lion's share of *Lyrical Ballads* amounted to little in monetary terms. But then there had been the ticklish question of Coleridge's pride and professional self-confidence.

But that was Coleridge's affair, not William's. And Coleridge never objected or lifted a finger in protest. He never complained that Wordsworth had lured him to the Lakes with the false promise that *their* book's authorship was of no importance at all to him. And while Coleridge was plagued with regrets over his decision to move north after William brusquely canceled *Christabel* and wrote his insulting apology for the *Mariner*, he was too paralyzed by then to alter his plans. But no one had forced him to continue working on the book once he knew where things stood—even if he was blind to the reasons behind William's high-handed behavior.

If Coleridge had behaved generously, he had chosen to do so and Wordsworth was duly grateful. And by the time of their nightlong conversation, neither was in a position to bail out of their friendship, or inclined in that direction.

William worried about Coleridge's deteriorating health, morbid outlook, and financial problems. Grateful for Coleridge's services with the new edition, William would do anything he could to help his friend—lend him money, assume his debts, plead with him to stop the optical experiments that were ruining his health, even urge him to complete and publish *Christabel*. While adamantly opposed to sharing the limelight in *Lyrical Ballads*, Wordsworth was unaware of any conscious desire on his part to stifle or destroy his friend's creativity.

And from where he lay, Coleridge needed all the help he

could get. Feeling weak, sick, and very much alone, he saw his marriage falling apart. Who else was there to rely on? Poole was hundreds of miles away, Southey was in Portugal, and the time had long since passed when he could turn to Ottery for help. Wordsworth was his closest friend and obviously wanted to be of assistance. William was optimistically reassuring him that he would recover from his strange affliction, while he was encouraging William to bolster his courage and take the plunge into matrimony. After all, that was what good friends were for.

Describing their one-week "melancholy visit" (LWDW I, p. 333), Dorothy Wordsworth described how she and William were both so deeply moved that "we both trembled, and till we entered the door durst hardly speak" (LWDW I, p. 333). And as Coleridge soon discovered, their loyalty knew no bounds. Sympathetic to their bedridden friend's plight, they were willing to take his side in all matters, including his domestic affairs. Appalled by Sarah Coleridge's cold-hearted treatment of her stricken husband, Dorothy relayed the sad news:

> Mrs. C. is in excellent health. She is indeed a bad nurse for C. but has several great merits. She is very much to be pitied, for when one party is ill matched the other necessarily must be so too. She would have made a very good wife to many another man, but for Coleridge!! Her radical fault is her want of sensibility and what can such a woman be to Coleridge? [LWDW I, p. 330]

Already alienated from Sarah and wounded by her criticisms, Coleridge divulged his marital problems to William and Dorothy and took comfort in their unswerving loyalty. But the more he turned to them for the sympathy he so sorely craved, the more savage his arguments with Sarah became. Armed with a second opinion, Coleridge now stood up to Sarah and dismissed her lamentations and criticisms by pointing out the "want of sensibility" that his good friend Dorothy had so astutely noted.

Coleridge was correct: in at least one sense, Sarah Coleridge did not understand him. Like Poole, Lamb, Wedgwood, Davy, and Southey, she was mystified by her husband's attachment to William Wordsworth. But unlike the others, Sarah had more at stake and so could not be objective. Robert Southey later gave an analysis of the Wordsworths' role in the Coleridges' problems:

> it is from his idolatry of that family [the Wordsworths] that this has begun,—they have always humored him in his follies,—listened to his complaints of his wife,—and when he has complained of the itch, helped him to scratch, instead of covering him with brimstone ointment, and shutting himself up by himself. Wordsworth and his sister who pride themselves upon having no selfishness, are of all human beings I have ever known the most intensely selfish. The one thing to which W. would sacrifice all others is his reputation, concerning which his anxiety is perfectly childish—like a woman of her beauty; and so he can get Coleridge to talk his own writings over with him, and criticise them and (without amending them) teach him how to do it—to be in fact the very rain and air and sunshine of his intellect, he thinks C. is very well employed and this arrangement a very good one. [CL III, p. 4]

While Southey's pungent description was of a later situation, the drastic polarization began with the Wordsworths' April visit.

After their departure, the widening gulf between Keswick and Grasmere began to loom large in Coleridge's laudanum-soaked consciousness: "Mind, shipwrecked by storms of doubt, now mastless, rudderless, shattered,—pulling in the dead swell of a dark and windless sea" (CNB 932). If life at Keswick was grim and lonely in spite of the children, Grasmere had genially beckoned. But given the strain he had set up between his wife and the Wordsworths, it would now be harder to meld the two worlds. Besides, William would soon marry and they would inevitably grow even further apart.

Unless, that is, something could be done to prevent it. Nothing is impossible in the mind of a man who can solve his nation's food shortages with acorns, who can dismiss Newton's discoveries by the light of his bedside candle. Coleridge began to ponder the situation.

Spring comes late to the Lakes, and Coleridge's health waned and waxed with the weather. Warm days he came to life like a "parlour fly" (CL II, p. 719), while on damp, gray days he took to his bed and sank into morbid fantasies of an early death at the age of twenty-eight. By mid-July, the blue skies of summer having finally arrived, he felt optimistic in spite of his arthritis and set out on the Keswick highway. But instead of heading for Grasmere, he turned toward Yorkshire and the solution to his problem of losing William Wordsworth.

Having told Sarah that he was off to Durham Cathedral library for six weeks to read the theological works of Duns Scotus, Coleridge spent much of his time with Sara and Mary Hutchinson, who lived nearby. He "frolicked in the billows" of the ocean (CL II, p. 751) and delighted over the return of his verse-making facility:

> O ye hopes, that stir within me,
> Health comes with you from above;
> God is with me, God is in me,
> I cannot die, if Life be Love! [CL II, p. 752]

Composing whimsical doggerel for the sisters and bantering back and forth flirtatiously, it felt great to be alive.

Coleridge's gaiety crashed to a halt upon his return home that September. Filled with nostalgic yearnings for Sara Hutchinson, he contemplated his wife with scorn. Barely able to abide her shortcomings, he catalogued them at great length in his diary, where he also began to doodle "W.W. M.H. D.W. S.H." (CNB 980). Soon his STC monogram would be added but his blueprint for happiness was: "Wordsworth and M—S and Coler." (CNB 1144). By striking out for Yorkshire, he had discovered a new route to Dove Cottage and William Wordsworth.

Torn by conflict, Coleridge confided to Southey: "If my wife loved me, and I my wife, half as well as we both love our children, I should be the happiest man alive—but this is not—will not be!" (CL II, p. 774). Early October found him building a stone love seat in William and Dorothy's backyard at Dove Cottage; they christened it Sara's Seat. Responsive to their unhappily married friend's craving for sympathetic love, the Wordsworths encouraged his dream: *Wouldn't it be lovely to all live together?*

But Coleridge was still of two minds: while half blaming his failing marriage on the opium and brandy he drank, he was half convinced that his stormy arguments with Sarah were driving him to those excesses. Hoping to gain perspective through a trial separation and a program of abstinence, Coleridge made arrangements to return to London and resume working for the *Post*.

Already off on a trip of her own, Sarah Coleridge was not at home to see her husband off for London that November. But William and Dorothy came over to bid their friend farewell. Nearly heartbroken, Dorothy confided to her diary:

> Poor C. left us and we came home together.... C. had a sweet day for his ride. Every sight and every sound reminded me of him dear dear fellow—of his many walks to us by day and by night—of all dear things. I was melancholy and could not talk, but at last I eased my heart by weeping—nervous blubbering says William. It is not so. O how many, many reasons have I to be anxious for him. [JDW, p. 57]

Arriving in London on the fifteenth, Coleridge began working for Stuart on a regular basis. But unable to get a grip on his opium intake or a fresh perspective on his marital conflict, he felt stymied and confused. Sorely in need of advice by the time Christmas rolled around, he caught a stage for Bristol and was at Poole's house well before the new year.

Having earlier confided to Poole his fits of "loathing" and "disgust" brought on by laudanum and brandy (CL II, p. 731), Coleridge discussed the matter in person. In fact his diary during this Stowey visit reveals Coleridge's first attempt at analyzing the physical side effects of opium.

Shortly after that visit, early in 1802, Coleridge sent Poole a long progress note dutifully describing his diminished drug intake and cheerfully promising that a new philosophical work would soon be winging its way to the publishers. Then he wrote Sarah a letter filled with his "tenderest yearning" and "frequent prayer . . . that we meet to part no more—and live together as affectionate husband and wife ought to do" (CL II, p. 786).

Poole's influence was remarkable. Coleridge began solicitously to remind Sarah to wear her warm flannel drawers and to gently chide her to "regularly and perseverantly" take her mustard pills (CL II, p. 779). Coleridge's letters to Sara Hutchinson included descriptions of his fretful concern for his wife's rheumatism and a warm anecdote describing Mrs. C. teaching Hartley the Bible.

But Poole's influence began to fade—particularly after Coleridge received the news from William in late February that his wedding would take place shortly after Coleridge's return to the Lakes. In fact, by the time he boarded the northbound coach for his return home that March, Coleridge's firm resolve to save his marriage had wilted; he was unable to resist his impulse to make a Yorkshire detour to see Sara Hutchinson, whom he visited for ten days. On leaving her, he mulled in his diary: "Can see nothing extraordinary in her—a poem noting all the virtues of the mild and retired kind" (CNB 1152). Mystified by the intensity of his attachment to this short, dumpy, mild, and retiring woman, Coleridge asked the wrong question. He might better have wondered *who* rather than *what* he saw in this woman. Although there was nothing extraordinary about Sara, she was his link to William Wordsworth.

Once again Coleridge was a divided man by the time he arrived at Keswick. Half intending to remain at Greta Hall and devote his energies exclusively to reconciling with Sarah after their four-month separation, he was at William's house within four days of his homecoming.

"Much affected by the sight of him," Dorothy was "agitated" by his "half stupefied" appearance (JDW, p. 105). Coleridge spent three days at Dove Cottage, taking long walks in the March countryside with William and having long heart-to-heart chats about their futures. Spring was just around the corner and William could feel it—he was about to marry and make a fresh start. But for heavily drugged Coleridge, gazing in glazed stupefaction with "how blank an eye," his senses numbed by "dull pain" (PW, pp. 363–364), the landscape was a barren wasteland. He faced the chilling prospect of returning to Sarah and a loveless life at Greta Hall.

Seen through Poole's eyes at Stowey, Coleridge's homecoming had taken on the cheerful domestic glow of snug flannels, mustard pills, and cozy bedtime stories with his imaginative children. But from the perspective of Dove Cottage, he contemplated returning to a moribund marriage and the inevitable death of his creative imagination with all the relish of a condemned man.

But Coleridge was by no means the only one at Dove Cottage feeling oppressed by a heavy burden. As his marriage approached, Wordsworth found himself brooding over Annette Vallon and memories of their baby. While listening to Coleridge's outpourings of guilt over his illicit love for Sara Hutchinson, William had darker feelings to get off his chest.

After hearing William's painful confession, Coleridge advised him to postpone his wedding and clear his conscience by seeing Annette in France before marrying Mary. The recent truce in the war made the visit possible, and Dorothy's diary informs us that it was on the morning after Coleridge's departure for Keswick that William announced his plan to see Annette.

Six days after Coleridge's departure, William composed the first four stanzas of his *Ode: Intimations of Immortality from Recollections of Early Childhood*. The next day, he stopped at Greta Hall for several days on his way to Yorkshire, where he planned to talk with Mary in person and explain his reason for postponing their wedding to the fourth of October.

On the eve of his departure for Yorkshire, Wordsworth shared his new ode with Coleridge. The results were electric—a creative spark was ignited just as it had been in the old Somerset days. Responding to Wordsworth's poem with one of his own, Coleridge immediately began drafting *Dejection: An Ode* in the form of a letter to Sara Hutchinson. It took several weeks to complete and while nominally addressed to Sara was clearly intended for William. But as Coleridge well knew, there would be plenty of time to readdress it before William's wedding day.

When William returned from Yorkshire, Coleridge walked over to Dove Cottage to read his new poem to his friends and elicit their reactions. When Coleridge had recited his melancholy verse, Dorothy noted, "the green fields and the fair sky made me sadder; even the little happy sporting lambs seemed but sorrowful to me" (JDW, p. 102).

But if listening to Coleridge's poem depressed Dorothy, writing it provided Coleridge enormous relief. He had been tormented by feelings of inner deadness and sterility until he finally managed to capture them on paper. Afterward, he began to craft and shape these raw emotions into a great poem.

Exhilarated by the process of mastering his depression creatively, and justifiably proud of the results, Coleridge trumpeted the good news to Southey. Forwarding a copy, he wrote: "Having written these lines, I rejoice for you as well as for myself, that I am able to inform you, that now for a long time there has been more love and concord in my house, than I have known for years before" (CL II, p. 832). No longer a beaten man, Coleridge had recaptured his self-esteem as a writer by turning out a masterly work—nineteen months after having become blocked following the *Christabel* rejection.

The carry-over into his personal life was dramatic. Finally able to respond to Sarah's criticisms, he stood up, fought back, and reasserted his dominance. Delighted to see him back on his feet as a poet and feeling his oats, Sarah became cordial and solicitous. So cordial, in fact, that she soon became pregnant.

Dorothy Wordsworth's response to the Coleridges' attempts to salvage their marriage was remarkable. During one of Coleridge's stays at Dove Cottage that spring, Sarah sent over a fresh supply of laundry for Samuel accompanied by a note. Dorothy reacted:

> Mrs Coleridge is a most extraordinary character—She is the lightest, weakest, silliest woman! She sent some clean clothes on Thursday to meet C. (the first time she ever did such a thing in her life) from which I guess she is determined to be attentive to him—she wrote a note . . . all in her very lightest style . . . she concludes 'my love to the W's—' Is not it a hopeless case? So insensible and poor C! [LWDW I, p. 363]

Dorothy's scornful note reveals that she was unable to resist the temptation to disparage, if subtly, Coleridge's resolve to save his marriage. Increasingly glum over William's wedding, Dorothy had begun to anticipate her future status as maiden-aunt boarder in her brother's home. It would be a far cry from her exalted role as muse for two antic poets roaming the woodlands by day and by night. She had her reasons for feeling bitter.

Wittingly or otherwise, both William and Dorothy systematically undercut Coleridge's attempts to improve his relationship with Sarah. Their contempt for *Mrs. C.*, their excesses of sympathy for *Poor C.*, and their outright encouragement of

Coleridge's phantom pursuit of Sara Hutchinson all contributed.

Shortly before leaving for France, William and Dorothy had a secret rendezvous with Coleridge by a huge boulder, nicknamed Sara's Rock, which lay by the side of the Grasmere-Keswick road. Including Sara and Mary Hutchinson in his magic circle of names, Coleridge carved the group's initials into the stone. Then he displayed his handiwork for the Wordsworths' approval, whereupon William solemnly deepened the *T* in STC, followed by Dorothy's kissing all the sets of initials as if to conclude the ceremony.

In spite of the fact that they were inciting him to fly in the face of his moral scruples and religious beliefs, William and Dorothy justified their encouragement as loyalty to *Poor C*. In part they were influenced by the ugly picture Coleridge painted of his marriage.

Coleridge made the fatal double error of confiding his dissatisfactions to William and Dorothy and then tactlessly transmitting their confidences back to Sarah. To make matters even worse, he revealed Sarah's opinions to the Wordsworths. Apart from her own bitterness, then, Dorothy had reason to sneer skeptically at Sarah's "love to the W's" (LWDW, I, p. 363).

One of the reasons for the secret meeting at Sarah's Rock was the fact that Coleridge had let the Wordsworths know they were not welcome at Greta Hall. Not welcome, that is, if they preferred to play out such conspiratorial scenes with their opium-pixilated friend. It was not the first time that Coleridge had slipped out of the house with an air of cloak-and-dagger secrecy and met Wordsworth in private to complain of mistreatment by his wife.

While this drastic split in his loyalties was largely of Coleridge's own design, he did not see it that way. Declaring himself a "creature of mere impact" lacking "due powers of resistance to impulses from without" (CL II, p. 782), Coleridge refused to recognize the role he played in pitting his wife and closest friends against each other. Instead, buffeted by their opinions, he ricocheted between Keswick and Grasmere. And the opium he took facilitated the ease with which he merged with others and shifted his allegiances.

Was he revealing his "true" feelings for Sara Hutchinson

at that solemn ceremony at the rock? Or was his farewell gesture intended to please William and Dorothy, who were about to leave for France? And were the Wordsworths behaving strictly out of loyalty? Or did they harbor an ulterior motive for wishing to see Coleridge's marriage fall apart? A wish to become one big happy family, with William as its head, of course.

Not surprisingly, Coleridge cut down drastically on his opium after the Wordsworths' departure that July. In "a melancholy parting . . . having sat together in silence by the roadside" (JDW, p. 147), William and Dorothy bid *Poor C.* farewell and began their odyssey. No longer afforded the dubious luxury of friends who answered his excessive craving for sympathy with a pity he could ill afford, Coleridge blossomed and thrived.

Reformulating his views on poetry, Coleridge began contemplating a more separate existence from William:

> Altho' Wordsworth's Preface is half a child of my own brain . . . I rather suspect that somewhere or other there is a radical difference in our theoretical opinions respecting poetry. This I shall endeavour to go to the bottom of—and acting the arbitrator between the old school and the new school hope to lay some plain, and perspicuous, tho' not superficial, canons of criticism respecting poetry. [CL II, p. 830]

Intent on enjoying robust good health now that his opium intake was reduced, Coleridge took long solitary hikes and made overnight expeditions in the Cumberland countryside. Exhilarated by strenuous exercise, he satisfied his hunger for reckless, highwire excitement by mountain climbing. At night he slept better than he had in many years.

And while he missed the Wordsworths and Sara Hutchinson, he hit upon a way to deal with these feelings. As he sat, pausing for a rest on a mountaintop, Coleridge penned an entry into his diary. He would write a poem called the *Soother of Absence*. If he had been able to master his depression by capturing it artistically in *Dejection: An Ode*, why not try the same tactic with his loneliness?

And while Sarah Coleridge fretted over the risks her mountain climbing husband took, she was relieved to see his health blossoming and joined in with her sons' enthusiasm over their daredevil Papa's tales of his alpine adventures. But no matter how much she cared, or how hard she tried, Sarah was incapable of satisfying her husband's cravings for masculine companionship.

Feeling the void left by Wordsworth's departure, Coleridge tried to persuade Southey to relocate in the Lakes. Not only did he describe the grandeur of the scenery, he also painted a warm, cheerful picture of his current domestic situation. Emphasizing the spaciousness of Greta Hall, he noted how easily the two families could permanently combine their households under one roof.

While Southey would ultimately succumb to Coleridge's overtures, he was not currently in a position to embark on such an undertaking. So, forced to turn elsewhere to satisfy his hunger for male friends, Coleridge was surprised and delighted when his old friends, the Agnus Dei and the Virgin Mary, turned up for a three-week summer holiday that August.

Although Lamb's daily company briefly helped to take Coleridge's mind off the missing occupant of Dove Cottage, his feelings of loneliness returned when Lamb departed for London that September. Wordsworth would not be returning to Grasmere until after his wedding. And as he rattled around the Lakes that fall awaiting the returning honeymooners, Coleridge realized that William's marriage meant that they inevitably would be seeing less of each other. Unless, that is, his wildest dreams came true and he could somehow establish a domestic connection to William.

As a matter of fact, on the night of October 3, Coleridge dreamt of that connection to Wordsworth and his failure to establish it. On that night, William Wordsworth lay asleep in a Yorkshire farmhouse. He would be marrying in the morning. Meanwhile, Coleridge tossed and turned. Awaking in the middle of the night, he penned a note in his diary:

> October 3—Night—My dreams uncommonly illustrative of the non-existence of surprise in sleep—I dreamt that I was asleep in the Cloister at Christ's Hospital and had awoken with a pain in my hand from some corrosion. Boys and nurses' daughters peeping at me. On their implying that I was not in the school, I answered yes I am. I am only twenty—I then recollected that I was thirty, and of course could not be in the school—and was perplexed—but not the least surprise that I could fall into such

an error. So I dreamt of Dorothy, William and Mary—and that Dorothy was altered in every feature, a fat, thick-limbed and rather red-haired—in short, no resemblance to her at all—and I said, if I did not *know* you to be Dorothy, I never should *suppose* it. Why, says she—I have not a feature the same. And yet I was surprised—

I was followed up and down by a frightful pale woman who, I thought, wanted to kiss me, and had the property of giving a shameful disease by breathing in the face.

And again I dreamt that a figure of a woman of gigantic height, dim and indefinite and snakelike appeared—and that I was forced to run up toward it—and then it changed to a stool—and then appeared again in another place—and again I went up in great fright—and it changed to some other common thing, yet I felt no surprise. [CNB 1250]

Feeling powerless to prevent his loss of Wordsworth, Coleridge depicted his dilemma in his dreams. Turning back time, he could again become twenty, return to Christ's Hospital and start over again. But that locale was filled with memories of homesickness and had long come to symbolize his loneliness. In fact, his dream vividly reminded him that as he wandered the cloisters among his classmates, he had never felt he was really one of them. His metaphorically corroded hand, doubtless the symbol of secret masturbation, had helped set him—in dream, at least—apart from the others. Arousing himself for self-consolation, the youngster perhaps discovered that this activity only made him lonelier by increasing his sense of shame and alienation. If Coleridge was sorely tempted to comfort himself similarly on the eve of William's wedding, his dream seemed to be telling him that he was too old for that now. Recourse to his adolescent solace still had the power to make him feel tainted, an outsider.

But how could he become an insider? The second dream scene posed this question. The prospect of becoming bonded to William and Mary through Dorothy struck him as unnatural. His dream reminded him that Dorothy's recent meddling in his marriage had revealed an unfamiliar and unflattering aspect of her. In the dream she appeared coarse, fat, and thick-limbed. Given the fact that in some of Coleridge's other dreams people with such physiques are taunting, aggressive boys, there is room to wonder if Coleridge had found something unappealingly masculine in Dorothy's recent behavior. If Dorothy's treatment of Sarah reflected her secret interest in undermining the Coleridges' marriage in order to have Coleridge for herself, the dream suggests that Coleridge found Dorothy's behavior unattractively out of character.

The third dream scene seems to explore this reaction to Sara Hutchinson as an alternative link to Wordsworth. Indistinct and faceless but beckoning, Coleridge's dream figure is the receptively warm but immemorably featured Sara Hutchinson. Moreover, while the dream woman invites a liaison, Coleridge recoils in fear of venereal disease—a symbol, and a particularly powerful one in the eighteenth century, of illicit love.

If the first three dreams reviewed his options, Coleridge's fourth dream reminded him of the female forces who had always controlled his life. As all-powerful as an Arabian Nights genie, the towering dream woman can summon him to her side against his will. Three women in his life had exercised such a hold over him: his mother, the nursemaid Molly, and his wife. The eerie feminine spectre stands for a composite of these controlling women—the powerful objects of his feelings of helpless resentment, past and present.

As a small boy, he could be forced by malicious Molly, or by his fickle mother, to do her bidding. Now, as a grown man, he finds himself in the same predicament: he feels as bound to his wife as he once felt to the others. Sarah's twin powers consist of their matrimonial bond—a holy one—and the compelling fact of her current pregnancy, which has swollen her to enormous proportions, at least in his dream.

Like it or not, he is Sarah Fricker's for life. The dream woman's chimerical ability to transform her physical shape at will, suggests Sarah's pregnancy and the powerful grip it held over him. The phallic shapes into which she materializes—snakes or stools—are emblems of her magical procreative powers. Yet in the end, awesome as she is, Coleridge's dream woman is not the woman of his dreams: she is a "common thing," wife and mother.

And so, lonely and about to be excluded even further on the dawn of William's wedding day, Coleridge seemed unable to find a way out of his dilemma. He could not return to his adolescence. A connection with Dorothy Wordsworth filled him with distaste—it would be as unnatural as marrying a man. A liaison with Sara Hutchinson filled him with fear—he would be ostracized for his illicit love. To remain with Sarah Fricker was a form of perpetual bondage—a helpless boy being forced to a gigantic mother's side at a time in the dimly remembered past when female control over him had seemed infinite. What was he to do?

Chapter 12

Troubled Sleep

> *But yester-night I pray'd aloud*
> *In anguish or in agony,*
> *Up-starting from the fiendish crowd*
> *Of shapes and thoughts that tortured me:*
> *A lurid light, a trampling throng,*
> *Sense of intolerable wrong,*
> *And whom I scorned, those only strong!*
> *Thirst of revenge, the powerless will*
> *Still baffled, and yet burning still!*
> *Desire with loathing strangely mixed*
> *On wild or hateful objects fixed.*
> *Fantastic passions! maddening brawl!*
> *And shame and terror over all!*
> *Deeds to be hid which were not hid,*
> *Which all confused I could not know*
> *Whether I suffered, or I did:*
> *For all seemed guilt, remorse or woe,*
> *My own or others still the same*
> *Life-stifling fear, soul-stifling shame.*
> —from *The Pains of Sleep* [PW, pp. 389–390]

Weary and wet, but pleased to be home with his new bride, William Wordsworth arrived at Dove Cottage at six in the evening in a pouring rain. Overjoyed by "Maister" William's two-day-old marriage, his housekeeper Molly Ashburner was waiting to greet the three members of the wedding party (LWDW I, p. 381).

Determined that their honeymoon cottage would be wreathed with blossoming fall bushes and garlanded with flowers, Dorothy had labored long and hard in the garden before leaving with William for France that July. After taking her new sister-in-law on a candlelight tour of the garden, Dorothy was satisfied with the luxurious growth of the broom and Portugal laurels. Then she discreetly bid the newlyweds good night and retired.

The following morning, refreshed after a night's sleep in her own bed, Dorothy helped Mary unpack her belongings. William was undoubtedly as pleased as his sister to have slept under his own roof once more after so many months on the road. Transforming his bachelor's couch into his and Mary's nuptial bed, he wasted no time in starting a family—Mary was pregnant within days of her arrival.

Although he was anxious to resume his regular writing schedule after such a long break in his daily routine, William set aside time to take Mary on long walks, introduce her to his favorite local haunts, and show her some of the more spectacular lakeside views. The out-of-doors was ablaze with unusually beautiful fall colors that year—a dappled patchwork of browns, rusts, oranges, yellows, and greens.

When William was too busy with his writing to be with his new bride, Mary and Dorothy visited the neighbors, baked cakes and bread, or puttered in the garden. Given William's desire to keep Dorothy on as a permanent member of his household—both for her own welfare and the sake of his literary career—he had been wise to select one of her oldest and closest friends as his bride. Sweet-tempered and good-natured, Mary did not appear to resent the constant presence of her sister-in-law and could abide Dorothy's doting over William—sometimes serving him breakfast in bed or listening reverentially as he recited his poetry.

And for her part, Dorothy had already begun to address Mary as "my sister" (LWDW I, p. 350). Having managed to find two women willing to devote themselves to him and to join forces amicably in looking after him, William contemplated a life of domestic peace and prosperity. If such an arrangement meant that Wordsworth took more than he gave, neither woman seemed to object to this one-sidedness. Whatever companionship William might not offer they would supply one another. Both Mary and Dorothy were looking forward to their new life.

While his tiny cottage hummed with the bustle of domestic activity, William rapidly learned to adapt to these background sounds and to work undisturbed. When he needed complete privacy in order to concentrate, he composed out-of-doors, regardless of the weather. Although he was still nagged by tension and anxiety that took the form of chest pains whenever he sat down to write poetry, Wordsworth was content if not happy.

The Dove Cottage honeymooners had already begun to settle into their cozy routine by the time "Poor Coleridge"—their unhappily married friend whose shrewish wife's recent conciliatory attempts to pamper him with fresh laundry had seemed so pathetically ludicrous to Dorothy—turned up to greet them. Learning that the coast was clear, as Sarah Coleridge was off on a short trip, Dorothy and William reluctantly "consented" to pay a return three-day visit to Greta Hall (JDW, p. 161).

During that stay Wordsworth did not mention having read Coleridge's satirical poem, *Spots in the Sun*, which had been tactlessly published in the *Post* exactly one week after Coleridge's grandly sentimental wedding-day gesture of *Dejection: An Ode*. Yet there had been much in that jesting poem to irk William:

> My father confessor is strict and holy,
> *Mi Fili*, still he cries, *peccare noli*.
> And yet how oft I find the pious man
> At Annette's door, the lovely courtesan! [PW, p. 969]

Given the fact that Wordsworth brought up another poem of Coleridge's that had recently appeared in the *Post*, it is probable that William had been reading the paper regularly since his return from France.

Wordsworth told Coleridge he had found his *Hymn Before Sunrise in the Vale of Chamonix* artificial, "a specimen of the mock sublime" (CL IV, p. 974). Tactful enough to overlook the most flagrantly personal signs of Coleridge's recent bitterness, Wordsworth focused instead on an even more unfortunate example of his friend's growing cynicism. While falsely implying in his introduction that he had actually visited Chamonix, Coleridge neglected to inform his readers that *Hymn Before Sunrise* was in fact closely based on a poem by a Swiss poet.

Openly acknowledging that source in a letter to a friend, Coleridge was not yet plagiarizing in the strictest sense. But *Hymn Before Sunrise* does mark the start of a pattern of unacknowledged borrowings that was about to become a habit. Subsequent critics have been baffled by Coleridge's behavior, rightfully asking how—having just written what he knew to be a masterpiece, *Dejection: An Ode*—Coleridge could stoop to borrowing heavily from a second-rate poem and attempt to palm off the result as his own composition?

As with his marriage and family life, Coleridge had reached a bitter turning point with his poetry—he no longer valued what was his in comparison to Wordsworth's. In part, Coleridge's envy operated as a self-fulfilling prophecy: the happier William's family seemed, the gloomier his own marriage became. But regarding Wordsworth's superiority as a poet, Coleridge was faced with tangible evidence: during the same spring in which he had managed to write *Dejection*, Wordsworth had written thirty poems of quality, some of them great.

There was much to covet about William's life, and Coleridge could not keep from noticing *everything*. But he had also seen what a relief it was to be free of envy during the three months Wordsworth had been gone. Clearly, one way out of his dilemma—his sour feelings, aching joints, and escalating opium intake—was to get away, far away.

And so, when he heard of Tom Wedgwood's plans to go abroad for his health, Coleridge lost no time in offering his services. Tom gratefully accepted, with the proviso that they first test their compatibility by traveling in England. Although eight months pregnant, Sarah Coleridge raised no serious objection. Faced with the prospect of the rheumy chills of another Lake District winter, which played such havoc with his arthritis, Coleridge convinced Sarah that a trip south or abroad would do wonders for his health. In addition, as the trip might cement Coleridge's tie with his benefactor, her husband's plan struck Sarah as eminently sensible.

Until, that is, she learned of his Yorkshire detour. The irksome, insouciant innocence with which he informed her of his one-day stopover with Sara Hutchinson was enough to unleash Sarah Coleridge's fury. He in turn pretended to be outraged by her unwarranted jealousy, protests of innocence alternating with sanctimonious lectures. Apparently he could not resist the temptation to goad Sarah into suffering the same morbid feelings of envy and jealousy that plagued him.

Back and forth by mail, the pair battled through the months

of November and December. Half spiteful but half tender—and pickled in laudanum from his gizzard to his zatch, Coleridge wallowed in his conflicted emotions toward Sarah: deeply solicitous about her pregnancy but horrified at the prospect of spending the rest of his life with her. On learning of Sarah's fainting spells as her third trimester drew to a close, he urged her to get a nurse to look after herself and young Derwent. But with remarkable *sangfroid*, he suggested that Sara Hutchinson might also help with her lying-in. Feeling beyond reproach because his relationship with Sara Hutchinson was in fact asexual, Coleridge could see nothing provocative about his dreamy fantasy that the two women might become good friends and devote themselves to him. It was asking for no more, after all, than what his good friend William had.

Coleridge's letters to Sarah also contained dutiful reports of how much opium he was using, suggesting that his addiction was now an openly acknowledged problem between them. Reassuring her that his habit was under control, he painted a rosy picture of his remarkable rehabilitation under Tom Wedgwood's genial companionship and the tranquil country life they led.

But about to confide to his brother Josiah that "the dullness in my life is unsupportable without" opium (Wedgwood and Wedgwood, 1980, p. 129), Tom was as hooked on that drug as Coleridge and had already begun to suffer bouts of suicidal depression and psychotic paranoia. Following the best medical advice that money could buy, Tom retreated into his temperature-controlled, soundproofed, hermetically sealed apartment where—soothing his nerves—he became obsessed with his own death. At other times—also following his croakers' advice—he had recently traveled to Europe and the West Indies, to no avail. As bereft of appetite for food as for life, Tom had begun losing weight at an alarming rate and was by now quite emaciated.

Still hoping to turn the tide of misery with the daily company of a sympathetic friend, Tom had welcomed Coleridge's overture. But destined to reinforce each other's self-destructive tendencies rather than cheer each other up, Coleridge and Wedgwood drifted aimlessly through the West Country and Wales, making and breaking plans. A note from Coleridge to

Tom, informing him of the arrival of a secret stash of *bhang* (a form of marijuana), conveys the conspiratorial tone of their adventures:

> We go off early tomorrow morning. I shall hear from you of course.—Respectful remembrances to the family at Cote.—We will have a fair trial of *Bang*—Do bring down some of the hycosamine pills—and I will give a fair trial of opium, henbane and nepenthe. By the bye, I always considered Homer's account of the *Nepenthe* as a *Banging* lie. [CL II, p. 934]

As a houseguest on the great country estates of Tom's wealthy friends, Coleridge spent his days in the drawing rooms amusing himself with the companionship of fashionable ladies, reading, or taking long walks while Wedgwood hunted. In the evenings they attended lavish dinner parties, listened to piano and voice recitals given by eligible young ladies, and embroiled themselves in fireside discussions of the three P's: politics, poetry, and philosophy. On their solitary evenings, Coleridge read aloud to Tom to soothe his nerves.

Nothing if not a monologist, Coleridge was the life of the party and no doubt assumed others were spellbound by his conversational glitter. But Tom's sister Kitty was offended by the flip manner in which he referred to his early Bristol days as the time "when I had the misfortune to meet my wife" (Cornwell, 1973, p. 371). Moreover, Kitty was put off by the fact that while he claimed to be at death's door he was making no realistic plans for his family. As she saw things, Coleridge was all too willing to take advantage of Tom's generosity—a charge made plausible by the Wedgwood family ledgers, which reveal that in the year about to begin (1803), Tom would spend a total of 505 pounds on Coleridge. But whether Tom was Coleridge's pigeon, or Coleridge Tom's canary, is a matter of interpretation.

By the new year both men were back in the Lake District, where they had gone to see Coleridge's baby daughter, whom he named Sara and nicknamed "Sariola" and "Coleridgiella." But whatever emotional satisfactions his newborn child provided, they were not enough to keep Coleridge at home that winter. Restless, if not on the run, he remained in the Lake District three weeks—shuttling between Grasmere and Keswick.

Then, wracked by arthritic pains, he headed south in search of a warmer climate.

Describing his attachment to Wedgwood as a "comet tied to a comet's tail" (CL II, p. 919), Coleridge found his own inner sense of frenzy and restless dissatisfaction matched in Tom. They talked of going to France, Italy, the Canary Islands, the West Indies, and other points south. But by February the peripatetic pair was still in Bristol with their final destination undecided.

Before leaving Keswick, Coleridge tried to prepare Southey for their reunion in Bristol, the scene of their past glories: "O Southey! I am not the Coleridge, which you knew me" (CL II, p. 913). But it was not until Coleridge arrived that Southey could begin to fathom what he had meant. He wrote a friend:

> I am grieved that you never met Coleridge; all other men whom I have ever known are mere children to him, and yet all is palsied by a total want of moral strength. He will leave nothing behind him to justify the opinion of his friends to the world; yet many of his scattered poems are such, that a man of feeling will see that the author was capable of executing the greatest works. [Chambers, 1938, p. 166]

After Coleridge's departure, still haunted by the eerie encounter, Southey wrote:

> Coleridge only talks, and poor fellow! he will not do that long, I fear. . . . It provokes me when I hear a set of puppies yelping at him upon whom he, a great, good-natured mastiff, if he came up to them, would just lift up his leg and pass on. It vexes and grieves me to the heart, that when he is gone, as go he will, nobody will believe what a mind goes with him,—how infinitely and ten thousand-thousand fold the mightiest of his generation. [Chambers, 1938, p. 166]

Poole, who saw Coleridge shortly after his visit with Southey, was equally powerless to help him get a grip on his drug habit. Hooked on opium, he wriggled and squirmed. The unpleasant physical symptoms he suffered when he tried to reduce his intake forced him back to the drug for relief. Or, as he put it, stopping opium led to a "diarrhoesima con frurore," or "slishslosh!" (CL II, p. 924).

By mid-March Coleridge and Wedgwood were in London. Their plans for a continental tour fluctuated daily, according to each man's health and vacillations of mood. Amusing himself while waiting for Wedgwood to decide their destination, sometimes Coleridge sallied forth high as a kite into the fashionable London drawing rooms, radiating a false gaiety and singing for his supper "as a singer does, to amuse the guests by his talent" (Armour and Howes, 1940, p. 72).

Their volatile travel plans were at the mercy not only of their whims, but also of a rapidly unfolding international chain of events. The truce with France, less than one year old, that had allowed Wordsworth to visit Annette in Calais before his wedding was about to end. A hollow peace, cynically designed as a measure to buy time, the Treaty of Amiens had allowed both England and France to recuperate. Both nations' economies had become overheated and each government had felt sorely pressed to appease temporarily the widespread unrest caused by the financial and emotional hardships of a nine-year war.

But now England and France were once more on the verge of war. Napoleon was already rearming and had found a pretext to invade Switzerland. For her part, England was strategically holding on to the tiny Mediterranean island of Malta, which she had promised to evacuate as part of the treaty. Britain was the mightiest naval power in the world, while Bonaparte's brilliantly directed armies knew no match. Neither country had any serious intention of foregoing its long-range imperialistic ambitions. A showdown seemed unavoidable.

After much debate over the pros and cons of a continental tour, Coleridge and Wedgwood finally decided to part company. Too ill himself to properly tend to Tom, Coleridge agreed that Wedgwood required someone more physically fit to accompany him to France. There had been servants galore to look after Tom in England, but what if an emergency arose in France? Coleridge was in no condition to nurse a dying man.

Parting in late March, the two friends would never see one another again. Twenty-eight months later, Tom would die on the eve of his departure for Jamaica, another voyage intended to regain his health. At the time of his death, Tom would be involved in preparing a portable collection of nightingales, thrushes, robins, blackbirds, and larks—hoping to cheer himself with the familiar sounds of English songbirds while recuperating in the tropics.

Coleridge arrived home from London on Good Friday and was immediately laid low by a bad case of influenza which lasted a month. Up and about by mid-May, he continued reading philosophy and resumed corresponding with friends, but otherwise his mind was strangely shut up. While continually proposing and promising new literary and philosophical projects, he was doing no serious writing. In a letter to Southey that summer, he described how opium was turning him into a vegetable:

> A sense of weakness—a haunting sense, that I was an herbaceous plant, as large as a large tree, with a trunk of the same girth, and branches as large as shadowing—but *pith within* the trunk, not heart of wood—that I had *power* not *strength*—an involuntary impostor—that I had no real genius, no real depth.—This on my honor is as fair a statement of my habitual haunting as I could give before the tribunal of heaven. How it arose in me, I have but lately discovered.—Still it works within me. But only as a disease, the cause and meaning of which I know. [CL II, p. 959]

Long aware of the havoc laudanum played on his bowels, Coleridge's gloomy note suggests he was becoming aware that it was poisoning his faculties as well.

Depressed over the grim prospect of becoming a self-aware but helpless spectator, gradually witnessing his faculties grow duller, Coleridge leapt at the opportunity to make a tour of Scotland with Wordsworth and his sister, in the desperate hope of regaining his health. If that trip failed, it was curtains for Coleridge. Unless, that is, he could find his way to a southern climate.

Before leaving for Scotland, he consulted his physician, who heartily endorsed the trip. Basing his opinion on the still-prevailing medical concept of toxic humors trapped within the body, Coleridge's doctor hoped that strenuous exercise would discharge the mysterious gouty poisons that lurked inside his patient. Similar rationales were given for cupping, bleeding, blistering, and leeching—all of which were commonly prescribed for various forms of gout, which no doubt was his croaker's diagnosis. While Coleridge half knew the truth, he still hoped it might be "atonic gout" he was suffering from.

Sarah described Coleridge's departure to Southey:

> Last Monday my husband, W. Wordsworth and D.W. set off for Scotland in an Irish-car and one horse—W. is to drive all the way, for poor Samuel is too weak to undertake the fatigue of driving—he was very unwell when he went off, and was to return in the Mail if he grew worse. . . . I hope he will be able to go for if the weather be tolerable it will do him much good, so Mr. Edmonson [Coleridge's doctor] thinks. . . . My husband is a good man—his prejudices—and his prepossessions sometimes give me pain, but . . . I should be a very, very happy woman if it were not for a few things—and my husband's health stands at the head of those evils. [CL II, p. 975]

From the start things went poorly for the three travelers: their rustic jaunting cart implied a spirit of adventurous gaiety that was not to be. Grouchy and out of sorts, Wordsworth struck Coleridge as silent and preoccupied—"a brooder over his painful hypochondriacal sensations . . . not my fittest companion" (Moorman, 1957, p. 591). And William described Coleridge: "in bad spirits, and somewhat too *much in love with his own dejection*" (Cornwell, 1973, p. 387).

And whether she realized it or not, Dorothy managed to strike the raw nerve of Coleridge's envy of William when, by the banks of Loch Lomond, she suddenly felt moved to rapturously recite *Ruth*—the very poem Coleridge had confided to Davy that he "would rather have written" at the time of the *Christabel* debacle (CL I, p. 632). Filled with self-pity, Coleridge confided to his diary: "What? tho' the world praise me, I have no dear heart that loves my verses—I never hear them in snatches from a beloved voice, fitted to some sweet occasion, of natural prospect, in wind at night . . ." (CNB 1463). And it was by the same bonnie banks that William first brought to Coleridge's mind the image of a pig: "selfish—feeling all fire respecting every trifle of his own. . . . The *up*, askance, pig look, in the boat etc." (CNB 1606).

Masking his hostility as best he could, while politely apologizing for being a "burthen" to the Wordsworths because of his ill health (CL II, p. 994), Coleridge was relieved when William suggested they part company. No mention was made of the underlying resentments on both sides. Instead they decided that traveling in an open cart was hazardous to Coleridge's health. Dividing the remaining joint travel funds, William and Dorothy kept twenty-nine guineas and gave Coleridge six.

Relieved of the Wordsworths' irritating presence, Coleridge was pleased to be alone in the Highlands. If it was the atonic gout he was suffering from, he would give that disease a run for its money. Shipping his trunk to Edinburgh, he struck out for the north of Scotland with little more than his journal, the shirt on his back, and a ruined pair of walking shoes that had been scorched while drying too close to the fire.

Through the Scottish heather, over moorlands and mountains, he tramped a sickle-shaped itinerary across Scotland, covering 263 miles in eight days. Though "a little stiffish" (CL II, p. 981) in the morning, thirty-year-old Coleridge was by no means a crippled arthritic. But he lost the battle with his mystifying ailment. Unable to force the toxic humors to settle in his big toe—the classic symptom of true gout—Coleridge succeeded only in making his feet raw and sorely blistered by his ill-fitting shoes.

Unfortunately, he misdirected his trial of willpower toward vigorous exercise rather than against opiates. But throughout the hike he had been plagued by nightmares and diarrhea whenever his laudanum dose fell below a critical maintenance level. Unable to fend off those nightmares, he did manage however to turn them to a creative purpose by capturing their essence in *The Pains of Sleep*, a poem he drafted before leaving Scotland.

Fortunately, there was little opportunity for either Coleridge or Sarah to dwell upon the sorry failure of his drastic effort at self-cure. Greta Hall was bulging with people and bustling with activity by the time Coleridge returned. Sorely in need of consolation over the tragic loss of their only child, the grief-stricken Southeys had just arrived from Bristol for an extended visit.

In spite of the inevitable frictions of a shared household, the Coleridges got along well with the Southeys, who unlike the Wordsworths did not provoke drastic polarizations and bitter flashes of animosity between Coleridge and Sarah. Nor were Coleridge and Southey covertly competitive with one another about their respective poetic abilities.

Tan and more fit after his walking tour of the Highlands, Coleridge was in the best athletic shape he could remember. Taking Southey on daily rambles to help distract him from his recent tragedy, Coleridge was instinctively generous with his brother-in-law. Hiking long distances and skipping rocks on the river Derwent like a boy with his playmate, Robert Southey cheered up: "Coleridge and I are the best of companions possible, in almost all moods of mind, for all kinds of wisdom, and all kinds of nonsense, to the very heights and depths thereof" (Chambers, 1938, p. 174).

The Southeys' daily company tended to diminish the loneliness in the Coleridge household, and Coleridge was able to write Poole: "Mrs Coleridge enjoys her old state of excellent health. We go on, as usual—except that tho' I do not love her a bit better, I quarrel with her much less. We cannot be said to live at all as husband and wife, but we are peaceable housemates . . ." (CL II, p. 1015). Soon he would be referring to his bed as his "celibate couch" (CNB 1718n). Clearly the Coleridges' erotic romance had waned with the passage of time and the almost inevitable tedious familiarity that long-term domesticity can breed. Painfully recollecting those earlier Maydays when Eros and Priapus had stood guard over their home as protective household gods, Coleridge would in 1808 confide to Sarah that he had never

> known any woman for whom I had an equal personal fondness—that till the very latest period, when my health and spirits rendered me dead to everything, I had a PRIDE in you, and that I never saw you at the top of our hill, when I returned from a walk, without a sort of pleasurable feeling of sight, which woe be to the wretch! who confounds with vulgar feelings, and which is some little akin to the delight in a beautiful flower joined with the consciousness—'And it is in my garden.' [CL III, p. 77]

But after three young children and seven years of matrimony, the Coleridges—now both in their early thirties—were going through that familiar turning point that confronts most marriages in that season of life. Unfortunately, as they also were discovering, the odds were stacked against them.

Nothing if not a libido poison—both physiologically and emotionally—the opium he was using was indeed lethal enough to render Coleridge "dead to everything," depending on the dose. While he tried conscientiously to curb his drug intake during his hike in Scotland, his laudanum consumption began to escalate in early October. Judging from Coleridge's diary, he began to increase his use of opium immediately after another visit from his old friend William Wordsworth.

Back from Scotland in late September, Wordsworth came on horseback to Greta Hall on the ninth of October. While he wanted to see how Coleridge's health was faring, he had come also to announce that he was on the verge of a momentous artistic decision. After lengthy deliberation, he was seriously considering giving up writing short poems and devoting himself exclusively to composing a full-length masterpiece of Miltonic proportions. His autobiographical epic would be a bold personal statement of his life and philosophy.

The daring scope of his latest undertaking made William anxious. Every time he picked up his pen to make his beginning, Wordsworth felt the old oppressiveness that began in his chest and spread in waves through his entire body until he was drenched in sweat. Anxious but determined, William sought Coleridge's encouragement and literary counsel. Satisfied, he returned to Dove Cottage where, after several weeks of false starts, he began to compose. His project would take two years to complete.

Meanwhile, back at Greta Hall, Coleridge went into a tailspin and reached for the laudanum bottle. Plagued by his aching joints, he nonetheless prided himself on lacking a mean or selfish bone in his body. Petty resentments were unworthy of him; Coleridge considered it a point of honor not to show such feelings. William had asked for help, and he had graciously consented to informally serve as his mentor and supporter through the entire project. In fact, the poem would be dedicated to Coleridge.

But what of Coleridge's envy? He penned a note in his diary:

> I am sincerely glad, that he has bidden farewell to all small poems—and is devoting himself to his great work. . . . In these little poems his own corrections, coming *of necessity* so often . . . wore him out. . . . But now he is at the helm of a noble bark; now he sails right onward—it is all open ocean, and a steady breeze; and he drives before it, unfretted by short tacks and unreefing the sails, hawling and disentangling the ropes. [CNB 1346]

Shortly after this description of his seafaring brother's latest daredevil voyage into uncharted poetic realms, Coleridge penned the following entries: "Impotence—Painful Sensation and Loss of Hope = castration of the self-generating Organ of the Soul—Continuousness a true foliation" (CNB 1552); and "the violent and vindictive passions. . . . emasculates and dwarfs" (CNB 1553).

The "violent and vindictive passions" Wordsworth evoked threatened Coleridge's self-image. William's latest burst of creative energy made Coleridge feel enviously impotent. Enthusiastically enjoying the thrill of his first child, Wordsworth was intent on climbing recklessly to new artistic heights by writing a poem about his own childhood, even if the dizzying prospect also frightened him. In contrast, Coleridge saw himself as a burned-out, second-rate poet whose stale domestic garden was choked with ugly weeds. And, of course, there was the ubiquitous white poppy lurking in the hedgerows. How had his life taken such a pernicious turn?

Shortly after Wordsworth's visit, Coleridge began reading and rereading his old diaries. Searching in part for an explanation of his dilemma and in part for a solution, he instinctively turned back the pages of time to 1799, a critical turning point in his life. Just back from Germany, he had lingered during August and September with Southey before visiting William in the Lakes. It had been a time of indecision, as he vacillated between the two in his desire to live in close association with a brother poet.

Now, in October 1803, Coleridge reread, recopied, and commented upon incident after incident from that earlier period in one entry after the next in his current diary. Exercising a writer's license to alter his story, and influenced both by the depressive's inclination to distort the past in maudlin ways and by the addict's hazy sense of time, place, and fact, Coleridge rewrote the events of that year in an attempt to lessen, explain, or shift the focus of the pain he now felt. Rationalizing his revision as preparation for a great epic poem of his own, to be titled *The Soother of Absence*, Coleridge penned the following note in his journal: "Mix up truth and imagination, so that the imagination may spread its own indefiniteness over that which really happened, and reality its sense of substance and distinctness to imagination" (CNB 1541).

It was at this crucial point—immediately after writing this note—that Coleridge penned the well-known entry describing how love had fatally pricked him with its poisoned arrow. Had he been able to write a tale—the tragedy of a married man, a poet, falling helplessly in love at first sight with another woman, and his life falling apart in consequence of that love—it might have made an interesting story. Given Coleridge's extraordinary talent, it might even have become a poem, one that might have rescued his creativity by freeing him of a dream and restoring his confidence. But unfortunately for Coleridge, it was a tale he would live and come to believe, rather than put on paper.

By the time his thirty-first birthday rolled around, he was fully blocked in his efforts to write his epic and totally absorbed in living out the plot of his newly revised life story. He had become the unhappily married poet who was unable to write because he missed his one true love:

Wed. Morn. tomorrow my birthday. . . . O me! my very heart dies!—This *year* has been one painful dream. I have done nothing! . . .

October 19, 1803. The general Fast Day—and all hearts anxious concerning the invasion.—A grey day, windy . . . and now the rain storm pelts against my study window! O Sara Sara [he writes the name in Greek script] why am I not happy! why have I not an unencumbered heart! . . . why for years have I not enjoyed one pure and sincere pleasure!—one full joy!—one genuine delight, that rings sharp to the beat of the finger! . . .

A day of storm. At dinner an explosion of temper from the sisters. A dead sleep after dinner. The rhubarb had its usual enfeebling-narcotic effect. I slept again with dreams of sorrow and pain, tho' not of downright fright and prostration. I was worsted but not conquered—in sorrows and in sadness and in sore and angry struggles—but not trampled down. But this will all come again if I do not take care.

Storm all night—the wind scourging and lashing the rain, with the pauses of self-wearying violence that returns to its wild work as if maddened by the necessity of the pause. I, half-dozing, list'ning to the same, not without solicitations of the poetic feeling. . . . October 20, 1803 on Thursday morning 40 minutes past 2 o'clock. [CNB 1577]

While Coleridge—high on opium—played at his make-believe character, the lovesick poet of *The Soother of Absence*, his world was again playing its own mad game of war. By now, the print shops of Keswick were filled with pictures depicting Napoleon as a bloodthirsty ogre who had replaced the bogeyman in the minds of naughty girls and boys, whose scolding parents threatened that "Old Boney" (Cooper, 1964, p. 84) would get them if they didn't watch out. After giving their fretful infants a dose of "mother's blessing," working class mothers crooned their babes to sleep:

Baby, baby, naughty baby,
Hush you naughty thing, I say,
Hush your squalling or it may be
Bonaparte will come this way.

Baby, baby, he's a giant
Tall and dark as Rouen steeple
And he'll dine and sup, rely on't
Every day on naughty people.

Baby, baby, he will hear you
As he passes by the house.
And he limb from limb will tear you
Just as pussy tears a mouse. [Cooper, 1964, p. 84]

All of England lay coiled, tensely poised to repel the daily expected invasion of French troops led by the rabid Corsican. Faced with a threat unparalleled since the Normans, and which would be matched in the next century only by the Nazis, England waited for Napoleon's *Grande Armée*, some two hundred thousand strong, to cross the Channel. Throughout Britain, a vast sentinel network was set up, with huge woodpiles ready to be kindled at a moment's notice to announce the invasion. In peacetime such bonfires were used to announce Royal Coronations. Had he given it some thought, Coleridge would have had good reason to wonder whether he or others in his world were saner.

But while his friends and fellow countrymen prepared to repel the French hordes, Coleridge remained in his study, reading and transcribing his 1799 diaries, concentrating his attention on ideas for *The Soother of Absence*. The mood would be one of timeless sorrow:

> One excellent use of communication of sorrows to a friend is this: that in relating what ails us we ourselves first know what the real grief is—and see it for itself, in its own form and limits.... Perhaps, at certain moments a single most insignificant sorrow may, by association, bring together all the little relicts of pain and discomfort, bodily and mental, that we have endured even from infancy [CNB 1599]

Having established the tone for his epic with this remarkably insightful description of the way in which grief experienced in the present telescopes with childhood memories of grief, Coleridge blocked out a scene for his tale:

> Sara! Sara! ... If I have not heard from you very recently, and if the last letter had not happened to be full of explicit love and feeling, then I conjure up shadows into substances—and am miserable. Misery conjures up other forms, and binds them into tales and events—activity is always pleasure—the tale grows pleasanter—and at length you come to me. You are by my bed side, in some lonely inn, where I lie deserted—there you have found me—there you are weeping over me!—Dear, dear, woman! [CNB 1601]

The pathetic inn scene was clearly a daydream intended for his poem's plot and no letters survive—not even heavily edited fragments—to suggest even a remote kernel of reality to the idea that Coleridge and Sara were actually corresponding at this time.

Coleridge's dramatic upsurge in yearnings for Sara Hutchinson were again triggered by his desperate wish to reknit his failing ties to Wordsworth. Faced with the knowledge that his feelings of envy were poisoning his bond with William, Coleridge turned to her, half as the heroine of his poem and half as a flesh-and-blood woman. Had he succeeded in either area his jealousy might have abated. Ridding himself of his obsession with Sara by writing a great epic poem about her might have blunted his envy of Wordsworth, while becoming his friend's brother-in-law by bonding with Sara might have allowed him to bask in William's glory more graciously.

Unfortunately, Coleridge felt no more ready to write *The Soother of Absence* than to pursue Sara Hutchinson in real life. Instead he decided to confront his envy more directly—at least in his notebooks. He would write down his childish feelings and subject them to rational analysis. Coding his own name as A. and William's as B., he approached the problem as if it were an impersonal logical theorem in what amounted to a no-fault system of personality analysis:

> I have had some *Lights* lately respecting envy. A. thought himself unkindly used by B.—he had exerted himself for B. with what warmth! honoring, praising B. beyond himself.—etc, etc—B. selfish—The *up*, askance, pig look, in the boat, etc. Soon after this A. felt distinctly ugly touchlets of pain and little shrinkings back at the heart, at the report that B. had written a new poem, an excellent one!—and he saw the faults of B. [CNB 1606]

After further soul-searching and some semantic quibbling, Coleridge concluded in his entry that his was the "vice of personal uncharitableness, not envy" and that his feelings were a matter of "mere resentment" (CNB 1606).

Coleridge hoped that logical analysis of his feelings and cool forecasting of future hurts would desensitize him to his bitterness. But matters went from bad to worse, and envy and opiates gnawed at his bowels. As he put it, "Something there is in my stomach or guts that transubstantiates my bread and wine into the body and blood of the devil" (CL II, p. 992). He was torn between religion and psychology as he sought to make sense of experiences that were equally open to analysis by either approach: "December 6, 1803—Adam travelling in his old age came to a set of the descendants of Cain, ignorant of the origin of the world; and treating him as a madman killed him. A sort of dream, which I had this night" (CNB 1698).

Culture-bound and deeply influenced by his early religious upbringing, it makes sense that Coleridge dreamt in biblical images. But what did his dream of Cain mean to him? Enough of a modern psychologist to half sense that dreams pictorialize "a scattered mob of obscure feelings" associatively linked to "little relicts of pain . . . that we have endured from infancy" (CNB 1599), Coleridge was also half attracted to the medieval incubus theory that dreams, nightmares in particular, derive from possession of the sleeper by evil spirits: the devil's work. Given the biblical imagery of his dream(s), both explanations fit his data equally well.

In Christian terms, he could chastize himself: his dream confirmed that he was suffering from the "vice of personal uncharitableness" (CNB 1606)—the devil was at work in his guts. Psychologically, of course, it makes sense that "childhood relicts" of his old Cain and Abel memories were being stirred by his rivalrous conflict with William. Unable directly to connect his feelings toward William with his old ones toward Frank, he linked them symbolically in his dream, taking upon himself once more the role of Cain.

Faced with the threatened reemergence of these violent feelings, Coleridge's instinctive reaction was to look for an escape from his pernicious friendship with Wordsworth and from the conflicts it evoked. In a sunny climate maybe he could conquer his escalating addiction, as well. He made up his mind to head south.

Before leaving his family and Greta Hall, he often went to sleep hugging his pillow as if it were, he wrote, a giant breast. On his last night home he bade farewell to his pillow by hallucinating "a phantom of my face . . . in the middle of it" (CNB 1731). The next morning he said good-bye to Sarah and the children and caught a post chaise to Grasmere, where he planned to spend a few days. But laid low by a sudden recurrence of his mysterious ailment, he remained at Dove Cottage for several weeks while Dorothy and Mary nursed him.

Winter had arrived in the Lakes and everyone at Dove Cottage agreed that his mind and body worked like a perfectly tuned barometer, sensitive to the most minute changes in atmospheric conditions. Could anyone who saw it for himself doubt Coleridge's need for a consistently warm climate?

As he lay on his sickbed, his opiate intake increased even further during the midnight-to-dawn vigils of "delirium" (CNB 1770) which he attributed to his "feverous brain" (CNB 1782). Resting fitfully, he candle-gazed nightly while the rest of the household slept. By mid-January he had recuperated sufficiently to travel and began to take long walks with William.

During one of their outings, Wordsworth read the recently completed sections of his autobiographical poem to Coleridge, who pronounced them "divine" (CNB 1801); he graciously promised to send William an elaborate critique of the passages as well as extensive notes blocking out a future strategy for the sections yet to be written. Deeply grateful, William generously "forced" a hundred pounds on Coleridge to help defray the cost of his long voyage (CL II, p. 1040). On the surface at least, they seemed the best of friends.

On the eve of his departure from Dove Cottage, Coleridge had a dream:

> I dreamt among other wild melancholy things, all steeped in a deep dejection but not wholly unmingled with pleasure, that I came up into one of our Christ's Hospital wards, and sitting by a bed was told that Davy was in it, who in attempts to enlighten mankind had inflicted ghastly wounds on himself, and must henceforward live bed-ridden. The image before my eyes instead of Davy was a wretched dwarf with only three fingers; which however produced as always in dreams, no surprise. I however burst at once into loud and vehement weeping, which at length, but after considerable continuance, awakened me. My cheeks were drowned in tears, my pillow and shirt collar quite wet. And the hysterical sob was lingering in my breast. [CL II, p. 1028]

Coleridge's choice of Davy as a stand-in for himself made sense: he had felt a deep identification with Davy when they first met. Like Coleridge, he had been experimenting on himself with consciousness-altering drugs. But while Coleridge had been using opium, Davy had been lucky enough to be using nitrous oxide. By now Davy had made his scientific reputation on that early work, just as Coleridge had secured his literary reputation with the early poems written during the honeymoon phase of his opium experiments.

Recently, however, Coleridge had claimed to be disillusioned with Davy for "prostituting the name of philosopher" (CL II, p. 1032) and for failing to live up to the promise of his youthful genius. Instead, Coleridge felt, Davy was trading on his early experiments for popular success. If, then, Davy is taken as Coleridge's double, the dream suggests that Coleridge was feeling dwarfed, grotesque, and castrated whenever faced with any reminder of his faded youthful Christ's Hospital promise. And Wordsworth's flourishing poetic abilities were a constant reminder.

Coleridge took his leave from the Wordsworths the next morning. Promising to write often and to send his notes for William's masterpiece, he departed on foot, with William accompanying him part of the way before they bade each other good-bye. Afterward, Coleridge walked nineteen miles in the "mud and drizzle, fog and stifling air" (CL II, p. 1040).

If he mused upon the curious details of his farewell dream as he walked along, Coleridge might have recalled that the dwarf had shown him only three fingers. While Coleridge may not have recognized that the missing fingers signified castration, he might well have made something of the wounded dwarf holding up three fingers as if showing him a sign. If the digits were consecutive, they spelled the letter W—William's initial. And regardless of their location, they signified the number three. As Coleridge well knew, in Christian numerology that number stood for the Trinity. Did they also suggest, then, the only remaining solace for Coleridge?

There was much for him to ponder as he set out on the first leg of his Mediterranean pilgrimage. Earlier—when Coleridge had left London to settle in the Lakes—Lamb had teased that he was off to see "his god Wordsworth" (Hanson, 1962, p. 409). And while Coleridge had allowed his friend to dwarf him, Wordsworth had shown himself to be imperfectly human—less than a diety and incapable of offering the protective generosity that Coleridge might reasonably have expected from one.

Was the dwarf trying to tell him that the time had come for Coleridge to look elsewhere if he still craved a personal God?

Chapter 13

Bargaining with God

*When my Triplets you see
Think not of my Poesy
But of the holy Trinity.*

[CNB 1904]

Never never did I feel such a shock as at first sight of him. We all felt exactly in the same way—as if he were different from what we have expected to see. . . . He is utterly changed; and yet sometimes, when he was animated in conversation concerning things removed from him, I saw something of his former self. But never when we were alone with him. He then scarcely ever spoke of anything that concerned him, or us, or our common friends nearly, except we forced him to it; and immediately he changed the conversation to Malta. . . . His fatness has quite changed him—it is more like the flesh of a person in dropsy than one in health; his eyes are lost in it. . . .—a shadow, a gleam there was at times, but how faint and transitory! [LWDW II, p. 86]

Having shared his dream that he would come "back to dear old England, a sample of the first resurrection" (CL II, p. 307), Dorothy Wordsworth was dismayed and heartbroken at her first meeting with Coleridge after his return from Malta. One glance told her he had regained neither his health nor his youthful vigor. The ravages of those three years were striking: his pudgy, boyish face had become flabby, haggard, and bloated. Age, opium, alcohol, and depression were etched upon it.

Had she searched her memory more carefully, Dorothy might have been less shocked. She had noticed signs even before his departure. But nothing is more telling than the first glimpse of an old friend after a long absence. And while he was gone, Dorothy had nostalgically remembered Coleridge as he had been when they first met, in Dorset back in 1797. The two images did not superimpose easily.

Dorothy had been captivated by Coleridge's emotional spontaneity as he soared over the fence and bounded across the pathless field in his rush to greet her on that June day eight years ago. Now he lacked both the agility and the exuberance for such encounters. And his impulsive tendency to cut corners, which she had so admired, had proven fatal. The shortcut to euphoria originally facilitated by opium had detoured abruptly into flattened moods. At best he was subdued: "At Malta . . . I have earned the general character of being a quiet well meaning man, rather dull indeed—and who would have thought, that he had been a *Poet!*" (CNB 2372).

Dorothy's intuition that Coleridge had undergone a fundamental transformation was correct. Her description of their reunion emphasizes her shock and pity over what he had become, but there was also a constructive outcome to Coleridge's stormy passage into midlife that began with the voyage to Malta.

Other pilgrims had sought refuge on that remote stretch of barren rock long before Coleridge. Dramatically converted to Christianity by the miracle of having his sight restored after being struck blind by lightning on his way to Damascus, Saint Paul had later been shipwrecked and stranded on Malta while on his way to Rome. "The inhabitants showed us no small courtesy" (Markham, 1980, p. 1), wrote Luke, describing the sanctuary given them.

It was a sancturary the Maltese provided again, when —during an occupation that lasted several centuries—The Order of the Knights of St. John of Jerusalem, an international group of hospitalers and crusaders, decided to make Malta their home base after being expelled from Rhodes by the Ottoman Turks in 1522. Determined not to suffer another defeat at the hands of the infidels, The Order strengthened and rebuilt Malta's crumbling fortifications so that by the time of Coleridge's arrival the port of Valletta was impregnable to direct military assault and could be conquered only by wars of attrition through systematic naval blockade.

It had been through such a blockade that Napoleon had confiscated the island from The Order while on his way to Egypt. And two years later—after Nelson's victory on the Nile—the English had taken Malta from the French by means of a similar strategy. Napoleon's declaration that he would sooner see the English in a suburb of Paris than in possession of Malta testified to the tiny island's strategic value. Whoever possessed Malta dominated the Mediterranean, and at the time of Coleridge's departure France and England were in the process of settling the issue.

Nelson, in command of the Mediterranean fleet, was playing a cat-and-mouse game, hoping to lure the French squadron out of its lair in the port of Toulon. But determined to spring his divided fleets from Brest, Cadiz, and Toulon and unite them in an armada powerful enough to dominate the Channel and provide coverage for his Army of England, Napoleon had placed his admirals under strict orders to avoid any engagement with the enemy. The war of nerves had been sustained for months; while other French warships and privateers, along with pirate ships from the Barbary Coast had been doing their share to divert Nelson by systematically harassing English commerce in the Mediterranean. Ships like the *Speedwell*, which Coleridge took from England to Malta, were permitted to travel only in convoys.

Fifteen merchantmen and the *H.M.S. Leviathan*, a seventy-four-gun ship of the line—made up the convoy. Their departure from Portsmouth was delayed several days by gale force headwinds but on the morning of April 9, 1804 a favoring breeze blew up from south-southwest, and the caravan weighed anchors and headed down the Channel with every hope of a fair voyage.

In a constructive mood, Coleridge had taken as his motto "no health or happiness without work" (CNB 1993) and carefully outlined his plan for a daily regimen of shipboard activity to avoid idleness, boredom, and depression. He would wake at the crack of dawn; wash, shave, and dress; take tea and study Italian until breakfast. Then he would read philosophy, take journal notes, and work on prose pieces. After lunch it would be more Italian until teatime; afterward, poetry composition. It was all part of an optimistic plan—the new beginning he hoped for if "God grant me fortitude and a perseverant spirit of industry!" (CNB 1993).

Coleridge's major prose project was to be a book entitled *Consolations and Comforts from the exercise and right application of the Reason, the Imagination, and the Moral Feelings addressed to those in Sickness, Adversity or Distress of Mind, from Speculative Gloom.* It was to be a nineteenth-century version of modern self-help books. Coleridge hoped to master his depression by writing about it and by using himself as an example for others. It was a book he would never finish. As the voyage wore on, his subject matter decidedly got the upper hand.

By the third night at sea, the nightmares had returned. Attacked by three menacing hags in a murky passageway, Coleridge awoke shrieking in the middle of the night. A week later, he awoke from another dream, filled with grief, openly weeping, his pillow soaked with tears. The following morning he tried to begin a poem describing the experience but managed only a few lines. Still, it was enough to reassure him that he was a professional writer and that his tormenting experiences were all grist for the mill. Meticulously recording his homesickness, night terrors, and loneliness, he told himself that he was simply getting it down on paper for future use—for his two major projects, *The Soother of Absence* and *Consolations and Comforts.*

Though he slept poorly, things looked better in the light of day, at least during the first leg of the voyage, from Portsmouth to Gibraltar. There was only one bad time, when he gloomily fantasized Mary Hutchinson's death and Wordsworth's then marrying Sara. Otherwise, he avoided morbid daydreams by devoting his energies to recording his immediate impressions of the voyage. Improvising a duck crate as a ringside seat and the ship's rudder case as his writing desk, he stationed himself in the center of the *Speedwell*'s daily bustle and action.

But his ambitious program of work fell by the wayside as he became absorbed in the beauty of the sea. He carefully noted the movement, color, and texture of the waves; the skyscape from dawn to sunset; the night sky and evening stars; and the changing patterns of the coastal shapes of Spain and Portugal far away on the horizon.

The *Speedwell* was a compact, twin-masted merchant brig bound for the Adriatic and the port of Trieste by way of Malta and Venice. She carried sixty-four cannon in her hold—a load which imparted a lurching motion to the one-hundred-thirty-ton vessel as she pitched and rolled in the swells of the sea. Her rhythm reminded Coleridge of "a wench kept home on some gay day to nurse a fretful infant, and who having long rocked in vain, at length rocks in spite" (CL II, p. 1126). Nevertheless she was a fast, trim ship and tended to keep up with her escort, at times even threatening to pass her.

As they approached Gibraltar and the Pillars of Hercules, Coleridge was exhilarated by his sense of cosmic overview on glimpsing the land masses of Europe and Africa at the same time. They spent six days at Gibraltar before weighing anchor and entering the Mediterranean. Greeted by favoring winds their first day back at sea, the convoy progressed steadily. Although he felt queasy, Coleridge focused his attention on the ship's course and remained cheerful.

Then the breeze died down. The *Speedwell* lay in irons, and Coleridge spent the better part of a day staring at the sun's reflection on the water. He was back into his old habit of firegazing. That night he dreamt of Sara Hutchinson.

The next morning the wind had risen, but it was blowing directly against them. The *Speedwell* was forced to tack and veer endlessly to avoid losing ground. Head winds prevailed for almost a week, along with foul weather, which confined Coleridge and his two fellow passengers to their tiny, steamy cabin.

One of his travel companions was a Mr. Hastings, a lieutenant on half pay and a small-time merchant, whose blotchy purple face was "gemm'd" with pimples and black, shining eyes—signs Coleridge attributed to rum, brandy, and a rotting liver (CNB 2072). The other passenger was a Mrs. Ireland, a mammoth woman who worked as housekeeper for a general's family. Christening her "Mrs. Carnosity" because of her bizarre eating habits and obsessive preoccupation with food, Coleridge declared her "an unconscientiously fat woman, who would have wanted elbow room on Salisbury Plain" (CL II, p. 1127).

The ship pitched unpleasantly and Coleridge, withdrawn from his cabin mates, lay on his bunk, increasing his daily opium intake. Groggy from laudanum almost to the point of somnolence, yet unable to sleep because of the thoughts racing through his feverish brain, Coleridge dozed in fits and starts.

During his hazy vigils, fragmentary images of the Wordsworths and Sara Hutchinson floated before him. He tried to summon clear visual pictures of them but was frustrated and tantalized in his efforts. Finally, he managed to capture clear images of their faces but was dismayed by his inability to combine those mental pictures with feelings for his friends. Then his time sense decomposed until he was haunted by a vivid impression that it was a hot July day. He was forced to remind himself of exactly where he was on a half dozen different occasions throughout that long, feverish day.

Struck by the similarity between his own ordeal and the *Speedwell*'s, Coleridge compared his deteriorating thought processes to the Sisyphean futility of the ship's motion. Finally, the wind shifted and the *Speedwell* began gaining on her destination—but in gale force winds and high seas. Part of her rigging was sheared off by the storm and the entire ship's crew was seasick except for the captain. Crouching in terror on his bunk, Coleridge imagined a horrible death by drowning, his fear relieved only when he nodded off in opium dozes.

The storm died down as rapidly as it had come up, but two days later Coleridge was delirious and visually hallucinating. Mouth open, teeth bared menacingly, a savage image of his own face hovered above him. With equal suddenness, a woman's face materialized in the floral patterns in the curtains of his bunk.

Shortly afterward, he became sorely constipated as a result of the heavy doses of opium he had been taking. On the ninth of May—"a day of horror" (CNB 2085)—the military surgeon was rowed over to the *Speedwell* to manually disimpact Coleridge. Although filled with tears of gratitude, Coleridge made no mention of the role opium had played in his emergency, though his diary reveals he was clearly aware of the drug's responsibility for both his delirium and his constipation.

Unable to discontinue opium, he chastized himself for his lack of willpower and vowed to make an all-out effort once back on dry land, safe and sound. The following night he had another screaming nightmare and was eternally grateful to Mrs. Ireland for waking him. By now "Mrs. Carnosity" had become "good Mrs. I." (CNB 2087).

Coleridge's voyage to Malta had begun on a hopeful note of confidence in his capacity for self-discipline. In a spirit of determined optimism, he had sneered arrogantly at the weaknesses of his two fellow passengers and their inability to control their vices. But now, as the *Speedwell* rapidly approached the coast of Malta, he was of a different frame of mind:

> O dear God! give me strength of Soul to make one thorough trial—If I land at Malta, spite of all horrors to go through one month of unstimulated nature—yielding to nothing but manifest danger of life!—O great God! Grant me grace truly to look into myself, and to begin the serious work of self-amendment —accounting to conscience for the hours of every day. Let me live in *Truth*—manifesting that alone which *is*, even as it *is*, and striving to be that which only reason shows to be lovely—that which my imagination would delight to manifest!—I am loving and kind-hearted and cannot do wrong with impunity, but o! I am very, very weak—from my infancy have been so—and I exist for the moment!—Have mercy on me, have mercy on me, Father and God! omnipresent, incomprehensible, who with undeviating laws eternal yet carest for the falling of the feather from the sparrow's wing.—Sunday Midnight, May 13th, 1804. [CNB 2091]

Five days later the *Speedwell* dropped anchor at Malta. After spending the night in quarantine aboard ship, Coleridge was rowed ashore the next morning. Feeling "light as a blessed ghost" (CNB 2100), he somehow managed to weave his woozy way through the town to the villa of an acquaintance from England, John Stoddart. Distorted as in a funhouse mirror, Valletta's steep streets and towering fortifications loomed up, "all height and depth—you can walk nowhere without having whispers of suicide, toys of desperation. Explosive cries of the Maltese vendors—shot up, broad and bulky noises, sudden and violent" (CNB 2100).

After settling in at the Stoddarts, he attended services the next day at a small Anglican chapel where he was horrified to discover the altar cross painted in the baroque Roman Catholic manner rather than the bare, simple English style. He had not come to Malta to worship a popish God. But he was better pleased to find white freestone houses that reminded him of Bath during a tour of the town made later that day. It was late spring and the entire island was an exotic botanical garden, filled with tropical trees and flamboyant flowers he had never before seen. Delighted with the dates, pomegranates, almonds, and carobs, Coleridge enthusiastically noted that the orange and lemon trees were already thick with fruit.

He found the commercial district less attractive than the residential section. Its noisy thoroughfares were packed with Maltese citizens, English soldiers, and an odd assortment of vagabonds, adventurers, and refugees from Africa, Europe, and the Levant. The market passages were lined with shops of tradesmen and artisans interspersed with tavernas and cafes. Beggars, urchins, dogs, cats, pigs, and roosters all added to the traffic while swarthy vendors hawked their wares, shouting descriptions of their offerings at an ear-splitting pitch in order to be heard above the braying of the donkeys and the tinkle of mandolins.

As the Stoddart's new houseguest, Coleridge met other members of the tightly knit British colony. They led an active social life, with salons, card parties, balls, theatricals, dinner parties, and government receptions, but he was in no condition for a heavy social schedule. His first order of business was his long-promised showdown with his addiction.

He wasted no time in starting his withdrawal program, going "cold turkey" instead of tapering off gradually. As part of his new regimen, he awoke daily at dawn and bathed in the sea. By the third day he began to feel "unwellish" and went on to spend "a wretched and debilitating night" (CNB 2101). Toward the end of the first week he became severely ill, rushing home from a dinner party and taking to his bed with a "raging fever" (CL II, p. 1137) until one of the servants became alarmed and called Stoddart, who rushed to his bedside. Feebly instructing his host to give him thirty drops of laudanum in a glass of lemonade, Coleridge was better within twenty minutes.

His trial with opium was excruciating. To do without it was an agony, and while the next dose brought relief, the hypersensitivity to sound it induced was an acoustic nightmare. His nerves were jangled by the deafening racket of "jack asses—cats—cocks—bells—day cries—night-bellowings—guns" (CNB 2114). "But the worst of all, and the only thing at all alarming in my case, is the now constant oppression in my breathing—so that I walk up and down, like a leopard in his den" (CL II, p. 1138). Feeling suicidal and lacking both medical supervision and emotional support, he terminated his trial and was candle-gazing within days. The "thorough trial" of abstinence he promised himself on board the *Speedwell* lasted less than a week (CNB 2091). Nonetheless, it helped his morale to be on doses less astronomical.

Well aware that boredom and idleness invariably led to escalating doses, Coleridge was pleased to obtain the post of temporary private secretary to Sir Alexander Ball, Malta's civil governor. His duties consisted of helping Ball prepare reports and bulletins which were sent back to Whitehall with each departing convoy.

Malta was an important observation post for gathering information on French naval operations, and Ball's dispatches were considered vital to British military intelligence and foreign policy. And by prearrangement with Stuart, Coleridge would occasionally be sending pieces based on nonclassified data to the *Post*. Given the fact that Pitt had just returned to office and Napoleon had crowned himself Emperor of France, Coleridge was excited by the novelty of the adventure, at least for the moment.

In early July Coleridge was given quarters in the lavish Governor's mansion. But nine days out of ten were spent living and working at Ball's summer residence at St. Antonio, four miles out of town. Summer had arrived and the intense heat of the infernal Mediterranean sun beat down mercilessly on Valletta. By midday its sweltering, dusty streets were motionless; only gradually did they come back to life with the growing shade created by the slanting afternoon sun. By sunset the entire town was noisily reanimated, and in the late evenings everyone went to bed surrounded by tangles of mosquito curtains that only seemed to trap the thick, motionless night air. By dawn the baked outer crust of the earth's shell had cooled off as it dissipated the collected heat of the previous day; but by then the entire process was ready to begin all over again.

Once that July an earthquake tremor shook the island, breaking the torpidly monotonous routine. Occasionally, lightning storms lit up the night sky, but rarely was there rain. Periodically, the hot, humid breezes of a sirocco made their way from the deserts of North Africa. While other Englishmen cursed the unkind climate, Coleridge declared himself content. He had had not one bout of arthritis since arriving on Malta.

In spite of the heat, Coleridge and Ball worked diligently. Ball dictated and Coleridge reworked the papers into final form, subject to Ball's approval. On his days off, Coleridge walked over to nearby St. Julian's Bay to visit the Stoddarts, who had taken refuge from Valletta and were summering there.

In early August Coleridge set out on a long-awaited three-month tour of Sicily armed with a semi-official letter of introduction from Ball to the British Consul in Syracuse, G.F. Leckie. Coleridge remained as the Leckies' houseguest for his entire stay, using their villa as his base of operations for day trips and extended visits into the countryside as far north as Mount Etna. By now his spoken Italian was seviceable enough for him to get around, though he was frustrated that his range of conversation was limited to the opera and the weather.

Attending the opera almost nightly, Coleridge was struck by the naturalistic way in which it served as the popular poetry of Sicily, in contrast to the elitist appeal of Covent Garden productions. Even the most ragged urchins sang snatches of arias as they roamed the streets of Syracuse.

But Coleridge's ardor for opera took on deeper personal significance after his encounter with Cecilia Bertozzoli, the prima donna of the local company. Their torrid friendship rapidly progressed from a flirtation to a romance which ended abruptly in her boudoir—where, in a fit of conscience, Coleridge abruptly terminated their dalliance and fled from her bedside before their lovemaking could be consummated.

Neither did he have sufficient presence of mind or command of the subtleties of the Italian language to explain his complex reasons for withdrawing from "la P. D." (CNB 2196). And in the awkwardness of the moment, it is not likely that she would have been sympathetic. It happened in a flash: in the midst of the erotic preliminaries an image of Sara Hutchinson's face passed before him:

> gracious Heaven! when I call to mind that heavenly vision of her face, which came to me as the guardian angel of my innocence and peace of mind, at Syracuse, at the bedside of the too fascinating Siren, against whose witcheries Ulysses's wax would have proved but a half-protection, poor Cecilia Bertozzoli. Yet neither her beauty with all her power of employing it, neither heavenly

song, were as dangerous as her sincere vehemence . . . of *attachment*—for it was not mere *passion*, and yet Heaven forbid! that I should call it *love*. [CNB 3404]

While Coleridge rationalized his behavior by telling himself he was acting out of loyalty to Sara Hutchinson, there is no evidence that his fidelity was based on a sexually consummated relationship with her. All of Coleridge's biographers agree that they were not physically involved. In fact, during those final days before leaving Dove Cottage to depart for Malta, Coleridge had *wishfully* daydreamed of returning to Sara with "a deforming eruption" on his face and body (CNB 1826) that would render him so repulsive as to guarantee the asexual love he yearned to have with her. He prided himself on the platonically disembodied, spiritual nature of his feelings.

And at the time of his misadventure with Cecilia, Coleridge was a young man of thirty-one, hundreds of miles from home, feeling very much alone and sexually frustrated. While nobly justifying his prudishness on the basis of moral scruples, he himself had begun to observe his extreme finickiness toward women and his repugnance with physical passion. Commenting on the sultry sensuality of the Maltese, he was struck by the contrast between their lust and his "English hauteur"—his *"horror carnis humanae,"* or dread of human flesh (CNB 2123). This horror was most apparent in his nightmares, which were replete with images of the infecting touch, kiss, and breath of tempting sirens and frightening hags. Nor was the traditional safety valve of masturbation—which he referred to as "many a man's secret harm" (CNB 2747)—an outlet he would permit himself to enjoy guiltlessly. Instead, pent up and frustrated, he was in the process of becoming prissy and compulsive: "I cannot endure the least atom or imagination of dirt on my person, but wash my body all over 20 times, where 8 or 9 years I washed half of it once" (CNB 2531). And so, growing old before his time, his chief form of recreation and entertainment was to debauch himself with bouts of libido-deadening laudanum followed by recriminatory orgies of self-flagellation.

Ten days after his sexually frustrating encounter with Cecilia Bertozzoli, he reached one of his climaxes of opium confession. It was his thirty-second birthday:

> O my God! ... So help me heaven! ... O sorrow and shame! I am not worthy to live.... I have done nothing! No I have not even layed up any material, any inward stores,—of after action!—O no! still worse! body and mind, habit of bedrugging the feelings, and bodily movements, and habit of dreaming. ... [CNB 2237]

He returned to Malta in early November. The Mediterranean fall was filled with clear radiant days as the street vendors hawked their cool-weather crop of peas in the brilliant sunshine, shouting in Arabic to passersby. As winter came on, the days became gray, wet, and windy. Evenings when he did not go out to socialize, he spent his time musing by the fireside of the Governor's Palace. Feeling lonely and homesick, he increased his opium dose and doodled the initials *WW DW MH SH STC* on page after page of his notebooks as he vacantly firegazed. And in a remarkable journal passage that winter, Coleridge spoke to future busybodies and snooping biographers who he imagined might some day be thumbing through his private diaries:

> If I should perish without having the power of destroying these and my other pocket books, the history of my own mind for my own improvement. O friend! Truth! Truth! but yet Charity! Charity! I have never loved Evil for its own sake; no! nor ever sought pleasure for its own sake, but only as the means of escaping from pains that coiled round my mental powers, as a serpent around the body and wings of an eagle. My sole sensuality was *not* to be in pain! [CNB 2368]

But if one eye was on posterity, his other was becoming firmly fixed on eternity. Rereading his old diaries by the Palace fireside that winter, he was reviewing his life, putting it in perspective and clarifying his faith:

> Christianity an imposture, the scriptures a forgery, the worship of God superstition, Hell a fable, Heaven a dream, our Life without providence and our death without Hope—etc.
>
> (I wrote this quotation from Bentley Dec. 1797. With what different thoughts I re-peruse it Jan. 1805—yet the feelings the same.) [CNB 312]

Bargaining with God

Feelings the same, different thoughts: what did Coleridge mean? Never an atheist, he had always believed in God. But back in his Unitarian days, the Trinity and the miracles had seemed so much Anglican mumbo jumbo, mystifying rhetoric designed to exploit ignorant working class men.

He had pictured Jesus as a proletarian radical at the barricades—a millenarian visionary like himself. But now his belief in himself was shattered and his faith in his fellow man lay dead. The glorious French Revolution had spawned a greedy dictator, nothing more. Pantisocracy, marriage, and *Lyrical Ballads* had soured into disillusioning partnerships. Addicted and unable to create, Coleridge had lost his pride in himself. Far worse, he was unable to change his life by exerting his free will—it would take a miracle to free him from this morass.

By now Coleridge *wanted* to believe in miracles and in a God who could perform them. And that God was the God of his childhood—an Anglican God. But the doctrine of the Trinity had always been his stumbling block: was Jesus a mere man or the Son of God. If Jesus was mortal, like himself, then Coleridge would have to save himself. But if Jesus were the divine Son—one of the persons of the Trinity—then Coleridge could pray for redemption.

Faith comes quickly to men under stress. As Coleridge reviewed his life by the Palace fireside, his need to believe grew more desperate:

> But yesternight I pray'd aloud
> In Anguish and in Agony
> Help Lord! or I perish.... [CNB 2482]

If modes of petition reflect degrees of faith, Coleridge had been climbing Jacob's ladder. Over the years his dialogues with his maker had run the gamut from silent passing thoughts about God, to fragmentary personal pleas, to formal silent prayers—until recently, when he had prayed aloud, just as he had done as a child. Back then it was:

> Matthew! Mark! Luke! and John!
> God bless the bed which I lie on.
> Four Angels round me spread.
> Two at my feet and two at my head.
> [CL I, p. 348]

Once more he found himself praying for a peaceful night's sleep.

Coleridge's diaries reveal this transition in his faith. His first direct petition to God occurred after his delirium on the *Speedwell*. But he had been bargaining with God. His faith in the Trinity was not settled, and he knew his prayer to be conditional, as if to say: *Give me the strength to resist opium and I, in turn, will believe in You and all of Your mysterious ways which my intellect cannot fathom.*

That prayer had gone unanswered, and now Coleridge was struggling to meet his God halfway by tackling the thorny problem of the Trinity. He chose Paul as a guide for his pilgrimage. Like Coleridge, Saint Paul was a skeptical nonbeliever until he had been blinded by lightning and restored to sight through amazing Grace. Hoping for a similar awakening, Coleridge searched for evidence that such miracles were possible. He found the proof he was looking for in a three-month-old English newspaper: "*Mr. R. Tower of Hempnall, Norfolk, was struck blind, as he was returning from Norwich, but has since received his sight*" (CNB 2272). Carefully transcribing the item in his diary, he concluded, "A case strictly the same in the only apparently miraculous part with the conversion of St. Paul" (CNB 2272). Afterward Coleridge meditated on Paul's teaching that God was not comprehensible through the senses or through reason, but only through revelation.

As winter wore on, the northwest winds kicked up whitecaps across the Mediterranean, while Coleridge opium-gazed into the nightly fires, musing on Paul, his fellow Maltese shipwreck victim. He groaned and prayed for God to grant him a "day of visitation" (CNB 2437). Three days later—on a wintry Tuesday afternoon in February—Coleridge's prayer was answered: "it burst upon me at once as an awful truth. . . . No Christ, No God!" He carefully wrote down 1:30 P.M., the exact moment of his revelation—"No Trinity, No God!" Now he could be sure, once and forever, that "Unitarianism in all its forms is idolatry" (CNB 2448).

But thunderstruck as he may have felt that day, Coleridge soon discovered that he had not been born again. While settling a crucial article of his faith in a remarkably self-dramatizing manner, he had not magically transformed his life. The downward spiral continued inexorably. The only difference was that he had returned to the religion of his father and his father's father and could take comfort in the Trinity when the going got rough.

As Easter approached, his depression worsened; he became suicidal. Outside the windows of his apartment Valletta buzzed with the Dionysian festivities of Carnival Week. The island was rioting with spring daisies, its craggy rocks carpeted with crimson and blue wildflowers, its orange and lemon trees dripping with fruit. But no more in tune with nature's annual resurrection than with its metaphorical celebration in the pageantry of the Roman Catholic Church, he growled and muttered to himself about the "mummery, processions, baptisms, etc—the immense noise and jingle jingle as if to frighten away the daemon" (CNB 2561). British to the bone, Coleridge was emphatically Anglican, *not* Catholic.

Homesick, he waited impatiently for his replacement to arrive from England. He had received almost no letters from home in a year and had recently been dismayed to discover that many of his own had never reached their destination. Some had been lost through French attacks on English convoys, while others had been burned as plague papers after the friend entrusted to carry them had contracted yellow fever and died. In fact, throughout most of that long lonely winter, Malta's communication with the outside world had been drastically curtailed because an epidemic of yellow fever had broken out on Gibraltar; quarantine restrictions slowed traffic to a standstill in ports throughout the Mediterranean.

As always when he was homesick or lonely, his nightly swigging from his laudanum bottle increased dramatically. Hung over one morning, he contritely asked himself: "Had I prayed and surrendered my whole heart to God and reason, could this have been the result?" (CNB 2458).

But the lost lamb was not left without guidance: Coleridge dreamt he was alone in a Christ's Hospital classroom until Middleton, his former mentor, appeared and greeted him warmly. After Middleton disappeared, Coleridge slumped beneath a desk and lay beside the flickering flames of a fire that had materialized at the foot of the desk. As he lay by that fireplace, a clergyman schoolmaster began to read aloud from a text of

Saint Paul. But instead of listening to the sermon, Coleridge continued to fire-gaze and daydream, though his lecturer was now Saint Paul himself. Then Middleton returned. Vexed by Coleridge's behavior, he scolded him severely until he woke up.

Coleridge's dream depicted his Faustian dilemma and the nightly battle taking place for his soul. Having forfeited it to an opium devil, he stared nightly into fires he believed to be the same as those in which he expected to be spending eternity. Unless, that is, Paul could drag him from the burning coals. But even if Saint Paul had not yet gained Coleridge's undivided attention in the matter of redemption, there were times when he appeared to be gaining some ground:

> I humbly thank God, that I have for some time past been more attentive.... There are few day-dreams that I dare allow myself at any time; and ... it is very seldom that I can think myself entitled to make lazy holiday with any one of them. I must have worked, hard, long, and well, to have earned that privilege. [CNB 2543]

Coleridge seesawed endlessly between despair and redemption, death and resurrection. Able to savor the fragrance of the orange blossoms, he feasted his senses on the multicolored brilliance of the wildflowers and "the hum of numberless bees" for days at a time (CNB 2569)—only to become numbed once more and sink back into a stupefied, cadaverous despair in which he became preoccupied with the degradation of his addiction and felt suicidal. During these zombielike periods his thoughts turned to his Soother of Absence, Sara Hutchinson. But his musings about her became more and more ethereal. And as time wore on it was God, not Sara, who soothed his soul when he hit rock bottom. If he could pray with conviction, his inner deadness lessened:

> To God
> Thou who the weak and bruised never breakest,
> Nor ever triumph in the yielding seekest,
> Pity my weak estate, o now or never,
> I ever yet was weak, and now more weak than ever.
>
> S.T.C.—The fish gasps on the glittering mud, the mud of this once full stream, now only moist enough to be glittering

mud. The tide will flow back, time enough to lift me up with straws and withered sticks and bear me down into the ocean. O me! that being what I have been I should be what I am! [CNB 2606]

All through that long hot summer Coleridge hung on as best he could, waiting for his replacement. By August the thermometer read eighty-eight in the shade and one hundred forty in the sun as the slats of the oak and mahogany chests in the Governor's Palace split with a popping noise like fireworks or pistol shots. Sometimes he meditated on Christ and Saint Theresa; other times he increased his laudanum. Finally, the new secretary arrived. Two weeks later, on September 23, 1805, Coleridge set out for the home he had not seen in eighteen months.

His plans were uncertain. If the British Consul in Naples agreed to declare him an official diplomatic courier and provide passage on a King's ship, he would sail home. Otherwise, he preferred to avoid repeating his harrowing experiences on the *Speedwell* by taking an overland route through Italy and Northern Europe, giving France and her territories a wide berth.

But as Coleridge discovered by the time he hit Naples, Bonaparte's legions were even then pouring into Italy and Austria. On the twenty-first of October Nelson and his "band of brothers" had inflicted devastating damage on the French armada at Trafalgar, decisively foiling Napoleon's plans to invade England. Wheeling in his fury, Bonaparte had only just begun to concentrate his thirst for glory and revenge on the rest of Europe.

Soon to be given a place of honor next to the Imperial Guard's pennants commemorating the carnage at Ulm and Austerlitz would be the banner announcing France's victory over Prussia on the bloody battlefields of Jena. Having already demonstrated that he could carve up the troops and lands of the Holy Roman and Austro-Hungarian Empires as suited his whim, Napoleon was setting his sights on total continental victory.

Convinced that his own name was among those on the Emperor's most-wanted list for the unflattering articles he had written on the Corsican upstart in the *Post* back in 1799–1800, Coleridge toured Southern Italy for the winter but abandoned his plan to weave his way through Napoleon's columns. By spring he had arrived as far north as Florence and from there made his way to the port of Livorno, where he booked passage home on the *Gosport*, an American ship.

Looking at himself in the mirror at his *pensione* while waiting for his ship to sail, he "made the melancholy observation" that at thirty-three his protuberant abdomen revealed the telltale signs of middle age (CNB 2701). But it would be two more years before Coleridge could see through the looking glass and put his Malta experiences into perspective:

> there is a period in a man's life, varying in various men from 35 to 45 . . . in which a man finds himself at the *Top of the Hill*—and having attained perhaps what he wishes begins to ask himself—What is all this for?—begins to feel the *vanity* of his pursuits—becomes half-melancholy, gives in to wild dissipation, or self-regardless drinking—and some not content with these—not *slow*—poisons, destroy themselves—and leave their ingenious female, or female-minded friends to fish out some *motive*. . . . I had *felt* this truth; but never saw it before so clearly; it came upon me at Malta, under the melancholy dreadful feeling of finding myself to be *Man*, by a distinct division from Boyhood, Youth, and "*Young Man*"—Dreadful was the feeling—before that life had flown on so that I had always been *a Boy*, as it were. . . . Yet if men survive this period, they commonly become cheerful again—that is a comfort—for mankind—*not for me!* [CNB 3322]

The *Gosport* left Livorno on June 23, 1806, and reached Portsmouth the eleventh of August. After spending six days in quarantine, Coleridge came ashore "shirtless and almost penniless" (CL II, p. 1177). He hurried to a small deserted chapel and offered up "as deep a prayer as ever without words or thoughts was sent up by a human being" (CL II, p. 1176).

Like the mariner, who shrived himself, Coleridge prayed upon his safe return to his homeland. His "exile" (CL II, p. 1174), as he put it, was over. There had been moments when he had relived the mariner's ordeals. His crises of faith and delirium were like the old navigator's trials. At times his poem struck him as uncannily prophetic, as scenes from the *Mariner* materialized before him: a young boy scrambling up the *Speed-*

well's rigging with a leg of mutton hung from his neck "albatross fashion" (CNB 1997); the time he pondered the "strange lust of murder in man" (CNB 2090) as the ship's crew tried to kill a helpless seahawk as it wheeled from ship to ship looking for a safe perch; the evening star dogging the crescent moon; the eerie illumination of the helmsman's lantern at night; the sun pouring through the gossamer sails of the becalmed convoy; the rushing sound of porpoises hissing like a ghost ship accelerating from some inner source of mysterious power on a windless sea; the nautical lore of the superstitious crew. Time and again his thoughts returned to his ballad. But was there really anything uncanny about that?

Common sense suggests that the voyage he made would remind him of the one he had written about. One need not pose a deep unconscious motive to explain why his experiences at sea reverberated with his poem about the sea. In fact, he later used his recorded observations for important revisions in the *Mariner*, making it more vivid, more seaworthy. He was an artist practicing his craft.

But he also began to feel an identification with the mariner which went beyond a series of associations to his poem. Stepping off the ship at Malta, he felt "light as a blessed ghost" (CNB 2100), the mariner's words as well. And for over two years he had been metaphorically alone on a wide, wide sea. He had discovered the relief that prayer could bring.

Yet even if there were moments of deeply felt connection with the mariner, what do they signify? Coleridge was an artist with a lively imagination, capable of forming intense identifications with a wide range of characters. In the prima donna's boudoir he became Ulysses struggling to remain faithful to Penelope by stuffing wax in his ears to avoid the temptation of the Siren's sweet song. In his apartment at the Treasury he made a similar identification with Saint Paul as he searched for his faith in God's mysteries.

But the Mariner's experiences had been a myth of his own making—and a myth not yet completed with his return to solid ground. Like the mariner, Coleridge was about to become a refugee in his own land. For the next eight years he would be a displaced person without a permanent home. He would roam, searching for domestic peace, compulsively reliving his ordeals and telling the tale of his suffering.

Had the mythmaker merged with his myth? Or, to put it less mystically, was Coleridge adopting the myth of his character as part of his unconscious sense of identity as he made the transition into midlife?

Coleridge's earlier identity crisis in adolescence offers clues about his midlife turmoil. His passage into adulthood had been stormy. The news of Frank's suicide triggered the Comberbache episode as he set out to undo his fratricidal guilt by nursing a delirious stranger. After that, he had attempted to repair his loss by finding a brother, first with Southey, then Lloyd.

His quest ended in Somerset, where life and art conspired to bring him the relief he sought—he met Wordsworth and wrote *The Rime of the Ancient Mariner*. Successfully establishing his identity, he became a professional writer who told symbolically his tale of fratricidal conflict. At the same time, he deeply believed in the social ideal of brotherhood and unselfishly lived up to it in his friendship with William. Coleridge went through his identity crisis and achieved dignity, peace of mind, and a stable sense of who he was.

Afterward, whenever his old fratricidal conflict threatened to reemerge, he bent over backward to keep up his friendship with Wordsworth, regardless of the personal expense. While his poem *Christabel* began to express his Christ-Abel feelings of being the sacrificial victim, he avoided any direct recognition of his growing feelings of resentment. But despite his efforts, their ideal brotherhood began to deteriorate and *Christabel* became blocked.

He began to sense a growing hostility toward William and to rue having subjugated his professional identity to him. He began to realize that they were not of one mind in their views on poetry. In Scotland, William had appeared pig-faced and petty. Shortly afterward, his old fratricidal feelings began to reemerge. Not too long before his departure for Malta, Coleridge dreamt of two brothers caught in a life-and-death struggle over their birthright, followed later by his dream of the murderer Cain.

Frightened and guilty at these ominous signs of his childhood conflict resurfacing, Coleridge fled. The hostility toward

Wordsworth beginning to obtrude into his consciousness appalled him—its bewildering power threatened to disrupt the most treasured relationship of his adult life. Coleridge's complexly constructed symbolic solution to his childhood problem had operated with clockwork efficiency on many levels at once. Now the intricate mechanisms threatened to become unsprung and fall into a thousand pieces that could never be reassembled.

While his voyage to Malta was consciously intended to gain perspective by removing himself from an overheated situation, it was also a symbolic repetition of his old childhood story: he was reliving the exodus of victim and victimizer. The small boy ran from the scene of the crime after erupting with murderous feelings toward his big brother. Later the exiled older brother sailed away on a sea voyage from which he would never return unless brought back from the dead. Earlier, Coleridge had clumsily reconstructed the story in *Osorio* and then artfully synthesized it in the *Ancient Mariner*. Was he now reliving it in life?

Like Frank, Coleridge fell into a delirium and became suicidal, guiltily turning his hatred upon himself. In his delirium on board the *Speedwell* he hallucinated an ugly image of himself—his own face, greedy and menacing, mouth open, teeth bared. While the pharmacology of opium best explains the fact *that* he hallucinated, the shape of his terrors was idiosyncratic and by no means random.

Opium disoriented him until his feverish perspiration seemed the sweat of a hot summer's day—but why did his delirium specify July and not August? On just such a hot July's day, he had been thrown helter-skelter back into the feverish agonies of childhood:

> Tuesday Night, July 19, 1803—Intensely hot day—left off a waistcoat, and for yarn wore silk stockings—about 9 o'clock had unpleasant chilliness—heard a noise which I thought Derwent's in sleep—listened anxiously, found it was a calf bellowing — instantly came on my mind that night, I slept out at Ottery—and the calf in the field across the river whose lowing had so deeply impressed me—Chill + Child + Calf-lowing probably the rivers Greta and Otter. [CNB 1416]

Ever since reading the *Arabian Nights* Coleridge had been impressed by the "impossibility of baffling destiny" (CNB 2537).

While he sought to escape his conflicts by fleeing to Malta, they were there waiting for him. On first entering the Governor's Palace, his attention was immediately seized by a painting of Cain slaying Abel. Shortly afterward, a woman on the street reminded him of one he had known at the Henley pesthouse; he considered weaving the experience into a poem about Sara Hutchinson. Throughout his stay on Malta there had been similar flashbacks—fodder for his art, but tormenting and guilt-provoking as well.

If his addiction was not sufficient impediment, Coleridge's gnawing guilt filtered and screened out the joy of the events around him. Like the mariner at the wedding feast, he made himself the outsider. On a Maltese festival day he rattled around the Governor's Palace "like a mouse in a cathedral on a fair or market day" (CL II, p. 1170). While everyone else enjoyed the gaiety of the holiday, Coleridge stood apart and mused to himself:

> It is a subject not unworthy of meditation to myself, what the reason is that these sounds and bustles of holidays, fairs, Easter-Mondays, and Tuesdays and Christmas Days, even when I was a child and when I was at Christ-Hospital, always made me so heart-sinking, so melancholy? Is it, that from my habits, or my want of all money all the first two or three and 20 years of my life I have been *alone* at such times?—That by poor Frank's dislike of me when a little child I was even from infancy forced to be by myself—or rather is it not, that from . . . my ill-health, as well as from sundry accidents of my life, I cannot be happy. . . . [CNB 2647]

As part of his midlife crisis Coleridge was struggling to trace and understand the childhood basis of his unhappiness, that he might fashion a new identity for himself. His intuition told him the answers lay buried in his past. But there he was baffled. How much of his present difficulties were due to an unhappy childhood, ill health, or the random accidents of life? Alienation from Frank, arthritis, and opium were the three sources of his misfortune woven in a Gordian knot, which thus far he found impossible to unravel.

At a loss to determine the significance of the past, where he knew the answers lay, Coleridge was forced to substitute an artistic meaning of his own creation. Aware that his conflicts were neurotic but unable to free himself from their grip by shedding light on their sources, Coleridge was compelled to state them symbolically by assuming the mariner's character—a fact which Dorothy Wordsworth recognized intuitively when she recoiled in pity and horror at the sight of him two months later, on the night of October 26, 1806.

Chapter 14

Exile's Return

*'Tis mine and it is likewise yours;
But and if this will not do
Let it be mine, because that I
Am the poorer of the Two!*
—from the *Notebooks* of STC [CNB 1003]

Throughout the winter and early spring of 1808, traffic periodically came to a standstill on Albemarle Street. At those times Londoners bound for Piccadilly did better to detour onto Dover or Old Bond Streets, which paralleled Albemarle. The traffic snarl crescendoed at number seven, the Royal Institution, where the roadway was jammed with the private carriages of wealthy, fashionable patrons of the arts who had come to hear Samuel Taylor Coleridge deliver a series of lectures on poetry and literature.

Often the coaches waited for what seemed like hours, while ladies and gentlemen sent their liveried footmen scurrying to ask the managers and porters whether Mr. Coleridge would be speaking. By now they were accustomed to long delays and last-minute cancellations due to ill health. Yet despite the irregularity of the speaker, large and enthusiastic crowds filled the auditorium for the fifteen or twenty lectures Coleridge managed to give.

By early spring the series was so popular that Coleridge was able to squeeze in friends without tickets only by arranging personally for them to sit in an upstairs gallery overlooking the crowded hall. One of those present recalled:

> He came unprepared to lecture. The subject was a literary one, and the poet had either forgotten to write, or left what he had written at home. His locks were ... trimmed, and a conscious importance gleamed in his eloquent eyes, as he turned them

> towards the fair and noble heads which bent down to receive his apology. Every whisper (and there were some hundreds of ladies present) was hushed, and the poet began. I remember there was a stateliness in his language, and the measured tones did not fall so pleasantly upon my ear as the half-whispered accents.... I began to think, as Coleridge went on, that the lecture had been left home on purpose; he was *so* eloquent—there was such a combination of wit and poetry in his similes—such fancy, such a finish in his illustrations; yet, as we walked home after the lecture, I remember that we could not call to mind any real instruction, distinct impression, or new fact imparted to us by the great theorist. It was all fancy, flourish, sentiment, that we heard. [Armour and Howes, 1940, p. 416]

At his best, Coleridge spoke with that same sweet musicality that would later make Dylan Thomas so pleasing to hear. Either would have sounded angelic reading a London Street Directory. Each was a theatrical performer who rose to the occasion even while suffering profoundly from the nightmarish effects of his addiction.

De Quincey, who attended the early lectures, described Coleridge's ordeal:

> His lips were baked with feverish heat, and often black in colour; and in spite of the water he continued drinking through the whole course of his lecture, he often seemed to labour under an almost paralytic inability to raise the upper jaw from the lower. [De Quincey, 1970, p. 78]

"With throats unslaked, with black lips baked" (PW, p. 192)—the passage suggests that there were others besides Coleridge himself who had begun to identify him with the Ancient Mariner.

De Quincey's observations were accurate. At other lectures Coleridge was forced to suck oranges; and his diaries describe moments when he suffered from the DT's, with visual hallucinations of bugs crawling in the wallpaper of his room. At times, in the aptly descriptive language of a more contemporary drug culture, he was "spaced out": "I feel like a child—nay, rather like an inhabitant of another planet—their very faces all act upon me, sometimes as if they were ghosts, but more often as if I were a ghost, among them—at all times, as if we were not *consubstantial*" (CNB 3324). One wonders how that sea of faces appeared in the opium mist as the mariner blinked and peered over the rostrum.

Coleridge found the prospect of lecturing nerve-wracking. The audience's attentiveness was no consolation. They had not come to hear his poems but to consider his ideas as a critic—an untried role, and one at which he was desperate to succeed. Aware that his muse had fled permanently, he was trying to stage a comeback as a critic rather than live off his laurels as a burned-out poet at the age of thirty-five. As always, under stress he turned to opium.

But as De Quincey pointed out after his death, Coleridge relied on other aids besides drugs to fortify his courage. One of Coleridge's props, De Quincey revealed, was other men's ideas. He denounced Coleridge as a plagiarist.

Coleridge focused on Shakespeare's plays, which he subjected to formal, scene-by-scene analysis, carefully dissecting the tightly constructed dramas. His lectures were a pioneering effort at a scholarly approach to literature on a systematic basis. They *almost* marked the initiation of that approach, which, however, must actually be credited to a German, Augustus Schlegel, whose ideas Coleridge had previously encountered. And as Coleridge was delivering his lectures at the Royal Institution, Schlegel was giving his in Vienna. The meticulous efforts of modern scholars have clearly determined Schlegel's priority, not only in the critical approach, but in content as well. (For a systematic tracing of Coleridge's borrowings see Fruman, 1974.)

While Coleridge's plagiarisms were intentional rather than accidental, they occurred in a setting of desperation and confusion. He felt himself a man with his back to the wall. Shedding a wife, friends, or career involves a great deal of turmoil and distress, and by the time he mounted the speaker's platform that January, Coleridge was in the process of doing all three.

It had been a year and a half since his return from Malta, and apart from staging a comeback as a critic, he had recently dissolved his marriage and vowed as well to emancipate himself from his "faithful self-sacrificing friendship" (CNB 3232) with Wordsworth. He was striking out on his own. Or was he?

Some viewed him as a pathetic figure whose literary ideas

were the charred remains of the career of a poet whose creative imagination had burned itself out from too much opium and fire-gazing. Was he actually *shedding* his oldest and dearest friends, or was he merely wearing out their patience and goodwill?

William and Dorothy Wordsworth would become the most vocal members of the school that pitied Coleridge. Their letters are riddled with comments of "poor Coleridge" and "poor creature!" (LWDW II, pp. 84, 101, 109, 329; also JDW, 54, 74, 105). But there were others who chafed at that notion. As Lamb put it, "He is a fine fellow in spite of all his faults and weaknesses. Call him Coleridge—I hate 'poor Coleridge.' I cannot bear to hear pity applied to such a one" (CL III, p. 310). Given the divided reactions of Coleridge's friends, it is not surprising that his biographers have been roughly split in similar camps. Those who do not pity him tend to emphasize Coleridge's development as a thinker, while those who emphasize his deterioration focus on the squalor of his addiction.

Both views contain elements of truth: Coleridge was both growing and degenerating. Phoenix-like, he bewildered his friends. As Dorothy once put it, "yet how Coleridge does rise up, as it were, almost from the dead!" (LWDW II, p. 310). Beyond the role played by his unconscious identification with the Mariner in this cyclical return from the deep, much of this confusing, contradictory picture was due to the ebb and flow of Coleridge's addiction. Since opium often leaves no noticeably permanent effects on the mind, it is not surprising that Coleridge could resurrect himself during periods when his drug intake was under better control.

There were times when he could pack lecture halls and spellbind his audiences. But he could also become maudlin, infantile, and virtually incoherent. Those who saw him at his worst were sorely tempted to step in, take over, and manage his life. However, anyone unable to calibrate his attitude to correspond with Coleridge's mercurial shifts might find himself patronizing an extremely intelligent man who was resentfully sensitive about such high-handed treatment. Saving Coleridge from himself could be a touchy proposition.

The rescue mission had begun soon after his return from Malta. Coleridge raised distress signals and William responded by declaring himself in charge of salvage operations. Or, as he put it, "I believe if anything good is to be done for him, it must be done by me" (LWDW II, p. 79). Instead of returning home, Coleridge lingered in London. Like Southey years before, Wordsworth was sorely tempted to fetch his dawdling friend, who once again was busy catching up on old times with the Agnus Dei.

The warm letters Coleridge wrote Sarah described how homesick he felt and how much he missed the children. He was *forced* to delay his return because he was working out arrangements with Humphry Davy to deliver an important lecture series at the Royal Institution. But in his letters to William and Dorothy "homesick" became "heartsick": he was remaining in London because he dreaded the prospect of returning home to Sarah and their scalding arguments.

And so while Sarah Coleridge more positively anticipated their reunion, William and Dorothy braced themselves for the painful ordeal of saving their friend from the grasping clutches of his unsympathetic wife. The stage was set for the old Grasmere-Keswick tug-of-war: The Wordsworths had been cast as the helpful but smug missionaries, and Sarah had the part of the shrew. Coleridge himself was of three minds: he wanted to return to his wife and family, he wanted to be absorbed in the charmed *WW MH SH STC* quartet, and he wanted to remain in London and start a new life. Clinging to all options, he continued to beam his dissonant messages.

On the evening of his return to the Lakes, on the twenty-sixth of October, William and Coleridge talked long into the night. Convinced he knew what was best, Wordsworth adamantly counseled Coleridge to publicly announce his separation from Sarah at once, so there would be no doubt in anyone's mind that his decision was final.

And while Dorothy fretted over Coleridge's vacant, dropsical appearance, she remained unflappably optimistic about the remedy, confident that she and William could rehabilitate their addicted friend. After all, they knew the cause: Sarah Coleridge tormented her husband, driving him to laudanum and brandy. The cure was evident: if Coleridge would make a clean and final break with Sarah and move in with them, they would have him straightened out in no time. If only he would act decisively, they were entirely behind him.

Three days later the Wordsworth entourage set out on their journey south to Coleorton, where they would be spending the winter at a friend's farmhouse. Coleridge, his courage braced, headed home for his showdown with Sarah. His son Derwent later recalled the emotional climate that awaited his father:

> I well remember his expected arrival, my mother had taken my pillow for my father's bed, who required several. In her telling me this, I exclaimed—'Oh! by all means. I would lie on straw for my father,' greatly to my mother's delight and amusement.... [CL II, p. 1199]

But the festive homecoming atmosphere rapidly degenerated into one of bitterness and recrimination. Coleridge's diaries reveal that in the midst of his harangues with Sarah, he visited the rock where he had carved his initials with those of the Grasmere circle shortly before William's wedding. Other entries indicate that he began fire-gazing and daydreaming of Sara Hutchinson.

Aware that Coleridge was deeply conflicted about leaving his children, Wordsworth wrote suggesting that he bring Hartley with him to Coleorton. Three days later, Coleridge replied with a rambling, almost incoherent letter saying that everything was settled and they would soon be on their way. Dorothy breathed a sigh of relief and announced the good news to a friend:

> I have at last the comfort of writing to you with a settled hope that poor Coleridge may be restored to himself and his friends. Lost he has been, oppressed even to the death of all his noble faculties ... but Heaven be praised, his weakness is conquered (I trust it is) and all will be well.... [LWDW II, p. 101]

If the Wordsworths' analysis of Coleridge's predicament was based on an uncharitable view of Sarah Coleridge and, perhaps, William's unconscious guilt over his earlier treatment of Coleridge, the perspective from Keswick was equally unsympathetic. Blaming the Wordsworths for meddling, Southey saw them as motivated by selfishness, not altruism. Wordsworth, Southey claimed, liked nothing better than having the intellectual services of Coleridge's crippled genius at his beck and call—to have Coleridge dedicate himself as William's critic, editor, and source of ideas. According to Southey, Coleridge was all too willing to live through Wordsworth—a claim supported by a note in Coleridge's diary at the time: "To W. . . . O that my spirit purged by death of its weaknesses, which are alas! my *identity* might flow into *thine*, and live and act in thee, and be Thou" (CNB 2712). Nevertheless, Southey was not an unbiased observer and part of his outrage may have stemmed from his resentment that he was about to become de facto head of the Coleridge household. But it would be as much an oversimplification to lay sole blame for the Coleridges' marital problems at the Wordsworths' doorstep as it was for Coleridge to blame Southey for having forced him to marry Sarah Fricker in the first place.

Coleridge had first proposed to Sarah on a whim, his impulse having been to cement a brotherly relationship with Southey. But his infatuation with Southey had turned sour three months before his marriage. Long before he and Sarah went to the altar it was clear there would be no double wedding.

Coleridge and Sarah were in love at the time of their marriage. But there were irrational elements to their idealistic match, as there so often are in marriages based on romantic feelings more than practical considerations or material convenience. Sarah was twenty-five and Coleridge twenty-two at the time of their wedding. Moreover, Sarah was the oldest of five children while Coleridge was the youngest of ten. The baby of one family and the responsible eldest daughter of another were marrying, with the stage set for an unequal emotional dependence. They each retained role models from their parents' marriages that shaped their expectations.

Coleridge remembered his mother as "an admirable economist who managed exclusively" for his dreamy, impractical father (CL I, p. 310). In theory Sarah Fricker had been well prepared to play a similarly complementary role by her mother, who managed singlehandedly after her feckless husband squandered her dowry. But Mrs. Fricker had done so as an embittered martyr—an attitude which apparently had not been part of the script for Coleridge's parents. Then there had been Berkeley's death, Coleridge's addiction, Sarah's temper, meddlesome friends, and another woman to compound their problems. But in the end there are no first causes and postmortem analyses of failed marriages leave much to be desired, whether done from a distance of two hundred years or in the heat of separation.

As she waited triumphantly for Coleridge to arrive, Dorothy Wordsworth was not only certain about her diagnosis of the Coleridges' marital problems; she was equally confident about the Wordsworths' ability to manage their friend's addictions:

> As to drinking brandy, I hope that he has already given over that practice; but *here* I think, he will be tolerably safe. . . . I think if he is not inclined to manage himself, *we* can manage him, and he will take no harm, while he has not the temptations which variety of company leads him into of taking stimulants to keep him in spirits while he is talking. [LWDW II, p. 110]

Coleridge and Hartley arrived on Christmas Day, and over the holidays William read aloud his recently completed autobiographical poem. Barely able to contain himself, William could hardly wait to get his friend's reactions. Coleridge recognized *The Prelude* as the masterpiece it is and told William so, both directly and in a short poem.

But apart from his reaction to the literary merits of the work, Coleridge had a more personal response. The contrast between William's productivity and his own sterility was painfully reemphasized. And while listening to William read his poem was itself enough to make Coleridge jealous, he found something irksome as well in the self-centeredness with which Wordsworth had single-mindedly pursued his goal. On the eve of Coleridge's departure for Malta, having learned that Coleridge had fallen seriously ill in London, William's final letter of farewell had been to beg his stricken friend to send his notes and outlines for William's projected autobiographical masterpiece:

> Your last letter but one informing us of your late attack was the severest shock to me, I think, I have ever received. I walked

over for the letter myself to Rydale and had a most affecting return home in thinking of you and your narrow escape. I will not speak of other thoughts that passed through me; but I cannot help saying that I would gladly have given 3 fourths of my possessions for your letter on The Recluse at that time. I cannot say what a load it would be to me, should I survive you and you die without this memorial left behind. Do for heaven's sake, put this out of the reach of accident immediately. We are most happy that you have gotten the poems, and that they have already given you so much pleasure. Heaven bless you for ever and ever. No words can express what I feel at this moment. Farewell farewell farewell. [LWDW I, p. 464]

But if William's letter had not irritated Coleridge at that time, it is more than likely that Wordsworth's dogmatic ideas concerning his friend's future plans intensified Coleridge's resentment.

It seems that William and Dorothy's rehabilitation agenda included very definite views on Coleridge's career. "Entreating" him not to commit himself to the lecture series at the Royal Institution, they told him that they would "fain see him address the whole powers of his soul to some great work in prose or verse, of which the effect would be permanent, and not personal or transitory" (LWDW II, p. 83).

Well intentioned as they may have been, their disapproval of his plans to deliver his lectures on literary criticism, coupled with the expectation that he write a great work for posterity, as William had just done, served only to demoralize Coleridge even further.

Virtually from the moment of his arrival, Coleridge began to discover that the love between himself and the Wordsworths was poisoned—although he was not yet able to clearly and directly express that perception to himself. Instead, his sense of betrayal came out indirectly, in the form of an angry paranoid fantasy: he imagined that he saw William in bed with Sara Hutchinson. Sensing the delusional nature of his suspicions, he confined his seething outrage to his diary.

Under the influence of opium, Coleridge's imagination was running amok. If formerly Sara had been Coleridge's vehicle for pining to be united with William, she now became his means of expressing his feelings of hatred and betrayal. Unable to admit openly that he envied Wordsworth's poem and was vexed by his friend's smug contempt for his own career plans, Coleridge could only rage at him impotently, in diary entries written in Latin.

In Coleridge's paranoid imaginings, Wordsworth forbade his having Sara as a flesh-and-blood love of his own. Coleridge was galled by the way the doting circle of women in the household (Dorothy, Mary, and Sara) all playfully referred to William as "the Master" and demurely dubbed themselves "we females" (LWDW II, p. 75). But judging from Coleridge's journal, Sara found him unappealing and pathetic, and kept her distance for this reason rather than, as Coleridge suspected, on Wordsworth's instructions.

Tormented by jealousy, he maintained his composure by withdrawing and saving his most irrational moments for his diary, where he could safely let off steam. "Like a volcano beneath a sea" (CNB 2984), he struggled to disguise his seething resentments by presenting a calm surface. As a result, Coleridge often appeared gloomy to the Wordsworths, who apparently were unaware of the feelings that lay behind his vacant, remote preoccupation. They knew only that he was not himself and blamed it on the opium he was taking. It had been three years since they had last lived with Coleridge, and they were only beginning to fathom how much he had changed.

The visit to Coleorton proved as painful and disillusioning as the homecoming to Keswick. Had Coleridge attempted to unburden himself by trying to explain his unhappiness to his old friend, William would have dismissed it as "nervous blubbering" (JDW, p. 57). For while Wordsworth's poems express fine nuances of feeling and sensitivity, he had little tolerance for such sentimentality in his personal relationships. He was an inflexibly practical, hard-headed man with very definite ideas about how his friend should solve his problems.

Wordsworth saw the next step in Coleridge's rehabilitation to be the public announcement of his separation from his wife. Urging Coleridge to visit his family in Ottery, Wordsworth persuaded him to write a letter to his brother George making their parting known. George responded by refusing to see his brother, as he viewed marital separation as the violation of a holy bond. But by the time Coleridge learned of George's response, he had already gone to the West Country, where he remained throughout the summer and fall of 1807. During a visit to Stowey, Poole helped him deal with his nervousness about his forthcoming lectures at the Royal Institution by giving him pointers on how to make the task more manageable. To avoid the jitters that last-minute deadlines always brought on, Poole suggested that he prepare the talks in advance and narrow the scope of his topics.

After leaving Poole, Coleridge consulted Dr. Beddoes, a Bristol physician, about his escalating addiction, but did not place himself under his care. Instead, a series of diary entries systematically recording his pulse, skin color and texture, and other physical parameters suggests that he attempted to become his own physician, but to no avail.

At times he felt suicidal and had drug-induced flashbacks to the paranoid episode at Coleorton:

> O Agony! O the vision of that Saturday Morning—of the bed.—O cruel! is he not beloved, adored by two—and two such beings—. And must I not be beloved *near* him except as a satellite?—But O mercy mercy! is he not better, greater, more *manly*, and altogether more attractive to any the purest woman? ... W, is greater, better, manlier, more dear, by nature, to woman, than I—I—miserable I! [CNB 3148]

Although by no means prepared to make a break with Wordsworth, it was at this point that Coleridge vowed to serve him with a "blank heart" (CNB 3232), as the first step in lessening his subservience.

Now that his idealistic dream of a quartet with William and the Hutchinsons was as moribund as his former attempt with Southey and the Frickers, Coleridge instinctively turned elsewhere in search of his childhood dream of a fraternal foursome. He didn't have far to go.

In Bristol that fall Coleridge had become reacquainted with John Morgan, an old friend and admirer who had been one of the original backers of *The Watchman* ten years earlier. Apart from friendship, Morgan met the important unconscious criterion of being married to one of a pair of sisters, Mary and Charlotte Brent. The emotional geometry clicked and in no time at all the Brent sisters began to occupy the same place in Coleridge's imagination that their predecessors—the Evans, Fricker, and Hutchinson sisters—had held before. Feeling part of a harmonious brotherly quartet was vital for Coleridge in preparing for a creative enterprise, and he was filled with anxiety at the prospect of his new role as lecturer and literary critic.

Debilitated by opium, melancholia and, malaise, Coleridge depended on the Brent sisters to nurse him back to health and self-confidence. He remained with Morgan for three weeks, flirting and punning outrageously with the two sisters as he began to feel better. He even wrote Dorothy a letter extolling the virtues of this latest pair of sisters and also wrote a poem for them. Then, feeling chipper and armed with locks of hair and miniature portraits of his two latest conquests, he headed for London and the lectures.

After two postponements of the series, Coleridge shuttled back to Bristol and the Morgans to refuel emotionally. In London he lived in a room, which Stuart had lent him, above the editorial offices of *The Courier*. Often he did not receive callers until four in the afternoon, as he padded and wobbled around the room in a nightshirt and cap with festoons of handkerchiefs pinned to his gown.

There were times that winter when Coleridge considered hospitalizing himself in a lunatic asylum, as he struggled to control his opium intake and prepare his lectures. Desperate, dazed, and unfettered by any sense of scrupulosity, Coleridge elaborated his and Schlegel's views on Shakespeare and no doubt considered them entirely his own. Feeling pressured to succeed, Coleridge was preoccupied with the important life-and-death issue of economic survival and did not have time for the intellectual niceties of academic scholarship. Thinking that he was dying, he wrote his wife a long, operatic deathbed letter of farewell, forgiving her for everything and begging her forgiveness as well. He was outraged when she replied, in *"frisking high spirits,"* saying *"Lord how often you are ill! You must be more careful about colds!"* (CL III, p. 61).

Opium also continued to fuel Coleridge's flashbacks. As he neared the end of the lecture series, he relived the paranoid episode at Coleorton. But this time he wrote Wordsworth a long, angry letter which has not survived. Wordsworth's reply was equally sharp. He scolded Coleridge for his "pernicious" habit of voicing his "most lawless thoughts" and "wildest fancies." He would not "sully" his own letter by repeating the "rubbish" of Coleridge's accusations, since Coleridge's letter obviously was written by a man "in a lamentably insane state of mind." Only the manuscript draft of Wordsworth's letter survives (LWDW II, p. 240). The final copy, if it was sent, has been destroyed.

Tempers had flared openly, and by now each man had taken his measure of the other's ambivalence. However, by September of 1808, when Coleridge arrived at Allan Bank, the Wordsworths' spacious new home in Grasmere, the conflict had died down. Coleridge was in good spirits and feeling optimistically self-confident after his successful lecture series and an extended summer visit with friends. He settled into the domestic routine at Allan Bank without apparent friction. Weekends, Hartley and Derwent were regular visitors.

"There came this morning," Charles Lamb wrote to a friend, "a printed prospectus from S. T. Coleridge, Grasmere, of a weekly paper, to be called The Friend—a flaming prospectus—I have no time to give the heads of it—to commence first Saturday in January. There came also a notice of a turkey from Mr. Clarkson, which I am more sanguine in expecting the accomplishment of than I am of Coleridge's prophecy" (Coleridge, 1818, p. xxxix).

While all of Coleridge's friends were skeptical regarding his latest plan, conceived in the fall of 1808, to publish a one-man newspaper, they pitched in and lent their support. Poole, Lamb, and Morgan recruited subscribers. Stuart provided free printing paper and publishing advice. Southey and Wordsworth cosigned a note of four hundred pounds as a security bond and agreed to serve as occasional contributors to the sixteen-page weekly.

Unlike *The Watchman*, *The Friend* was to be more philosophical than political. In keeping with accepted practice, the six hundred or so subscribers were to receive the first twenty numbers before paying the one-pound subscription charge. They could then either cancel or renew as they saw fit. The expenses were high, the margin of profit small, and Coleridge realized that the first twenty issues would be the hardest. He cut down on narcotics and went to work.

While encouraging Coleridge's efforts, Wordsworth appointed himself the unofficial behind-the-scenes coordinator who kept Poole, Stuart, and the others informed of Coleridge's actual progress, that they might gauge how much financial help and personal support they would lend to the effort.

Wordsworth was of the opinion "that Coleridge is not sufficiently master of his own efforts to execute anything which requires a regular course of application to one object" (Coleridge 1818, p. lii). When the first issue came out in June of 1809, Wordsworth wrote Stuart: "The Friend has at last appeared. I am sorry for it as I have not the least hope that it can proceed" (LWDW II, p. 534). By the third issue Wordsworth informed Stuart that he was "encouraged to entertain more favorable hopes of his exerting himself steadily" (LWDW II, p. 539), whereupon Stuart dispatched more paper.

As time went on, publication became regular, and Coleridge managed to complete twenty-seven issues before the enterprise folded. The vast majority of essays were written by Coleridge, who dictated the articles to Sara Hutchinson. The prose was dense, and he lost some subscribers and failed to collect from many others. The work was draining, and by early March of 1810 Sara gave up and returned to her brother's farm in Wales. The last issue appeared on the fifteenth of that month. In April Dorothy described Coleridge:

> We have no hope of him—none that he will ever do anything more than he has already done. If he were not under our roof, he would be just as much the slave of stimulants as ever; and his whole time and thoughts, (except when he is reading and he reads a great deal), are employed in deceiving himself, and seeking to deceive others. He will tell me that he has been writing, that he *has* written half a Friend: when I *know* that he has not written a single line.... He speaks of *The Friend* always as if it were going on, and would go on.... do not think it is his love for Sara which has stopped him in his work—do not believe it: his love for her is no more than a fanciful dream. [LWDW II, p. 599]

While Dorothy's estimate of the dreamy nature of Coleridge's "love" for Sara is essentially accurate, it is peculiar that she minimized the role that Sara's departure played in the folding of the newspaper. But Dorothy had been relieved to see Sara go, as she felt Coleridge had been wearing her out. Moreover, Dorothy herself felt worn out by Coleridge. She resented him as a boarder in their house and looked forward to getting rid of him. He had become a nuisance.

But catering to Coleridge was nothing new, and there is room to wonder if her statement "we have no hope of him" might better read, "we have no further *use* for him." For it is a much overlooked fact that her brother William had by now passed his own prime in his career as a poet. While he would continue to compose verses for the rest of his life, there would be no more masterpieces for him either. William had enjoyed a steadier, longer, much more productive career than Coleridge, but now there would be reason to envy the new directions Coleridge's career was to take.

Wordsworth elected to continue writing, remaining in rural seclusion and awaiting posterity's verdict, while Coleridge turned to London and popular success, trying his hand as a journalist, playwright, and lecturer. Dorothy could "only grieve at the waste and prostitution of his genius" (LWDW II, p. 495), while William, for his part, was about to give his old friend a gratuitous and less than gracious send-off.

In May Coleridge moved from Allan Bank to Greta Hall, just as Mary Wordsworth was due to deliver another baby. Although he said he would be gone for ten days, his stay with his estranged wife stretched on for five months. During this time Sarah described her husband as "in an almost uniform kind disposition towards us all, his spirits . . . in general better than I have known them for years" (Campbell, 1905, p. lxxxi). Meanwhile, Dorothy acidly reported that "Coleridge is still at Keswick where, as at Grasmere, he has done nothing but read" (LWDW II, p. 412).

In October of 1810 Basil Montague, an old college friend of William's and an only slightly more recent friend and admirer of Coleridge's, stopped at Greta Hall on his way to London from Scotland. Offering Coleridge a spare place in his coach, he invited him to remain on in London as his houseguest for as long as he liked. Coleridge accepted and they set out for town, stopping at Grasmere on the way.

At some point during their stopover, Wordsworth took Montague aside and had a long talk with him. It was his duty, William thought, to put Montague on his guard by informing him of Coleridge's addiction and alcoholism. Documenting his claims by furnishing Montague with blow-by-blow details of Coleridge's past excesses, William told Montague that Coleridge had become a nuisance as a boarder at Grasmere and said he no longer held out any hope for Coleridge's recovery. William advised Montague not to allow Coleridge into his home.

Montague made no mention of this conversation until they had reached London, where he retracted his invitation and brusquely explained his reasons. The graphic details of the incidents Montague mentioned were of such a decidedly personal nature that Coleridge instantly realized that they could only have come from Wordsworth. Hurt and offended, he left the Montagues' home and took a hotel room in Covent Garden.

A few days later he moved into the home of John Morgan and the Brent sisters, who were now living in London. Without dropping a beat, Coleridge had managed to insert himself into a domestic quartet he had laid the groundwork for during his stay in Bristol three years previous. While Coleridge's diaries reveal that he felt hurt and betrayed by Wordsworth's perfidy, there were two new forces that mitigated his desperation—God and a new pair of sisters. Interspersed among entries for the Brent sisters, Coleridge wrote out a long declaration of his faith, stating his unswerving belief in the Trinity and confessing his sense of frailty as a human being.

Describing those frailties, Charles Lamb wrote Dorothy: "Coleridge has powdered his hair, and looks like Bacchus, Bacchus ever sleek and young. He is going to turn sober, but his clock has not yet struck; meantime he pours down goblet after goblet" (CL III, p. 75). Relying upon mutual friends for news, neither Coleridge nor the Wordsworths made any attempt to contact each other directly. Coleridge expected a full apology, while William and Dorothy confidently waited for him to come crawling back to the Lakes, dilapidated by his addiction and sorely in need of their charity. He never came. And when Dorothy later heard he had consulted a physician for his addiction, she declared it a "farce." "For my part," she wrote, "I am hopeless of him, and I dismiss him as much as possible from my thoughts" (LWDW II, p. 540).

Knowing of Coleridge's estrangement from Wordsworth, Mary Lamb took it upon herself to ask William to come to London and heal the rift in their friendship. Her letter drew a "sneer" from Wordsworth, who had heard of Coleridge's high spirits and considered the fact that he now powdered his hair "proof positive" that Coleridge's injured feelings were mere pretense (CL III, p. 909).

But the Wordsworths' dire prophecy, that Coleridge would be hopelessly lost once he was no longer under their care, did not prove true. Although he was, as they put it, as much a "slave to stimulants" as ever (LWDW II, p. 399), Coleridge appeared to be thriving now that he was liberated from William and Dorothy's protective custody.

Within a month of arriving in London he wrote his first piece for *The Courier* and by the following spring (1811) was working for Stuart on a full-time basis. Knocking out over ninety articles on domestic and foreign affairs during this stint, Coleridge lived with the Morgans in Hammersmith except for brief intervals when, mixing the poppy with the grape, he went off on binges.

His *Courier* articles reflected his growing conservatism, most notably on the war effort. Skeptical about the virtue of pacifism, unlike the new generation of radicals, who chanted antiwar slogans and taunted the red-coated "Piccadilly Butchers" who contained them behind barricades in the streets of London (Bryant, 1954, p. 260), Coleridge was in favor of an all-out effort to destroy Napoleon. Except for the toehold that Wellington had gained in Portugal, Bonaparte's armies dominated Western Europe, having marched into every continental capital except St. Petersburg, Stockholm, and Constantinople. As Coleridge's pieces on the Iberian Campaign suggested, England's hopes lay with Wellington—whose task of advancing through Spain and across the Pyrenees was about to be eased by Napoleon's setting his sights on Russia.

Coleridge wrote a total of thirteen articles on Bonaparte and eighteen on the war with France in addition to covering the Parliamentary debates on the monetary crisis of 1811 and commenting on the widespread domestic unrest. More than ever, England was becoming a country of haves and have-nots. Factory owners amassed untold wealth as their huge ironworks, operated by steam-driven engines, belched out ten thousand gun barrels a month to feed England's frenzied war effort, while the indigent lined up in droves at the soup kitchens that had sprung up all over London after a wave of bank failures.

Meanwhile, still lacking the franchise and prevented from collective bargaining by the Combination Acts, hungry, unemployed workers in less war-stable industries like textiles had begun to rise up in frustration and to destroy the hated machinery that was displacing them. As far as they could tell, the industrial revolution and eighteen years of war had failed to bring them anything but miserable living conditions, an inflationary economy, and families torn apart by the loss of two generations of fathers and sons—killed, missing in action, or taken prisoners of war.

At the same time, signs of prosperity and progress were everywhere. Coal was being separated into coke, which drove the blast furnaces of the war foundries under an intense white heat, and coal gas, which was used to create a pleasing effect for ladies and gentlemen of fashion who strolled along the streets and browsed in the exclusive shops and arcades that it illuminated.

H.R.H. The Prince of Wales had become Regent, and the elegant age that bears the name of his reign had just begun. Brighton Pavilion was under construction and plans for Regent Park were being developed. Beau Brummell set the trend in fashion, while "mad, bad and dangerous" Lord Byron (Cecil, 1955, p. 85) "awoke to find himself famous" (Low, 1977, p. 243) as he set Regency London on fire with his scandals and satirical verse—lampooning Coleridge, among others, for having sold out. For while Napoleon may have become an archfiend in Coleridge's eyes, he was the archetypal romantic hero in George Gordon's.

Near the end of September Coleridge temporarily resigned from *The Courier* staff, protesting the suppression of his controversial article criticizing the reappointment of the Regent's brother, the Duke of York, as Commander-in-Chief of the Army. The Duke had earlier lost that post when it was proved that his mistress had used her royal connection to peddle military commissions—a scandal that made a mockery of Britain's war effort. After returning briefly to *The Courier*, Coleridge made up his mind to leave political journalism and resume his career as a lecturer; he planned to deliver a series of talks on Shakespeare and Milton at the London Philosophical Society.

Lord Byron wrote to a friend that he had seen Coleridge, "who is sort of a rage at present," and described how he had gone "to hear the new Art of Poetry by the reformed schismatic" (Campbell, 1905, p. lxxxiv). After one of the lectures a recently arrived German visitor in the audience enthusiastically told the speaker of the remarkable resemblance his ideas bore to his fellow countryman Schlegel's recently published book on Shakespeare.

Politely commenting on the felicitous coincidence, Coleridge expressed an interest in reading the work. There was a brief flurry of controversy until a red-blooded patriotic bystander in the crowd blusteringly vouched for the fact that he had heard Coleridge present the very same ideas at the Royal Institution before Schlegel's book had even been published. Apparently no one present thought to mention an earlier essay Schlegel had published outlining his critical approach to Shakespeare, and the incident died down.

The series ended in late January *"with eclat"* (Campbell, 1905, p. lxxxiv). During this period, Coleridge had also been sitting for a bust and a portrait that were scheduled to be exhibited at the Royal Academy the following spring. He was the talk of the town.

Armed with his recent success and the afterglow of his audience's admiration, Coleridge returned to Keswick in early February to pick up a hundred copies of *The Friend*, which he intended to publish as bound volumes. During the six weeks he remained at Greta Hall, Dorothy wrote several letters to Sarah Coleridge entreating her to urge her husband to write and visit before returning to London.

In their full pride, neither Wordsworth nor Coleridge would take the initiative to seek the other out. Both had shared their side of the story with friends, and by now the gossip had begun to spread in literary circles. Dorothy's version ran thus:

William for the most benevolent purposes communicated to a friend a small part of what was known to the whole town of Penrith—sneered and laughed at there, to our great mortification—and we would have made any sacrifice to draw him away from Penrith. William communicated this to a friend, who, in three days travelling with C., saw the whole with his own eyes; and William is therefore treacherous!!! He does not *deny* the truth of what William said, but William ought not to have said it; though in fact by so doing he believed that he was taking the best means of preventing the spreading further, and to fresh persons what it was so distressing to him to know. [LWDW II, p. 523]

And Coleridge's side of the story was that Basil Montague told him that he had been "commissioned" by Wordsworth to tell Coleridge that he was a "rotten drunkard" (CL III, p. 296).

Each man stood his ground, and Coleridge returned to London without a meeting. By May, after he had begun a new series of lectures, William Wordsworth came to town, determined to put an end to the gossip. Communicating through intermediaries, their negotiations rapidly degenerated into a schoolboy quarrel. Wordsworth proposed that Josiah Wedgwood serve as an impartial judge in a mock trial, while Coleridge proposed to challenge Montague to a duel to settle the affair honorably.

Their mutual friends patiently worked at effecting a compromise, and in the end the two made up by modifying their accusations and designating Basil the villain in the piece. Afterward they took a long walk to Hampstead together, and William even managed to attend one of Coleridge's lectures before leaving town. But the old days were gone forever, and Coleridge would never return to the Lakes again, while Basil would become one of his faithful cronies in old age.

Shortly after William's departure, Coleridge picked up where he had been at the time of Wordsworth's first visit to Stowey. He began rewriting *Osorio*—the play that told his boyhood story and *fore*told the tormented friendship he had lived out with Wordsworth.

Little had either man realized, fifteen years earlier, that reading their juvenile plays to one another had been like exchanging calling cards from the unconscious and finding complementary themes. For if Coleridge had been ripe to cast himself as a guilt-ridden wanderer and have William play his older brother, a similar casting had been done for Wordsworth's play, *The Borderers*. Also telling the tale of a smoldering, brotherlike rivalry, Wordsworth's play had a similar outcome to Coleridge's: manipulated by his cunning rival into tripping himself up on his own foibles, Mortimer goes into self-exile as a guilt-ridden wanderer. Interestingly, on the eve of his departure for Malta, Coleridge had told William he had had a vague premonition about himself, "something you have given to Mortimer . . . in your tragedy" (CL II, p. 115). But if it dawned on Coleridge at all, it had dawned on him far too late, just how much he had bought into Wordsworth's scripting of his life story.

All through the summer of 1812 Coleridge diligently reworked *Osorio* and continued to live with the Morgans in Hammersmith. By late fall he was lecturing again and his play, with the new title *Remorse*, had been accepted for the stage and scheduled to open in January.

On the first of December, Wordsworth's six-year-old son Thomas died. Coleridge immediately wrote William:

> There is a sense of the word, love, in which I never felt it but to you and one of your household—! I am distant from you some hundred miles, but glad I am, that I am no longer distant in spirit, and have faith, that as it has happened *but once* so it never can happen again. An awful truth it seems to me, and prophetic of our future, as well as declarative of our present *real* nature, that one mere thought, one feeling of suspicion or jealousy or resentment can remove two human beings farther from each other, than winds or seas can separate their bodies. [CL III, p. 437]

But committed to his lectures and the last-minute preparations and rewrites involved in mounting the *Remorse* production, Coleridge felt unable to take the time to visit Wordsworth. While his immediate outpouring of emotion had been sincere, he knew their friendship could never be the same. As he put it to Poole, "All outward actions, all inward wishes, all thoughts and admirations, will be the same—*are* the same—but—aye there remains an immedicable *But*" (CL III, p. 437).

In what was considered a highly successful run by the commercial theatrical standards of the day, *Remorse* opened at the Drury Lane in January of 1813 and played to packed houses for twenty nights in spite of the winter weather. The reviews were favorable and the theatergoing public proved to be in an unusually receptive mood that January, as indeed was the rest of London. On the seventeenth of December the entire city had erupted with joy as the cannon at the Tower and at Hyde Park boomed out the announcement of Bonaparte's retreat.

Having marched his invincible *Grande Armée* of half a million men on a two-thousand-mile trek from Paris to Moscow, Napoleon had triumphantly installed himself in the Kremlin in mid-September and awaited, as was his custom, the familiar trumpet blare announcing the arrival of the inevitable train of fawning monarchs, ministers, and ambassadors—tripping over one another in their rush to surrender and curry the Corsican's favor with obsequious promises to do his bidding.

Unaccustomed to being kept waiting, Bonaparte had been nonplussed by their failure to materialize and had stared absentmindedly at the first few lazy drifts of snowflakes in the September sky as he waited for them to arrive. They never came. And by now Napoleon and his men were learning a terrible lesson, from both the punishing Russian winter and the equally fierce Cossack cavalry who stalked them in their retreat, appearing from nowhere and vanishing into blinding sheets of falling snow, like phantom Horsemen of the Apocalypse.

Back in London, the city went wild, celebrating Wellington's success during Bonaparte's Russian campaign, as he marched his men across Spain, his sights on the Pyrenees and the lands beyond. And for Coleridge there were the playwright's laurels—the nightly applause and four hundred pounds he received for his play (the equivalent of fourteen thousand 1980 dollars).

But as Bonaparte had just learned and Coleridge was about to rediscover, fortune is not a dependable companion. By the next fall, he was attempting to sell his personal library in order to survive. Having declared bankruptcy and transferred his residual business holdings to his sister-in-law, John Morgan had fled to Ireland to escape his creditors and avoid debtor's prison. With Morgan's departure Coleridge suddenly found himself on his own once more—without that cherished domestic security in which his creativity had flowered over the previous three years.

By now Coleridge had exhausted the London market for his lectures and would have to take his show on the road. Moreover, whatever his earnings might prove to be, there was his drug habit to support in addition to bed and board. Consuming as much as a pint of laudanum a day, almost a gallon a week, his habit cost roughly five pounds per week, or two hundred sixty per year.* Coleridge was in trouble.

But it was Morgan and the Brent sisters who were in trouble as he saw it, and now it was his turn to repay them. Heading for the West Country, where there were fresh audiences for his lecture series, he sought refuge with old friends. In Bristol he hoped to earn money to send to the Brent sisters and also to help Morgan's affairs by reestablishing his business connections so that he might resume his law practice once it was safe to return.

Keeping up the sisters' sagging spirits with a series of letters written in a tone of mock gaiety, Coleridge offered advice on how to manage the bankruptcy proceedings as well as small sums of money from his lecture earnings. In November of 1813 he interrupted his lecture schedule to escort his "two proteges" (CL III, p. 461) to modest lodgings he helped them find in Ashley, on the outskirts of Bath, where he wanted to keep a watchful eye over them. His gallantry held out until they

---

*According to Southey, Coleridge regularly took at least "two quarts of laudanum a week, the cost of which is 5 pounds, and sometimes he swallowed a pint a day" during this period of his life (Campbell, 1905, p. lxxxiv). These figures—both dose and price—struck me as so astronomical that I cross-calculated them (see Appendix C, p. 326) and found that they hold up on both counts: One English pint (20 ounces) of laudanum contained approximately 3 *grams* of *morphine*—modern pharmacology texts reveal that addicts in advanced stages have taken as much as 5 grams daily, without fatal effects.

Reckoning cost independently of Southey, based on Berridge's statement that "laudanum had been sixpence an ounce early in the nineteenth century," the figure comes out to the equivalent of $123 a week, or $6,400 a year by 1980 standards. Based on Southey, it amounts to $175 a week or $8,900 a year.

reached Ashley where, judging from his later notes of profuse apology, his chivalry collapsed.

Opium and alcohol took over. Though unable to recall exactly what he had said or done, Coleridge was mortified over having offended the Brents by his intoxicated behavior. But the fact was that he needed to be taken care of himself and had no real reserve to meet the practical needs of others on a daily basis.

After settling the sisters, he suffered a full-blown alcohol and/or opium withdrawal psychosis. For seven days and seven nights "the terrors of the almighty" (CL III, p. 463) rained down upon him in his hallucinations, as he prayed for redemption through Christ and paced like a caged leopard.

Feeling more like a sick kitten by the time he limped back to Bristol a week later, he wrote the Brents, saying he hoped to spend Christmas with them. But when the time came he felt too ill and too ashamed to put in an appearance. His siege lasted all winter. He would not resume his lectures until the spring of 1814, just as Napoleon was making his way through France, cowering under a hail of curses and stones from his former subjects en route to his exile on Elba.

During his six-month ordeal, Coleridge remained under a physician's care and lived in a friend's home. At times he required constant supervision to keep him from razors and narcotics. Although there were moments of wily desperation, he cooperated with the plan of gradually tapered doses. It is not known if he achieved total abstinence.

In the meantime, John Morgan had returned from Ireland and joined his wife and sister-in-law at Ashley, where they awaited Coleridge's return. Sheepish over what had transpired, Coleridge was anxious to rejoin them but unsure if they would ever want to see his face again. He remained in Bristol under his doctor's care until September.

By the time he rejoined the Morgans, Coleridge's creative juices had begun to flow. He stimulated them once more with his old fantasy of a harmonious foursome:

> Suppose me married to little Megrim, and that a Brentus Coleridge should discover the North West Passage, or (he being by the Mother's side of a ship-building generation) a power and

machinery capable of rendering a vessel on the open seas independent of the winds—can you conceive of a nobler sound than Baron Coleridge of Coleridge, in the County of Devon?—But if Charlotte prefers it, he shall be a Baronet, Sir Brentus Coleridge, of Coleridge Hall, the son of the celebrated S.T. Coleridge lawfully, et on the etc of Charlotte Brent of *Brain Town*? [CL III, p. 518]

Coleridge was feeling that old procreative urge stirring within. This time his issue would be a book of prose. Producing it would prove an arduous labor, but John Morgan would be there to serve steadily as midwife, assisting in the delivery. Opium would dull the labor pains as Coleridge scoured his old notebooks for ideas—and ransacked other men's works as well. Although his newest brainchild would not discover the North West Passage, *Biographia Literaria* would explore new frontiers of its own.

Coleridge did not begin his opus until the spring of 1815, a time of triumphant rejoicing in England. Napoleon, decisively defeated in his attempt to return to power, was awaiting transportation to St. Helena, where he would spend the rest of his life in the permanent custody of his keepers.

By the time of Bonaparte's swan song, Coleridge had been back with the Morgans for almost a year and was comfortably settled into a domestic routine in a rural retreat. Wordsworth had recently published a two-volume edition of his own poems and, by mutual agreement, Coleridge's works were no longer included. Instead, Coleridge had decided to publish his own collected poems and intended to write a brief introduction clarifying his theoretical differences with Wordsworth to set the record straight.

He began dictating his short preface to Morgan and, as was so often the case, he discovered he had more to say than he had anticipated. He did not stop talking for six months, working steadily nine hours a day, from eleven o'clock to four and again from six to ten, with Morgan keeping him to the task. He ran out of conversation and finished *Biographia Literaria* in September 1815.

In one sense the book is a rambling hodgepodge of personal memoirs, literary criticism, and philosophical ideas written by a boozy ex-poet turned literary thief. It is sprawling, digressive, and, as Coleridge realized when he christened it an "immethodical miscellany" (Chambers 1938, p. 241), lacking in organization; he had not had the mental reserve to cut, redraft, and rework his opus. Nonetheless, it is a remarkable document which contains strikingly modern insights into the psychological nature of the creative process, insights that anticipate current psychoanalytic thinking by a century and a half (see Chapter 17).

As to the question of the originality of his ideas, Coleridge stated his view in *Biographia Literaria:* "I regard truth as a divine ventriloquist: I care not from whose mouth the sounds are supposed to proceed" (Coleridge, 1817a, p. 89). While he may well be correct that this process underlies the history of ideas, less wholesome motives lay behind his modest disclaimer than might appear at first glance. For as Coleridge well knew, he purposefully plagiarized large sections of other writers' books word for word. Given his highly original insights into psychology, Coleridge's thefts were a case of petty larceny. Unfortunately, he was not a great believer in himself and felt the need to puff up his book with other people's ideas.

Unfettered by any sense of scrupulosity, Coleridge did not see himself as bound by the canons and ethics of the academy. Writing for posterity might be a matter of art: but composing for lucre was a trade. He did not feel he could afford to be concerned over the certainty that his plagiarisms would ultimately be discovered. Coleridge sorely needed cash to meet his expenses and pragmatically viewed plagiarism as part of the trade aspect of his craft.

Usually it was a criticism he leveled at those he considered hacks. But it was also one of the less lofty ways in which he viewed his profession as a whole. He wryly referred to publishers as "the angels of Paternoster Row" who sat like "cormorants on the tree of knowledge" (Chambers, 1938, p. 241). He would deal with such vultures by looking out for "STC and his three little ones." In fact, in *Biographia Literaria* itself he launches into a long digression about the lack of financial reward writers encounter and discusses his bitterness over the hardships involved in becoming an "author by trade" (CL I, p.

185). No doubt he wrote the work with an eye more toward raising cash than toward posterity.

Coleridge was beginning to contend with feelings of cynicism and disillusionment in his personal relationships by the time he completed *Biographia Literaria*. He remained with the Morgans till March of the next year, 1816, but his notebooks reflect a growing sense of bitterness toward the Brent sisters, whose domination he had come to resent. He was finally growing weary of the old dream of a foursome and was filled with negative feelings toward women in general. It seems no coincidence that within weeks of his final departure from Morgan, Coleridge recorded in his notebooks a memo on his favorite childhood fable of the two misogynist brothers, the sons "of the Sassanian King in the Arabian Nights" (CNB 4315).

A chapter of his life was drawing to a close. Apparently he was disillusioned with his lifelong quest for a fantasied foursome, and from now on there would be no more such relationships. By the time Coleridge arrived in London he was again using astronomical amounts of opium. Describing his friend's latest lodgings, Lamb wrote:

> Nature who conducts every creature by instinct to its best end, has skillfully directed C. to take up his abode at a Chemist's laboratory in Norfolk Street. She might as well have sent a Helluo Librorum for cure to the Vatican. God keep him inviolate from the traps and pitfalls. He has done pretty well as yet. [Campbell, 1905, p. xcvii]

Chapter 15

An Archangel a Little Damaged

A few weeks after Coleridge's arrival in London, the Agnus Dei updated his report on his friend's latest misadventures:

> He is at present under the medical care of a Mr Gillman (Killman?) a Highgate apothecary where he plays at leaving off laudanum. I think his essentials not touched: he is very bad, and his face when he repeats his verse hath its ancient glory, an Archangel a little damaged. [Campbell, 1905, p. cxvii]

Convinced his old schoolmate had found a dangerous if convenient solution to the problem of supply and demand by lodging *inside* a pharmacy, Lamb was chary of Coleridge's latest domestic arrangement. After all, his earlier prophecy had proven correct—within days of moving above the Norfolk Street chemist's, Coleridge had become bedridden and debilitated as he sank into another opium crisis.

And while Lamb's "Killman" pun indicates his fears for his friend's life, his demotion of the Highgate croaker to an apothecary's status reflects a skepticism that was widespread among Coleridge's cronies. Put off by the fact that Gillman and his wife Ann behaved like a pair of snooping busybodies, warily checking on the comings and goings of his visitors, Coleridge's friends were starting to wonder if he had fallen into the clutches of a pair of unscrupulous quacks. As Morgan put it, maybe Gillman was "speculating upon him and hoping to ride upon his reputation with notoriety and practice" (CNB 4466n).

Another acquaintance described the highjinks at Highgate:

> I have lately heard a curious anecdote of Mr Coleridge, which at the risk—at the certainty—of spoiling it in the telling, I cannot

forbear sending you. . . . He put himself under watch and ward; went to lodge at an apothecary's at Highgate, whom he cautioned to lock up his opiates; gave his money to a friend to keep; and desired the druggist not to trust him. For some days all went on well. Our poet was ready to hang himself; could not write, could not eat, could not—incredible as it may seem—could not talk. The stimulus was wanting, and the apothecary contented. Suddenly, however, he began to mend; he wrote, he read, he talked, he harangued; Coleridge was himself again! And the apothecary began to watch within doors and without. The next day the culprit was detected; for the next day a second supply of laudanum from Murray's, well wrapped up in proof-sheets of the "Quarterly Review." [CL IV, p. 633]

Although Dr. James Gillman already had five years' experience in private practice, he had little experience in treating narcotics addiction. In fact, opium dependence had not yet become recognized as a bona fide medical illness, and it is unlikely that Gillman received any formal instruction in drug abuse, either at his medical school, the Royal College of Surgeons, or at the Westminster Hospital, where he took his clinical training.

Instead he was forced to take his lead from his patient, who was teaching him how to manage his condition. Just before moving into his doctor's house, Coleridge wrote Gillman a note warning him that his word was never to be trusted in any matter pertaining to opium. In all other affairs, Coleridge added, he was a gentleman who could be taken at his word. Both doctor and patient assumed that it would be a short time before the forty-three-year-old poet was back on his feet.

But as the thirty-four-year-old Gillman was discovering, treating Coleridge's addiction without placing him under lock and key was a full-time job. And while it was important for Coleridge's rehabilitation to encourage his efforts at completing several publishing projects that were then pending, distinguishing a legitimate visitor from an opium smuggler was no easy matter. Sometimes they were one and the same, as was the case with his publisher, John Murray, who was working with Coleridge on an edition of *Christabel, Kubla Khan,* and *The Pains of Sleep.* Apparently Murray had no compunction about bootlegging a steady supply of opium to ease his author's prepublication jitters and thereby insure the smooth flow of final copy.

Coleridge had reason to be nervous: the critical response to *Christabel* proved overwhelmingly hostile. Hazlitt found "something disgusting at the bottom of his subject, which is but ill glossed over by a veil of Della Cruscan sentiment and fine writing" (CL IV, p. 686). Another reviewer found it a poem "which sin[s] as heinously against purity and decency as it is well possible to imagine" (CL IV, p. 918), while a third critic condemned it as a piece of "impertinence . . . utterly destitute of value" (CL IV, p. 693). Given that the plot of the ballad was based on a strange relationship between two women—apparently a vampire-victim relationship, but with considerable homosexual implications—it is easy to see why it provoked such an outcry.

Of all the readings of the poem, Hazlitt's hunch that Geraldine was actually a man came closest to the mark from a psychological point of view. Although Coleridge never completed the poem, he confided to James Gillman that his plan was to have Geraldine turn herself into a man in the next episode. In fact when Gillman discussed *Christabel* in the biography of Coleridge he would eventually write, he prefaced his comments with a discussion of talks he and Coleridge had about the principal characters in the ballad and of the Elizabethan practice of having men play the parts of women on the stage.

And so it would seem that Coleridge, Gillman, and Hazlitt each intuitively sensed that at an unconscious level *Christabel* was the story of a homosexual relationship between two men disguised as a tale about two women. The Christ-Abel title suggests hidden male identities.*

---

*As does the poetic fragment *The Wanderings of Cain*. Written at about the same time as *Christabel*, *Cain* bears a striking resemblance to that poem in mood, plot, tone, cadence, meter, setting, and narrative technique. These similarities suggest that Coleridge may originally have intended to tell his tale of innocent homosexual love turned sour in the form of a ballad about two young boys: unconsciously, himself and Frank, himself and Wordsworth. If so, he found the subject too emotionally charged, which explains why he managed only a fragment. Instead, he unconsciously told his deeply personal story of the love between two men by disguising it as a tale about two women. Interestingly, after *Christabel* was published, Wordsworth called it "an indelicate poem." Was he aware, intuitively, that *Christabel* told the story of his and Coleridge's love? And was that why Coleridge was able to publish the ballad only after the break in their friendship?

And if *Christabel* tells the tale of homosexual love between two men, one need not look far to locate its most immediate source—Coleridge's infatuation with William Wordsworth. Written when Coleridge was twenty-four and twenty-seven (Book I in 1798, Book II in 1800), the poem describes interactions between the characters Christabel and Geraldine that bear an uncanny resemblance to those between Coleridge and Wordsworth.

Having just completed the *Ancient Mariner* when he began *Christabel*, Coleridge was in the innocent honeymoon phase of his intellectual love affair with William. And while he selflessly idolized William back in 1798, there was no reason for Coleridge to feel dominated or in a dependent position of disadvantage.

Wordsworth had been the one to move to Somerset so that they could be near each other, Coleridge's ballad would be given pride of place in *Lyrical Ballads*, and even in Germany Coleridge had taken it for granted that William would later join him in the West Country. Feelings of competition, envy, and dominated dependency had not yet infected Coleridge's side of their love for one another.

Written under the sway of still idyllic emotions, the first book of his ballad tells a tale of blissful homosexual love between a young maiden, Christabel, and a lady, Geraldine. Geraldine is a woman in distress to whom the innocent Christabel generously offers her hospitality. Later, just before Christabel surrenders herself sexually, she glimpses Geraldine's half-deformed bosom for a split second. The withered half of Geraldine's torso is a metaphor for the ugly side of her personality. In the supernatural lore the poem trades in, it is evidence that she is a witch-vampire. But, like the exuberant Coleridge, plunging headlong into the relationship with William, Christabel gives herself over fully to the lovemaking. Having ignored the warning sign, she awakes the next morning to find herself under the spell of a fascinating creature who can now dominate her at will.

By 1800, as he set about writing the second book, Coleridge was unconsciously attuned to the warnings that Southey, Lamb, Davy, Poole, Wedgwood, and others had given him all along:

that he had fallen fatally under Wordsworth's spell. To the detriment of his marriage and to his later regret, Coleridge had been lured to the Lakes. That the place names in the second book are the names of actual locations in the Lake District is rather telling: this was where the emotions and real-life events shaping the ballad's plot were being experienced.

Like Christ or Abel, and like Christabel, Coleridge was caught in the process of becoming the "innocent victim," largely by his own neurotic design. And while the poem clearly expresses Coleridge's intuition that generous feelings of homosexual love can turn sour as the result of greed, power, pride, and dominance, he remained a helpless spectator as his relationship with William underwent a similarly malevolent transformation.

The vampire motif employed to explain the relationship between Christabel and Geraldine fits equally well the friendship between the two poets. A vampire sucks his victim's blood in order to incorporate the other's vitality, in order to live forever. And if Christabel literally surrenders her lifeblood to Geraldine as a human sacrifice, it is easy to picture Coleridge as beginning to see himself in that same light.

Did Coleridge feel, at least unconsciously, that he was allowing himself to be sucked dry of his creative juices so that Wordsworth might slake his thirst for literary immortality? Recall the tirelessly self-sacrificing way in which Coleridge slaved over the second edition of *Lyrical Ballads*, a book he knew was to be published in Wordsworth's name alone. While Coleridge consciously prided himself on his selfless devotion to William's reputation, it is psychologically implausible that his unconscious feelings were not more ambivalent. Not surprisingly, he vented those feelings in his poem.*

Since *Christabel* was a parable of his friendship with Words-

---

*The relation between vampire and victim is that of a symbiotic bond—they are connected by the flow of lifeblood. The vampire needs the victim in order to support his own existence. However, by the act of feeding and penetration he also makes the victim immortal. The closest Coleridge came to conscious recognition of these feelings was on his way back from Malta when he wrote: "To W.—in the progression of spirit.... O that my spirit purged by death of its weaknesses, which are alas! my *identity* might flow into *thine*, and live and act in thee, and be Thou" (CNB 2712).

worth, it is easy to see why he found it harder and harder to complete as their relationship deteriorated. So much under William's "spell" that he took Wordsworth's rejection of his poem as a reflection of its true artistic merits, Coleridge became blocked. This was a turning point at which a less neurotically bewitched man might have ended the friendship, completed his poem, and published what he had written.

But time and again Coleridge had postponed publishing *Christabel*. Not until the spring of 1816 did it finally see the light of day. And each of the three poems published then was deeply revealing: *Kubla Khan* expressed Coleridge's bisexuality, *Christabel* told the tale of his love for William Wordsworth, and *The Pains of Sleep* confessed his opium addiction. One reviewer scornfully commented that *Kubla Khan* demonstrated that Coleridge could write better nonsense verse than any other poet in England, while another branded *Christabel* "the most obscene poem in the English language" (CL IV, p. 919).

In the face of such denunciatory vehemence from the critics, Coleridge decided to change publishers. All of his forthcoming works would be issued by what he called a "religious house" (Chambers, 1938, p. 278). While *Christabel* had provoked charges of obscenity, the public's awareness of his addiction also weighed heavily. Even in his own eyes Coleridge bore the stigma of a notorious opium eater and sot who had abandoned his wife and children, thereby forfeiting his claim to respectability in an increasingly moralistic society.

One way to polish his tarnished public image was by acquiring the aura of ecclesiastical respectability. He began sprucing up his paunchy and dissipated appearance by dressing like a man of the cloth, sporting black breeches, black coat, black silk stockings, and black shoes as his daily garb. People meeting him for the first time took him for a clergyman and he confided to his brother George that he had "a feeling, one third pride and two thirds tenderness," when friends commented on the striking resemblance he bore to their clergyman father "in person and mind" (CL III, p. 104).

Always an excessively sociable animal, with a flair for grandstanding and a compulsive need to talk, Coleridge was unable to resist the temptation to pulpitize to any who would listen. In fact, to lure Coleridge away from Murray and to celebrate their partnership, Coleridge's new, "religious" publishers gave him an advance to compose three lay sermons, one to each of the social classes, instructing them on how to cope with the massive upheavals taking place in the aftermath of the Napoleonic Wars.

No longer unified by the patriotic goal of defeating a common enemy, England's social classes were at each other's throats once more. While the war had turned shopkeepers into millionaires, no such success stories were coming from the lower classes, whose abominable standard of living stood in sharp contrast to the wealth and prosperity that surrounded them.

With peace, the bottom had fallen out of the armaments market, dropping the price of iron and idling two thirds of England's blast furnaces, as well as devaluing all other commodities. All, that is, but bread. The dismal harvest had led to astronomical food prices which the hungry masses of unemployed workers, their ranks swollen daily by mustered-out soldiers and sailors, could ill afford.

Mass open-air demonstrations had been followed by minor riots and incidents of looting. And in a window-smashing flashback to 1795, the Regent's carriage had been attacked. Responding in predictable fashion, the government had come up with its traditional remedy for dissent: habeas corpus was suspended and a new Seditious Meetings Bill passed.

Still ready to quote chapter and verse as once again he preached his nostrums to his fellow countrymen, this time Coleridge found himself on the other side. If the former firebrand's politics were now Tory, the brand of religion he was peddling was based on the underlying assumption that the existing social order was sanctioned by God and that to tamper with it was a sin.

Lay Sermons drew a mixed reception. Angry over Coleridge's turncoat politics, Hazlitt charged him with apostasy, wryly commenting that he was "fit to take up the deep pauses of conversations between Cardinals and Angels" (Chambers, 1938, p. 296). In America, James Russell Lowell claimed he had tried the experiment of reading Coleridge's sermons to a group of his Rhode Island Red hens who had become delinquent in meeting their daily quota of eggs. Lowell declared the effect "magical," though he cautiously added that he did not know "whether their consciences were touched or they wished to escape the preaching" (Coleridge, 1817b, p. xxxiv).

Though he vowed strict doctrinal obedience to the teachings of the Anglican Church and advocated literal interpretation of the scriptures, Coleridge wagged that he was not so much a fundamendalist that he believed that possessing a pair of angel's wings implied the ability to flap around heaven like "a sort of celestial poultry" (Armour and Howes, 1940, p. 264). Independent as a thinker, Coleridge was fashioning his own mystical religious views, which many found difficult to understand. While some of his listeners blamed their difficulty in understanding him on their own intellectual limitations, Carlyle was one skeptic who threw up his hands in exasperation at Coleridge's "thrice-refined pabulum of transcendental moonshine"; he characterized Coleridge as a thinker who "knew the sublime secret of believing by 'the reason' what 'the understanding' had been obliged to fling out as incredible" (Coleridge, 1817b, p. xxxix).

If Coleridge was returning to a facsimile of his paternal religion, he was also identifying with his father's tactic of baffling his rural congregation with incomprehensible displays of erudition. While John Coleridge accomplished that by delivering snatches of his sermons in Hebrew, advertised as the original language of the Holy Ghost, his son achieved the same end with erudite razzle-dazzle of a different sort. Still, Coleridge could be good-natured about his foibles and was amused when, upon asking Charles Lamb if he had ever heard him preach, Lamb replied that he had never heard him do anything else.

In fact, while Coleridge was bitter over Hazlitt's lampoons in print, Lamb's sharp satires only enhanced their friendship:

> I was going from my house at Enfield to the India-house one morning, and was hurrying, for I was rather late, when I met Coleridge, on his way to pay me a visit; he was brimful of some new idea, and in spite of my assuring him that time was precious, he drew me within the door of an unoccupied garden by the road-side, and there, sheltered from observation by a hedge of evergreens, he took me by the button of my coat, and closing his eyes commenced an eloquent discourse, waving his right hand gently, as the musical words flowed in an unbroken stream from his lips. I listened entranced; but the striking of a churchclock

recalled me to a sense of duty. I saw it was of no use to attempt to break away, so taking advantage of his absorption in his subject, I, with my penknife, quietly severed the button from my coat and decamped. Five hours afterwards, in passing the same garden, on my way home, I heard Coleridge's voice, and on looking in, there he was, with closed eyes,—the button in his fingers,—and his right hand gracefully waving, just as when I left him. He had never missed me! [Armour and Howes, 1940, p. 279]

By now Coleridge had become a full-fledged member of the Gillman family in addition to being a patient. Accompanying them on their annual seaside holidays to Ramsgate, Coleridge had begun to develop a deep attachment to Ann Gillman, whom he described as "an affectionate and sisterly nurse" (CL IV, p. 669).* Quick to nickname Ann's toddler "Hen Pen" (CNB 4341), Coleridge had taken a deep interest in both of the Gillmans' boys from the start. And by now, the Gillmans were repaying that warm concern in kind.

Hartley Coleridge was already spending his holidays from Oxford with his father as a guest of the Gillmans, and Derwent would be joining them once he began university. For his part, Coleridge tutored young Henry in Latin and Greek and offered an uncle's advice to James Jr. And since Coleridge wrote his wife Sarah infrequently, Ann Gillman took on the role of epistolary go-between for the estranged couple, helping to reknit a sense of family between them in matters concerning their children.

The Gillmans also opened their home to Coleridge's friends. Lamb, Stuart, Montague, and Morgan were regulars among Coleridge's frequent visitors. Apart from having the run of the house, he sometimes made use of Gillman's horse-drawn gig to take his friends on outings. The Gillmans had long since ceased to keep strict financial tallies, and their generosity was the natural expression of feelings of love and friendship.

*While it appears that by this point in his life Coleridge had given up his lifelong quest for a fantasied foursome, this conclusion is only tentative as his diaries for this period have not yet been published. In point of fact, Ann Gillman did have a sister (Lucy Harding) who resided in her home. It is conceivable that, in his domestic arrangements at Highgate, Coleridge took a final fantasy fling with yet another pair of sisters.

When Coleridge's three-volume edition of *The Friend* was reissued, it was gratefully dedicated to James Gillman. By the end of 1818, Coleridge, through lecturing and publications, had carved out a place for himself as a contemporary dramatist, poet, philosopher, theologian, and literary critic. In the first three years of his residence with the Gillmans he published his three poems with Murray, *Sybilline Leaves, Biographia Literaria, The Friend, Lay Sermons*, and the drama *Zapolya*. While he was often the target of crossfire from the critics, Coleridge had reestablished himself as a writer.

Under the Gillmans' careful management, Coleridge's sickly look of dissipated paunchiness had given way to a sleek appearance of corpulent prosperity. Dressed in black, with his flowing mane of prematurely white hair, he shows a trace of venerability in the 1818 portrait by C. R. Leslie.

But the younger generation's response to Coleridge's dense literary style, his theologian's costume, and his social message was by no means universally positive. Beau Brummell had already issued the dernier cri in matters sartorial and pronounced clerical garb outré, while Lord Byron, enfant terrible of the scandal-ridden Regency, served as its intellectual and spiritual spokesman. His verdict on the Right-Reverend-Professor Coleridge was:

> Coleridge, too, has lately taken wing,
> But like a hawk encumbered with his hood,—
> Explaining metaphysics to the nation—
> I wish he would explain his Explanation. [Low, 1977, p. 125]

Like the prototypes of the Jazz Age of the 1920s, the postwar generation of the Regency had plunged into a cult of hedonism. Cynical and disillusioned, they asserted their individualism through mock-military dress rather than the sans-culotte uniform of Coleridge's generation. And it was the Pavilion at Brighton, with its domes and oriental pagodas—not the Bastille—that was the symbol of their age. Commenting on that miracle of rare device which was the Prince of Wales's personal pleasure dome, a wag of the day marveled that it was "as if St. Paul's had gone to the sea and pupped" (Bryant, 1954, p. 111).

Coleridge was not the only one of his circle offended by the spiritual bankruptcy of the age and the degeneracy of its obese, three-hundred-pound Regent. Lamb wrote a quatrain entitled *The Triumph of the Whale:*

By his bulk and by his size
By his oily qualities
This (or else my eyesight fails)
This should be the Prince of Whales. [Low, 1977, p. 110]

It was an age of irreverence. So much so in fact that after his falling out with "Prinny" (Cole, 1970, p. 131) Beau Brummell had quipped to a mutual acquaintance, on encountering him with the Prince at a social gathering, "Who's your fat friend?" (Cole, 1970, p. 89). But much to Coleridge's relief and delight, he discovered that there were also serious young men in search of guidance in their pursuit of philosophical principles and religious ideals.

By 1818 the forty-six-year-old Coleridge's quest for youthful followers and spiritual heirs had become focused on two newly recruited admirers: Thomas Allsop, a twenty-three-year-old London businessman, and Joseph Henry Green, a twenty-six-year-old surgeon. While both were destined to become faithful personal friends, Green would rapidly become Coleridge's philosophical disciple and ultimately his literary executor.

After hearing Coleridge deliver a series of lectures on philosophy, Green began making weekly trips to Highgate. Soon he began to record and transcribe his master's thoughts with the dream of serving as junior collaborator and amanuensis for what was projected to be Coleridge's philosophical magnum opus.

The spring of 1820 was perhaps the richest period in Coleridge's later life. He was enjoying a reprieve in his health after an ominous attack of pleuritic pain the previous year. Having published many books, he believed that his intellectual reputation was now secured. Surrounded by youthful admirers, he worked steadily five to six hours a day on his magnum opus while enjoying his secure domestic status in the Gillman household. Old London friends dropped by regularly, while Poole looked in on him whenever he was in town. And much to Coleridge's delight, his two boys were spending the spring holidays with him as the Gillmans' guests.

Twenty-two-year-old Derwent was about to become a Cantab, and Coleridge was already nursing fond hopes that he would eventually take Holy Orders. Hartley, at twenty-four, had graduated from Oxford the year before and was completing his probationary year as academic fellow at prestigious Oriel College. Delighted with Hartley's success, the proud father was pleased to see his son pursuing a sensible career plan, something he deeply regretted not having done himself. And he was hopeful that his two sons might develop friendships with their Ottery cousins, thereby healing the rift of the previous generation. After many chaotic years and personal trials, Coleridge was beginning to count himself lucky, believing that life was proving surprisingly kind to him. But on the morning of June 30, 1820—a number of weeks after the departure of his sons—Coleridge's mellow sense of harmony was shattered by a piece of news that arrived in the form of a letter from his nephew John Taylor Coleridge. Knowing that his uncle would be upset, John addressed the letter to Gillman so that Coleridge could be prepared for the shock. Later, Coleridge would rank this misfortune as one of the four "griping and grasping sorrows" (CL IV, p. 249) of his life—along with the unhappy outcomes of his relationships with Sarah Fricker, William Wordsworth, and Sara Hutchinson.

John Coleridge's letter revealed the month-old news that Hartley had been rejected for a permanent fellowship on the grounds of "sottishness, a love of low company, [and] general inattention to college rules" (CL V, p. 67). Shocked and mortified, Coleridge attempted to contact Hartley only to discover that he had vanished, leaving neither explanation nor destination. Haunted by memories of his own Comberbache escapade, Coleridge immediately dispatched Derwent to locate and retrieve his brother.

The mission proved easy, as Hartley was headed for the Lakes and had never planned to disappear. Hartley was frank with Derwent about the chain of events leading to his dismissal. From his first day at Oriel, he had felt a strong repugnance for the sanctimonious faculty and never bothered to hide his contempt. The other fellows were "bigots, ignorant deciders upon the conduct of others, conceited of their own dignity, and rather disposed to tyrannize. . . . I was induced . . . to vent my chagrin in certain impotent, but I dare say not forgotten threats of great reformations to take place in the college and University when my unripe fortunes came of age" (CL V, p. 71).

Since he had been so open about his dissatisfaction, Hartley was not surprised at the faculty's decision to deny him a permanent position. But they had behaved hypocritically, Hartley thought, by disguising their disapproval of his rebelliousness behind trumped-up charges of alcoholism, and by revenging themselves by casting aspersions on his moral character. Denounced as a "sot" who could not be safely trusted with a bedside candle lest he set his room on fire, Hartley had been advised to immigrate to the colonies by a senior colleague who informed him that damaged goods did better in Canada.

While awaiting Hartley's return to Highgate, Coleridge searched his soul. Depressed and beset by nightmares, he prayed to God for Hartley's deliverance. At the same time, he wrote:

> My conscience indeed bears me witness, that from the time I quitted Cambridge no human being was more indifferent to the pleasures of the table than myself, or less needed any stimulation to my spirits; and that by a most unhappy quackery after having been bedrid for six months with swollen knees and other distressing symptoms . . . and through that most pernicious form of ignorance, medical half-knowledge, I was *seduced* into the use of narcotics. [CL V, p. 79]

On arriving at Highgate, Hartley reviewed the circumstances of his dismissal for his father. Convinced that his boy's intemperance amounted to nothing more than one or two innocent bouts of "tipsy" (CL V, p. 62) undergraduate revelry, Coleridge made up his mind to go to Oxford, clear Hartley's good name, and have him reinstated. Plagued by memories of his own youthful scandals and troubled by a gnawing sense that the sins of the father were being visited on the son, Coleridge seemed determined to reinstate Hartley into a respectable way of life even though Hartley had made it emphatically clear that he wished to remain in London and become a poet and professional writer.

But Coleridge was equally clear that he did not want to see his firstborn follow in his footsteps and become an "author by trade" (CL I, p. 185). In opting for a literary career, Hartley was nostalgically emulating the imaginative, high-spirited, unconventional poet-father of his boyhood—the doting, carefree father who had helped him compose his first verse as a boy of ten. With his proud Papa's encouragement, Hartley had sent that poem to his Uncle Southey.

But the father Hartley Coleridge was now dealing with was of a different kidney on matters literary. No longer whimsical, Coleridge stood for sobriety, propriety, and austerity. For if Hartley was molding himself in the image of his boyhood father, Coleridge was engaged in an identical process. He was shaping himself in the image of his own warm-hearted but respectable clergyman father. And it was this new, later-life image of himself that Coleridge wanted both of his boys to emulate and confirm.

Before leaving for Oxford, Coleridge wrote a long letter to the Provost outlining his arguments on Hartley's behalf. Analyzing degrees of alcohol abuse, he pointed out that occasional social drinking to convivial excess was not the same as steady, solitary drunkenness and that the term "habitual intemperance" should be reserved for the latter (CL V, p. 62). Suggesting that Poole, Wordsworth, and Southey could vouch for his son's moral character, he offered his own analysis of Hartley's childhood "habits and dispositions" (CL V, p. 107).

While his fatherly letter was filled with sentimental anecdotes, he also tried to make the Oriel faculty understand the enlightened philosophical principles underlying the system of progressive education with which he had raised his boy. He feared that they had misinterpreted Hartley's restless, intellectually challenging manners as disrespect for their authority. To document his child-rearing credo, he quoted extensively from *Frost at Midnight*, his poem so filled with hopes for Hartley.

But it was a voyage in vain. His boy was not reinstated, nor was the charge of sottishness dropped. Hoping to soften the blow, the Provost told Coleridge that the fellows of Oriel did not want their decision to be construed as a moral verdict on Hartley's character, but only as recognition of his temperamental unsuitability for the austere, cloistered life of an academic fellow. And while they could plainly document drunken incidents, the Provost agreed that these had never amounted to habitual, solitary intemperance.

Still feeling that his son had been "cruelly wronged and then calumniated" (CL V, p. 108), Coleridge set about fostering Hartley's literary career. Settling him in Montague's house, he began collaborating with him on an essay on poetic meter and furnished him with notes for a long poem on Prometheus. On his own, Hartley also began contributing poetry and essays to the *London Magazine*.

Within a year of his moving in, Hartley was asked to leave Montague's home because of his tendency to vanish for days at a time without explanation. Moving in with a friend then, he maintained the same pattern of spasmodic writing alternating with episodic drinking bouts. In January of 1822 one of Hartley's cousins described him as penniless and eating irregularly.

But what Coleridge could least abide were those times when he was unable to contact Hartley and the young man's friends were unable to account for his whereabouts. As Coleridge knew but could never openly admit, his son's behavior toward him bore an uncanny resemblance to the way he had treated Hartley during the period between his return from Malta and his settling in with the Gillmans at Highgate. Over those years there had been long stretches of time when, lost in a haze of alcohol and narcotics, Coleridge had faded in and out of Hartley's life in a confusing fashion. If Hartley had elected to follow in the footsteps of the poet-father of his boyhood, the identification ran deeper than literary interests; it included the career of black sheep of the family. Of course, Hartley's choice of that role demanded that he be driven out of the fold by his father.

As he reviewed Hartley's progress after two years in London, Coleridge was vexed and perplexed by the many familiar elements he was discovering in his son's character. Sometimes Hartley's mood disorder bordered on suicidal despair. Alternating between paralyzing insecurity and grandiose daydreams, he tended to procrastinate on literary projects. Most distressing was what Coleridge called Hartley's "fatalism" (CL V, p. 78) —his superstitiously guilty reaction in response to success. That "feeling or fantasy of an adverse destiny" had occurred at the time of Hartley's original election as an Oriel fellow: "after the first flush of success" he had been "seized with an uneasy melancholy" (CL V, p. 58).

Coleridge had felt the same way when he was awarded the Wedgwood annuity. In fact, it was that same superstitious dread that had prompted him to write *Frost at Midnight*, the poem in which he had passionately vowed to protect his vulnerable infant son from ever knowing similar insecurities. Appalled to see his grown son a slave to that familiar superstitious quirk, and unable to protect him from the temptations of city life, Coleridge made up his mind that Hartley had to return permanently to the simple country life of the Lakes, where he could live among a community of people who had known him since childhood and who could be counted on to look after him.

After some initial protest, Hartley gave in and returned to the Lake District, where he obtained a post as an assistant schoolmaster. His London stay had proven a bitter experience for Coleridge, who was relieved to be rid of him. After 1824 father and son never corresponded with one another and would never meet again. Yet for the rest of his life, Coleridge claimed, no day went by without his thinking of his boy.

Hartley Coleridge remained a schoolmaster for three years and was an alcoholic poet for the rest of his life. Although direct communication between them was severed, Coleridge continued to take an active interest in Hartley's works, reading and annotating them. A few months before his father's death, Hartley would publish his *Biographia Borealis* and a volume of collected poems dedicated to his father.

Much to Coleridge's relief, he was more successful at influencing his second son, who eventually took Holy Orders and became a respectable West Country curate and schoolmaster like his grandfather before him. And much to Coleridge's delight, he was pleased to discover that his twenty-year-old daughter Sara had grown up into a graceful, attractive woman as well as a gifted translator of ancient and modern languages.

During her first visit to Highgate in 1823, Sara met and fell in love with her cousin Henry Nelson Coleridge and became secretly engaged. It was at that time that Henry also became smitten with his uncle—so much so in fact that he began keeping a faithful record of Coleridge's remarkable conversations, which he later published as *Table Talk*.

Thursday night at the Gillmans' was known as "attic night" (CL V, p. 13), since that was when Coleridge regularly held an informal open house in his attic study for "*con*versazione," or as he puckishly corrected himself, "*one*versazione," referring to his addiction to the monologue (CL V, p. xxxix). Over the years, Carlyle, Emerson, Mill, and a variety of other writers, known and unknown, made pilgrimages to hear the aging poet whose conversation had become legendary.

Encountering Coleridge one day while out on a stroll on Hampstead Heath, Keats recorded his impressions:

> I joined them, after enquiring by a look whether it would be agreeable—I walked with him at his alderman-after-dinner pace for near two miles I suppose. In those two miles he broached a thousand things—let me see if I can give you a list—nightingales, poetry,—on poetical sensation—metaphysics—different genera and species of dreams—nightmares—a dream accompanied by a sense of touch—single and double touch—a dream related—first and second consciousness—monsters—the kraken— mermaids — Southey believes in them—Southey's belief too much diluted—a ghost story—good morning—I heard it as he moved away—I had heard it all the interval—if it may be so called. He was civil enough to ask me to call on him at Highgate. [Armour and Howes, 1940, p. 277]

It is well established that in his youth Coleridge had relied on laudanum to lubricate the flow of his conversational brilliance, and there is every reason to believe that the aging bard never changed in that regard.

One day in 1828 Ann Gillman stormed into the shop of T. H. Dunn, a Highgate chemist, and adamantly insisted upon interviewing the proprietor in the presence of his assembled assistants. Because, she said, wheeling in her fury, she intended to extract a promise from each and every one of them that they would never sell Mr. Coleridge another drop of opium.

By no means intimidated by this outburst, Dunn rose to the occasion and told Mrs. Gillman that he had long anticipated such an interview and had carefully made up his mind on the matter. The facts were, Dunn claimed, that the Gillmans had suspected all along that Mr. Coleridge had regularly supplemented his daily maintenance dose with a steady supply from the shop over many years. It was Dunn's opinion that to withhold it now might prove fatal. He would agree to no such ultimatum and told Mrs. Gillman, before she left in a huff, that if there were to be any further discussion her husband would have to come in person.

The record shows no evidence that such a meeting took place, while Coleridge's correspondence reveals that he remained Dunn's faithful client until his final days. Eleven surviving letters to Dunn document the fact that Coleridge had regularly purchased the drug all along. Giving his preferred customer a three-shilling discount on the bottle, Dunn permitted him to go into arrears as much as twenty-six pounds at a time. The records indicate also that Coleridge's average purchase rate was twelve ounces every five or six days, or two ounces per day (approximately 300 mg. of oral morphine)—far less than his three-grams-a-day debaucheries before his domestication with the Gillmans.

Given that Coleridge would steadily use "Old Black" (his nickname for laudanum) to the very end (Lefebure, 1975, p. 334), there is room to wonder what role it may have played in his grand scheme for his magnum opus. Did opium stimulate his ambitious plan to write the definitive philosophical synthesis while paving the way for its inevitable failure?

Devouring book after book in preparation for this project, Coleridge would remain an avid reader for the rest of his life. For seventeen years J. H. Green would come weekly to discuss and transcribe Coleridge's philosophical ideas for the great work. As Coleridge never published his reams of notes, it is impossible to state with certainty to what extent he was deluding himself.

Modern psychopharmacological research on opiates reveals that grandiose cosmic ambitions, mood swings, thought deterioration, and compulsive loquacity are well-known and predictable responses to the acute or chronic administration of that drug. But the social testimony of Coleridge's contemporaries presents conflicting evidence of opium's role in the failure of Coleridge's magnificent dream.

Carlyle's exasperated descriptions of Coleridge would suggest that laudanum turned Coleridge's mind into "pabulum" (Coleridge 1817b, p. xxxix). But Green's commitment suggests otherwise. While he may have been a hero-worshipping youngster when they first met, Green was a mature man in his mid-forties and Chairman of the Department of Surgery at King's College by the time he inherited Coleridge's endless reams of notes and drafts in his role as literary executor. Independently wealthy thanks to an inheritance, Green would devote the remaining thirty years of his life to Coleridge's opus.

While Green's maturity and level of professional achievement suggest he was not one to chase transcendental moonbeams, the fact that he was never able to organize Coleridge's papers into coherent publishable form might suggest otherwise. And over the years since Green's death no one else has succeeded in making sense of them.

Chapter 16

Coleridge the Psychologist

While Coleridge's philosophical opus continues to defy summary, synthesis, and publication, his contribution to psychoanalysis is less resistant to description. Some of his most original psychological ideas are elaborated in *Biographia Literaria;* the rest lie scattered in his letters and diaries as a series of observations.

His insights into the nature of dreaming and the creative process anticipate current psychoanalytic thinking by a century and a half. But at the same time, Coleridge emerges as a reactionary medievalist filled with antiquated superstitions on the nature of human experience.

For if his life straddled two centuries, his mind evinced the cultural prejudices of both. While proclaiming a literal, abiding belief in the gospel of the immaculate conception, Colderidge in the next breath could struggle to achieve what he himself termed "an accurate psycho-analytical understanding" (CNB 2670) of the ways in which ancient fertility myths like Leda and the Swan were woven into the biblical tale of the Virgin Birth. More often than not, the religious mystic in him was at war with the rational psychologist. Nowhere was the split between psyche and soul more apparent than in his psychology of dreams.

Dreams had baffled and fascinated human beings for centuries, and it is not surprising that Coleridge attempted to unlock their mysteries as both theologian and psychologist. Apart from his intellectual curiosity, Coleridge had a more deeply personal reason for his obsessive interest: throughout his life he was haunted by disturbing nightmares and vivid opium dreams that he struggled to comprehend.

He carefully recorded those dreams in his diaries, where

he also took copious notes on his own and other people's thoughts on the nature of sleep and the dream process. His poetry reflects this preoccupation as well. *The Ancient Mariner, Kubla Khan, The Pains of Sleep*—even *Christabel*—are based on actual dreams or dreamlike states that are re-created as supernatural tales.

In view of this close connection between his intellectual interest in dreams and the art he was creating, it is hardly surprising that Coleridge began to suspect that artistic creativity and the dream process interconnect. He became intrigued by the role that bodily states play in the formation of dream images. How, for instance, could a sharp physical sensation be *verbally interpreted* as a stabbing pain and then *visually translated* into a dream image of being attacked by an assassin's dagger? He labeled such images "allegorical personifications" of bodily sensations (CL VI, p. 607).

He was fascinated by another similarity between literary and dream processes. The dreamer is both author and audience—first producing the dream and then responding to it much as a spectator views a work of art created by another. Like successful art, dreams have an irrationally compelling impact on their beholder. The theatergoer overlooks the glaring artificialities of the stage and becomes rapidly absorbed in the play as easily as a dreamer becomes absorbed in the sequence of illogical dream images unfolding before his eyes. In both dreaming and the theater, the viewer compensates for the disruption of logic, time, and space. He accepts the rapidly shifting sequence of scenes without losing his absorption in the story being told.

What accounts for this capacity of dreams and art to compel the viewer? In both cases, Coleridge reasoned, there is a temporary alteration of the rational, judgmental faculties which ordinarily accompany waking consciousness. The involuntary nature of that change seemed self-evident in sleep:

> The truth is, that images and thoughts possess a power in and of themselves ... such is the ordinary state of mind in dreams. It is not strictly accurate to say, that we believe our dreams to be actual while we are dreaming. We neither believe it nor disbelieve it. [CL IV, p. 641]

Unlike this automatic relaxation of logical judgment that led to what he called "the non-existence of surprise in sleep" (CNB 1250), Coleridge postulated that a "voluntary lending of the will to this suspension" takes place in art (CL IV, p. 642). He labeled the audience's role in this process "the suspension of disbelief" and declared it the "true theory of stage illusion" (Gillman, 1838, p. 105).

Translated into its modern psychoanalytic equivalent, Coleridge's "willing suspension of disbelief" is roughly the same as Ernst Kris's "regression in the service of the ego" (Kris, 1935, p. 64). In order to enter the world of the imagination—that land of make-believe—the audience suspends its disbelief and meets the creator halfway.

In his intuitive, nonsystematic way, Coleridge touched on many of the fundamental issues in the modern psychology of dreaming and creativity. Yet there is a crucial sense in which Coleridge understood the meaning of the dream process no better than he appreciated the personal significance of the vivid dreams and nightmares that tormented him. Deeply divided, his faith told him one thing, his reason another.

While confidently asserting that dreams are simple wish fulfillments* he was equally persuaded by Swedenborg's mystical view that dreams are caused by "impure spirits" (CL VI, p. 207)—"foul spirits of the lowest order" which are attracted to "the precious exviands" of the bowels (CL V, p. 391). At times skeptical of the virtues of common sense, Coleridge flung his psychologist's logic to the winds and asserted his mystic's faith in the medieval incubus theory that dreams are the result of demonic possession by evil spirits. Given the fact that Coleridge often expressed his psychological conflicts by dreaming in biblical imagery, the conflicting theological and psychological explanations he proposed fit his data equally well.

*In a letter written in 1826 Coleridge described sleep as "the time when you are Fancy's rather than the Fancy's yours" (CL VI, p. 615). At first glance this statement might appear to be little more than a poetic conceit. But since he had already taken great pains to make his careful semantic distinction between *fancy* and *imagination* (see below), we have to assume that he was using his words precisely. In nominating *fancy* as the dream mechanism, Coleridge clearly implied that he considered dreams simple wish fulfillments.

Considering the painful content of his guilt-ridden nightmares, it is easy to see why Coleridge was sorely tempted to join Swedenborg and blame his troubled sleep on the devil playing havoc with his bowels. Troubled by the "vile gossip" of the persecutory forms that expressed his moods of self-loathing (CL VI, p. 616), Coleridge was drawn to an explanation that located the source of the problem outside himself:

> I have too often experienced in a dream . . . myself in chains, or in rags, shunned or passed by, with looks of horror blended with sadness, by friends and acquaintances, and convinced that in some alienation of mind I must have perpetrated some crime, which I strove to recollect. . . . [CL V, p. 716]

It was at times like these that he was attracted to the still prevalent incubus theory of demonic possession.

Cultural biases impelled him toward both scientific reasoning and superstitious thinking. Raised as a child in an eighteenth-century Devonshire village that had a town crier, he grew up in a rural vicarage heated by wood fires, where the amenities consisted of a well and an outhouse. But he lived to see gaslight, indoor plumbing, and steam heat in nineteenth-century London.

When Coleridge's brother Frank sailed from Portsmouth in 1781, his three-masted ship was totally wind-driven. By the 1820s, Coleridge watched with skeptical fascination as newfangled steam vessels cut graceful arcs in Ramsgate's water, as if in total defiance of prevailing breezes. And while apocryphal tales abounded in his boyhood—such as Death appearing to his father and announcing his selection—enlightened medical science was busily combating any fatalistic resignation to the forces of death and disease by developing new techniques like Jenner's smallpox vaccine.

Coleridge grew up and lived among rapid changes: locomotives, mechanical reapers, spinning jennies, and power looms were all invented in his lifetime. Even the process for generating electricity would be discovered before he died.

He had witnessed the transformation of the eighteenth-century English countryside of his boyhood as factories began to dot and then clutter the landscape; manufacturing towns sprang up overnight. While Coleridge the progressive thinker would advocate social reforms to combat the growing slums, squalid working conditions, and cruel child labor practices Coleridge the reactionary escapist would turn to Swedenborg's medievalism and retreat from the dubious social progress that surrounded him.

Nowhere was Coleridge more modern a thinker than in his groundbreaking work on the creative imagination published in *Biographia Literaria*. Seeking to describe and explain the special mechanisms involved in creativity, he distinguished between two mental activities, *fancy* and the *imagination*.

His English readers have always found this semantic distinction easier to understand than his American audience, as the word "fancy" has different meanings in the two countries. In colloquial British usage the word expresses desire: one fancies a blackberry tart, or a pair of shoes in a shop window.

Using that difference of connotation, Coleridge described the fancy and the imagination as overlapping mental functions which both produce fantasy. But while all great art consists of fantasy, not all fantasy leads to great art. *Fancy*, in Coleridge's terminology, is simple wish fulfillment and more or less automatically produces unoriginal images which are fixed and predictable.

The imagination, as Coleridge conceived it, is spontaneous, energetic, active, and capable of great plasticity. The fantasies produced by the imagination have infinite variety, complexity, and originality. They are creative fantasies.

In making this careful semantic distinction, Coleridge suggested that the psychological mechanism in simple wish fulfillment (fancy) is not the same process whereby complex creative fantasies are born (imagination). Modern psychoanalysis has had to address itself to this critical distinction.

But if Coleridge's views as a psychologist are capable of being stated systematically, it is also the case that Coleridge was incapable of systematically stating them. His mind clouded by opium, he lacked the mental reserve to organize his insights into the nature of dreams and the creative process.

It would be another fifty years before a young Viennese neurologist, self-experimenting with cocaine and carefully describing his dreams, would record similar insights into the nature of the human mind and elaborate them in a comprehensive theory of his own. Scientifically trained, he would also be lucky enough to be toying with a drug with less addivtive potential than has opium, and he would be blessed with a more stubbornly disciplined temperament than was his anticipator.

Chapter 17

The Final Years

> *Stop, Christian Passer-by! Stop, Child of God!*
> *And read with gentle heart. Beneath this sod*
> *A poet lies: or that which once was he.*
> *O lift one thought in prayer for S.T.C.*
> *That he, who many a year, with toil of breath*
> *Found Death in Life, may here find Life in Death.*
> *Mercy for Praise, to be forgiven for Fame*
> *He ask'd, and hop'd thro' Christ. Do Thou the Same!*
> —*Epitaph* [CL VI, p. 963]

By early 1828 Coleridge knew his days were numbered. Although he had recently recovered from a serious illness, that brush with death prompted him to take Holy Communion for the first time since his Cambridge days. The gravity of his siege had been underscored by the urgency with which Gillman began to speed up arrangements for a definitive edition of Coleridge's works to be issued by William Pickering, a London publisher.

Just before the New Year another painful reminder that time was running out had arrived, in the form of a letter from Ottery informing Coleridge that his brother George lay dying of dropsy on the chest. Although Coleridge wanted to make the trip to Devon, he was too infirm and arthritic to travel alone, and it was not possible to find someone to accompany him on such short notice. Acutely aware that George's death signified the lifting of a generational screen, Coleridge knew he was next in line.

With one eye on eternity and the other on posterity, he divided his attention between his *Poetical Works*, his philosophical magnum opus, and his spiritual preparations for the next life. Focusing much of his irony on his publisher, whom he realized was about to become his literary taxidermist, Coleridge took to absentmindedly referring to him as Mr. Pickleherring. Playing at being in his dotage was a prerogative of old age which Coleridge fully intended to enjoy in the time remaining.

Although Gillman would not permit his charge to make long trips unescorted, he was unable to keep as tight a rein over Coleridge's highjinks at Highgate. An overnight visit with Charles and Mary Lamb resulted in a ruefully blistering twelve-mile ramble, while the all-male dinner parties which Coleridge managed to attend with his cronies and other literary lions of the day sometimes ended in ribald nights out on the town.

On one of those rare but glorious evenings, Coleridge was delighted when—after many rounds of punch and claret—one of the younger men at table improvised a comic song in his honor. "Like a wild schoolboy at play" (Armour and Howes, 1940, p. 274), Coleridge entered into the merriment by following the younger man's example and smashing window panes with wine glasses. Then—after some good-natured teasing about his aim— Coleridge obliged all present by using one of the remaining goblets as a target: "the roseate face of Coleridge, lit up with animation, his large grey eye beaming, his white hair floating, and his whole frame, as it were, radiating with intense interest, as he poised the fork in his hand, and launched it at the fragile object" (Chambers, 1938, p. 308).

On other occasions Coleridge entertained his companions by reciting his poems from memory, which he was always able to do, except twice when he was dead drunk. His tongue loosened by the grape, Coleridge loved to reminisce about his boyhood days and to regale his listeners with stories of Wordsworth and himself. Most of his colorful anecdotes were based on the old days in Somerset and the Lake District. But the fact that he and William had resumed their friendship and were about to embark on a trip to Germany with William's daughter Dora allowed Coleridge to update his repertoire with fresh Wordsworth stories.

While their formal reconciliation had taken place in 1812, the rift in their friendship had taken a much longer time to heal. Patching a quarrel had proven easier than mending a friendship. Sixteen years had passed since William's original visit to London to squelch the rumors about his breach with Coleridge. The "immedicable *but*" that Coleridge described in their love for one another had expressed itself in different forms of disappointment and betrayal over the years.

When Wordsworth published his collected poems in 1814, he had taken a pointed swipe at Coleridge's controversial claim to originality by gratuitously commenting in his preface that the English were indebted to the Germans for the latest innovations in Shakespeare criticism. Coleridge picked up the literary gauntlet and took William to task in *Biographia Literaria* by pointing out the naive way Wordsworth exalted the sensitive wisdom of young children. According to Coleridge, Wordsworth's view of children was based upon an adultomorphic fallacy: he attributed an abstract, complex reasoning process to young children as if they were miniature philosophers. In addition, Coleridge went on to point out, Wordsworth's theory of poetic diction was equally absurd—his characters spoke in poetic language and not in the idiomatic prose Wordsworth claimed they used.

While Coleridge deftly balanced his surgically accurate critique of Wordsworth's shortcomings as a theoretician with enthusiastic praise for him as a poet, he nonetheless found his mark. It rankled William to have his pet theories contradicted. Given their long-standing friendship, it is not surprising that each knew how best to hurt the other.

Over the years that followed, their estrangement in print continued in person. Henry Crabb Robinson, their mutual friend, chronicled the rift between them whenever their paths happened to cross at London dinner parties, musicales and receptions. At those chance encounters, Wordsworth's stiff reserve and intense pride stood in sharp contrast to Coleridge's affable, facile warmth. William seemed ill at ease while Coleridge delighted in collecting a rapt group of listeners as he recited Wordsworth's poems with lavish praise.

At such unplanned meetings, Robinson perceived Coleridge as "respectful," while Wordsworth seemed "cold and scornful" (CL IV, p. 757), meeting all of Coleridge's propositions with "dry unfeeling contradiction" (Moorman, 1965, p. 313). However, on occasions when William was not present, Coleridge's private remarks to Robinson suggested that he too was operating "under personal feelings of unkindness" (CL V, p. 261).

Realizing that the gulf between them could be closed only in private, William took the initiative one day late in the fall of 1821 and walked over from Hampstead to Highgate. While Coleridge was pleased by Wordsworth's gesture, he was later irked to learn of William's stiffly worded appraisal that he "perceived an amendment in me. In self-management, in the power of keeping my eyes more, and my heart less open, in aversion to baseness, intrigue, in detestation of apostasy" (CL V, p. 272).

Although Wordsworth's overture may have been marred, in Coleridge's eyes, by his sanctimonious big-brother tendency to pronounce judgments on Coleridge's character, he had nonetheless broken the ice. By 1824 William had felt comfortable enough to send Coleridge a manuscript of his preliminary translation of the *Aeneid* with a request for criticism. Coleridge promptly obliged—flattered by the request and pleased to have a chance to repay Wordsworth for the kindness he was showing to Hartley.

Ever since Hartley's 1822 banishment to the Lakes, Wordsworth had unofficially taken on the combined role of literary mentor and guardian angel. Besides giving Hartley advice and encouragement with his poetry, Wordsworth took an interest in his welfare. As Hartley knew, he could count on his Uncle William to bail him out of the inevitable financial scrapes that were the aftermath of periodic binges on which he wandered the countryside, drank in taverns, slept in barns, and left a collection of petty debts in his hazy wake.

And so by the time they departed on their two-month continental tour that June, both Coleridge and Wordsworth were aware of their strong ties, deep mutual debts, and the painful fact that time was running out. His weatherworn face now furrowed by his coarsening features and his bald crown surrounded by thinning, scraggly tufts of gray hair, Wordsworth looked as old as Coleridge. However, William's less destructive living habits and stronger constitution told the difference. Obese and arthritic, Coleridge stooped and shuffled while Wordsworth, still wiry and active, strode erect with pride of bearing.

Dressed in baggy trousers with thick shoes, William gave the appearance of a provincial farmer, while Coleridge, in his habitual cleric's black, was often mistaken for a dissenting minister. An observer who met the pair on their tour through the Low Countries and Germany remarked that Wordsworth "seemed satisfied to let his friend take the lead" in conversations (Moorman, 1965, p. 435) and that Coleridge seemed "to breathe in words" (Armour and Howes, 1940, p. 226).

Their interests as tourists proved as different as their appearances: William was fascinated by the soldiers' graves at Waterloo while Coleridge lingered and rhapsodized over the angelic faces of the peasant children. William's daughter Dora reported:

> They got on famously, but Mr C sometimes detains us with his fiddle-faddling, and he likes prosing to the folks better than exerting himself to see the face of the country and father with his half-dozen words of German makes himself much better understood than Mr C with all his weight of German literature. [Moorman, 1965, p. 435]

When the peripatetic poets arrived in Bonn—accompanied by a younger version of Dorothy—they were greeted by the local literati, who turned out in full force for the occasion. Among those present was Augustus Schlegel, who seemed delighted to meet Coleridge in person. Filled with expressions of admiration for each other's works, the two Shakespeare critics in their encounter displayed none of the acrimony over priorities that has characterized the subsequent debates of their academic advocates and apologists.

By the end of August the travelers had returned to London. Afterward Dora sent Coleridge a souvenir copy of her journal notes describing the trip. Coleridge was pleased to arrive home in time to inspect the freshly printed, handsome three-volume edition of his *Poetical Works* that Gillman and "Pickleherring" had arranged in his honor. But the most exciting news that fall was the birth of his first grandson, Derwent Coleridge, Jr.

Settling back into his comfortable routine, Coleridge worked steadily on his magnum opus and began his pamphlet *On Church and State*, which addressed the hotly debated issue of Catholic emancipation. Attending one of the Thursday soirees, a young visitor by the name of John Stuart Mill heard

Coleridge pontificate on the topic and came away declaring him one of "the two great seminal minds of England," the other being Bentham (Willey, 1973, p. 256).

While working steadily on his pamphlet, Coleridge began to complain of a bronchitic early-morning cough and "a continued oppression on my chest" which confined him to his bed for long stretches of time (CL VI, p. 786). Although he recovered by August, the Thursday night open houses were permanently suspended; by mid-September he was writing his will.

The will reflected the fact that Hartley was the only one of his three children whose economic future remained a source of anxiety to Coleridge. In spite of his painful memories of their earlier attempt at collaboration, he could not help dreaming of "what a comfort and delight it would be to have him with me as a Literary Partner!" (CL VI, p. 551). But he was forced to console himself with the knowledge that his old friend William had always cared for the boy and could be counted on to look after him: "I can never read Wordsworth's delightful lines 'To H.C. at six years old' without a feeling of awe, blended with tenderer emotions" (CL VI, p. 798). Having written his last will and testament, Coleridge returned to *On Church and State*. Taking advantage of a reprieve in his health, he finished the project by the new year (1830). It would be his last published work.

By now he was a semi-invalid, confined to his attic bedroom-study for long stretches of time. Receiving callers in his chambers, he was forced to content himself with the charming views from his bedroom windows and was eternally grateful to Ann Gillman for the steady supply of plants and fresh flowers she provided.

Although they were housemates separated by only one floor, there were moments when Ann seemed to drift further away and Coleridge felt the need to communicate through letters and notes. One Saturday night in May, feeling "weighed down by a heavy presentiment respecting my own sojourn here," Coleridge wrote a warm letter thanking her for her kindness over the years (CL VI, p. 832). A week later he reported to a friend that he had just returned from "the very brink of the grave" after having been found "on the floor pulseless and senseless" by a servant who had been awakened by a dull thud in the middle of the night; "animation was restored" by the application of mustard plasters (CL VI, p. 836).

A few days later—resassured after an unscheduled emergency visit to see for himself—Lamb breathed a sigh of relief over the false alarm. While Lamb feared lest his old friend's attack prove to be a case of paralytic apoplexy, a more likely explanation was that Coleridge had taken too strong a dose of "Old Black" and had fallen out of bed in his sleep. Wracked by sciatic and arthritic pains at night, Coleridge was dealing with his nocturnal anguish by secretly stepping up his opiate intake with the help of T. H. Dunn.

As his health grew worse, Coleridge's family knitted themselves more tightly around him. In June his daughter Sara, four months pregnant, moved to Hampstead with her husband and her mother to be near her father. In July Coleridge proudly sent Poole "manuscript proof that I am yet in the land of the living" (CL VI, p. 841)—an autographed copy of *On Church and State*. And on that same summer day—still troubled by thoughts of death and nagging concerns over Hartley—he added a codicil to his will placing Hartley's small share of inheritance in protective trust.

By the winter of 1831 Wordsworth was in town and, having heard of his friend's worsening health, paid Coleridge a visit. Their meetings stretched out over two or three days and took the form of several long private conversations. It is likely that they discussed Coleridge's concerns about Hartley's future and that William promised to look after him. Afterward Wordsworth commented that Coleridge's "constitution seems much broken up" although "his mind has lost none of its vigour" (Campbell, 1905, p. cxix). It was the last time they would meet.

William put Coleridge's physical suffering into perspective: "He and my beloved sister are the two beings to whom my intellect is most indebted, and they are now proceeding as it were, *pari passu*, along the path of sickness—I will not say towards the grave, but I trust towards a blessed immortality" (Armour and Howes, 1940, p. 378). Like Coleridge, Dorothy had become a semi-invalid. Already confined to a wheelchair, she would soon retreat into the twilight world of senile paranoia, subject to "frequent outbursts of anger, shouts and screams" directed at her brother and Mary Hutchinson (Davies, 1980,

p. 303). But, it was said, that in spite of her failing faculties she was able to quote long passages of William's poems from memory. She had devoted her lifetime to transcribing them.

During Coleridge's long stretches of confinement to his bedroom, his friends and family kept up his spirits. Visiting him regularly, they kept him abreast—or rather were kept abreast by him—of the important social and political issues of the day. As loquacious as ever, Coleridge was determined not to lose touch with the outside world. Henry Crabb Robinson described one of his regular visits to Highgate in April 1832: "Saw Coleridge in bed. He looked beautifully—his eye remarkably brilliant—and he talked eloquently as ever. His declamation was against the [Reform] Bill" (Campbell, 1905, p. cxix).

A drastic upheaval was taking place in the English system of government, Coleridge realized, as he expounded his increasingly conservative monarchist point of view to all who would listen. Through bloodless or through violent means, revolution seemed inevitable—it was the will of the people.

Bristol had already erupted in flames, as angry demonstrators rampaged for more than a week. Frustrated in their desire to see Parliament reformed and suffrage extended, they set their torches to the Bishop's Palace and the Custom House. The night sky had glowed with a red hue that could be seen as far away as Bath, as those hated symbols of church and state were reduced to ashes along with other buildings in that city.

And while Coleridge lay on his Highgate sickbed delivering his analysis of the situation, cavalry units like his old regiment, the King's Fifteenth Light Dragoons, had canceled all leave and ordered the troopers to "rough sharpen" their bayonets (Cooper, 1964, p. 287). As the old-timers explained to the frightened young recruits, the purpose was to leave a jagged cutting edge in order to inflict more savage wounds. The last time that order had been given had been on the eve of Waterloo.

England was on the brink of civil war. As nervous as the enlisted men under them, many company commanders wondered whether, if called upon to suppress a riot, their troops would obey orders to use their bayonets on their fellow countrymen, or whether they would turn them against their officers.

The mood of the people was one of steadily rising indignation. Having returned two Parliaments in rapid succession

The Final Years

with clear mandates to extend the suffrage and reform the corrupt and outmoded electoral system, the people were enraged by the indifference with which the King and the House of Lords ignored their demands for greater democracy.

Hoping to avoid a violent confrontation but determined to have their reforms, the middle classes were exerting economic pressure by refusing to pay taxes and by threatening England's credit by withdrawing gold from the banks until such time as the Bill was passed. It was the recognition of impending bankruptcy that finally drove the Establishment into submission. On June 7, 1832, the Reform Bill became the law of the land.

Looking down from his Highgate window on the London of his boyhood, Coleridge realized that the England he had known was a thing of the past. Although it was only men of his own class who had been given the vote, he knew what would follow.

Of all of Coleridge's faithful friends, Charles Lamb and he went back the farthest; and it was with his former fellow Grecian that he indulged in his most nostalgic reminiscing on days gone by. For his part, Lamb was deeply affected by the grim spectacle of his friend's decline. From their bluecoat days at Christ's Hospital, Coleridge had always been the object of Lamb's admiration, notwithstanding the affectionate irony with which he loved to chide his hero for his foibles. And now as they were older, the slightly senior Coleridge served as Lamb's generational screen: any worsening of Coleridge's physical condition made Lamb painfully aware of his own vulnerability. As time wore on, he found it trying to witness Coleridge's afflictions.

Suffering from severe arthritis, restricted access to contraband opium, and increasing shortness of breath from chronic congestive heart failure, Coleridge's outlook grew darker and more desperately religious:

> I have for more than 18 months been on the brink of the grave, under sufferings which have rendered the grave an object of my wishes and only not of my prayers, because I commit myself, poor dark creature, to an omniscient and all-merciful, in whom are the issues of life and death.... O trust, o trust in your

Redeemer! In the co-eternal *Word*, the only-begotten, the living NAME of the Eternal I AM, Jehovah, Jesus! [CL VI, p. 890]

But if there were times when Lamb had to fight his temptation to stay away from Highgate and the spectacle of his boyhood friend morosely inching his way toward eternity, he no doubt rejoiced at the news of his old friend's deliverance from opium. Dramatically announcing that his prayers had been miraculously answered and that he was at last free of "any craving for the poison" (CL VI, p. 894), Coleridge wrote:

> I hope, that this fearful night storm is subsiding—as you will have heard from Mr Green or dear Charles Lamb. I write to say, that if God in his fatherly compassion, and thro' the love wherewith he hath beheld and loved me in Christ, in whom alone he can love the world, hath worked almost a miracle of grace in and for me by a sudden emancipation from a 33 years' fearful slavery. [CL VI, p. 901]

But as Green knew and Coleridge soon discovered, his reprieve was the immediate result of Gillman's mercy, not God's. His miraculous sense of well-being was due to the fact that Gillman had decided to switch him from laudanum to pure morphine, a much stronger narcotic. While Coleridge was disheartened by the "too apparent failure of the experiment" of stopping opium (CL VI, p. 908), he nonetheless enjoyed the euphoria and was delighted to have a new lease on life.

In August 1832 Coleridge friskily informed Green that he was off to Hampstead to stand with his wife at their new granddaughter's christening. He and Sarah would show the world "that the lack of oil or anti-friction powder in our conjugal carriage wheels did not extend to our parental relations." "In fact," he added breezily, "bating living in the same house with her there are few women, that I have a greater respect and *ratherish* liking for, than Mrs C" (CL VI, p. 918).

Sarah sent her own description of the blessed event to Poole:

> The grandfather came from Highgate to be present and to pass the rest of the day here! . . . His power of continuous talking seems unabated, for he talked incessantly for full 5 hours to the

great entertainment of . . . friends who were present, and did not leave us till 10. . . . when Henry called to see him yesterday he appeared no worse for the exertion he had made. Coleridge talked a good deal of you, as he always does when he speaks of early days. . . . [Armour and Howes, 1940, p. 163]

Afterward Coleridge continued in his loquacious "hyperbolizing" mood (CL VI, p. 907), playfully composing doggerel that he signed with names like *Demophilus Mudlarkius* and *Philodemus Coprophilus*. Feeling spritely, he began taking twice-weekly air baths at a health spa in downtown London. Hopping the Highgate Stage to Tottenham Court Road, he caught a hackney to the establishment in preference to the newfangled horse-drawn buses. Signs of change were everywhere. Even London Bridge had fallen down (or rather, had been torn down, a new one having been completed in 1831).

Given the zippy tone of Coleridge's letters and his sudden burst of physical energy, it appears that Gillman had humanely decided to keep Coleridge on high doses of morphine for the rest of his life. And as might be expected, once he was up and about, Coleridge resumed his faithful patronage of T. H. Dunn's establishment.

In July 1833 Coleridge was touring the town on his annual seaside holiday at Ramsgate with the Gillmans:

As I was crawling up the hill towards Belle Vue, where we lodge, a stately old lady, certainly not less than 80, was coming down—I was making way to give her the wall—when with an unexpected alacrity of motion she made the outward curve, and with grave solemnity said—No, Sir! You are the far elder. It is my *Duty* to make way for the *Aged*. [CL VI, p. 947]

But of all Coleridge's outings that year, his return to Cambridge was the most gratifying. Accompanied by Gillman, he attended the third annual meeting of the British Association:

My emotions at revisting the university were at first overwhelming. I could not speak for an hour; yet my feelings upon the whole very pleasurable, and I have not passed, of late years at least, three days of such great enjoyment and healthful excitement of mind and body. The bed in which I slept—and slept soundly too—was, as near as I can describe it, a couple of sacks full of potatoes tied together. I understand the young men think it hardens them. Truly I lay down at night a man, and arose in the morning a bruise. [CL VI, p. 953]

Although unable to get out of bed until the afternoons, he was flattered by the crowd of admirers that flocked to his bedside each morning to listen to him pontificate. One of them later recalled the occasion: "I said to Coleridge . . . that I had read most of his published works: but, by way of being very honest, I added, But sir, I am not sure that I understand them all. 'The question is, sir,' said he, 'whether I understand them all myself' " (Armour and Howes, 1940, p. 235).

A few months after that Cambridge outing, Coleridge sent J. H. Green a copy of the epitaph he had composed for his tombstone. Despite the ambiguous apology for having sought praise and fame that it contained (see the epigraph to this chapter), he had no intention of relinquishing those ambitions as he went through the process of dying. Still determined to leave his mark as a philosopher by penetrating the unknown mysteries of the universe, Coleridge hoped to record any chance glimpses he might have as he made the passage into the next world. Toward that end, his strategy was to dictate his last-minute revelations to Green.

At nine in the evening one Monday in March 1834, Coleridge summoned Green to deploy their final philosophical gambit. Alarmed by the sudden eruption of a nasty red streak of erysipelas across his face—which he took for a sure sign of impending death—he urgently requested Green to come to him. He and God were about to enter upon their final collaboration and he wanted Green present in case God came up with a philosophical suggestion worth recording.

The rash proved a false alarm and Green's visit a dry run. All through that spring and early summer, Coleridge continued revising the third edition of his *Poetical Works* and laboring on his magnum opus. Although he was growing weaker, there were still occasional sunny days when he felt strong enough to take a tour of the garden. In May, Poole made a trip from Stowey to pay a visit and left with the impression that Coleridge's mind was "as strong as ever, seeming impatient to take leave of its encumbrance" (Sandford, 1888, p. 294).

In early August, Hartley Coleridge received a letter from his sister Sara:

> On the evening of the 19th he appeared very ill and on Sunday the 20th of July came a note. . . . from the tone of the note I mourned him as one about to be taken from us. Henry returned in a few hours. My father since he first felt his end approaching had expressed a desire that he might be as little disturbed as possible. He took leave of Mrs Gillman and did not wish even to see his beloved friend Mr Green. The agitation of nerves at the sight of those dear to him disturbed his meditations on his Redeemer to whose bosom he was hastening and then he said that he wished to evince in the manner of his death the depth and sincerity of his faith in Christ. Henry, however, was resolved to enter his room and see him for the last time. He was just able to send his blessing to my mother and me, though he articulated with difficulty and speaking seemed to increase his pain. Henry kissed him again and withdrew—never to see him living again. . . . On Thursday Henry brought word that by injections of laudanum the medical attendants had succeeded in easing my father's sufferings. This was a great relief indeed to our minds. . . . He had . . . feared his end would be long and painful. Thank God this was not so. . . . he saw Mrs Gillman for the last time and took leave of James Gillman. James then saw him raise his head in the air—looking upwards as in prayer—he then fell asleep—from sleep into a state of coma . . . and ceased to breathe at half past six in the morning Friday. [CL VI, p. 991]

Keeping his promise, J. H. Green remained by Coleridge's bedside throughout those final hours. He later told Sara that for as long as he had remained conscious, her father's mind was lucid—in fact at one point Coleridge had commented "I could even be witty." His final words, according to Green, had been to repeat "his formula on the Trinity" (CL VI, p. 991).

On learning the news. Hartley Coleridge sent his mother a long letter of consolation accompanied by a requiem poem for his father. In his letter Hartley reassured his mother that the Wordsworths had been very kind to him and that he intended to go there on the morrow. And it is said that on first reading the news of Coleridge's death to a friend, Wordsworth's voice cracked. All he could say was that Coleridge was "the most *wonderful* man he had ever known" (Campbell, 1905, p. cxxi). William had never been one to indulge in "nervous blubbering."

Epilogue

Posterity's Verdict: A Postmortem

> *Have you ever heard of a man whose hypochondriasis consisted in a constant craving to have himself opened before his own eyes? . . . Wounded by the frequent assertions—'all his complaints are owing to the use of opium' and yet . . . certain . . . that my complaints in genere were antecedent to my unfortunate (but God knows! most innocent) resort to that palliative. . . . if I could be present while my viscera were laid open!*
>
> [CL IV, p. 578]

In her letter to Hartley, Sara included a summary of Coleridge's autopsy. Their father had insisted on a postmortem examination, she told Hartley, and had made Gillman solemnly promise to carry out his last wish. Like her father, Sara had been anxious to know whether his addiction had originally been provoked by his physical pain.

Untrained in medicine, Sara relied on Dr. Gillman to explain the significance of the autopsy findings. Relaying the information to Hartley, she wrote that "nothing was observed which could be ascribed to laudanum." She added: "the internal pain and uneasiness which he had suffered from all his life and which my mother remembers his complaining of before he ever had recourse to opium is supposed to have been some sympathetic nervous affliction" (CL VI, p. 992).

The physical findings of Coleridge's postmortem examination were as follows:

External Appearances

Abdomen tympanitic and very tense—Body loaded with fat—

Internal—Thorax

Adhesions between the surfaces of the left pleura to a small extent—left lung crepitating—healthy—left bronchial tubes contained a small quantity of fluid but not over charged. Right pleura strongly adherent in many places—between it and the cartilages of the 5th, 6th, and 7th ribs was a cyst containing about half a pint of bloody serum of a very deep colour. The cavity of the right side contained at least three quarts of bloody serum. Right lung gorged with serous fluid—bronchia tubes dilated. The air tubes through-out exhibited marks of former inflammation, by the thickened and congested state of the lining membrane. Heart loaded with fat—half as large again as natural. Dilatation of both ventricles and hypertrophy of the left. Valves healthy. A deposit of caseous matter not quite amounting in hardness to cartilage was found beneath the lining membrane of the aorta, the sinus of which was dilated more than usual.

Abdomen

Liver pale—of exceeding softness, so as to break down on the slightest pressure. Gall bladder enormously distended with pale-coloured bile. Stomach empty, with patches of ulceration towards the cardiac extremity. Intestines natural—some congestion to the coats of the caput coli—but hardly amounting to inflammation. Other viscera healthy. [CL VI, p. 998]

The autopsy results indicate Coleridge probably died of heart failure and that he might have had an arrested case of tuberculosis. But while the anatomists thoroughly examined Coleridge's chest and abdominal cavities, they never inspected his bones and joints. Considering that Coleridge claimed to have been driven to drugs by arthritic pain during the early Lake District days when he was becoming addicted, the omission is surprising. While the examination of his heart revealed normal valves, making rheumatic fever somewhat less likely, there are other causes of arthritis that this limited postmortem could not have detected.

Coleridge's letters from the 1800–1801 period contain descriptions that suggest his pains were not imaginary. He reported that his knees were periodically painful and swollen, his fingers stiff.

In view of the fact that Coleridge himself coined the word *psychosomatic*, he would no doubt have been intrigued by the possibility that he was suffering from such a process—a disease lying at the mysterious interface between mind and body, provoked perhaps by emotional stress but very definitely physical in its manifestations. If Coleridge could have been present at his own autopsy—as he sorely wished to be—he could not have restrained himself from his habitual inclination to search for first causes and to speculate on mechanisms.

He would have wanted to ask: *When did it begin? Why?* If we ask these questions for him, we come up with an enigmatic hint of what might have happened.

In his autobiographical letter to Poole written in 1797—long before he was addicted or in search of rationalizations to explain his drug use—Coleridge described his harrowing ordeal as an eight-year-old on that stormy night by the banks of the Otter. He had suffered the physical shock of exposure, joint pains, muscle stiffness, and the emotional aftereffects of his nocturnal terror. Summarizing the sequelae, Coleridge wrote: "I was put to bed—and recovered in a day or so—but I was certainly injured—For I was weakly, and subject to the ague for many years after" (CL I, p. 354).

Was Sam, like so many other British children of that time, given "Mother's Blessing" to calm his nerves and soothe his pains? If so, how often was that treatment repeated for his recurring agues? It is a matter of record that laudanum was routinely prescribed as the treatment of choice for childhood agues by physicians in the late eighteenth century.

And if the arthritic pains that drove Coleridge to laudanum as a grown man were psychosomatic, or at least stress-related, what predisposed him to develop that particular symptom? His first experience with stiff joints began the night he tried to stab Frank. Was it a coincidence that at a time when he felt like murdering William, the arthritis flared so severely? Priding himself on having not a mean or selfish bone in his body, Coleridge took to his sickbed and nursed his grievances and aching joints with "Mother's Blessing." Were his arthritic symptoms in part a subconscious warning about the anger he was feeling toward William, a reminder of the mark of Cain he already bore?

While the theory cannot be substantiated, there are times when it beckons as an hypothesis. No one can read Coleridge's later claims concerning his addiction without hearing the faint, plaintive ring of a little boy protesting that he is being unfairly accused of a crime he did not commit.

As a bedridden old man, reduced once more to the helplessness of childhood, Coleridge had euphorically greeted his miraculous liberation from "Old Black" by exclaiming that "this fearful night storm is subsiding" (CL VI, p. 901). To what night storm was Coleridge referring? Was he unwittingly alluding to that harrowing boyhood storm after which his parents put him to bed and gave him laudanum for the first time, on the morning after his frightening encounter with Frank?

And what really happened back in 1801, at the bewildering time when his relationship with Wordsworth took its fatal turn? Resentment and jealousy welled up in him, and Coleridge became addicted before he knew what was happening. Was it fear of his murderous anger, of another impending storm like the one of his childhood, that prompted Coleridge to bow out of the fraternal competition with Wordsworth? He was bearing his pain *"like a woman"* (CL II, p. 774) when he wrote his note to Poole describing "the tune of this night wind that pipes its thin doleful sinking notes like a child that has lost its way and is crying aloud, half in grief and half in hope to be heard by its mother" (CL I, p. 669).

Were those night storm images of Ottery, Keswick, and Highgate a telescoping of memories? We will never know to what extent his addiction might have emerged from that stormy night in Devon.

It is only fitting to give Coleridge the last word on the question of his addiction and the role it played in his life:

> My character has been repeatedly attacked . . . as of a man incorrigibly idle . . . who, intrusted not only with ample talents, but favoured with unusual opportunities of improving them, had nevertheless suffered them to rust away without any sufficient exertion, either for his own good or that of his fellow-creatures. . . . By what I have effected am I to be judged by my fellow-man; what I *could* have done, is a question for my own conscience. [CL VI, p. 902]

Appendices

Appendix A
The Arabian Nights Tale: Shahryar and Shahzeman

It is of course impossible to state with absolute certainty which *Arabian Nights* tale Coleridge was referring to as the one that haunted him as a child. According to Lowes (1927), Coleridge read a small, one-volume, abridged version. That version must have included the Shahzeman–Shahryar tale, as it is the frame device for the rest of the book and occurs at the beginning.

A note penned in his notebook in 1816 reveals that Coleridge knew this tale (CNB 4315). It is the only tale he mentions that has to do with a compulsive seeker of virgins. The psychological context in which Coleridge recalled it in 1816 suggests the lifelong role this tale played as an unconscious motif in Coleridge's pattern of quartets.

Finally, personal correspondence with Kathleen Coburn informs me that she agrees that the tale is the most likely bet. In a letter dated, appropriately enough, October 4, 1978, she wrote: "congratulations on finding the Arabian Nights story. Your King Shahryar sounds very likely."

Appendix B
The Value of the English Pound

In search of an approximate conversion figure for the English pound of 1790 to modern standards, I enquired of Dr. Maeva Marcus, Historian of the U.S. Supreme Court. She in turn contacted Professor John J. McCusker of the History Department of the University of Maryland, who replied:

> You asked me how much one pound sterling in the 1790s could be said to be worth in United States dollars of the present. During our telephone conversation I told you of the problems inherent in making such comparisons: the math is easy but the results, however sound mathematically, can be deceptive. Put simply, in a less complicated time or place a sum of money of precisely the same value (purchasing power) might be considered to be "more." What we can do, however, is to convert sums to a common base on their comparative purchasing power using a commodity price index (CPI).
>
> On that basis, comparing the 1790s with July 1980, one pound sterling was worth about $35.00. The pound at par in the 1790s was worth $4.44. The CPI for the 1790s averaged 134.8; the CPI-U for July 1980 (which will be close to the average value for the whole of 1980) was 989; and the ratio between them 7.34. That ratio times $4.44 equals $32.58. As a check we can do the same calculations using a British CPI and exchanging the currencies in our own time. In that way the pound equals $38.89. The average of the two is $35.74. I would round that for convenience' sake to $35.

Clearly, Professor McCusker's figures are approximate, and the reader is cautioned not to take them too literally. Nonetheless, it is useful in thinking about Coleridge's life and times to have some way of comparing them to our own. Two evident shortcomings in the calculations are as follows. First, it was a time of rampant inflation due to the Napoleonic Wars, the Industrial Revolution, etc., and by the time Coleridge died in 1834, the value of the pound had changed rather drastically.

A second factor in limiting the usefulness of a 1790 pound–1980 dollar translation is the fact that the cultures were different. For example: Parson Woodforde's diaries reveal that on an income of 400 pounds a year ($14,000 by 1980 standards), he kept a large establishment for his family, lived quite well, traveled extensively and kept several servants. Presumably his vicarage came with the job. Even so, a modern Englishman living rent free would be hard pressed to match this on a comparable income. But would he have to? If his $14,000 came tax free and he purchased a dishwasher, vacuum cleaner, washer-dryer, refrigerator, food processor, modern stove, etc., he would remove many of the needs that Parson Woodforde's staff of low-paid servants was meant to provide.

Appendix C
Opium: Dose and Cost

As with money, the translation of the cost of opium and dosage is approximate. But according to J. W. Estes, M.D. of the Department of Pharmacology at Boston University Medical Center, my "computation of the dose of Coleridge's laudanum as morphine sulfate equivalents is impeccable." But, as Professor Estes adds, "I'd probably now give it a plus-or-minus 20 percent, however, because the more I see of eighteenth- and early nineteenth-century physicians' accounts books, etc., the less reliable their doses appear."

Based on Estes's "John Jones' *Mysteries of Opium Reveal'd* (1701): Key to Historical Studies of Opiates" in the *Journal of the History of Medicine,* April 1979, the following dose calculations apply:

Liquid Drops and Ounces

1 drop = 1/20 ml.
20 drops = 1 ml.
1 fluid ounce = 29.5 ml.
1 fluid ounce = 590 drops
20 fluid ounces = 1 English Pint

Laudanum to Morphine

Opium is 10 percent morphine by weight
25 drops laudanum = 1 grain opium = 64 mg. opium
1 grain opium = 64 mg. opium = 6.4 mg. morphine
1 liquid ounce laudanum = 590 drops laudanum
590 drops of laudanum = 23¾ grains of opium
23¾ grains of opium = 1520 mg. of opium
1520 mg of opium = 152 mg. of morphine

therefore

1 liquid ounce of laudanum = 152 mg. of morphine
1 English Pint laudanum = 3040 mg. morphine = 3.04 grams

The figure of 1 grain of opium = 25 drops of laudanum is based on De Quincey's description. According to Goodman and Gillman's *The Pharmacological Basis of Therapeutics* (1970), the tolerance of a drug addict can run as high as 5 grams of morphine per day.

Cost

According to Berridge (1979), "laudanum had been sixpence an ounce early in the 19th century." The following calculations apply:

English Currency

12 pence = 1 shilling
20 shillings = 1 pound
1 pound = 240 pence

Price of Laudanum

1 ounce laudanum = 6 pence
20 ounces laudanum = 1 pint = 120 pence = ½ pound
7 pints/week (aver. pint/day) = daily dose of 3 gms. morphine
= ave. weekly cost 3½ pounds
= ave. yearly cost of 182 pounds
U.S. dollars 1980 @ $35/pound = $123/week or $6400/year cost of a one-pint-a-day laudanum addiction.

References

Armour, R. W., & Howes, R. F. (1940), *Coleridge the Talker*. Ithaca: Cornell University Press.
Bate, W. J. (1968), *Coleridge*. New York: Macmillan.
Beer, J., ed. (1974), *Coleridge's Variety: Bicentenary Studies*. London, Macmillan.
Beres, D. (1951), A dream, a vision, and a poem: A psychoanalytic study of the origins of the Rime of the Ancient Mariner. *Internat. J. Psycho-Anal.*, 32:97–106.
Berridge, V. (1979), Opium in the fens in nineteenth-century England. *J. History of Medicine and Allied Sciences*, 34:298–305.
Blouett, B. (1967), *The Story of Malta*. London: Faber & Faber.
Blunden, E., & Grigg, E. L., eds. (1970), *Coleridge, Studies by Several Hands*. New York: Russell & Russell.
Borer, M. C. (1977), *The City of London*. New York: McKay.
Bryant, A. (1954), *The Age of Elegance*. London: Reprint Society of London.
Campbell, J. D. (1905), Samuel Taylor Coleridge: A biographical introduction. In: *Coleridge's Poetical Works*. New York: Macmillan, pp. xi–cxxiv.
Carpenter, M. (1954), *The Indifferent Horseman: The Divine Comedy of Samuel Taylor Coleridge*, London: Elek.
Cecil, D. (1955), *Melbourne*. London: Reprint Society of London.
Chambers, E. K. (1938), *Samuel Taylor Coleridge: A Biographical Study*. Oxford: Clarendon Press.
Cobbett, W. (1967), *Rural Rides*. London: Penguin.
Coburn, K. (1977), *In Pursuit of Coleridge*. London: Bodley Head.
───── (1979a), *Experience into Thought: Perspective in the Coleridge Notebooks*. Toronto: University of Toronto Press.
───── ed. (1979b), *Inquiring Spirit*. Toronto: University of Toronto Press.
Cole, H. (1970), *Beau Brummell*. New York: Mason/Charter.
Coleridge, Lord (1905), *The Story of a Devonshire House*. London: Unwin.
Coleridge, S. T. (1795), Lectures of 1795 on Politics and Religion. *The Collected Works of Samuel Taylor Coleridge*, Vol. 1, ed. L. Patton & P. Mann. New York: Pantheon, 1969.
───── (1796), The Watchman. *The Collected Works of Samuel Taylor Coleridge*, Vol. 2, ed. L. Patton. New York: Pantheon, 1970.
───── (1817a), *Biographia Literaria*. London: Dent, 1977.
───── (1817b), Lay Sermons. *The Collected Works of Samuel Taylor Coleridge*, Vol. 6, ed. R. J. White. New York, Pantheon, 1972.

——— (1818), The Friend. *The Collected Works of Samuel Taylor Coleridge*, Vol. 4 (2 Parts), ed. B. E. Rooke. New York: Pantheon, 1969.
——— (1829), On the Constitution of Church and State. *The Collected Works of Samuel Taylor Coleridge*, Vol. 10, ed. J. Colmer. New York, Pantheon, 1970.
——— (1850), Essays on His Own Times. *The Collected Works of Samuel Taylor Coleridge*, Vol. 3 (3 Parts), ed. D. V. Erdman. New York, Pantheon, 1969.
——— (1956), *Collected Letters of Samuel Taylor Coleridge*, Vols. 1–6, ed. E. L. Grigg. Oxford: Clarendon Press, 1956–1971.
——— (1957), *The Notebooks of Samuel Taylor Coleridge*, Vols. 1–3, ed. K. Coburn. New York: Pantheon.
——— (1968), *The Complete Works of Samuel Taylor Coleridge*, ed. E. H. Coleridge. Oxford: Clarendon Press.
Cooper, L. (1964), *The Age of Wellington*. London: Macmillan.
Cornwell, J. (1973), *Coleridge: Poet and Revolutionary*. London: Allen Lane.
Cottle, J. (1847), *Reminiscences of Samuel Taylor Coleridge and Robert Southey*. New York: Wiley Putnam.
Curry, K. (1975), *Southey*. London: Routledge & Kegan Paul.
Davey, R. (1906), *The Pageant of London*. London, James Pott.
Davies, H. (1980), *William Wordsworth: A Biography*. London: Weidenfeld & Nicolson.
Defoe, D. (1724–1727), *A Tour Through the Whole Island of Great Britain*. London: Penguin, 1771.
De Quincey, T. (1970), *Recollections of the Lakes and the Lake Poets*. London, Penguin.
Dickens, C. (1859), A Tale of Two Cities. London: Penguin, 1971.
Ellis, A. M. (1967), *Rebels and Conservatives*. Bloomington: Indiana University Press.
Erikson, K. T. (1976), Loss of community at Buffalo Creek. *Amer. J. Psychiat.*, 133:243–246.
Estes, J. W. (1979), John Jones' *Mysteries of Opium Reveal'd* (1701): Key to Historical Studies of Opiates. *Journal of History of Medicine*, 22:243–257.
Fruman, N. (1974), *Coleridge: The Damaged Archangel*. New York: Braziller.
Furneaux, R. (1974), *William Wilberforce*. London: Hamish Hamilton.
Gathorne-Hardy, J. (1977), *The Old School Tie*. New York: Viking.
Gillman, J. (1838), *The Life of Samuel Taylor Coleridge*. London: William Pickering.
Gimpel, H. J. (1966), *Lord Nelson*. New York: Franklin Watts.
Goodman, L. S., & Gillman, A. (1970), *The Pharmacological Basis of Therapeutics*. 4th ed. New York: Macmillan.
Goodwin, A. (1979), *The Friends of Liberty: The English Democratic Movement in the Age of the French Revolution*. Boston: Harvard University Press.
Haller, W. (1966), *The Early Life of Robert Southey*. New York: Octagon.
Hanson, L. (1962), *The Life of S.T. Coleridge: The Early Years*. New York: Russell & Russell.
Harper, G. M. (1960), *William Wordsworth: His Works, Life and Influence*. New York: Russell & Russell.

References

Hayter, A. (1970), *Opium and the Romantic Imagination*. Berkeley: University of California Press.
——— (1973), *A Voyage in Vain: Coleridge's Journey to Malta in 1804*. London: Faber & Faber.
Ignatieff, M. (1978), *A Just Measure of Pain: The Penitentiary in the Industrial Revolution*. New York: Pantheon.
Kessler, E. (1979), *Coleridge's Metaphors of Being*. Princeton: Princeton University Press.
Kevles, B. (1977), Interview with Anne Sexton. In: *Paris Review Interviews: Writers at Work (Fourth Series)*, ed. G. Plimpton. New York: Penguin, pp. 399–424.
Kris, E. (1935), *Psychoanalytic Explorations in Art*. New York: International Universities Press.
Lamb, C. (1820–1825), *Essays of Elia*. London: Chatto & Windus, 1905.
——— (1848), *Charles Lamb: Literary Sketches and Letters*, ed. T. N. Talfourd. New York: Appleton.
——— (1980), *The Portable Charles Lamb*, ed. J. M. Brown. New York: Penguin.
Lawrence, B. (1970), *Coleridge and Wordsworth in Somerset*. London: David & Charles.
Lefebure, M. (1975), *Samuel Taylor Coleridge: A Bondage of Opium*. New York: Stein & Day.
Lloyd, O. (1798), *Edmund Oliver*. Bristol: Cottle.
Loomis, S. (1968), *Paris in the Terror*. New York: Lippincott.
Low, D. A. (1977), *That Sunny Pleasure Dome: A Portrait of Regency Britain*. London: Dent.
Lowes, J. L. (1927), *The Road to Xanadu*. Boston: Houghton Miflin, 1950.
Mansky, P. A. (1978), Opiates: Human psychopharmacology. In: *Handbook of Psychopharmacology: Vol. 12. Drugs of Abuse*, ed. C. Iversen & S. Snyder. New York: Plenum, pp. 95–185.
Marcovitz, E. (1964), Bemoaning the lost dream: Coleridge's 'Kubla Khan' and addiction. *Internat. J. Psycho-Anal.*, 45:455–418.
Markham, J., (1980), Getting to know Malta. *New York Times Travel Section*, January 27, 1980, p. 1.
Mayhew, H. (1851–1864), *London Labour and the London Poor*. 4 vols. New York: Dover, 1968.
McFarland, T. (1974), Coleridge's plagiarisms once more: A review essay. *The Yale Review*, Vol. 63:243–248.
Moorhead, A. (1962), *The Blue Nile*. New York: Dell.
Moorman, M. (1957), *William Wordsworth: A Biography*, Vol. 1. Oxford: Clarendon Press.
——— (1965), *William Wordsworth: A Biography*, Vol. 2. Oxford: Clarendon Press.
Purkis, J. (1970), *A Preface to Wordsworth*. London: Longmans.
Quennell, M., & Quennell, C. H. B. (1977), *A History of Everyday Things in England*, Vol. 3. London: B. T. Batsford.
Reilly, R. (1979), *William Pitt the Younger*. New York: Putnam.
Roper, D. (1940), *Wordsworth and Coleridge: Lyrical Ballads*. London: Collins.

Sandford, H. (1888), *Thomas Poole and His Friends*. 2 vols. London: Macmillan.
Schneider, E. (1970), *Coleridge, Opium and Kubla Khan*. New York: Octagon.
Sherwin, O. (1960), *Uncorking Old Sherry: The Life and Times of Richard Brinsley Sheridan*. New York: Twayne.
Sultana, D. (1969), *Samuel Taylor Coleridge in Malta and Italy*. Oxford: Clarendon Press.
Titchener, J. L., & Ross, D. W. (1974), Acute or chronic stress as determinants of behavior, character and neurosis. In: *American Handbook of Psychiatry*, Vol. 3, ed. S. Arieti & E. Brodie. New York: Basic Books, pp. 39–60.
Trevelyan, G. M. (1922), *British History in the Nineteenth Century*. London: Longmans.
Warren, R. P. (1958), *Selected Essays*. New York: Random House.
Watson, J. S. (1960), *The Reign of George III*. Oxford: Clarendon Press.
Wedgwood, B., & Wedgwood, H. (1980), *The Wedgwood Circle*. London: Studio Vista.
Weissman, S. M. (1986), Review of Literature and Psychoanalysis, *Psychoanal. Q.*, 55:191–193.
Woodforde, J. (1979), *The Diary of a Country Parson*, Oxford: Clarendon Press.
Wordsworth, D. (1800), *Journals of Dorothy Wordsworth*, ed. M. Moorman. Oxford: Clarendon Press, 1971.
Wordsworth, W., & Wordsworth, D. (1967), *The Letters of William and Dorothy Wordsworth*, Vols. 1–3, ed. C. L. Shaver. Oxford: Clarendon Press.
Willey, B. (1973), *Samuel Taylor Coleridge*. New York: Norton.

Author Index

Armour, R.W., 132, 216, 256, 291, 299, 310, 313, 315, 319, 320, 333

Bate, W.J., 333
Beer, J., 333
Beres, D., 333
Berridge, V., 26, 330, 333
Blouett, B., 333
Blunden, E., 92, 333
Borer, M.C., 333
Bryant, A., 271, 292, 333

Campbell, J.D., 21, 114, 269, 273, 277n, 281, 283, 315, 316, 322, 333
Carpenter, M., 333
Cecil, D., 272, 333
Chambers, E.K., 41, 66, 215, 220, 288, 289, 310, 333
Cobbett, W., 333
Coburn, K., 22, 114, 333
Cole, H., 293, 333
Coleridge, L., 4, 8, 30, 333
Cooper, L., 224, 316, 334
Cornwell, J., 103, 169, 214, 218, 334
Cottle, J., 334
Curry, K., 334

Davey, R., 334
Davies, H., 101, 184n, 315, 334
De Quincey, T., 2, 141, 256, 334
Defoe, D., 334
Dickens, C., 334

Ellis, A.M., 94, 99, 101, 104, 147, 334
Erikson, K.T., 334
Estes, J.W., 334

Fruman, N., 334
Furneaux, R., 334

Gathorne-Hardy, J., 334
Gillman, A., 83, 330, 334
Gillman, J., 21, 34, 305, 334
Gimpel, H.J., 334
Goodman, L.S., 83, 330, 334

Goodwin, A., 41, 51, 334
Grigg, E.L., 92, 333

Haller, W., 48, 49, 56, 57, 159, 334
Hanson, L., 134, 141, 143, 145, 146, 147, 155, 162, 229, 334
Harper, G.M., 334
Hayter, A., 335
Howes, R.F., 132, 216, 256, 291, 299, 310, 313, 315, 319, 320, 333

Ignatieff, M., 335

Kessler, E., 335
Kevles, B., 335
Kris, E., 305, 335

Lamb, C., 19, 65, 161, 335
Lawrence, B., 91, 335
Lefebure, M., 51, 94, 113, 300, 335
Lloyd, O., 335
Loomis, S., 78, 335
Low, D.A., 272, 292, 293, 335
Lowes, J.L., 327, 335

McFarland, T., 335
Mansky, P.A., 335
Marcovitz, E., 335
Markham, J., 232, 335
Mayhew, H., 25, 335
Moorhead, A., 335
Moorman, M., 99, 150, 193, 218, 311, 313, 335

Pollock, G.H., ii, x
Purkis, J., 98, 335

Quennell, C.H.B., 17, 335
Quennell, M., 17, 335

Reilly, R., 17, 158, 335
Roper, D., 171, 172, 335
Ross, D.W., 336

Sandford, H., 321, 336

Schneider, E., 336
Sherwin, O., 16, 336
Sultana, D., 336

Titchener, J.L., 336
Trevelyan, G.M., 336

Warren, R.P., 336

Watson, J.S., 336
Wedgwood, B., 133, 213, 336
Wedgwood, H., 133, 213, 336
Weissman, S.M., iii, xv, 336
Willey, B., 314, 336
Woodforde, J., 336
Wordsworth, D., 336
Wordsworth, W., 336

Subject Index

Abyssinian Maid, *Kubla Khan* and, 113
Adam, STC dreams of, 226
Addiction, role in STC's life, 326; *see also* Laudanum; Opium
Aeneid, STC helps Wordsworth translate, 312
The Aeolian Harp, 74
Agnus Dei (Charles Lamb), 160
Ague, STC and, 325
Akibah, Rabbi, 13
Alfoxton, STC and Wordsworth suspected of spying at, 92
Allen, Robert
 STC's school friendship with, 22, 23
 STC visits: in London, 28; at Oxford, 48-49
Allsop, Thomas, as young follower of STC, 293
Androgyny, *Kubla Khan* images and, 114, 115
Animus and *anima*, harmony between, 111, 113, 115
Annuity offered by Wedgwoods, 132-133
Antiwar demonstration, Bristol Guildhall and, 75
Antiwar fervor at Cambridge, 41
Arabian Nights, tales of, 10-11
 stir STC's imagination, 110
Arthritis, STC and, 188
 unexplained pain and, 324
Artistic block, 188, 191
 STC undergoes, 179-180
Aspheterism, 51
Atonement, eternal, theme of, 120, 123
Autobiography, *Rime of the Ancient Mariner* and, 122-123
Autopsy of STC, findings of, 323-324

Ball, Sir Alexander, Malta Governor, 239
Bastille, impact on England of, 23-24
Bertozzoli, Cecilia, STC's romance with, 240-241
Biblical imagery of STC dreams, 227
Biographia Borealis (Hartley Coleridge), 298

Biographia Literaria, 279-280
 creative imagination and, 307
 published while living with Gillmans, 292
Bisexual reveries, *Kubla Khan* and, 115
Bowden, John, uncle of STC, 15-18
Bowyer, Rev. James
 Master of Upper Grammar School, 20-21
 and STC's poetry, 22
Brent, Charlotte and Mary
 domination of, 281
 STC flirts with, 266
 STC offends, 278
Brighton as symbol of Regency, 292
Bristol
 series of lectures at, 277-278
 Southey and STC at, 53-56
Bristol Channel, honeymoon at, 73-89
Bristol Guildhall, antiwar demonstration and, 75
Brother figure, Wordsworth as, 98, 104-105
Browne Greek Prize competition, 28
Brunton, Miss, actress, STC dallies with, 59
Burke, Edmond, debates Paine, 39-40
Burnette, George, and Pantisocracy, 51

Cain and Abel
 STC and Frank and, xvii-xx, 91-106
 STC dreams of, 226-227
Cambridge University
 STC returns to, in last illness, 319-320
 STC's life at, 24-31
 turmoil with antiwar sentiment and, 41
Carlyle, Thomas, on *Lay Sermons*, 290
Castration in STC dream, 228-229
Catastrophe, survival after, 123-125, 129
Catholic emancipation, STC on, 313-314
Childhood myth of STC, 3, 4
Childhood recollections as raw material for *Kubla Khan*, 110

339

Children, STC attacks Wordsworth's view of, 311
Christabel, 140
  based on strange relationship of two women, 285, 286
  Christ-Abel, Cain, and STC, 250
  and infatuation with Wordsworth, 286-288
  length as reason for rejection, 177
  negative critical response to, 285, 288
  plan to finish, 170
  as story of male homosexual relationship, 285-286
  struggle to complete, 173
Christ-Abel title suggests male identities, 285
Christmas at Dove Cottage, 189-190
Christ's Hospital School, 18-24
  STC dreams of, in Malta, 245-246
Church-and-King clubs, 27
On Church and State, work begins on, 313
Coleorton, Wordsworths at, 260
Coleridge, Anne
  death of, 13
  mother of STC, 4-5
  STC's distance from, 12-14
  STC visits, from Cambridge, 28
Coleridge, Berkeley
  born, 140
  dies of consumption, 145
Coleridge, Derwent
  born, 172
  enters Cambridge, 294
  takes Holy Orders, 298
Coleridge, Derwent, Jr., born, 313
Coleridge, Edward, brother of Rev. John, 4
Coleridge, Frank
  bright career prospects of, 29-30
  Comberbache as substitute for, 45
  delirium and suicide of, compared to STC's own experiences, 44
  early relationships of STC with, 8-11
  goes to sea, 11-12
  renews acquaintance with John, 21
  Rime of the Ancient Mariner and, 121-123
  STC compared to, 251
  STC's attempt to kill, 44-45; letter to Poole and, 116
  suicide of, 38-39, 44
Coleridge, George
  arrives in London, 21
  brother of Rev. John, 4
  death of, 309
  has Mary Evans write to STC, 60
  relationship with STC, 80-81
  STC writes about separation from Sarah, 264-265
  worries of STC's friends at Cambridge, 26
Coleridge, Hartley
  binges of, 312
  compared to STC, 297-298
  disappoints STC, 294-298
  mood disorder of, 297-298
  and STC letter about Anne, 13
  STC tries to foster literary career of, 297
  Wordsworth and, 314
Coleridge, Henry Nelson, admires STC, 298
Coleridge, James, brother of STC, mother's relationship with, 4
Coleridge, John, 12
  brother of STC, mother's relationship with, 4
  renews acquaintance with Frank, 21
Coleridge, Rev. John
  ambitions of, 3-4, 6
  death of, 12; Poole letter and, 117
  early life of, 5-6
  father of STC, 1-14
  hopes of, for STC, 2-3
  influences on STC, Poole letter and, 117
  STC's tales of, 3-4
  writings of, 6
Coleridge, Luke, 12
  arrives in London, 21
  brother of STC, mother's relationship with, 4
Coleridge, Nancy, 12
  death of, 28
Coleridge, Samuel Taylor
  age of, error in, 74
  anguish over defeat by younger scholar, 36-37
  assumes irrational guilt after son's death, 148-149
  attempt to kill Frank, 44-45; flees home after, 116; letter to Poole, 116
  attraction between Thomas Wedgwood and, 133
  begins *Osorio*, 86
  and brotherly conquests, 187
  Cain and Abel legend and, xvii-xx
  Christianity and, 68
  Christ's Hospital School and, 18-24
  dreams of, in Malta, 245-246
  composes own epitaph, 320
  conflict in household, 261-262
  conservative monarchist views of, 316

considers Unitarian ministry, 131-132
contradicts goal of reconciling with Mary Evans, 63-64
death of, 321
decides to change publishers, 288
declares death of his poetic imagination, 167-168
depression of; see Depression
dreams of; see Dreams
early friendship with Dorothy Wordsworth, 97
enlists in dragoons, 43-44
father and, relationships of, 1-14
favors destruction of Napoleon, 271-272
first grandson born, 313
Hartley compared to, 297-298
Hartley's birth and, 82
hears of Frank's suicide, 38-39
honeymoon of, 73-89
identifies with working class, 40-41
insecurity about own masculinity, 104-105
justifies George's concerns about Jacobinism, 63
learns managerial skills from Poole, 85
learns of prospective fatherhood, 77-78
loses Craven Fellowship, 36
married sex life diminishes, 220
meets Friedrich Klopstock, 141
moves to Ratzeburg, 142
name of, and *Smu-El*, 2-3
nurses comrade in dragoons, 34-35, 44
opium addiction begins, 165-166
and plagiarism, 211-212, 280-281
plans magnum opus, 300
pretends *Christabel* rejected because of length, 177
Priestly as political hero of, 47
as private secretary to Governor of Malta, 239-247
Pro-French leanings of, 78-79
as psychologist, 303-308
radicalization of, 47-53
reappraises his earlier poetry, 103-104
regrets move to Lake district, 178-179
rejected by Mary Evans, 64
relationship with Thomas Poole, 80-81
religion and, during Malta experience, 242-244
retreats to Somerset after autobiographic letter, 111
returns from Gottingen, 151
returns to London to work for *Post*, 199
reviews diaries, 222-223
rewrites diary events, 223
ribald nights of, 310
Sara H. and: believes himself in love with, 184; enchantment continues, 198-199; yearns for, 225-226
Sarah and: attend grandchild's christening, 318-319; conflict grows, 198-199; at Greta Hall, 269; letters to console, 146; marriage, 70; no longer loves, 184; pitted against Wordsworths, 202-203; proposal, 57; trade angry letters about visit to Sara H., 212-213; turns to Mary Evans from, 59
sexually frustrated in Malta, 241
as Silas Tomkyn Comberbache, 33-35
and Southey: bitterness between, 69; develop subscription lectures, 66-68; reconciliation with, 154; on relations with Mary and Sarah, 64-65; tries to persuade to move to Lakes, 205
spring, 1820, as rich period for, 293-294
starts *The Watchman*, 76, 77
stays in Germany after Berkeley's death, 148
suicidal impulses of, 43
takes opium to Somerset, 111
and tales of his father, 3-4
travels with Tom Wedgwood, 212-216
tries to clear Hartley's name, 295-297
as tutor of Charles Lloyd, 81-82
visits cave on summer holiday, 42
visits Wedgwoods, 133-134
and 4-way relationships with Anne, Molly, and Frank, 9-11
wears clerical apparel, 288
withdrawal program in Malta begins, 238
and Wordsworth: agent for, in publisher negotiations, 138-139; ambivalent relationship of, 227-228; angry exchange of letters, 266-267; both attend boarding schools, 100; continue mutual need and support, 195-196; develop mutual artistic debt, 136-137; differing views of children,

311; estrangement, 269-271; gossip of separation from, 273-274; infatuation with, *Christabel* and, 286-288; insist on anonymous publication, 138-139; intensely idealizes, 172-173; interprets nature of misunderstanding, 194-195; misinterprets rejection, 179; misses wedding, 184; moves North to be near, 168-169; patch up quarrel, 274; reunited, 310; seeks escape from, 227; share political views, 95-96; STC contemplates separation, 204; suspected of spying, 92; tour continent, 312-313; tour Lake country, 156-157
and Wordsworths: become friends, 94-96; begin Scotland tour, 217; divulges marital problems, 196; efforts to improve relations with Sarah undercut, 202-203; separate on Scotland tour, 219; trip to Germany with, 140-151 writes burlesque of Lamb and Lloyd, 104

Coleridge, Sara (daughter), 214
as gifted translator, 298
in love with H.N. Coleridge, 298
moves to Hampstead, 315

Coleridge, Sarah; *see also* Fricker, Sarah
financial responsibility of, 74-75
and financial worries, 190-191
honeymoon with, 73-89
hostess to Lambs and Wordsworths, 101-102
miscarries, 103
misses Germany trip, 140
pregnancy of, 77
on STC's frequent illnesses, 266
and STC trade angry letters about visit to Sara H., 212-213
STC writes to, about homesickness, 259
and Wordsworths, STC sends mixed messages to, 259
writes to STC about Berkeley's death, 146-147

Coleridge, William, brother of Rev. John, 4

Comberbache, Silas Tomkyn
as British dragoon, 33-35
as substitute for Frank, 45

Commodity price index in converting English pound, 238-239

Conflict in STC household, 261-262

Consolations and Comforts from the Exercise and Right Application of the Reason . . ., 233-234

Constipation by opium use on trip to Malta, 236

Consumption and death of Berkeley, 145

Cookson, Anne, mother of Wordsworth, 99

Cottle, Joseph
negotiates second edition of *Lyrical Ballads*, 138-139
provides living for STC and Southey, 69
publishes *The Fall of Robespierre*, 56
supports lecture series, 66

The Courier
STC resigns from, in protest, 272-273
STC writes for, 271-272

Craven Fellowship
STC loses, 36
STC practices for, 28-29

Creative mind, *Kubla Khan* as psychologic commentary on, 114

Crime hidden by symbolism, *Rime of the Ancient Mariner* and, 122

Davy, Humphry
prints second edition of *Lyrical Ballads*, 169-173
regrets STC's move North, 169
shows STC nitrous oxide, 155
in STC dream, 228-229
STC meets, 155

Death
of Anne Coleridge, 13
of Berkeley Coleridge, 145
of Frank Coleridge, 38-39, 44, 121-122
of George Coleridge, 309
of Rev. John Coleridge, 12, 117
of Nancy Coleridge, 28
of STC, 321

Death of Abel, influence of, 119

Debts after move to Keswick, 170

Degeneracy of Regency period, 293

Dejection: An Ode
describes STC's depression, 184-185
helps STC recapture self-esteem, 201-202
STC begins draft of, 201
written for Wordsworth's wedding, 184

Delirium on Malta voyage, 236

Delirium tremens, 256

Depression
after illness of Lloyd, 86-87
after Lloyd leaves, 86-87

at Christ's Hospital, 19
described in *Dejection: an Ode*, 184-185
in Malta, 244-245
and news of children's illness, 143-144
over losses and debt, 42-43
at time of Wordsworth's wedding, 185-186
"Destruction of the Bastille," 24
Disbelief, willing suspension of, 305
Dreams; *see also* Nightmare
of becoming bedridden, 228-229
of domestic connection with Wordsworth, 205-208
dwarf in, 228-229
first nightmare described, 181
Humphry Davy in, 228-229
and literary process, 304
of Mrs. Southey, 58
study of, 303-305
as wish fulfillment, 305, 307
Drug addict, drug tolerance of, 330
Duke of York, STC criticizes appointment of, 272-273
"Dura Navis," theme of, 22
Dwarf in STC dream, 228-229

Economic unrest in England at turn of century, 190-191
Ego, regression in service of, 305
Ends justifying means, debate on, 39-40
England
and France on brink of war, 216
moves from agrarian to industrial period, 306-307
prepares for French invasion, 91-92
socioeconomic gap widens in, 272
English pound, value of, 238-239
Epitaph, STC composes, 320
Erskine, Thomas, one of Twelve Apostles, 61-62
Erysipelas in STC's last illness, 320
Estrangement from Wordsworth, 269-271
Eunuch fears, 23
Europe, STC and Wordsworth tour, 312-313
Evans, Anne, 22
Evans, Mary
rejects STC, 64
rekindles STC's love, 59
STC hides from, 53
STC in love with memory of, 60
STC's courtship of, 22-23

Fagging at Christ's Hospital, 20
Faith, STC and, 242-244, 245-246

The Fall of Robespierre, 56
financial failure of, 61
Fantasy of Wordsworth in bed with Sara, 263
Femininity, landscape transformed through sexual imagery to depict, 112
Field, Rev. Matthew, Master of Lower Grammar School, 18-19
Financial problems, failure of *The Watchman* and, 79
Fire, fascination with, 166-167
Flogging at Christ's Hospital, 20
France
and England, on brink of war, 216
prepares to invade England, 91
threatens invasion of England, 224-225
Freedom of speech, Gagging Acts and, 76
French Armada, 247
French Revolution becomes anarchy, 40
Frend, William
early contact with, 76
as friend at Cambridge, 26
STC supports cause of, 41
The Watchman and, 78
Fricker
Edith, Southey's fiancee, 54
Eliza, 54
George, 54
Martha, 54
Mary, 54; marries Robert Lovell, 54
Sarah, 54; *see also* Coleridge, Sarah; character of, 55; STC proposes to, 57; STC turns from, to Mary Evans, 59
The Friend
published while living with Gillmans, 292
reissue of, dedicated to Gillman, 292
STC plans and publishes, 267-268
Friends of Liberty, 27-28
Frost at Midnight, 135-136

Gagging Acts, 76
loophole in, 77
Garrick, David, Rev. John's letter to, 6
Geraldine and Christabel, strange relationship of, 285, 286
Gessner, *Death of Abel*, influence of, 119
Gillman, Anne, 314
Gillman, Dr. James
cares for Coleridge's illness and addiction, 283-320
learns to care for addiction, 284
STC joins family of, 291-292
God, *The Aeolian Harp* and, 74

344 Subject Index

Goody Blake, 136
Gossip of separation of STC and Wordsworth, 273-274
Gottingen University, STC enrolls in, 144
Gout, STC's physician endorses Scotland trip for, 217
Grasmere, STC visits Wordsworths at, 267
Green, Joseph Henry
  with STC during final hours, 321
  STC gives copy of his epitaph to, 320
  STC plans to dictate last revelations to, 320
  as young follower of STC, 293
Greta Hall, STC's new home in Keswick, 169
Guilt
  STC and, 252
  theme of perpetual, *Rime of the Ancient Mariner* and, 120, 123

Hallucinations, 278
  of bugs, 256
  on Malta voyage, 236
Hardy, Thomas, one of Twelve Apostles, 62, 63
Hazlitt, William, lampoons *Lay Sermons*, 289-290
Heart failure, STC and, 324
History of Hindostan, influence of, on STC, 112
Honeymoon, 73-89
Horror carnis humanae, 241
Hutchinson, Mary, STC meets, 156
Hutchinson, Sara
  role in *The Friend*, 268
  STC and Sarah trade angry letters over, 212-213
  STC believes himself in love with, 184
  STC enchantment with, 198-199
  STC has upsurge of yearning for, 225-226
  STC's asexual love of, 241
  visits Coleridges at Greta Hall, 192
Hymn Before Sunrise in the Vale of Chamonix, 211
Hypochondriasis, self-pity and, 191-192

Imagination
  creative, *Biographia Literaria* and, 307
  fantasies and, 307
Italy, Southern, STC tours, 247-248

Jealousy of Wordsworth, 264
Jesus, STC's view of, 243
Jesus College, Cambridge, STC's life at, 24-31

Joint pains, STC and, 325

Klopstock, Friedrich, STC and Wordsworth meet, 141
Kubla Khan
  adverse criticism of, 288
  ambiguous sexual mysteries and, 113-114
  androgyny of STC and, 114-115
  opium and daydreaming before composition of, 111-112
  as psychologic commentary on creative mind, 114
  STC's bisexuality and, 288
  symbolic of STC's relationship with Frank, 106

Lamb, Charles
  on Christ's Hospital, 19
  and dying STC, 315, 317
  on *Lay Sermons*, 290
  and sister Mary: STC moves in with, 160; visit STC, 102
  STC reminisces with, 65
  STC's early friendship with, 22-23
  visits STC at Greta Hall, 205
  on Wordsworth's preface to *Lyrical Ballads*, 172
Landscape, transformation of, by sexual imagery, 112
Laudanum; *see also* Opium
  childhood agues and, 325
  costs of, 277
  quantity STC consumed, 277
  ratio to morphine, 330
  STC use of, after Hartley's birth, 83
  used into STC's old age, 299-300
Lay Sermons
  content of, 289-290
  published, 289, 292
LCS; *see* London Corresponding Society
Leckie, G.F., hosts Coleridge in Sicily, 240-242
Lectures in London, 255-258
Leech gatherer, William and Dorothy meet, 174-175, 176
Light, fascination with, 166-167
Literary process and dream process compared, 304
Lloyd, Charles
  delirium of, 82, 83
  forced to leave by illness, 86
  and fraternal theme of *Osorio*, 87
  renews arrangement with STC, 86
  as student of STC, 81-82
  writes *Edmond Oliver* for revenge, 104
London, Coleridges move to, 157

London Corresponding Society, 41, 50, 75, 76
London Revolutionary Society, 23-24
Lovell, Robert
    and Mary, as first married Pantisocrats, 54
    and Pantisocracy, 51
Lowell, James Russell, and *Lay Sermons*, 289-290
Lowther, Sir James
    employer of Wordsworth's father, 98-99
    refuses to pay debts to John Wordsworth, 100
Lyrical Ballads
    planning publication of, 94
    publication of second edition of, 140
    STC and Wordsworth plan preface on views of poetry, 171

Magical undoing, symbolic act of, Comberbache episode as, 45
Malta, 232
    Coleridge in, 237-247
    STC returns from, 231, 248
    voyage to, 233-237
Marat, Jean Paul, 40
Maria, fiancee of Frank, 11-12
Mariner (in *Rime*), STC compared to, 248-250, 252-253
Masculinity
    insecurity about, 104-105
    landscape transformed through sexual imagery to depict, 112
Masturbation, 241
Materialist philosophers, STC opposes, 163-164
Maurice, Thomas, *History of Hindostan*, 112
Middleton, Thomas
    inspires STC at Cambridge, 28
    STC as Grecian to, 20
    STC meets again at Cambridge, 25
Mill, John Stuart, hears STC on Catholic emancipation, 314
Miracles
    STC reads of, 244
    STC's view of, 243
Molly, Frank's nurse, relationships of, with Frank and STC, 9, 11
Montague, Basil, warned by Wordsworth and alienates STC, 269-270
Mood disorder, of Hartley Coleridge, 297-298
Morgan, John
    is bankrupt, 276-277
    as patron of STC, 80

STC moves in with, 270
STC rejoins, 278
STC's reacquaintance with, 265-266
Morning Post, STC reporter for, 156-157
Morphine
    Gillman switches STC from laudanum to, 318
    ratio to laudanum, 330
Murray, John
    acts as opium smuggler for STC, 284-285
    publisher of STC's verse, 284
Myth, childhood, of STC, 3, 4

Napoleon
    appoints self First Consul, 158
    fights in Mediterranean, 142
    and Malta, 232
    retreat of, 276
    STC favors destruction of, 271-272
    threatens invasion of England, 224-225
Nelson
    and French Armada, 247
    and Malta, 232
    maneuvers in Mediterranean, 233
    Nile victory of, 142
Nether Stowey
    Coleridges move to, 84
    as focus of rural simplicity, 81
    STC and Wordsworth suspected of spying at, 92
Newton's experiments, STC plans to replicate, 164
Nightmare; *see also* Dreams
    at Dove Cottage, 189
    STC's first, 181
Nightmares, on voyage to Malta, 234
Nitrous oxide, Davy introduces STC to, 155
"The Nose, an Odaic Rhapsody," 24

Ode: Intimations of Immortality from Recollections of Early Childhood, composition begun, 201
Ode on the Slave Trade, 28
Opium
    addiction to: childhood and, 326; heavy, 178-179, 180-181
    attempt to withdraw from, 238
    Cambridge and, 25-26
    in disruption of STC's relationships, 263-264
    dose and cost of, 329-331
    as libido poison, 221
    in Malta, 238-239
    smuggled to STC, 284-285

STC discovers mood elevation by, 37-38
STC tries to analyze side effects of, 199
use of: connected with Wordsworth visits, 221; in letter to Southey, 217; and Sarah's first pregnancy, 78; topic in letters to Sarah, 213; on trip to Malta, 235-236; Wedgwood and STC, on tour, 213-216
Wedgwood acknowledges addiction to, 213
Opium withdrawal psychosis, 278
Osorio
autobiographical nature of, 87-88
completion of, 107
dissatisfaction with, 107-108
renamed *Remorse*, 275
rewriting of, 274-275
story of, 87
Wordsworth praises, 95
Ottery, vacation at, from Cambridge, 42

Paine, Thomas, debates Burke, 39-40
The Pains of Sleep, 219
and STC's addiction, 288
Pantisocracy, 49-71
Southey and STC plan for, 51
Paranoia, Dorothy Wordsworth and, 315
Personal identity, remembered childhood experiences and, 88-89
Peter Bell, 136
Philosophy
materialist, STC opposes, 163-164
Western, STC attempts synthesis of, 163-164
Pickering, William, STC's last publisher, 309-310
Pitt, William
alcoholism of, 16
and Gagging Acts, 76-79
suspends habeas corpus and imprisons enemies, 50
war strategy of, 158
Pixies' Parlor cave, 42
Plagiarism, 211-212, 280-281
Pneumatic Institute, STC attends, 155
Poems on Various Subjects, 79
Literary Fund of London award for, 80
Poetical Works, STC revises third edition of, 320
Poetic brotherhood, STC's search for, 89
Poetic diction, STC and Wordsworth experiment with, 106
Poetic imagination

death of, attributed to Wordsworth, 167-168
remembered childhood experiences and, 89
STC declares death of, 167-168
Poole, Thomas
agricultural advice of, 83
autobiographic letters to: comments on first and second, 88-89; fourth, 115-118; last, 135; third, 107-110
character of, 85-86
criticizes STC's adulation of Wordsworth, 159-160
early contact with, 76
as father figure, 83
and grieving Coleridges, 145
influences STC to return to Sarah, 199-200
as patron of STC, 79-80
receives autographed copy of *On Church and State*, 315
relationship with STC, 80-81
on rural living, 82-83
STC and Southey meet, 56-57
STC sees as anchor, 149
The Watchman and, 76
worsens relationship between STC and Sarah, 153
Pound sterling, conversion of, 238-239
Pox, fear of, 23
Priestly, Joseph, as political hero of Southey and STC, 47
Psychoanalysis, STC's contributions to, 303-308
Psychological and theological explanations of dreams, 305
Psychologist, STC as, 303-308
Psychosomatic, STC coins word, 325
Public assembly, right of, Gagging Acts and, 76
Punishment, self, for surviving disaster, 123
Purchas' Pilgrimage, 111

Quartets, STC's pattern of, Shahryar and Shahzeman and, 327

Reform Bill becomes law, 317
Regency
degeneracy of, 293
as postwar generation, 292-293
Regression in service of ego, 305
Religion
during last illness of STC, 317-318
during Malta experience, 242-244, 246-247

mysticism of, and rational psychology, 303
Remorse
  accepted for stage, 275
  success of, 276
Retrospective falsification of feelings for Sarah, 186-187
Revelation, STC has, in Malta, 244
Revolution, England near, 316
Rheumatic fever during Bristol visit, 155
Right of public assembly, Gagging Acts and, 76
Rime of the Ancient Mariner
  completed, 140
  connected with Frank's death, 121-123
  creation of, 119-121
  criticized in Wordsworth's preface to Lyrical Ballads, 171-172
  events preceding writing of, 125-127
  STC revises, 171
  symbolic of STC's relationship with Frank, 106
Rivals, STC and Frank as, 1-14
Robespierre, Maximilien
  death of, 55-56
  and Reign of Terror, 49-51
  Southey and STC write about, 56
Robinson, Henry Crabb, and rift between STC and Wordsworth, 311
Rural life style, appeal to STC, 82

Sara's Rock, secret meeting at, 203
Schlegel, Augustus
  STC meets, 313
  and STC's lectures, 257, 273
SCI; see Society for Constitutional Information
Self-pity
  STC and, 178
  at time of Wordsworth's wedding, 186
Sex life
  frustration at Malta, 241
  wanes, 220
Sexual insecurities, adolescent, 23
Shahryar and Shahzeman, 327
  tale of, and STC family relationships, 10-11
Sicily, Coleridge in, 240-242
SMUL, STC spelling of his name, 2-3
Social issues, STC and Cambridge friends discuss, 39
Society for Constitutional Information, 50
  Rev. Horne Tooke and, 62-63
Sockburn, STC visits, 186, 187

"Song of the Pixies," 42
The Soother of Absence, 224
  STC tries to gather ideas for, 225
Southey, Robert
  analyzes Wordsworth role in STC's problems, 196-197
  character of, 48, 49
  completes Joan of Arc, 49
  Greta Hall visit, 219-220
  helps Sarah at Berkeley's death, 147-148
  leaves STC and England, 69
  marries Edith Fricker, 70
  nervous exhaustion of, 159
  Priestly as hero of, 47
  relatives throw him out, 60-61
  and STC: bitterness between, 69; as brother figure, 65; develop subscription lectures, 66-68; questions commitment to Pantisocracy, 59; reconciliation, 80, 154; on relations with Mary and Sarah, 64-65
  on Wordsworths' meddling, 260-261
  writes of STC's deterioration, 215
Speech, freedom of, Gagging Acts and, 76
Speedwell, STC's ship to Malta, 234-235
Spiritual brother, Wordsworth as, 98
Spots in the Sun, 211
Stoddart, John, provides lodgings for STC in Malta, 237-239
Stowey; see Nether Stowey
Stuart, Daniel
  hires STC as reporter, 156-157
  offers STC permanent job, 161
Suffering for past deeds, 123-125, 128-129
Suffrage, universal male, 75, 76
Suicidal impulses
  in Bristol, 278
  in Malta, 244-245
Suspension of disbelief, 305
Sybilline Leaves published, 292
Symbolic act of magical undoing, Comberbache episode as, 45
Symbolic crime, Rime of the Ancient Mariner and, 120, 123

Table Talk (H.N. Coleridge), 299
The Borderers, Wordsworth writing, 94-95
Thelwall, John
  one of Twelve Apostles, 63
  visits Coleridges, 102-103
Theological explanations of dreams, psychological explanations and, 305
This Lime-Tree Bower My Prison, 102

Tintern Abbey, 136
Tooke, Rev. Horne, one of Twelve Apostles and SCI leader, 62-63
Treason, Gagging Acts and, 76
Tuberculosis, STC and, 324
Twelve Apostles, 50-51
  becomes target of Pitt witch hunt, 61
  trials of, 61-63

Unitarian Church, STC considers ministry in, 131-132
Unitarianism
  accused of idolatry, 244
  vs Trinity, 26-27
Universe, *The Aeolian Harp* and, 74

Vampire motif, *Christabel* and, 287
Virgin Mary (Mary Lamb), 160
Virility of Wordsworth and his poetry, 104-105

Wade, Josiah, as patron of STC, 80
Wales, coast of, 73-74
Wallenstein (Schiller), STC undertakes translation of, 160
The Wanderings of Cain, 285
  STC and Wordsworth start on, 119
  turns into *Rime of the Ancient Mariner*, 119-120
War, civil, England near, 316
The Watchman
  content of, 78
  final edition of, 79
  origin of, 76
We are Seven, 136
Wedgwood, Josiah, and brother offer STC life annuity, 132-133
Wedgwood, Kitty, offended by STC reference about Sarah, 214
Wedgwood, Thomas
  and brother offer STC life annuity, 132-133
  scientific experiments of, 133
  and STC: attraction between, 133; travel together, 212-216; vacillate about European tour, 216
  suffers suicidal depression and paranoia, 213
Will
  codicil about Hartley's inheritance, 315
  STC writes, 314
Willing suspension of disbelief, 305
Wish fulfillment, dreams as, 305, 307
Wordsworth, Dora, tours with father and STC, 313
Wordsworth, Dorothy
  background of, 98-101
  continues to live with William and Mary, 209-210
  creates atmosphere of creative generosity with STC and William, 137
  misses William's wedding, 184
  as semi-invalid, 315
  and STC return from Malta, 231-232
  writings show Wordsworth's full support of STC, 196
Wordsworth, John, dies and leaves family impoverished, 100
Wordsworth, William
  Annette Vallon affair, 96; brooding over, 201
  aversion to solo publishing, 175-176
  background of, 98-101
  begins autobiographic poem, 221
  begins autobiography dedicated to STC, 150
  creative energy of, causes impotence feelings, 222
  determines to publish alone, 176
  and Dorothy: leave for France, 204; plan with Coleridges to move to Germany, 137; return to England, settle in North, 149-150; reunited after 10 years, 101; separate from STC on Scotland tour, 219; start Scotland tour with STC, 217; travel to Coleorton, 260; try to lure STC to Lake country, 159; undercut STC's efforts to improve relations with Sarah, 202-203; visit Greta Hall, 211
  fathers child, Caroline, 96-97
  financial problems of, 137-138
  grandparents make him scapegoat, 99
  listed as sole author of *Lyrical Ballads*, 170
  loses mother and becomes troublemaker, 99
  and Mary Hutchinson: courtship, 193-194; marriage, 183;
  settle in Dove Cottage, 209
  passes poetic prime, 269
  refuses to have *Christabel* in second edition of *Lyrical Ballads*, 176
  relationships to sister and wife, 210-211
  single-mindedness in pursuing goal, 262
  and STC: asks to help with *Aeneid*,

312; attraction for, 104-105; both attend boarding schools, 100; as brother figure, 98, 104-105; develop mutual artistic debt, 136-137; discuss his marrying Mary Hutchinson, 192-193; estrangement, 269-271; final visit, 315; gossip of separation, 273-274; insist on anonymous publication, 138-139; patch up quarrel, 274; read parts of autobiographic epic, 228; reunited, 310; share political views, 95-96; tour continent, 312-313; tour Lake country, 156-157; urges announcement of separation from Sarah, 264-265
on STC's death, 321-322
Stowey relocation, 97
writing first drama, 94-95
Writing, and sense of continuity with past, 88

Zapolya, published while living with Gillmans, 292

Made in the USA
Middletown, DE
08 October 2016